STRIKING BACK

BATTLES AND CAMPAIGNS

The Battles and Campaigns series examines the military and strategic results of particular combat techniques, strategies, and methods used by soldiers, sailors, and airmen throughout history. Focusing on different nations and branches of the armed services, this series aims to educate readers by detailed analysis of military engagements.

SERIES EDITOR: Roger Cirillo

AN AUSA BOOK

STRIKING BACK

COMBAT IN KOREA
March–April 1951

Edited by
William T. Bowers

THE UNIVERSITY PRESS OF KENTUCKY

Published by The University Press of Kentucky
Scholarly publisher for the Commonwealth,
serving Bellarmine University, Berea College, Centre
College of Kentucky, Eastern Kentucky University,
The Filson Historical Society, Georgetown College,
Kentucky Historical Society, Kentucky State University,
Morehead State University, Murray State University,
Northern Kentucky University, Transylvania University,
University of Kentucky, University of Louisville,
and Western Kentucky University.
All rights reserved.

Editorial and Sales Offices: The University Press of Kentucky
663 South Limestone Street, Lexington, Kentucky 40508-4008
www.kentuckypress.com

14 13 12 11 10   5 4 3 2 1

All photographs courtesy of the U.S. Army.

Library of Congress Cataloging-in-Publication Data

    Striking back : combat in Korea, March–April 1951 / edited by
William T. Bowers.
        p.   cm. — (Battles and campaigns)
    Includes bibliographical references and index.
    ISBN 978-0-8131-2564-0 (hardcover : alk. paper)
    1. Korean War, 1950–1953—Participation, American. 2. Korean
War, 1950–1953—Campaigns. 3. Korean War, 1950–1953—Personal
narratives, American. 4. United States. Army—History—Korean War,
1950–1953. I. Bowers, William T., 1946–
DS919.S775 2010
951.904'24—dc22
                                        2009031480

This book is printed on acid-free recycled paper meeting
the requirements of the American National Standard
for Permanence in Paper for Printed Library Materials.

Manufactured in the United States of America.

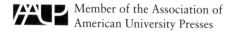

Member of the Association of
American University Presses

A NOTE ON THE TEXT

Colonel William T. (Tom) Bowers died September 18, 2008, at Bethesda Naval Medical Center at the age of sixty-two. Tom was a combat decorated soldier, scholar, and family man with an impressive military and educational background. As head of the Histories Division of the U.S. Army Center of Military History, he oversaw the writing of official histories of Vietnam and Korea, and mentored a large number of writing historians and students. His work on the Korean War and virtual battlefield staff rides for students was particularly impressive.

The editorial work for this book was completed by Tom's colleague Dr. John Greenwood, formerly of the Army History Program, as a tribute to Tom's work. Tom intended that America's "forgotten war," the Korean War, would be recorded in a published account of what the soldiers did, as told by the Army combat historians who were present to record the soldiers' actions.

Roger Cirillo
Series Editor

CONTENTS

Photo gallery follows page 230

PREFACE

Much can be learned about war from studying the thirty-eight months of fighting in Korea from June 1950 to July 1953. Military operations ranged from rapid advances and withdrawals and amphibious landings and evacuations, all reminiscent of World War II, to static operations interrupted by set-piece battles and vicious raids that recall the battles on the Western Front during World War I. The weather was often as brutal as the fighting: summers hot and humid, winters frigid with icy Siberian winds. The rugged terrain challenged even those who thought they were in good physical condition. Before Korea, U.S. strategic planners, and indeed most people in the United States, believed that such a war would never be fought again, and certainly not in Korea. Consequently, preparations were few, and the individuals who had to actually fight the battles paid the price.

This book takes a close look at some of the fighting that occurred over a two-month period in the late winter and early spring during the first year of the war. It is part of a series about the Korean War that focuses on combat at the lowest levels: battalion, company, platoon, squad, and individual soldiers. Although the spotlight is on tactical operations and frontline fighting, each combat action is placed in its own unique context, so that the reader is aware of the way in which events and decisions, both in Korea and elsewhere, influenced what happened on the battlefield.

Most of the material for this book is drawn from interviews conducted by Army historians soon after a combat action occurred, in some cases within hours or a few days. Additional information comes from official records, such as unit journals and periodic reports, and from unit and individual award recommendations, which include eyewitness accounts of heroic actions.

Army historians had to overcome many problems to collect the combat interviews that form the basis for this book. They worked on tight deadlines because the interviews and action summaries were needed not only to capture the historical record while events were still fresh, but also to provide information to other American units about enemy and friendly operations, namely, what tactics and methods the enemy was using and what procedures and tactics seemed to be effective or were failures in fighting the enemy. There were many combat actions, and little time was available to conduct interviews and compile the reports, which in most cases included maps, photographs, and a summary. Sometimes historians could not visit units until long after a battle had ended. Often the key individuals necessary to provide a complete understanding of the fight were not available for interviews due to death, illness, wounds, leave, or other reasons. The ideal was for the historian to walk the battlefield with the participants so that the resulting interviews, maps, and photographs brought the action alive. But this could not always be accomplished because of time or because the battlefield lay in enemy territory. Accounts by different participants were sometimes contradictory, even about routine matters such as orders, indicating that the confusion of combat remained after the fighting ended. Other statements were vague about the most recent actions or seemed to focus on one specific incident, indicating perhaps that the trauma produced by the immediate presence of danger and death in combat was still present.

Despite occasional shortcomings, this group of interviews provides a unique picture of the fighting in Korea. When soldiers describe what they saw and heard, it becomes clear that most narrative histories of the war fail to capture the confusion, uncertainty, fear, hardships, incompetence, dedication, professional skill, determination, and heroism that were everyday occurrences in most combat actions. When the interviews are compared with unit records, it appears that, on occasion, higher headquarters had an incomplete and erroneous understanding of what had actually happened. Taken as a whole, the interviews provide an explanation of why the UN forces prevailed in the difficult war that was fought in Korea. In most cases, soldiers and their leaders eventually found a way to overcome all problems and to succeed on the battlefield.

Chapter 1 provides the context needed to understand the fighting that took place during March and early April 1951. The stabilization of the front and the failure of enemy attacks in January and February gave General Ridgway an opportunity to launch several offensives designed to destroy enemy personnel and supplies while building confidence and fighting skills in the UN forces. The interviews in chapters 2, 3, and 4 focus on units of the U.S. 7th Infantry and 1st Cavalry Divisions fighting in the central mountains, where the ability to keep frontline units supplied was crucial to success. The next four chapters spotlight the attempt to use the 187th Airborne Regimental Combat Team, reinforced for a time with an armored-infantry task force, to trap and destroy a significant portion of the North Korean and Chinese forces above Seoul. The action in chapters 9, 10, 11, and 12 shifts back to the central region, to the U.S. 2d Infantry and 1st Cavalry Divisions and their efforts to trap enemy forces around the Hwach'on Reservoir and to capture the reservoir's dam, which controlled the waters of the rivers flowing through the UN forces' rear areas. Chapter 13 moves the action to the west to look at a regiment of the U.S. 25th Infantry Division as it conducts an assault crossing of the Hant'an River as part of the final operation before the enemy launched its spring offensive. The concluding chapter evaluates the success and failure of these offensives and provides an assessment of the situation as the UN forces faced another massive attack by the Chinese and North Koreans.

With the exception of the first and last chapters, the narrative is carried by the interviews, set off by brief remarks in italics to set the stage and link the interviews together. The interviews have undergone minor editing to remove repetitious and extraneous material not key to understanding the action, to correct obvious typographical and grammatical errors so that the reader is not distracted, and to make the interviews more readable by putting them in the form of a statement and changing map coordinates to recognizable locations. Under no circumstances has the meaning been changed. Notes at the end provide information for further research and study.

A number of individuals were of great assistance during the preparation of this book. Roger Cirillo, of the Association of the United States Army, initially proposed the project as a way not only to preserve the Korean War combat interviews, but also to provide an opportunity for a wider audience to become acquainted with their worth as a valuable source of historical information about the Korean War and about combat in general. Bob Wright, Mary Haynes, and Jim Knight provided expert assistance and cheerful encouragement and support while I conducted research in the archives and library of the U.S. Army Center of Military History (CMH). John Elsberg, Steve Hardyman, Sherry Dowdy, and Beth Mackenzie helped me to gain a better understanding of the cartographic support needed so that the combat interviews could be understood. David Rennie turned the sketches into maps. At the National Archives, Tim Nenninger, Rich Boylan, and Mitch Yockelson, all of the Modern Military Branch, provided invaluable assistance as I tracked down unit records and award recommendations, as did Richard Sommers and Dave Keough of the U.S. Army Military History Institute as I searched for additional material. As with my previous volume, *The Line: Combat in Korea, January–February 1951,* I must again extend my heartfelt thanks to Stephen M. Wrinn, Candace Chaney, and Ila McEntire at the University Press of Kentucky, and freelance copyeditor Stacey Lynn for transforming my manuscript into a book. While these individuals contributed immeasurably to this book, I alone am responsible for any errors in fact or omission that might appear.

NOTE ON MAPS

A number of the maps used in this work were rough sketches drawn by soldiers as they recounted their experiences during the Korean War. As such, the maps employ a variety of symbols for terrain and military operations. To ensure clarity, notations have been added to some sketches. Whenever possible, the standard military and topographical symbols shown below have been used, along with common abbreviations. Numbers on all contours are in meters.

▭	Unit symbol (enemy shown in gray or labeled)
⊓	Headquarters or command post
△	Observation post (OP)
⌒	Position area
●→	Machine gun or automatic weapon
♦ ♦	Mortar or gun
◇	Tank, self-propelled weapon
ᴫᴫᴫ ──	Front lines
──→	Route or direction of attack
⤬	Road block
⎍⎍⎍⎍	Trenches, fortified positions

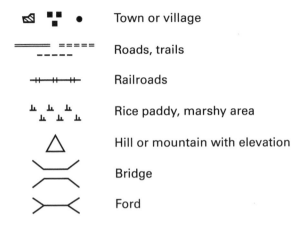

Town or village

Roads, trails

Railroads

Rice paddy, marshy area

Hill or mountain with elevation

Bridge

Ford

The following symbols placed in boundary lines or position area ovals or above the rectangle, triangle, or circle enclosing the identifying arm or service symbol indicate the size of military organizations.

●	Squad
●●	Section
●●●	Platoon
I	Company, troop, battery
II	Battalion, cavalry squadron
III	Regiment, group, combat team
X	Brigade
XX	Division
XXX	Corps
XXXX	Army
XXXXX	Army Group

Examples are given below. The letter or number to the left of the symbol indicates the unit designation; that to the right, the designation of the parent unit to which it belongs. Letters or numbers above or below boundary lines designate the units separated by the lines. Unit designations sometimes are shown as 3/A/9 (3d Platoon, Company A, 9th Infantry Regiment) or as 1–9 (1st Battalion, 9th Infantry Regiment).

A ⊠ 137   Company A, 137th Infantry

▢ 8   8th Field Artillery Battalion

⊠ 5   Command post, 5th Infantry Division

137
— ||| —   Boundary between 137th and 138th Infantry
138

ABBREVIATIONS

AA	Antiaircraft
AAA	Antiaircraft Artillery
AAA AW	Antiaircraft Artillery Automatic Weapons
A&P	Ammunition and Pioneer
ARCT	Airborne Regimental Combat Team
AST	Ammunition Supply Point
AT&M	Antitank and Mine
BAR	Browning Automatic Rifle
BCT	Battalion Combat Team
CCF	Chinese Communist Forces
CG	Commanding General
CO	Commanding Officer
CP	Command Post or Check Point
DivArty	Division Artillery
DUKW	Amphibious Truck
EMT	Emergency Medical Tag
FA	Field Artillery
FAC	Forward Air Controller
FM	Frequency Modulation
FO	Forward Observer
G-1/S-1	Personnel Officer
G-2/S-2	Intelligence Officer
G-3/S-3	Operations Officer
G-4/S-4	Supply Officer
HE	High Explosive

HEAT	High Explosive Antitank
HMG	Heavy Machine Gun
HQ	Headquarters
I&R	Intelligence and Reconnaissance
JCS	Joint Chiefs of Staff
KATUSA	Korean Augmentation Troops for the United States Army
KIA	Killed in Action
KMAG	Korean Military Advisory Group
LD	Line of Departure
LST	Landing Ship Tank
MG	Machine Gun
MIA	Missing in Action
MLR	Main Line of Resistance
MSR	Main Supply Road
NCO	Noncommissioned Officer
NK	North Korea
OP	Observation Post; Outpost
OPL	Outpost Line
OPLR	Outpost Line of Resistance
P&A	Pioneer and Ammunition
PLA	People's Liberation Army (Chinese Communist)
POL	Petroleum, Oil, and Lubrication
POW	Prisoner of War
RCT	Regimental Combat Team
Recon	Reconnaissance
ROK	Republic of Korea (South Korean)
R&R	Rest and Recreation
SCR	Signal Corps Radio
SOI	Signal Operating Instructions
SOP	Standard Operating Procedure
SP	Self-propelled
TACP	Tactical Air Control Party
TF	Task Force
T/O&E	Table of Organization and Equipment
UN	United Nations
VT	Variable Time Fuse

| WIA | Wounded in Action |
| WP | White Phosphorous |

RANKS

Pvt.	Private
PFC	Private 1st Class
Cpl.	Corporal
Sgt.	Sergeant
S. Sgt.	Staff Sergeant
SFC	Sergeant 1st Class
M. Sgt.	Master Sergeant
1st Sgt.	First Sergeant
WOJG	Warrant Officer Junior Grade
CWO	Chief Warrant Officer
Lt.	Lieutenant
LtJG	Lieutenant Junior Grade
2d Lt.	2d Lieutenant
1st Lt.	1st Lieutenant
Capt.	Captain
Maj.	Major
Lt. Col.	Lieutenant Colonel
Col.	Colonel
Gen.	General
Brig. Gen.	Brigadier General
Maj. Gen.	Major General
Lt. Gen.	Lieutenant General

Chapter 1

KOREA AND THE COLD WAR WORLD

March 1951 opened with UN forces on the move across the Korean peninsula. Two months earlier the situation was much different. The success of the Inch'on landing in September 1950 and the subsequent destruction of much of the North Korean army and its equipment had turned to stunning failure for UN forces with the massive Chinese intervention in November. Battlefield defeat and a hasty withdrawal from North Korea in late November and early December were costly in terms of manpower and material losses. Even more important, potentially, was the effect on morale among soldiers and their leaders at all levels, from the battlefields in Korea to Washington. The Chinese intervention dramatically changed the nature of the war. What had been termed a "police action" in June 1950, indicating a measured response to an unlawful but limited threat by North Korea, had now become a full-scale war, with the potential for escalation to a Third World War between the United States, its allies, and the Communist world.[1]

Almost from the beginning, the conflict in Korea had been of secondary concern to the United States and many of its allies, who saw the greatest threat in Europe, not in the Far East. The Soviet Union, which had exploded a nuclear device in September 1949, seemed poised to invade the almost defenseless Western European countries from its Eastern European satellite states. National Security Council (NSC) paper 68, a wide-ranging study of the global situation facing the United States completed shortly before the North Korean invasion, concluded that the Soviet Union was a di-

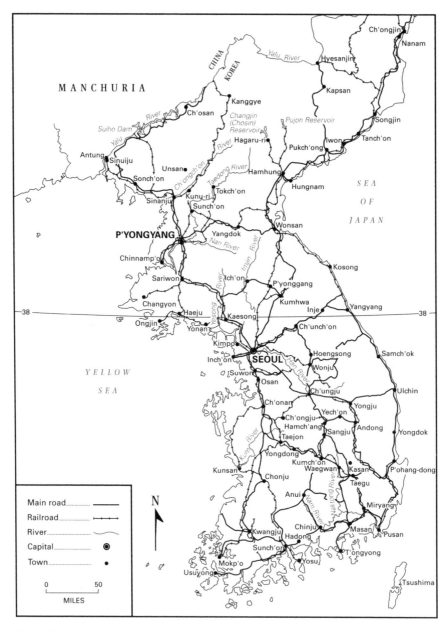

Korea (based on U.S. Army Center of Military History map).

rect threat to United States interests, especially in Europe, and that substantial increases in military forces and expenditures were required. United States defense policy prior to NSC 68 had rested on the assumption that its monopoly of atomic weapons would lessen the need for conventional forces. Consequently, air, ground, and naval forces were weak, not only in numbers, but also in terms of training and equipment. President Harry S. Truman was embroiled in domestic economic problems, and his administration was fighting off accusations from Republicans, such as Senator Joseph McCarthy, that Communist traitors in the United States government had contributed to the loss of China to the Communists. Truman did not see where money could be found for increases in defense spending. Consequently, the administration's priority of balancing the budget meant a one-third decline in projected Army spending for 1950.[2]

Truman was shocked in June 1950 when North Korea attacked South Korea, an area considered outside the range of vital United States strategic interests. Incensed with this flagrant example of naked aggression, Truman was also mindful of how the failure to deal swiftly with German, Italian, and Japanese aggression in the 1930s had led to World War II. To Truman, the surprise attack of North Korea offered an opportunity to mobilize the American people and obtain congressional backing to respond to a Communist threat and support the increases in defense spending called for by NSC 68. Truman ordered a rapid reaction to the North Korean attack, both in military and diplomatic terms. Understrength American divisions in Japan were quickly moved to Korea and reinforced with soldiers and units from the United States, including one Marine and two Army divisions. United States air and naval units began attacking North Korean forces, and the U.S. Seventh Fleet moved ships to the Formosa Strait to support Nationalist China against the threat of a Chinese Communist invasion. On the diplomatic front, the United States introduced a resolution in the United Nations, which was passed on 27 June, calling on its members to assist South Korea in repelling the North Korean attack. Eventually, fourteen nations provided combat support to United States and South Korean forces, and five others sent medical assistance.[3] But America's allies were greatly concerned with the possibility of an expansion of the war outside of the Korean peninsula, and, to some extent, allied contributions to the fighting in Korea were designed to give them some influence in American decisions.

By September 1950 the ability to immediately reinforce Korea with additional forces from the United States was exhausted. The draft was expanded to fill depleted troop units in the States, and four National Guard divisions were called into federal service, but several months would be needed before these forces would be ready for combat. The outbreak of the Korean War and the pressing defense demands it created seemed to confirm the conclusions of NSC 68. In early September President Truman announced that defense expenditures would balloon from an estimated $13 billion per year in June 1950 to $287 billion over five years and that American forces in Europe would be increased by several divisions and two corps headquarters.[4]

Gen. Douglas MacArthur, the American commander in the Far East and the Commander in Chief of the United Nations Command, was told that no additional forces would be sent to him. With the collapse of the North Korean army after the Inch'on landing in September, Truman directed MacArthur to cross into North Korea and move to the North Korean–Chinese border along the Yalu River, but to ensure that only South Korean forces entered the border area. Planning proceeded for withdrawing the bulk of United States forces from Korea, and one division, the 2d Infantry, was to be shipped to Europe. America's European allies reluctantly supported the United States' decision to turn from a policy of defending South Korea to occupying North Korea. As UN forces moved into North Korea, Soviet-built MIG jet fighter planes began to appear in the area, soon followed by Chinese Communist ground troops, which attacked United States and South Korean units in late October. Diplomatic signals by China, as well as intelligence reports, were disregarded, and the UN advance continued. MacArthur demanded and received permission from Washington to attack the bridges over the Yalu River, over which Chinese troops were crossing into North Korea. But on another matter, MacArthur disregarded his instructions and acted unilaterally by ordering United States forces to move directly to the Chinese border. After the fact, Washington approved this decision.

The Chinese attack in late November and the subsequent withdrawal of UN forces from North Korea greatly affected MacArthur and Truman. MacArthur's unrestrained optimism before the attack turned to deep pessimism. He requested massive reinforcements and said that without them he would likely be forced to withdraw to a beachhead around Pusan at the southern tip of the peninsula, hinting that complete withdrawal was possible. In contrast, Truman's fighting spirit was raised, and, at a news conference on 30 November, he told reporters that the United States would use every weapon in its arsenal, including the atomic bomb, to deal with the situation in Korea. The seriousness of the situation was apparent, with the danger of the fighting spreading to China and the Soviet Union and with the potential for the use of nuclear weapons.

Truman's public threat to use nuclear weapons drew an immediate response from America's closest ally, Britain. Prime Minister Clement Attlee immediately flew to Washington for meetings with the president. They reconfirmed that Europe remained the top priority and that they would strictly limit the scope of the war in Korea. Truman, however, refused to allow Britain a veto over the use of nuclear weapons, stating only that they would be informed before American use. MacArthur was told that no additional reinforcements would be sent to Korea. Truman then proceeded with a series of steps to mobilize the country. On 16 December he declared a state of national emergency. Gen. Dwight D. Eisenhower was appointed Supreme Allied Commander for the military forces of the North Atlantic Treaty Organization (NATO). European allies began to build up their military forces, including a limited rearmament of West Germany. Planning proceeded to move two corps headquarters (V and VII) and four divisions (2d Armored and 4th, 28th, and 43d Infantry) to Europe in 1951 to reinforce the U.S. Seventh Army, which had been activated in late November 1950 in Heidelberg, West Germany. The forces destined for Europe were to receive substantial training and the most modern equipment before their deployment.

In the midst of these measures, American public opinion, influenced by large casualty lists and a war with no clear end in sight, turned against the conflict in Korea. Criticism rose in Congress regarding the manner in which the Truman administration was prosecuting the war. There was little enthusiasm for the draft, for increased taxes, or for what seemed to be a greatly expanded activist role for the United States throughout the world. Reservists, many of whom were combat veterans of World War II, complained loudly that in Korea they were fighting their second war while new draftees were being readied for service in Europe. Because of pressure on Congress and the Army's desire to maintain morale in Korea, a troop rotation system was established that would permit frontline soldiers to leave Korea after serving nine months in a combat unit.

The Soviet Union and Communist China proceeded cautiously after the defeat of the UN forces in North Korea. In early December, China informed the United Nations that it would agree to an armistice in Korea if the following conditions were met: UN forces withdraw from the peninsula, United States naval forces move out of the Formosa straits, Nationalist China be expelled from the UN, and Nationalist China's UN seat be given to Communist China. The Soviet Union restricted its effort to logistical support of China and North Korea, and limited its participation in the air war over Korea, taking no steps to interdict American supply lines from Japan or to introduce its own forces into the ground war. China moved its forces forward toward the South Korean border, but it would take a number of weeks to build up the necessary logistical support for a renewed offensive to drive the United States and its allies from the peninsula.

On 23 December 1950, Lt. Gen. Walton H. Walker, the American commander in Korea, was killed in a traffic accident. His replacement, Lt. Gen. Matthew B. Ridgway, then the chief of operations on the Army staff in Washington, faced a formidable challenge. He was fully aware of the restrictions under which the war in Korea must be fought. There would be no reinforcements, although losses would be replaced; the war would not be expanded outside of Korea, effectively providing a sanctuary for enemy airfields and supply bases in China; and if defeats in Korea continued, in all likelihood a decision would be made to withdraw because Europe was the priority. En route to South Korea, Ridgway stopped briefly in Tokyo. MacArthur provided a pessimistic assessment: he was concerned that the UN lacked the capability to defend South Korea or even to erect a defensive line across the peninsula because of difficult terrain and a shortage of troops; air power could not be counted on to effectively interdict enemy supplies and forces; the Chinese must not be underestimated, for they were expected to re-new their attacks in overwhelming force at any moment.[5]

Arriving in Korea on 26 December, Ridgway sensed defeatism from the moment of his initial briefings at Eighth Army headquar-ters. The only planning taking place was for further withdrawals to Pusan and evacuation from the Korean peninsula. Information on enemy locations, strength, and intentions was almost nonexistent. Over the next four days, a series of visits by Ridgway to corps and division headquarters provided additional signs: men were exhausted; morale was low; many seemed to have an exaggerated idea of enemy capabilities. In American units, many of which had been hastily as-sembled and shipped to Korea to deal with the crisis in the summer of 1950, too many soldiers and their leaders lacked fundamental combat skills; Republic of Korea (ROK) forces, which held two-thirds of the UN line, were largely untrained and unreliable; and reserve forces consisted only of newly raised, untrained ROK units and the U.S. X Corps and 2d Infantry Division, which had sustained heavy casualties in North Korea and were in need of time to absorb replacements. There was a noticeable lack of aggression in all com-manders, except Maj. Gen. Ned Almond, commander of X Corps. But to balance this, there were reports that Almond was reckless, and the Marines, who had served under him in the harsh fighting around the Chosin Reservoir in North Korea, were firmly opposed to being part of Almond's X Corps in the future. To complete the picture of a desperate situation, the Chinese and the rebuilt North Korean army began their new offensive the night of 31 December.

Ridgway was a capable combat commander, who had proven his skills leading first the 82d Airborne Division and then the XVIII Airborne Corps through tough and extensive combat operations in the Mediterranean and Europe in World War II. He was confident that, with time, the morale and fighting abilities of the UN forces could be restored. But now there was no time. The main enemy blow fell on the U.S. I and IX Corps north of Seoul, but the greatest potential danger was pressure building in the mountainous center of the UN line held by the ROK II and III Corps, where a breakthrough by the enemy would endanger UN lines of supply and of retreat extending south from Seoul to the port of Pusan on the southern tip of the Korean Peninsula. As the fighting erupted in the New Year, there was a real question whether the UN forces would be able to hold back the enemy and retain their position in South Korea.

The initial enemy attacks were successful. In the west, UN forces conducted a fighting withdrawal to the Han River but could not stop the enemy onslaught. Seoul was abandoned on 4 January. With pressure building to the front and the threat of envelopment from the east, Ridgway ordered the U.S. I and IX Corps to withdraw to a new defensive line some fifty miles south of Seoul. This move was designed to keep United States forces intact and to stretch Chinese logistics, which did not have the capability to sustain lengthy offensive actions. Ridgway planned to slowly withdraw while inflicting maximum damage on pursuing enemy forces; at the appropriate time he would counterattack.

The day before the fall of the South Korean capital, to deal with a threatened breakthrough in the central mountains, Ridgway ordered Almond's X Corps to move into the area and take over a forty-mile front from the ROK II and III Corps, which had been badly mauled at the opening of the enemy offensive. With the U.S. 7th Infantry Division reorganizing from its withdrawal from North Korea, only the U.S. 2d Infantry Division was immediately available. On 7 January, North Korean forces attacked the 2d Division at Wonju, and over the next ten days fierce fighting took place just south of the town. To the east of the 2d Division, the enemy took advantage of a gap in the ROK lines to move the North Korean II Corps into the UN rear area between Yongwol and Andong, where it operated as a guerrilla force. Ridgway gave Almond the 187th Airborne Regimental Combat Team (RCT) to deal with this threat, while the U.S. 7th Infantry Division joined ROK units to close the gap in the UN defensive line. The 1st Marine Division was also sent

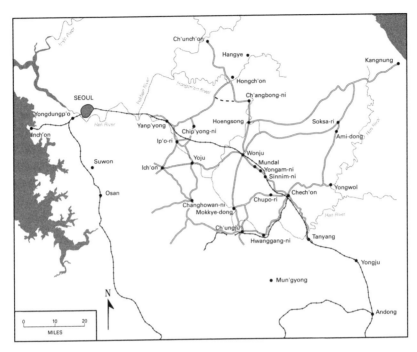

Area of operations, January–February 1951 (original map by author, based on U.S. Army Center of Military History map).

into the area to systematically eliminate the North Korean guerrillas. Late in January, the North Koreans pulled back to the Hongch'on area to regroup.

Meanwhile, south of Seoul, the Chinese had sent only patrols forward to follow the U.S. I and IX Corps. Ridgway was dissatisfied with the way his American units had conducted their withdrawal from Seoul; they had ignored his orders to maintain contact with the enemy and to inflict casualties whenever possible. To regain contact with the enemy and to restore a spirit of aggressiveness among his troops, he ordered a series of carefully planned reconnaissances in force. These actions began on 15 January; on 25 January Ridgway converted them into a deliberate coordinated advance called Operation Thunderbolt, which was designed to push north to the Han River to seek out and destroy enemy forces. On 29 January, Ridgway ordered X Corps to join the advance of I and IX Corps to protect their eastern flank.

General Almond planned to send ROK divisions assigned to his X Corps forward against the North Koreans reorganizing near Hongch'on. The ROKs were to be reinforced by American tank and artillery units and backed up by the U.S. 2d and 7th Infantry Divisions. Almond termed this eastward extension of Thunderbolt, Operation Roundup. The UN Command was unaware that the Chinese had moved into the central mountains to reinforce the North Koreans. Strong resistance developed along the IX and X Corps boundary. The IX Corps right flank unit, the 1st Cavalry Division, fought sharp engagements west of Ich'on at Hill 312 and elsewhere in late January. On 29 January and again on 1 February, the Chinese attacked elements of the U.S. 2d Infantry Division along the corps boundary just south of the key crossroads town of Chip'yong-ni. Despite indications of an enemy buildup and an awkward command control arrangement between the ROK divisions and their American artillery and tank support units, Ridgway allowed Almond to proceed with Operation Roundup. The ROK divisions began their advance on Hongch'on on 5 February.

Initially, the continuation of the UN advance proceeded smoothly. On the left, I Corps met little opposition as it reached the southern outskirts of Seoul. On the right, IX Corps advanced slowly against stiffening opposition and, by 9 February, had come upon a strong enemy defensive line along the high ground four to seven miles south of the Han River. Led by the 5th and 8th ROK Divisions, X Corps' advance moved north from Hoengsong along the roads running through the mountains to Hongch'on. The 23d Infantry Regiment of the U.S. 2d Infantry Division occupied Chip'yong-ni to maintain contact between IX and X Corps.

By 11 February, Ridgway was concerned. He ordered Almond to halt his advance toward Hongch'on until the enemy bridgehead between the Han River and Ich'on in the IX Corps sector was eliminated. Intelligence reports indicated that, in addition to the North Koreans, the Chinese had concentrated four armies, some 110,000 troops, in front of X Corps. The intelligence assessment was that the Chinese would move additional forces, the IX Army Group from Wonsan, into the area and then launch an attack south through Wonju and southwest into the Han River valley to cut the

UN line of supply to Pusan. It was expected that the enemy attack would begin about 15 February, when the Chinese IX Army Group was expected to arrive within supporting distance.

On the night of 11–12 February the Chinese struck the ROK divisions along the X Corps front. By morning the South Korean units were in retreat, and their American artillery and tank support units were in danger of being cut off and overrun. Heavy fighting ensued as the elements of the U.S. 2d and 7th Infantry Divisions fought their way south out of the trap. By 13 February a new X Corps defensive line was established on either side of Wonju. Almond wanted to withdraw the 23d Infantry Regiment from Chip'yong-ni because of its exposed position in advance of the main forces of IX and X Corps. Ridgway ordered the town held to block a possible enemy thrust into the Han River valley, but at the same time made arrangements to shift forces from IX Corps to X Corps for a possible relief operation if the 23d Infantry came under attack and was isolated.

On the night of 13 February the Chinese struck the 23d Infantry at Chip'yong-ni, and over the next two days three Chinese divisions sought to capture the key road junction. At the same time, the Chinese also tried to break through the 2d Division defensive positions immediately west of Wonju. Both attempts failed. Late on 15 February a tank-infantry task force of the 1st Cavalry Division reached the embattled garrison at Chip'yong-ni. The Chinese faded away into the mountains north of Chip'yong-ni and Wonju.

Ridgway believed that these successful defensive efforts against the Chinese, particularly at Chip'yong-ni, marked a turning point. They demonstrated that the Eighth Army had regained its confidence and that the enemy could be defeated. He quickly ordered a new offensive, Operation Killer, to take advantage of the enemy failures at Chip'yong-ni and Wonju. This advance, as its name indicated, was designed to methodically destroy enemy forces south of the Han River in the IX Corps sector and to disrupt the enemy in the X Corps area as they regrouped north of Hongch'on.

While UN forces in January and February 1951 fought to maintain their position in South Korea against renewed enemy attacks while taking the opportunity to launch limited offensives, Mac-

Arthur and decision makers in Washington struggled to settle on a policy for the war in Korea. In December, Truman and the Joint Chiefs of Staff had decided that the conflict in Korea would remain limited in scope and that no additional divisions would be deployed to the area for the foreseeable future. The Joint Chiefs of Staff and MacArthur wanted to retain a position in South Korea, but with unsettled battlefield conditions, they were uncertain if this was possible. Planning continued for an evacuation from the Korean peninsula, to include more than 700,000 ROK government officials and military personnel plus their dependents. At the same time, the South Korean government requested weapons to arm as many as 500,000 more of its citizens. MacArthur believed that this was unwise, since it could mean more Korean soldiers to evacuate, and he felt that the problem was not the size of the ROK army but the fighting ability of those forces already in existence. Rumors of a possible evacuation of UN forces from South Korea were already having a detrimental effect on the morale of the South Korean government and its army.[6]

When informed in late December that no additional U.S. troop units would be sent to the Far East, MacArthur responded with a recommendation of several measures that could be implemented against Communist China with a minimum use of military resources. These included a naval blockade of the Chinese coast, destruction of Chinese war industries by naval and air attacks, movement of Nationalist Chinese troops from Formosa to South Korea, and diversionary attacks by the Chinese Nationalists on mainland China. Additionally, MacArthur identified several targets in China and North Korea for attack with nuclear weapons. He believed that these actions would drastically reduce the Chinese ability to support their forces in Korea, and at the same time increase the UN military strength by the addition of Nationalist Chinese troops. Together, these measures could provide the margin for victory in Korea.

MacArthur discounted the possibility of Soviet intervention and reasoned that since Communist China was already committed to a major effort in Korea, her response to these attacks on her territory would not involve much greater resources than she was already expending. Moreover, MacArthur stated that, without these actions, the likely evacuation of Korea would involve a serious loss of prestige for the United States in all of Asia and would free up Chinese forces in Korea for attacks in other areas such as Formosa and Japan. In effect MacArthur was arguing that the stakes in Korea were much higher than Washington believed, and, on that basis, that the UN response should not be limited.

Washington carefully studied MacArthur's recommendations. Extending the war to China would exceed the authority granted by the United Nations and was strongly opposed by most U.S. allies. The Soviet Union and Communist China were linked by a security treaty signed in February 1950, and thus the chances for extension of the war outside of Asia were increased. A naval blockade of China would risk problems with the Soviet Union, which retained certain rights of trade in Manchuria, and with American allies who traded with China. Similar problems could arise with the bombardment of Chinese war industries along her coast. Nationalist China's military capability was weak, and she would require substantial assistance from the United States before being able to effectively launch attacks against China or provide useful reinforcements for UN forces in Korea. The introduction of Chinese Nationalist forces into Korea would certainly harden the Chinese Communist position and make it extremely difficult to obtain a negotiated end to the Korean conflict. MacArthur's assumption that attacks on China would not result in increased Chinese effort in Korea and elsewhere was dismissed by Truman as fantasy. Truman also believed that air attacks on Chinese war industries to stop the flow of supplies to Korea were doomed to failure. It appeared to Truman that MacArthur's recommendations would result in a widening of the war, something that the president was not prepared to accept.

On 9 January the Joint Chiefs of Staff rejected MacArthur's proposals, but the wording of the reply, couched as it was in terms of UN and allied acceptance and other conditions, gave MacArthur hope for future approval. This initiated a number of messages between MacArthur and Washington in which he asked for clarification of his orders, which at this time were to defend South Korea but to withdraw if his forces were in danger. In this exchange, Mac-

Arthur continued to argue for a change in national policy to expand the war to China. At one point he stated, "Their [American troops in Korea] morale will become a serious threat to their battle efficiency unless the political basis upon which they are asked to trade life for time is clearly delineated, fully understood, and so impelling that the hazards of battle are cheerfully accepted."[7]

As the UN forces fought the enemy to a standstill in January and February and cautiously began carefully coordinated advances, the questions of evacuation of Korea and appropriate measures to maintain the UN position in Korea became academic. Members of the Joint Chiefs of Staff, on visits to the war zone in January 1951, saw that Ridgway's leadership and policies were having a positive effect on the fighting ability of the UN troops. MacArthur agreed that conditions had improved and indicated that he believed that air and sea interdiction of Communist supplies in North Korea would prevent the Chinese from building up enough strength to overwhelm UN forces. Ridgway and MacArthur agreed that for now the UN forces should continue a cautious, carefully coordinated advance to the north until they met strong resistance by the enemy, indicating the enemy's main line of defense had been reached. This offensive movement would keep the enemy off balance and disrupt their preparations for a renewed attack, while at the same time instilling an offensive spirit and a will to win in the UN forces. Ridgway and MacArthur both cautioned against overoptimism by stating that it was only a matter of time before the enemy recovered and struck back in a renewed offensive.[8]

As UN forces continued their advance to the north in late February, the problems of fighting in Korea only increased. Intelligence concerning enemy location, strength, and intentions remained poor. There were indications that strong enemy reserve forces numbering some seven Chinese armies had entered North Korea from China and were moving south. But it was unclear where these forces were now located or what the Chinese plan of attack would be. It was thus particularly important that advancing UN forces, especially in the mountainous central region, not be drawn into a trap. Moreover, supply difficulties increased as UN troops moved farther north, away from their logistical support bases. In some instances air supply was utilized as a last resort, although the winter weather limited this capability. The harsh Korean winter also affected fighting capabilities. Air support could not always be counted upon in stormy weather, and the short hours of daylight limited air strikes even when planes could fly. Rugged terrain sometimes restricted the ability of artillery and armor to provide support to attacking infantry. Even the soldiers' winter clothing was inadequate, and therefore exposure to the elements produced large numbers of cold weather injuries in some units.

Ridgway aggressively pursued plans to make better use of his own resources. He slashed the number of personnel assigned to support duties in the U.S. Eighth Army to increase his combat fighting strength. At Ridgway's urging MacArthur did the same for the support units in Japan. Even with these efforts, the infantry in United States divisions in Korea remained at 20 to 50 percent below authorized strength. MacArthur strenuously argued for more replacements to fill his shortages, which in January 1951 amounted to 40,000. Washington reluctantly agreed to strip almost 15,000 men out of units called to active duty and send them to Korea in one to two months. This levy, and an increased flow of replacements, would bring the combat divisions close to their authorized strength by March 1951.

Combat veterans who had been fighting in Korea since the summer of 1950 were nearing the point of exhaustion. Medical statistics from World War II indicated that soldiers in combat without relief for 180 days or more suffered increased casualty rates. To maintain combat efficiency and morale and to prevent increased casualties either from battle or from combat fatigue, a rest and recreation (R&R) program consisting of five-day R&R leaves in Japan was developed. Initiated on New Year's Eve of 1950 with roughly 200 men per division per week, the R&R program participation increased in early 1951, eventually reaching a level of 500 arrivals per day in Japan.[9] The problem of combat exhaustion among senior commanders was more difficult to solve. On 15 January, Ridgway told the Army Chief of Staff, Gen. J. Lawton Collins, that he could not effectively implement his future combat plans with the current corps and division commanders in Korea. He recommended their gradual replacement with carefully selected generals from outside of Korea instead of wholesale, immediate relief, recognizing that massive turbulence in the high command could affect the fighting ability and morale of the entire Eighth Army.[10]

Planning was also under way to make more effective use of South Korean resources. For the people of Korea, the conflict was far from limited. For them, it was a total war that produced destruction and casualties rivaling that of World War II. Cities and villages were destroyed, and displaced people from both North and South totaled several million in South Korea.[11] Enormous resources were required to care for these refugees. Even with the extensive problems of South Korea, it was believed that the country could still provide more assistance for the war effort. Plans were developed to form units of Korean porters to haul supplies to UN troops in the mountainous regions of the country. At the same time, steps were undertaken to begin to improve the fighting efficiency of the ROK military forces by expanding the number of American advisors assigned to the Korean Military Advisory Group (KMAG) to provide expertise in training, logistics, and combat operations. New tables of organization and equipment (T/O&Es) were developed to convert the weak, lightly armed ROK divisions that existed before June 1950 into powerful fighting forces.

Ridgway called for help from outside the Eighth Army in Korea to improve the effectiveness of combat operations. Gen. Mark W. Clark, the commander of Army Field Forces, which was responsible for training in the United States, was given ideas for improving stateside training, including more emphasis on night operations. Ridgway requested that the air interdiction effort in North Korea be sustained and, if possible, increased. He also recommended naval diversionary operations to simulate amphibious landings behind enemy lines, timed to coincide with his planned offensive operations.

Ridgway's new offensive, Operation Killer, began on 21 February. The Army Chief of Staff was concerned over the name of the operation and feared a public-relations problem, but Ridgway said the objective was to kill the enemy and kept the name. The plan was to methodically destroy enemy forces up to Phase Line Arizona, which ran generally east from Chip'yong-ni to above Hoengsong

and continued east toward the upper Han River southwest of Kangnung. The main attack forces were the U.S. IX and X Corps; their
boundary was shifted eastward as was the boundary of the U.S. X
and the ROK III Corps. The 1st Marine Division was attached to IX
Corps and took over the sector of the 2d Infantry Division and the
187th Airborne RCT where they were scheduled to attack north
from Wonju toward Hoengsong. In X Corps the U.S. 7th Infantry
Division was to make the main attack north from Yongwol and then
swing west to trap the enemy between the U.S. 2d Infantry Division
and the ROK 5th Division advancing from the south. To the east of
the 7th Division, the ROK III Corps was to send its 7th, 9th, and
Capital Divisions north to secure the road running from the coast at
Kangnung into the interior. Ridgway planned to move the 187th
Airborne RCT to an airfield near Taegu to prepare them for possible
future airborne operations. He would seek opportunities to drop
the regiment to trap and destroy enemy forces between it and advancing UN ground units.

The offensive began with a winter thaw that made roads impassable and rivers unfordable. Airdrops were sometimes used to
supply UN forces in forward areas. Enemy resistance was light, but,
combined with the weather, it was sufficient to prevent the kind of
success that Ridgway had anticipated. The Marines cleared Hoengsong on 2 March and by 7 March all of IX and X Corps were on
Phase Line Arizona. Enemy losses were believed to be heavy. The IX
Corps, for example, reported 7,819 enemy killed, 1,469 wounded,
and 208 captured, but the stated objective of the operation was not
achieved. Sizable enemy forces were not trapped and destroyed, because they chose instead to withdraw. Countering the partial success of IX and X Corps, in the ROK III Corps area to the east, a
regiment of the Capital Division was caught in an ambush and suffered heavy casualties.

As UN forces approached Line Arizona and Operation Killer
began to wind down, Ridgway was busy planning a new effort. Intelligence reports indicated that the enemy was pulling back to positions just north of Line Arizona and that six Chinese armies and
four North Korean corps manned these defenses. To their rear in
the central sector the enemy had at least three Chinese armies and a

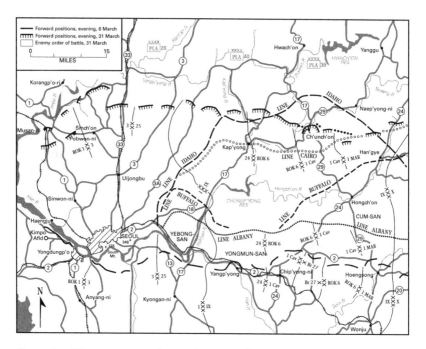

Operation Ripper, western front, 6–31 March 1951 (based on map in CMH manuscript, U.S. Army).

North Korean corps available for offensive operations, but it was unclear where other enemy reserves were located. It appeared that the Chinese were still continuing their buildup and that an immediate attack was not imminent. Ridgway's plan was to continue the drive to the north to destroy enemy forces and supplies and to disrupt the enemy preparations for a future offensive. The final objective was Phase Line Idaho, which began on the Han River just east of Seoul and ran northeast to a point about ten miles north of Ch'unch'on before turning southeast to the Korean coast about six miles north of Kangnung. There were two key aspects of the plan. First, it was expected that a crossing of the Han River east of Seoul by the U.S. 25th Infantry Division of I Corps would threaten to isolate the city to such an extent that the enemy might well abandon it without a serious fight. In the IX Corps sector the goal was the capture of Ch'unch'on, a major enemy supply center, by the 1st Cavalry and the 1st Marine Divisions. The 187th Airborne RCT would

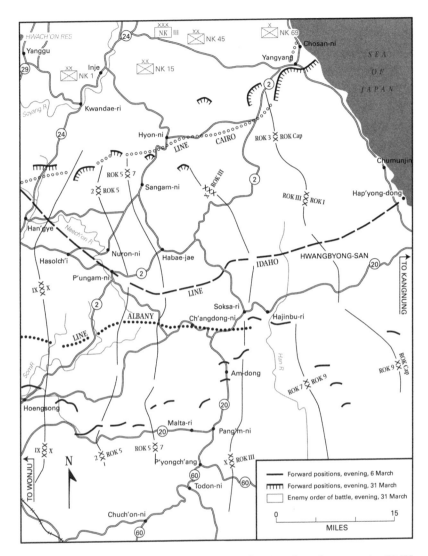

Operation Ripper, eastern front, 6–31 March 1951 (based on map in CMH manuscript, U.S. Army).

be available to drop north of Seoul or Ch'unch'on to trap any enemy forces attempting to withdraw. To the east, the U.S. X and ROK III Corps would also push forward to destroy the enemy forces in their sector. The entire advance would be carefully controlled through a series of phase lines to ensure that none of the UN forces would move too far in front of the others and be caught in a trap. The first of these intermediate phase lines, Albany, lay some five to ten miles beyond the starting positions and would allow Ridgway an opportunity to assess the progress of the operation and make changes. Ridgway arranged for amphibious demonstrations off both coasts of North Korea and ordered supplies pushed forward to support the new advance, which was called Operation Ripper.

The attack began on 7 March. In the I Corps sector the 25th Division successfully crossed the Han River after an artillery bombardment and pushed forward, reaching Phase Line Albany with advance elements on 11 March. Two days later the remainder of I Corps gained Albany. The IX Corps units advanced against light opposition, and most were on Albany late on 12 March. In X Corps, opposition was initially stiffer, and the terrain was more rugged; still, most of X Corps had reached the first phase line by 14 March. Intelligence reports indicated that additional Chinese troops began entering North Korea in early March, but there were still no signs of a major enemy offensive. The assessment was that the enemy would continue to delay until their buildup was complete and they were ready to attack. There were no clear signs as yet that the enemy was abandoning Seoul. With all of this in mind, Ridgway ordered Operation Ripper to continue above Phase Line Albany. The main attack for this phase would be in the IX Corps area, as the 1st Cavalry and 1st Marine Divisions used a double envelopment to overcome the main enemy defenses around Hongch'on and then strike quickly to capture Ch'unch'on. To the east the U.S. 2d and 7th and ROK 5th Divisions of X Corps would have to overcome difficult terrain as well as stiff enemy resistance in order to keep pace.

The second phase of Operation Ripper began on 14 March. The UN forces would have to surmount determined resistance as the enemy fought hard to gain time and protect their troops and supplies being built up for their own future offensive action. Equally challenging for the UN was the rugged terrain over which they would have to fight and supply their frontline soldiers.

Chapter 2

GRENADE HILL

3d Battalion, 32d Infantry Regiment, 14–16 March 1951

After reaching Line Albany (see map on page 19) on 13 March, the advance of Operation Ripper continued almost without pause to the north. In the 7th Infantry Division sector on the right flank of X Corps, the terrain to the north was mountainous with few roads. Securing the roads and passes was critical to keeping the advancing forces supplied. The 3d Battalion, 32d Infantry, drew the mission of capturing the key terrain along one of the routes. Capt. Pierce W. Briscoe, an Army combat historian who interviewed members of the unit about the subsequent action, describes the situation.

In the 3d Battalion sector, Hills 1286, 1577, and 1073 dominated the terrain and controlled the approaches to the pass. This pass on the MSR was vital to the continuing supply of units advancing northward. The 3d Battalion was to secure the pass and the surrounding area in order to keep open the lateral road from the Amidong sector to the east coast. This would permit supplies to be brought by LST to an east coast port, and from there to the west, and would therefore eliminate the necessity of using the long overland route from Pusan.

On 14 March 1951, the 7th Reconnaissance Company, together with Company I, 32d Infantry Regiment, was given the mission of reconnoitering and securing the pass. Company I was to take the high ground to the left of the road [Hill 1008].

At approximately 0400, 15 March, the 7th Reconnaissance Company moved out from Soksa-ri with two M4 tanks in the lead.

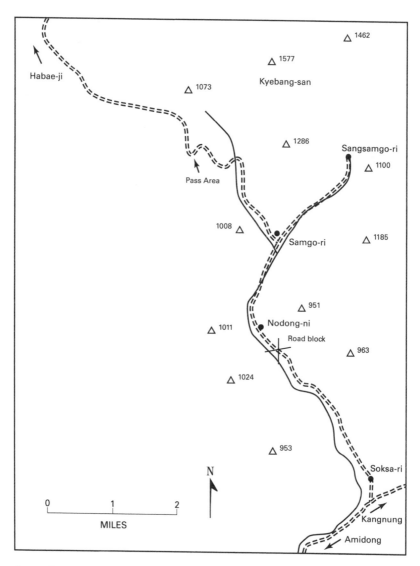

Area of operations, 3d Battalion, 32d Infantry, 15 March 1951 (original map by author, based on maps from the Army Map Service).

A scout section consisting of three jeeps with light machine guns and one radio jeep, and an 81mm mortar squad in two jeeps, and a rifle squad in a half-track followed. After moving approximately two and a half miles, the company encountered an enemy roadblock. The enemy had placed large boulders approximately three feet high across the road. Sergeant Rinehart, platoon sergeant, 1st Platoon, radioed to a squad of the 13th Engineers in the rear of the 1st Platoon to come forward and check the roadblock for mines and booby traps. After the engineer squad determined that there were no mines or booby traps, the company proceeded to clear the road-block. This required approximately four hours.

At 1015 the Reconnaissance Company arrived at the base of the ridgeline leading to Hill 1286. A liaison pilot in a plane overhead had spotted some enemy on this ridgeline, but he did not know whether they were alive or not. Sergeant Rinehart in the lead tank fired on these enemy positions with his .50-caliber machine gun. They responded with small-arms fire. Deploying at fifty-yard inter-vals, the company then from both sides of the road started to fire on the ridgeline.[1]

As the 7th Reconnaissance Company was exchanging fire with the enemy on Hill 1286, the 3d Battalion, 32d Infantry, moved forward. The battalion had arrived at Soksa-ri about 0900. Com-pany I quickly moved out in an approach march from Soksa-ri to Nodong-ni. While Company I secured Hill 1008, Company L was to join the 7th Reconnaissance Company at Samgo-ri and capture Hill 1286. The commanding officer of Company L, Capt. Freemont B. Hodson Jr., describes the situation when he received his orders.

In the early morning hours of March 15, Company I, together with the 7th Reconnaissance Company, went out to occupy the pass but did not succeed in doing so. A tank had gone through a bridge south of Nodong-ni and blocked the road. At 0900 hours the bat-talion arrived at Soksa-ri. At approximately 0930 Company L moved out in an approach march from Soksa-ri to the vicinity of Nodong-ni. At this point the battalion commander, Maj. Spencer Edwards, told me that I was to go to the top of Hill 1286, send people to Hill 1577, and then to cut down to Hill 1073. Samgo-ri was to be my line of departure. Company I was to be on the left of the road. Hill 1286 was to be the company objective for the day. After the pass was secured, the battalion was to secure the surrounding area and keep the lateral road from the Amidong sector to the east coast open. This road could be used as a supply route rather than the long overland route from Pusan.[2]

The company executive officer, 1st Lt. Jack D. Thomas, describes Company L's preparations for executing their mission.

At 0630 [15 March] we moved out by truck as far as Soksa-ri and unloaded. The company stayed approximately one hour. The company commander, Captain Hodson, was told to go approximately two miles farther up the road and meet the battalion commander, Maj. Spencer Edwards. The troops were to follow at once with the vehicles at the tail of the column. Upon reaching the command group, I met Captain Hodson. He gave the platoon leaders what information he had on the forthcoming attack. We dropped all unnecessary equipment including our packs. Ammunition of all types—grenades, bandoliers, machine-gun—was handed out. The company did not have enough ammunition on hand at the time because the attack had not been anticipated.

Company L moved up the road in a column of platoons. After marching approximately 700 yards we came upon the 7th Reconnaissance Company's position on the road and also saw Company I on the high ground to the left. Two air strikes had been placed on the objective for the day, Hill 1286.[3]

The platoon leader of the weapons platoon, 1st Lt. James F. Greer, provides additional details of Company L's approach to Hill 1286.

About 0930 Company L began its approach march from Soksa-ri to Hill 1286. The company moved up about five miles from Soksa-ri to the vicinity of Nodong-ni and at 1130 was given the attack order by Captain Hodson. We were issued C rations and dropped our packs and bedrolls. At 1215 we moved out with the 1st Platoon leading and with one squad on the high ground on the right as flank security. The rest of the company followed: mortar section, heavy-weapons attachment from Company M, followed by the 2d and 3d Platoons. A platoon of the 7th Reconnaissance Company—five tanks—was in front as advance guard of the company.

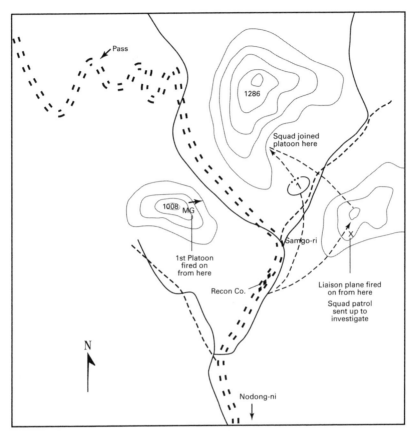

Initial deployment and attack (based on sketches in CMH manuscript, U.S. Army; not to scale).

Approximately 700 yards from the base of Hill 1286, a liaison plane came over and was fired on by the enemy from the high ground to the right and south of Hill 1286. The preceding day, air reconnaissance had reported the enemy position, but no enemy was sighted. The firing on the plane was the first indication that there were enemy on the hill or in the surrounding area.

As soon as the shots were heard, the squad on the right flank was sent up to reconnoiter and clear the ground, depending on the number of enemy there. When the squad reached the high ground they found no trace of the enemy. The squad rejoined the platoon.

The tanks in front of the company saw one lone enemy halfway up the ridgeline leading to Hill 1286. They fired three rounds of 76mm ammunition at the position, but results were undetermined.

The company in its original formation moved forward, with the 1st Platoon deploying in platoon column as they crossed the open ground leading to the base of Hill 1286. Upon reaching the base, they came under automatic-weapons fire from about 100 yards up the forward slope. Seeing this, I moved the 4th Platoon mortar section into a creek bed about 300 yards south of the hill. We started registering on the hill and immediately came under automatic-weapons fire from approximately 600 yards to our left flank in the sector of Company I. I displaced the mortar platoon forward about 200 yards to the base of Hill 1286 into a partially defiladed area. We proceeded to register on the hill.[4]

While Lieutenant Greer was moving his mortars into position, the 1st Platoon began the assault on the hill. The action is described by the company executive officer, Lieutenant Thomas, and members of the 1st Platoon: Sgt. Thomas G. Cline, 2d Squad leader; Cpl. Lawrence D. Swift, 1st Squad BAR man; and SFC Clyde J. Ging, 1st Squad leader.

LIEUTENANT THOMAS: Captain Hodson took the other three squads of the 1st Platoon up the road to the base of the ridgeline leading to Hill 1286. The squad sent to clear the high ground on the right of the road joined the platoon here. Captain Hodson, leading the 1st Platoon, deployed the platoon by squads and started up the slope. After advancing up the slope approximately 200 yards, the platoon received grenades and small-arms fire. This fire was coming from the forward slope short of the crest and from the right flank.[5]

MEMBERS OF 1ST PLATOON: The 1st Platoon, moving down the road from Soksa-ri, was informed by the company commander that it was to be the assault platoon in the attack on the ridgeline leading to Hill 1286. The 2d Squad had been sent on a patrol to a hill on the right of the road. The platoon continued on and reached the base of the ridgeline to Hill 1286. The 2d Squad joined the platoon here. At this time the platoon was fired on from a hill across the road in the sector of Company I. The platoon took cover around the base of the ridgeline and assembled for the assault.

Starting up the ridgeline in skirmish line four squads abreast, we advanced approximately a hundred yards. At this point we received a tremendous volume of grenades. The grenades were thrown from bunkers and foxholes near the top of the ridgeline. The 2d Squad received light-machine-gun fire from an enemy position on the ridgeline in their route of approach. The entire platoon then pulled back to the base of the ridgeline and reassembled.[6]

Captain Hodson describes his new plan of attack.

Not knowing the strength of the enemy, I pulled the platoon back approximately seventy-five yards to reorganize and formulate a new plan of attack. I called the battalion commander and told him I would like preparatory fires placed on the hill prior to jumping off again. The signal to start these fires would be a red star cluster. Another red star cluster would be the signal for supporting fires to cease.

I ordered that the 1st and 3d Platoon fix bayonets. In the meantime I instructed the 2d Platoon to work its way to the right and up the ridgeline to try to outflank the enemy. If this succeeded, fire could be brought on the enemy from two sides. I also gave the mortar section instructions that the 2d Platoon was to have priority of fires. The mortar section was to fire at twenty-five- to thirty-five-yard intervals from the lead elements of the 2d Platoon. I also arranged that two tanks, one quad 50, and one twin 40[7] were to fire on the ridgeline and any other targets of opportunity.[8]

The company executive officer, Lieutenant Thomas, provides more details of the attack plan.

The company commander called me via SCR300 radio[9] to bring the rest of the company up to the position. Upon arriving at the base of the hill we deployed, with the 1st Platoon on the left, the 3d Platoon in the center, and the 2d Platoon to proceed up a finger to the right to try and outflank the enemy positions.

The 1st and 3d Platoons were to attack up the forward slope and, if successful in securing any part of the ridge, were to pivot

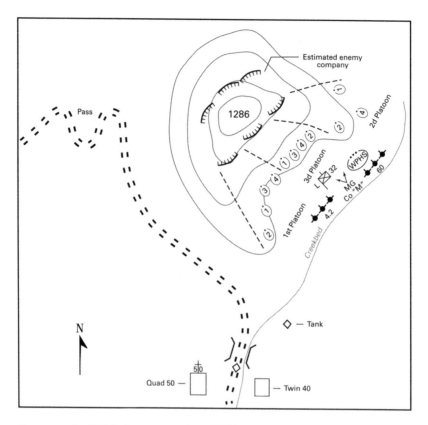

Company L, 32d Infantry, attack on Hill 1286, 15 March 1951 (based on sketches in CMH manuscript, U.S. Army; not to scale).

around and come up two platoons abreast and clean out the enemy on both sides of the ridgeline. The 2d Platoon was to proceed up the finger to the right. If they secured the ridgeline, they would stay there. While we were reorganizing, the company commander called the battalion commander and requested that all available supporting fires be placed on the hill at his signal.[10]

The weapons platoon leader, Lieutenant Greer, describes the supporting fires for the attack.

At this time, Captain Hodson called the battalion commander to arrange for supporting fires. Due to the immediate need of the supporting fires, we had approximately five minutes to arrange our signals and to get everyone prepared. We were informed by our artillery forward observer that due to the wide angle between his view of the target and the line from the guns to the target, it would endanger friendly troops to adjust artillery fire.

At 1315, a red star cluster was fired by Captain Hodson. This was the signal for the supporting fires to begin. Immediately, heavy concentrations of fire from 4.2-inch mortars, 81mm mortars, 60mm mortars, 76mm shells from the tanks, twin 40s, and quad 50s [along with .30- and .50-caliber machine guns mounted on jeeps] were brought to bear on the hill. At 1330 a second red star cluster was fired by Captain Hodson. This was the signal for all supporting fires to cease except organic weapons.[11]

Special measures were taken to silence the machine gun that had stopped the 2d Squad during the 1st Platoon's initial attack. Members of the 1st Platoon describe the situation.

Captain Hodson gave the tank commander the coordinates of the enemy machine-gun position that had fired on the 2d Squad. The tank fired on the position but did not silence it.

The platoon, after reassembling, was resupplied with grenades, approximately fifteen per man. At this time, the company commander told the squad leader of the 2d Squad to go up the ridgeline to a blind spot that was approximately twenty yards in front of the enemy machine-gun position. The squad was composed of four men. The 1st and 4th Squads and Company M's machine guns were to give supporting fires. The blind spot in front of the enemy machine-gun position was a small knoll that offered cover for approximately four men. The 2d Squad moved up in single file with approximately fifteen yards between men. Supporting fires were fired. The squad reached the knoll. The enemy machine gun was silenced after the squad had thrown about eight fragmentation grenades.[12]

Lieutenant Thomas describes the beginning of the attack.

At 1330, a second red star cluster was fired by the company commander, and all supporting fires were lifted. The 1st and 3d Platoons started forward and, after advancing approximately a hundred yards, came under heavy small-arms and automatic-weapons fire from enemy positions on the forward slope. Captain Hodson

was with the 1st Platoon; I was with the 3d Platoon. Hugging the
ground, we inched forward using BARs and light machine guns as
covering fire for the riflemen. The two platoons reached to within
twenty-five to fifty yards of the crest, when several hundred hand
grenades were thrown down on us. Grenades were thrown from
enemy positions on the forward slope. We threw what grenades we
had back at the enemy positions. Captain Hodson then called battalion for more grenades, bandoliers, and machine-gun ammunition. All during this period, Company M's heavy machine guns and
our 60mm mortars were placing fire on the crest of the hill.[13]

*The attack of the 3d Platoon is described by SFC Santos L.
Alecea, platoon guide; Sgt. Jimmy R. Hintz, 2d Squad leader; and
Cpl. Archie W. Fowler, light machine gunner in the 4th Squad.*

The enemy was well dug in, in log bunkers and foxholes. The
positions were camouflaged with pine needles, dry leaves, and dry
branches. Blending into the nature of the terrain, they were very
difficult to locate and fire on.

The platoon moved up the ridgeline in skirmish line, under protective overhead fire by Company M's light machine guns at the
base of the ridgeline. In the meantime, fire was being placed on the
hill by quad 50s, twin 40s, and .50-caliber machine guns. The quad
50s and twin 40s were from the 15th Antiaircraft Artillery unit attached to the battalion; the .50-caliber machine guns were from the
7th Reconnaissance Company, which formed the advance guard.
Moving up, creeping and crawling, the platoon advanced approximately a hundred yards. The enemy, estimated to be company size,
began throwing fragmentation and concussion grenades in tremendous volume from positions on the forward slope. Sergeant Alecea,
platoon guide, received fifteen grenades within fifteen feet of where
he was lying. The grenades were rolled down the hill, and many
were deflected by tree stumps and small culverts. Many of the grenades were duds. Sergeant Pearson, platoon sergeant and acting
platoon leader, was wounded by a fragmentation grenade. Sergeant
Alecea assumed command of the platoon and directed fire on the
enemy positions on the forward slope.

The platoon at this point was very low on ammunition and grenades. Knowing this, Captain Hodson, who was between the 1st and 3d Platoons, called down to First Sergeant MacGraff at the Company CP to get more grenades and ammunition up.[14]

As the 1st and 3d Platoons attacked up the ridge, the 2d Platoon worked its way around the right flank. Their attack is described by members of the unit: SFC Don R. LeSieur, 1st Squad leader; Cpl. Richard H. Neihardt, 1st Squad BAR man; and Cpl. Joe W. Powell, 4th Squad leader.

Having no platoon leader, the platoon sergeant, SFC Kenneth Patterson, organized the platoon into a line of skirmishers. The 1st Squad was on the right, the 2d on the left, and the 4th Squad in the center. The 3d Squad had been practically annihilated in another action a few days before, and replacements were not available. Our mission was to proceed up a finger to the right of the ridgeline leading to Hill 1286 and to clear the enemy, if any, on the right flank of the company. Sergeant Patterson told the squad leaders to keep the men dispersed as far as possible as we moved up the finger to avoid making good targets for the enemy. Sergeant Patterson assigned squad areas of attack.

At 1330 the second red star cluster was fired to stop the preparatory fires, but no one in the platoon saw it. However, Captain Hodson, with the 1st and 3d Platoons on our left, called to us, "Get up that hill." Creeping and crawling, we started moving up, two squads abreast with one in support. All members were firing their weapons, yelling "banzai," and blowing whistles. About halfway up the ridgeline, approximately 200 yards, everyone started yelling for more ammunition. The enemy was firing small-arms and automatic-weapons fire from the ridgeline to our left and from several positions above us on the forward slope. The enemy fire was ineffective due to the steepness of the terrain.[15]

Lieutenant Greer, weapons platoon leader, describes the supporting fires for the attack and the ammunition resupply effort.

The company started its attack. The enemy, having recovered somewhat from the concentrations of supporting fires, began firing heavy small-arms and automatic-weapons fire from all along the ridgeline and from the crest of Hill 1286. The 1st and 3d Platoon's advance was stopped. Captain Hodson had sent the 2d Platoon approximately 300 yards to the right in a flanking movement. The heavy machine guns of Company M were given a new sector of fire, covering the advance of the 2d Platoon to the crest of Hill 1286 and between the 2d and 3d Platoons, from which the mortar section at the base of the hill was receiving automatic-weapons fire.

The advance of the 1st and 3d Platoons was very slow due to the nature of the terrain. Hill 1286 was very steep, heavily wooded with very sharp and rocky ridgelines. All SCR536 radios[16] were nonoperative. There was no contact with the 2d Platoon on the right.

As the 1st and 3d Platoons crawled forward on their bellies they were met by heavy small-arms and automatic-weapons fire from enemy positions just above them on the forward slope. The 60mm mortars continued to fire on the ridgeline and the crest of Hill 1286 in support of the 1st and 3d Platoons. About this time the 2d Platoon came into view as they advanced up the ridgeline to the right of the 1st and 3d Platoons. They carried an identification panel with their lead elements. They came under heavy automatic-weapons fire from the crest of Hill 1286. The 60mm mortar fire was shifted to support the 2d Platoon, as they reported they were low on ammunition. By observing their panel, I was able to place 60mm mortar fire within twenty-five yards of their lead elements.

The company as a whole was running low on ammunition. The first sergeant took all available personnel from company headquarters to the ammunition trailer and brought up a resupply. He informed the battalion commander of the ammunition situation, and an M19 from the antiaircraft artillery unit was sent forward with a resupply of mortar, small-arms, and grenade ammunition.

The 57mm recoilless-rifle section could not be used in direct support of the company due to wooded terrain. The men from this section plus the ammunition bearers from the heavy-machine-gun section were used to carry the ammunition to the men on the hill.[17]

Members of the 2d Platoon describe how they resupplied themselves with ammunition.

The platoon had nine ROK soldiers as members of the unit. Realizing the need for additional ammunition, Sergeant Patterson sent these soldiers, together with the platoon guide, to the Company CP to secure a resupply. The carrying party started back up the ridgeline with the ammunition, but only machine-gun ammunition was received. The platoon guide, who was carrying the bandoliers for the BARs and riflemen, passed out on the way up and did not reach the platoon position. The BARs were forced to use the machine-gun ammunition. This was done by taking the rounds out of the belts and loading them into the BAR magazines.[18]

Members of the 3d Platoon describe the replenishment of their ammunition and the continuation of the attack.
Approximately ten minutes later the grenades and ammunition called for by Captain Hodson were brought up by two ammunition bearers of Company M. Approximately 400 grenades were brought up. Men from each squad crawled down the ridgeline approximately thirty feet from their positions and brought the grenades up. Approximately fifteen grenades were distributed to each man.

Resupplied with grenades and ammunition the platoon advanced with 1st, 3d, and 4th Squads on line. The 2d Squad on the right flank was pinned down by light-machine-gun fire from the forward slope and could not advance. The advancing squads, creeping and crawling, fired their weapons and threw grenades at the enemy positions. In the meantime Corporal Fowler, 4th Squad, fired his light machine gun at the enemy machine-gun position that was keeping the squad on the right pinned down. After firing three bursts from his light machine gun the enemy gun was silenced. The 2d Squad then crawled up on line with the other three squads.[19]

Members of the 1st Platoon describe their attack at this time.
At this time the enemy started firing burp guns, Russian BARs, and machine guns from foxholes and bunkers on top of the ridge. The platoon crawled forward to within twenty-five yards of the enemy positions. The company commander told the platoon not to throw grenades until they could see the trajectory of the enemy gre-

nades. The grenade battle lasted for approximately forty-five minutes. The company commander thought that the company could assault the enemy positions and take them without excessive casualties. The 3d Platoon had moved up on line with the 1st Platoon.

The whole platoon started forward in crouch silhouettes firing as they advanced. During the advance, grenades were still being thrown by the enemy but not in as great a quantity as before.[20]

Lieutenant Greer, with the weapons platoon at the base of the ridge, had a good view of the enemy grenade attack.

With the resupply of ammunition the attack gained momentum but was stopped cold approximately thirty yards from the ridgeline leading to Hill 1286. At this point approximately 100 to 150 fragmentation and other grenades resembling ink bottles were thrown by the enemy. The platoon sergeant of the 2d Platoon, SFC Ambrose P. Pearson, thought that the grenades were 60mm mortar rounds dropping in too close. He called down for me to cease fire, which I did immediately. After the mortars ceased fire the explosions continued, and I heard someone holler, "grenades." The men of the 1st and 3d Platoons watched the trajectory of the enemy grenades in flight and threw back accordingly. After several minutes of the grenade exchange, the enemy troops withdrew from the forward slope to positions on the reverse side of the ridgeline. Several were cut down by light-machine-gun fire from the 1st and 3d Platoons.[21]

Captain Hodson explained the reasoning behind his order not to throw grenades.

I then went along the line of the 1st and 2d Platoons and instructed them not to throw any more grenades until they could see the trajectory of the enemy grenades. The enemy was so well emplaced that grenades were thrown without the men being able to see exactly where they were coming from. A resupply of grenades was received by the platoons, and the attack continued.

At 1630 I ceased fire the entire company. I then called my ROK interpreter, and he called out to the enemy in Korean, "I'll give you two minutes to surrender or we'll kill every one of you." The enemy listened and didn't fire a shot. At the end of the two-minute period no enemy surrendered. We opened fire again.[22]

Lieutenant Greer describes the next phase of the grenade action.

The 1st and 3d Platoons were able to advance about fifteen yards without receiving any fire or grenades. When they were within approximately ten yards of the crest line, they were again met by a heavy volume of enemy grenades from positions on the reverse slope of the ridgeline. Using the same tactics as before, the platoons threw grenades back.

The company supply at this time was very low. Captain Hodson asked battalion for more grenades. Having about 500 in supply, these were brought up by the same people who brought up the initial supply of ammunition. Resupplied with grenades, the 1st Platoon started swinging around the flank across the ridgeline. The 2d Platoon on the right had overcome all resistance in its sector and was advancing rapidly to the crest of Hill 1286. As the 1st Platoon crossed the ridgeline, enemy resistance was broken. The 3d Platoon moved on to the ridgeline and advanced rapidly to the crest of Hill 1286.[23]

Members of the company describe what happened next.

3D PLATOON MEN: At the end of the two-minute period Captain Hodson hollered to the platoons, "Give 'em hell." Being approximately ten to twenty feet from the enemy positions on the crest of the ridgeline, the platoon rushed in and secured the position.[24]

1ST PLATOON MEN: A couple of enemy, hearing this, jumped out of their foxholes and started running down the reverse slope. The platoon then attacked the top of the ridgeline and overran the enemy positions. Some enemy still in their foxholes continued to fire on the platoon. These were eliminated by dropping grenades into the holes. The platoon cleared its area and tied into the left flank of the 3d Platoon.[25]

LIEUTENANT THOMAS: The 1st Platoon began to work its way around the left flank and over the slope. The 3d Platoon swung around to the right and came up on the enemy positions. As both platoons were securing the enemy positions the enemy was running down the reverse slope in the general direction of north.[26]

CAPTAIN HODSON: A few of the enemy began to get out of their foxholes and run back down the ridgeline. Our light machine guns killed six or eight of them as they ran. As the 1st and 3d Platoons began to overrun the enemy positions, the enemy began crawling out of their positions hollering "surrender." In the meantime the 2d Platoon had been successful in its mission and was on top of the ridgeline to our right. They had taken the ridge without suffering a casualty.[27]

Men of the 2d Platoon describe their final advance up the ridge.

Resupplied with ammunition, we started moving again on our bellies. At this time, approximately 1700, we noticed three or four enemy moving to the right on the ridgeline. We thought they were trying to outflank the platoon position. Corporal Neihardt fired two magazines from his BAR at the enemy, hitting two of them. The others ran over the crest of the ridgeline.

The platoon continued to advance with two squads on line. The 3d Squad supported the advance by firing their BARs as overhead covering fire. It was now approximately 1730 hours. At about 1800 hours we reached the top of the ridgeline. One enemy soldier was in position in his foxhole on top of the ridgeline. He was bayoneted and shot by one of the riflemen.

The platoon then moved to the right on the ridgeline to the northeast to clear the enemy out of positions approximately one hundred yards away. This was the ridgeline that led to Hill 1286. In its original formation the platoon secured the position and found only one North Korean soldier. He was taken prisoner. The platoon then deployed in a perimeter defense along the ridgeline for the night. One squad was sent out approximately 150 yards to set up an outpost. There was no further enemy activity during the night.[28]

Captain Hodson describes the enemy losses.

Thirty-two enemy dead were counted on the position along with eleven prisoners. We captured a large quantity of burp guns and automatic weapons. Included in the enemy dead was a regimental commander of the North Korean army. We found maps showing the enemy defenses in the area. The prisoners stated that a regiment of North Koreans was in the vicinity of Hill 1577, and their mission was to hold the pass at all costs.[29]

Company L lost two men killed and eight wounded during the attack, all due to grenade fire. On the ridgeline leading to Hill 1286 the company reorganized and established a defense perimeter against a possible counterattack. The next day, 16 March, the 2d Platoon led the advance on Hill 1577.

At 0930 the platoon started again working its way up the ridgeline. This was accomplished by leapfrogging squads. Moving across the crest of Hill 1286, the platoon continued on toward Hill 1577. At 1200 the platoon reached the crest of Hill 1577 encountering no enemy resistance.[30]

Clearing the enemy from the terrain along this supply route allowed the 7th Infantry Division advance to continue. The fight of Company L, 32d Infantry, for Hill 1286 was typical of actions fought across the front during Operation Ripper, as UN forces pushed north against Chinese Communist and North Korean rear guards. This particular fight for this hill stuck in the minds of many soldiers because of the prominent role that hand grenades played in it.

Chapter 3

BREAKING THE HONGCH'ON DEFENSE LINE

3d Battalion, 5th Cavalry Regiment, 13–18 March 1951

When the second phase of Operation Ripper began on 14 March 1951, the enemy initially fell back before the UN advance, except for small rearguard forces. These groups of Chinese and North Koreans sought to delay the progress of the UN troops to buy time to strengthen their main defensive positions on high ground north of the Hongch'on River and to evacuate supplies stockpiled at their base at Ch'unch'on. General Ridgway's main effort (see map on page 18), directed on Hongch'on and Ch'unch'on, consisted of two divisions from IX Corps, the 1st Cavalry on the left (west) and the 1st Marine on the right (east). The 1st Cavalry Division in turn directed the reinforced 5th Cavalry Regiment to attack early on 14 March. Regimental orders initially called for the 3d Battalion of the 5th Cavalry to remain on Phase Line Albany, some five miles south of the Hongch'on River. As the operation began to unfold, the 3d Battalion's role became dominant. The battalion commander, Maj. Charles J. Parziale, explains what happened.

On 13 March 1951, the relief of Australian elements by the 3d Battalion, 5th Cavalry Regiment, was a routine matter. One company of the battalion was placed on Hill 703. The remainder of the battalion was disposed on tactical positions to the east and west to maintain contact with a company of the 6th ROK Division on the left and the 5th Marine Regiment on the right.

On the afternoon of 13 March the regimental commander notified me of a pending move. I alerted Company I, which was on Hill 703, and the other battalion elements. Upon reporting to regimental

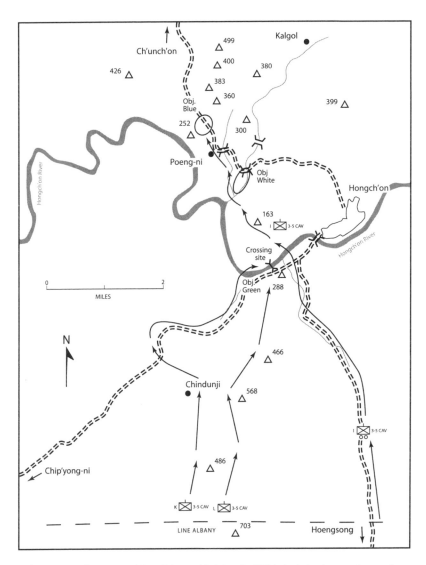

Advance to the Hongch'on River, 14 March 1951 (original map by author, based on maps from the Army Map Service).

headquarters, I was informed that the 3d Battalion would remain on Phase Line Albany while the other battalions, plus the 2d Battalion, 7th Cavalry Regiment, which was attached to the 5th Cavalry Regiment, moved forward.

When the regimental commander learned that 3d Battalion patrols were operating some 5,000 meters to the front during the day, he instructed me to send one company toward Objective Green (Hill 288) and assist the 1st Battalion in taking that objective. The remainder of the battalion was to occupy Phase Line Albany.

On my return to the battalion I ordered Company L to move at midnight toward Objective Green and assist the 1st Battalion in the capture of that objective. Company L was also to be prepared to take Objective Green itself.[1]

The Advance over the Hongch'on River

The commander of Company L, Capt. Robert J. Cook, describes his company's situation when the order to advance was received, and the subsequent night move to Objective Green.

On 13 March, when Company L relieved troops of the Australian Rifles on Hill 703, additional ammunition, a full day's C ration, and water were brought by a carrying detail of twenty men from the company. Each man carried a minimum of forty pounds from a point three miles distant. Extra batteries for the SCR 300 and SCR 536 radios were also carried.

That night at 2300, Company L was ordered to move as quickly as possible to Checkpoint 3, a small hill at the mouth of the junction of two valleys to the north [about 2,000 meters north of Hill 703]. The company then was to move across Hill 568 and Hill 466 in order. These points had to be cleared physically.

Company L moved at 0030, 14 March, from Hill 703 to the valley generally north. The company carried all its equipment including ammunition, mountain bedrolls, rations, individual and organizational weapons (including three 57mm [recoilless] rifles, three 60mm mortars, three 3.5-inch bazookas, three light machine guns, and nine BARs). Some extra rations and ammunition had to be left on Hill 703, and the battalion picked this up later that day. Company L at this time had an additional section of ROK personnel, comprising some twenty-five men, who were operating attached to the 2d Platoon. These men were armed with BARs, one Bren gun, and M-1 rifles.

On this move north from Hill 703 the night was cloudy, without moon or stars. Although searchlights had been requested and were turned on, they were ineffective. It took the company five and a half hours to reach the valley. Movement was made over very mountainous terrain, complicated by ice and snow on the northern slopes. In some places snowdrifts were between four and six feet deep. Some ridges were narrow and so icy that the ridgeline could not be followed. For the most part, the company advanced in single file. This advance was made tactically in enemy territory, under blackout conditions, and in silence. Because of previous white phosphorus shelling and tracer bullets, portions of the terrain were on fire, and the stifling smoke was a real hazard to the troops.

The only guide to the movement was the terrain itself, which was followed to lower ground. Because of the rapidity of the order and the move, no reconnaissance was possible. The reason for the rapidity of the action was the company could not afford to be caught in the valley under enemy observation and fire. Therefore, it was desired to reach the first objective before daylight.

The melting snow was packed into ice by the moving company, and men fell down as many as twenty or thirty times, often off the ridgeline into a gully. Silence was maintained surprisingly well.

Three-quarters of the way down the terrain became terraced rice paddies, over-crusted with a thin layer of ice, beneath which was thick mud.

Radio communication was not possible most of the way down.

Two casualties resulted on this march. One man sprained his ankle, but he hobbled down the mountain assisted by others. Another man, one-third of the way down, broke his leg by slipping off the route of march into a rocky streambed. He was carried down the mountain by litter to the valley where he was picked up later that day by helicopter called in by the battalion.

There were no stragglers.

While the company was reorganizing in the valley, a five-man patrol went ahead and reported back in twenty-five minutes. The company moved out immediately because only thirty minutes remained before daylight, and it was necessary to reach the next objective before that time.

A few minutes before dawn the company started up the objective [Hill 568], a high hill which rose abruptly from the valley floor. The company moved up tactically with one platoon on scout. Unoccupied enemy positions were found.

On this objective the company took its first break. The men rested an hour until about 0900.

The remainder of the day was spent crossing to Hill 466. The company was digging in on Hill 466 at 1530 when the order came to move the company north to Hill 288, south of and overlooking the Hongch'on River.

In the meantime I sent the executive officer and one man two or three miles to the nearest road to contact someone in the company rear and secure an indigenous [South Korean] carrying party to return with rations and water. While the executive officer was after rations, the battalion changed the company mission to that of having the company assemble in the vicinity of the river preparatory to crossing the stream and taking Objective White.

At 1700 Company L was off Hill 466 and assembled on the banks of the river west of the stream junction. The company crossed there at 1800.[2]

Major Parziale describes the additional orders received by the 3d Battalion.

By daylight, Company L had made very good progress; it had moved 5,000 meters in darkness. I instructed the company to expedite its movement, but to screen carefully so that no enemy units would be bypassed.

At 0800, 14 March, the regimental commander ordered me to move my entire battalion forward to secure Objective Green and establish a line south of the Hongch'on River. I ordered the other companies of the battalion to assist Company L on Objective Green. I requested eight trucks from regiment to motorize Company I. I ordered Company K to proceed overland by the best route available to the junction of the road and the river west of Hongch'on.

I joined the regimental commander about 1000 and informed him of my plan of movement. The regimental commander then instructed me to take Objective White, a hill mass across the Hongch'on

River. After securing Objective White the 3d Battalion was to secure Objective Blue, the valley south of the approaches to Hill 383.[3]

The S-3 of the 3d Battalion, Capt. James V. Marsh, provides additional details of the move of Company L and the subsequent missions received by the 3d Battalion.

At 0045, 14 March, Company L, with a machine-gun section from Company M attached, moved north to the high ground and crossed Hill 568 to Hill 466, arriving at the latter point at 1030. The company then moved to its objective [a hill about 700 meters northeast of Hill 466, overlooking the main road and Objective Green] and arrived there at 1230, without meeting the enemy. Freshly dug enemy positions, which had been abandoned, were found. This move on foot was made at night over very rugged mountainous terrain. No roads were available. One nonbattle casualty resulted. A man who broke his leg on the treacherous terrain was evacuated down the mountain by litter, and was later evacuated for hospital treatment by helicopter. The heavy-machine-gun section attached to Company L hand-carried its guns.

The other battalions of the regiment jumped off between 0700 and 0800, 14 March. At 1050, regiment ordered the 3d Battalion to Hill 288 [Objective Green]. Company K cleared the high ground north of its position to Hill 486, then moved to the high ground northeast of Chindunji. The company then proceeded northwest, emerged on the road, and advanced northeast to its objective. The heavy-machine-gun section attached to Company K hand-carried its guns.

At 1130 the regimental commander ordered the 3d Battalion to displace its CP to Hill 288, and from there to move later to the vicinity of Objective White [high ground about 2,000 meters northwest of Hongch'on].

The 3d Battalion headquarters secured six trucks from the regimental Service Company to transport Company I by road to a point on the river west of Hill 288. Company I departed its area at 1315 and arrived at 1500. Company M, with its mortars and 75mm rifles, and the 3d Platoon of the Heavy Mortar Company were ordered to accompany Company I on organic transportation. These elements arrived with Company I.

At 1330 the 3d Battalion was ordered to move on Objective Blue through the preceding Objectives Green and White. This order was transmitted by radio to the companies, which were in the process of displacement.[4]

Capt. Edward R. Stevens, commander of Company I, describes the crossing of the Hongch'on River and the advance north of the river.

Company I crossed the Hongch'on River between 1400 and 1500. Twelve prisoners were taken without resistance in a village just above the crossing. The company moved north about 2,000 yards to a hill. The company objective was Hill 383, but darkness was approaching, so the company moved to Company K's objective [Objective Blue], where it encountered enemy small-arms, automatic-weapons, and a great deal of mortar and artillery fire. Initial enemy fire from the lower approaches of Hill 380 caused eight wounded and one killed. The company withdrew to high ground where it remained that night and 15 March.[5]

Major Parziale recalls his plan for the move north of the river and the ensuing action. There was some misunderstanding between Parziale and Stevens as to the mission of Company I after crossing the river.

Company I arrived at the river at 1300, and the vehicles transported the company across, just west of the river-stream junction. The men dismounted from the trucks, and Captain Stevens, the company commander, joined me on Hill 163. I instructed Captain Stevens to secure Objective White and hold it until the remainder of the battalion arrived.

My plan at that time was to leave Company I on Objective White and pass Companies K and L (with Company L on the left) to secure Hills 383 and 380 that afternoon. However, due to the terrain over which Companies K and L were moving, those companies did not arrive prior to 1700.

Company I in the meantime had somehow bypassed Objective

White and, prior to darkness, engaged the enemy in a severe fire-fight, just southwest of the bridge. I ordered Company I to secure the high ground to the west and button up for the night. When Company L arrived, it was ordered to secure Objective White. Company K, arriving later, was ordered to secure the right flank and the rear of the battalion.

Both flanks were open, for the 2d Battalion was to the left rear, and the Marines had not yet crossed the river.

The battalion CP was immediately to the rear of Objective White. The supporting weapons of Company M, less the machine guns attached to the rifle companies, were also near Objective White. Two platoons of Company B, 70th Tank Battalion, initially with the battalion, were replaced on the following day by two platoons of Company A, the tank company that normally worked with the 3d Battalion.[6]

The push of Company I against the hills north of the river and the movement of the rest of the battalion across the Hongch'on awakened the enemy artillery and mortars. Both Companies K and L came under fire as they crossed the river and moved into position. The most affected were the 3d Battalion's mortars, as recounted by Major Parziale.

The heavy mortars and the 81mm mortars which moved up at 1400 within supporting range supported the attack of Company I. These weapons, however, came under an enemy counter-mortar and artillery barrage, and all members of the heavy-mortar fire direction center were either killed or wounded. The 81mm mortar platoon also suffered casualties from this fire. The mortars, however, remained in position during daylight in support of Company I. After dark they were ordered to withdraw to the rear of Objective White.[7]

The battalion S-3, Captain Marsh, provides more detail about the battalion's actions north of the river, the effect of the enemy fire, and the situation as the day ended.

Crossing the Hongch'on River immediately upon its arrival, Company I was on Objective White at 1700. Company L was moved off the high ground, and it followed Company I across the river just west of the stream junction.

At 1745 proceeding toward Objective Blue, and in the vicinity of the bridge, Company I received initial enemy fire of small arms and automatic weapons. Thirty minutes later, enemy mortar fire began to be received by the company.

In the meantime Company K was clearing the high ground south of the Hongch'on River. This was a slow process, even though the company met nothing but the terrain, which impeded its progress.

North of the Hongch'on River the 3d Platoon, Heavy Mortar Company, and the 81mm Mortar Platoon, Company M, moved across the valley floor to a point from which support could be rendered to Company I in its attack on Objective Blue [the mortar position was at the southwest base of Objective White, near the stream]. At 1815, as Company I was moving on its objective and the mortars were giving support, the heavy mortar platoon received enemy 120mm mortar fire and suffered two killed and eight wounded in action. At 1950 both the heavy mortar and the 81mm mortar forward observers with Company I were struck by enemy mortar bursts.

Due to the heavy enemy fire and the approaching darkness, Company I was instructed to button up for the night on the high ground near Poeng-ni instead of pushing on toward Hill 383. The battalion felt that the enemy main line of resistance, covering the river, had been contacted, and that the battalion was in a good position from which to continue its attack since the river had been crossed and the edge of Objective Blue had been reached.

Company L was moved on Objective White and instructed to button up there for the night. It completed organizing its position at 2000. Company K was placed on the high ground to protect the battalion right flank, and it closed at 2030.

No friendly forces [Marines] had crossed the river on the 3d Battalion right flank. Elements of the 2d Battalion, 5th Cavalry Regiment, had that day secured the left flank of the 3d Battalion by crossing the river and occupying the high ground in the loop of the river. A 1,000-yard north–south gap, however, existed between this 2d Battalion position and Company I.

During the evening of 14 March the enemy harassed Company I with small-arms and mortar fire. The remainder of the battalion received harassing enemy mortar fire. The battalion CP was moved to the vicinity of Objective White. A section of the 75mm rifles (two) from Company M was attached to Company I, and a section was attached to Company L. The communications section of the battalion headquarters worked constantly through the night of 14–15 March under enemy mortar and artillery fire. At 2000 the 3d and 4th Platoons, Company A, 70th Tank Battalion, reported to the battalion as attachments. The 61st Field Artillery Battalion was in direct support, and the batteries fired after Company I had made contact with the enemy.

The rapid movement of the battalion across the Hongch'on River established the bridgehead and made further advance possible. To achieve this, Companies K and L had traveled almost 10,000 map yards on foot on 14 March over the worst kind of mountainous terrain. Relay radio stations had had to be set up because of the difficulty of receiving communications in that rugged terrain.

Between the time of initial enemy contact and the morning of 15 March, approximately 300 rounds of all types of enemy mortar and artillery fire were received by the battalion.

The 1st Battalion remained south of the Hongch'on River in the vicinity of Objective Green, Hill 288. On the right flank the Marines were about 2,000 yards south of the river.[8]

The Hongch'on Defense Line

Although the 3d Battalion knew they had reached the enemy's main defensive position, they did not have a clear picture of its location and strength. The next day, 15 March, the battalion dispatched patrols to gather more information. Captain Marsh summarizes the day's activities.

On 15 March the battalion consolidated and improved its positions and sent out patrols to find, fix, and soften up the enemy. Company K moved north about 400 yards. Tank patrols moved up the northeast valley toward Kalgol, and also up the MSR to the northwest [the Ch'unch'on road] until mines were reached. Friendly

81mm and 4.2-inch mortars as well as artillery fired on suspected enemy positions. About thirty prisoners were taken by Company I and the tank patrols. The Tactical Air Control Liaison Officer who joined the battalion during the day called in three or four air strikes on Hills 383, 300, and 499. The battalion continued to receive heavy mortar fire.

The Marines advanced on the right flank to Hill 239. The 2d Battalion, 5th Cavalry, on the left remained in position and sent out patrols.[9]

On 15 March the battalion intelligence officer, 1st Lt. Alma G. Longstroth, set up an observation post on the hill above the CP, but smoke and haze made observation difficult. Patrol reports and prisoner interrogations provided little specific information about the enemy's defensive positions. After the battle Lieutenant Longstroth learned the extent of the enemy field fortifications and defensive preparations. He outlined them in a report dated 4 April 1951.

Songch'i Mountain, two miles west of Hongch'on and over 540 meters high, by its location controls the MSR to Ch'unch'on. It consists of the numbered hills 499, 383, and 380 and the unnumbered hills 300, 360, and 400. The unnumbered hills the enemy chose to defend with his main strength. From many of the enemy positions a commanding view of the corridor followed by the MSR can be obtained.

Songch'i Mountain with its strategic location was also very good ground for defense. The eastern slope of the ridge connecting 380 and 300 is very steep with many cliffs making ascent practically impossible. Hill 300, where the bulk of the defending enemy was entrenched, has only scattered lightly wooded areas making concealment of defensive positions easy, but affording little concealment for assaulting troops. The ridges running southwest from Hill 300, going from south to north, are inclined sharply near the top making overhead supporting fire by heavy machine guns ideal.

The fortifications on Songch'i Mountain consisted of well prepared camouflaged trenches, caves, bunkers, and dugouts. Communication trenches averaging five feet in depth were located just over the crest on the reverse slope of the defended ridges. This trench was linked with the firing positions on the forward slope by similar trenches. The majority of the firing positions were covered with logs and dirt.

Mortar positions, both 60mm and 81mm, were of three distinct types and were located on the ridgelines, probably to increase their range. Concealment of flash was accomplished by positioning mortars behind groves of trees. The three types of positions were: (a) dug-in positions with overhead cover for ammo and crews with only the tube visible from the air above; (b) large circular pits with communication trenches to covered ammo pits and sleeping quarters; and (c) circular gun pits with steps down to eight- to ten-foot-deep trenches with ammo and sleeping-quarter caves.

Command posts were placed in ravines to the rear of the entrenchments and were located in spacious dugouts and caves. U.S. Army field telephones were the main means of communication; however, many colored smoke grenades and some Very [flare] pistol ammunition were found in the CP installations.

Dug-in positions without communication trenches were everywhere on the mountain. Some were strategically located to guard flanks and rear and were mostly automatic-weapons positions. The others appeared to be for reserve elements.

The enemy was well equipped with weapons. Light machine guns were mostly of the Bren type as evidenced by the fact that seven web and leather gun covers for Bren guns were found by light-machine-gun positions. Heavy machine guns were the U.S. Army water-cooled type. Mortars were 81mm, 82mm, and 60mm and were employed in sections of two or three with OPs close to the gun positions. The enemy dead that were searched in the area were mostly carrying U.S. carbine, M-1, or caliber .45 ammunition. It is thought that the enemy was supported by artillery units located along the MSR to their right rear, as much artillery fire was received by friendly elements from that direction.

From the amount of fortifications on Songch'i Mountain it appears that a reinforced regiment prepared positions on the southern slopes with another regiment dug in on positions along the ridgelines extending west and east–southeast from Hill 540. The forward regiment's main line of resistance was dug in on Hills 360 and 300 with reserve elements on Hills 400 and 383 and an outpost line generally running east and west to the south of Hills 360 and 300.[10]

Unfortunately, the 3d Battalion did not know as much about the enemy positions on 15 March as they did a few days later. Other than artillery and mortar fire, the Chinese did little to reveal their strength or locations. Consequently, the 3d Battalion was ordered to conduct a reconnaissance in force against the hill mass on 16 March. Major Parziale describes the situation and his plan.

On 15 March aggressive patrolling was performed to find and fix the enemy. Infantry and tank patrols moved up both valley roads to the right and left of the hill mass. During the entire day and evening of 15 March the enemy subjected patrols, companies, and command posts to intense mortar and artillery fire. The supply route was almost untenable. Very few casualties, however, resulted.

That day regiment ordered the battalion to conduct a reconnaissance in force in order to gain better positions and to buy more real estate cheap.

That evening I briefed the company commanders, the tank platoon leaders, the platoon leader of the heavy mortar platoon, and the members of my staff. I instructed Company L to conduct a reconnaissance in force on Hill mass 383. The size of the reconnoitering force was to be a reinforced rifle platoon, supported by a tank platoon. Company K was given the same mission for Hill 380 with the same support. Company I was to secure the left flank of the battalion and support the advance of Company L by fire. Company I was to be prepared to pass through Company L, when that company attained its objective, and take Hill 499. The heavy mortar platoon was to be in direct support of one company; the 81mm Mortar Platoon in direct support of the other. Company M was to move the 75mm rifles into the Company I position to support Company L's advance and also to fire up the road toward Ch'unch'on.

I based my orders on the following facts: (1) the regiment had limited the battalion to making a reconnaissance in force, not a full-strength attack; (2) I felt a reconnaissance in force would enable the battalion to gain a toehold on the approaches to the enemy positions; (3) an all-out attack was not warranted because of the situation on the right and left flanks; (4) even if the reconnaissance in force gained no ground, it would determine enemy strength and the location of enemy flanks.

I felt that the hill mass comprising Hills 383, 380, and 499 was held by a reinforced enemy battalion. I was led to believe this because enemy mortars were not usually in support of an enemy company, and also because the enemy was firing at least two batteries of 105mm howitzers.[11]

The battalion S-3, Captain Marsh, provides more details of the plan of support for the attack.

The section of 75mm rifles with Company L remained in place to give long-range supporting fire. The machine-gun sections with Companies L and K accompanied the attack groups. Artillery, 4.2-inch, and 81mm mortar forward observers were with the rifle companies. The 3d Platoon, Company A, 70th Tank Battalion, was ordered to move northwest on the MSR in support of Company L. The 4th Platoon, Company A, 70th Tank Battalion, was ordered to move up the valley to the northeast to support Company K. A squad of the P&A Platoon, 3d Battalion, was to accompany each tank platoon to clear mines.[12]

Platoons' Reconnaissance in Force

Capt. R. M. Lohela, commander of Company K, describes the situation and the advance of his platoon during the reconnaissance in force.

On the night of 15 March the battalion commander ordered Company K to move one reinforced platoon to the ridge leading to Hill 380 with the mission of taking Hill 380. Company L would operate to the left of Company K; the Marines on the right were not abreast of the battalion. The enemy situation was not known.

That night I was informed by regiment that a possible case of typhus existed in Company K. Therefore, when I returned from the battalion briefing, I awoke the company and between 2400 and 0200 made certain that every man used DDT powder. The typhus case later turned out to be measles.

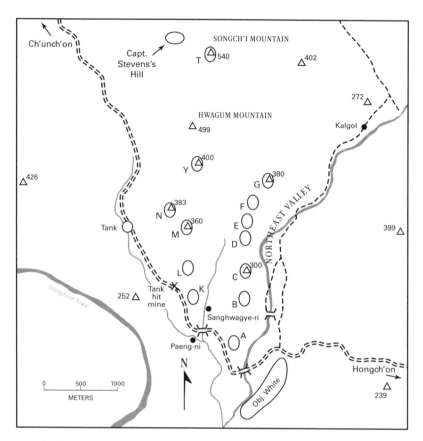

Attack of the 3d Battalion, 5th Cavalry, 16–18 March 1951 (original map by author, based on maps from the Army Map Service).

On 16 March, although an air and artillery preparation was to be made prior to the jump-off, atmospheric conditions [heavy ground haze or fog] prevented an air strike. I do not know why there was no artillery.

At 0715 the 1st Platoon, commanded by Second Lieutenant Barr and reinforced with one 57mm rifle, two extra BAR teams, and one section of light machine guns from Company M, moved out. Extra ammunition was carried by this group. Artillery and 81mm mortar observers accompanied the platoon, as did Lieutenant Delaney who was to coordinate the supporting weapons. Lieutenant Barr, who had radio communication with five tanks at the bridge, moved to join the tanks. The platoon forded the river just below the bridge and crossed the rice paddies. An enemy barrage just missed the platoon. The tanks went up the northeast valley between the river and the ridge along the valley floor.

At 0740 the 1st Platoon reached the base of the hill. There, enemy small-arms and machine-gun fire was received, some of it from the left, some of it from the point of the hill. Two casualties resulted.

At 0755 the platoon reached Objective A [see map on page 52] under mortar fire from the village to the left. At 0815 the platoon reached Objective B without making physical contact with the enemy. Enemy small-arms, machine-gun, and automatic-weapons fire was received by the platoon from the left and pinned down the platoon on Objective B for one hour and thirty minutes. The platoon suffered three wounded in action and five nonbattle casualties. Lieutenant Delaney was wounded but remained with the platoon.

The supporting tanks were receiving mortar fire and could fire only against the right side of the ridge, and not against enemy positions located on the fingers to the left of the ridge. Pinned down at 0945, Lieutenant Barr called for an air strike. An air strike was delivered against Objectives C and D at 1000.

At 1015 the 1st Platoon moved out toward Objective C. Machine guns, BARs, and the 57mm rifle were left on Objective B for supporting fire. The 57mm rifle knocked out an enemy bunker at the base of Objective C, and the tanks neutralized one enemy bunker on the right side of Objective D. A four-strand barbed wire obstacle existed at the base of Objective C. As the platoon assaulted through grenades, satchel charges, and small-arms fire from the objective, the supporting fires lifted, and the platoon gained Objective C with no further casualties. Enemy machine-gun fire was still being received from the left, the objective of the Company L attack.

At 1045 the supporting weapons moved from Objective B and joined the platoon on Objective C. From there, support was rendered while the platoon secured Objective D at 1100. The platoon then reorganized. Some enemy small-arms, automatic-weapons, and mortar fire was received on Objective D. But the majority of the enemy mortar fire fell on Objective C, just vacated. The supporting weapons and one rifle squad were then deployed to lay down a base of fire to support a further attack.

With most of the 1st Platoon noncommissioned officers lost, PFC Wilmer L. Sours helped the platoon leader reorganize the platoon.

In the meantime, I was in communication with the platoon at all times, and I coordinated artillery fire. The expenditure of ammunition by the assault platoon was great. A constant supply of ammunition had to be carried forward. Litters were also carried forward. Much mortar and machine-gun ammunition was expended in addition to small-arms ammunition.

The 1st Platoon on Objective D could not advance. Enemy forces apparently had withdrawn from Objective C to Objective E prior to the air strike on Objectives C and D and were in strong defensive positions. At 1330 it was apparent that the 1st Platoon was stalemated on Objective D.[13]

The experience of the assault platoon of Company L was similar. Captain Cook, the company commander, describes the action of the platoon, which he accompanied.

At dark I learned the mission of the company for the following day. On 16 March, shortly after 0700, after both air and artillery preparation had failed to materialize, the 1st Platoon with an attached section of ROK personnel and one 57mm rifle from the Weapons Platoon, and accompanied by me and radio personnel, jumped off toward Hill 383. I was anxious to move across the open valley to take advantage of the prevailing ground haze and mist that partially obscured enemy observation from the high ground. I did not take my supporting tanks with me for I did not want the noise of the tank motors to give away my move. Furthermore, visibility was so limited that tank fire would not be observed. Yet the tanks were in position for immediate use if needed.

The first intermediate objective of the Company L reinforced platoon was Objective K, the long finger ridge extending in the direction of Hill 383. The immediate approach to K was a gradual slope.

At 0755, on approaching Objective K, the platoon received ten to fifteen rounds of enemy artillery, resulting in two casualties. At about the same time the squad on the right flank picked up ten prisoners in the village of Sanghwagye-ri. The prisoners were sent back, and the platoon passed Objective K and started up the steep slope to Objective L. At this time the platoon was under sporadic enemy artillery and heavy-mortar fire.

The platoon crossed Objective L without meeting stabilized resistance, but saw enemy withdrawing from the immediate front without firing small arms. The platoon passed several dug-in individual positions, two- and three-man positions, and well-camouflaged and elaborate observation posts and outposts.

By 0900 the platoon cleared all the ground on Objective L, and portions of the platoon were moving toward Objective M. From Objective L to Objective M there was a steep incline, sparsely wooded, with extremely soft ground.

About a hundred yards from Objective M the platoon came under intense enemy small-arms fire from the crest of the hill. Grenades were hurled down by the enemy. Automatic-weapons fire from the enemy came from the immediate left of the objective. The platoon pushed to within ten yards of the crest of Objective M, where a firefight and a grenade fight with the Chinese took place. Sgt. Frank B. McKeever, squad leader, after hurling a grenade, bayoneted a Chinese attempting to escape from a pillbox and in general sparked the attack against Objective M. The machine-gun position to the left of Objective M was grenaded, and the platoon assaulted the objective with success. On this objective I observed some of the best defensive positions I have ever seen. Some enemy light mortar was being fired, and the platoon received several tree bursts. Enemy troops were seen running from Objective M to Hill 383. The enemy from the vicinity of Hill 380 on the right flank had placed sporadic automatic-weapons and small-arms fire on the Company L platoon.

The platoon, in making its advance, had hit the flank of a very elaborate defensive trench running north and south between Objectives L and M. Fire and communication trenches with six or seven heavy pillboxes existed. This trench was constructed by the enemy to meet an attack up the draw from the west.

About 1000 or 1030, the platoon was consolidated on Objective

M. Ammunition was distributed. By the number of enemy I had seen, those defending Objective M and those observed on Hill 383, it seemed to me that more than a platoon would be needed to make an additional advance.

Meanwhile, about one-half hour after the 1st Platoon moved from Objective White, the platoon of four tanks attached to Company L moved out to the north, generally in the direction of Objective K and then northwest on the MSR. One tank was disabled by a mine. The other three continued along the MSR watching Objectives L and M. At about 1030 I asked the tanks to fire on the northern and western slopes of M, in the saddle, and also on the forward nose of Hill 383, in addition to firing on targets of opportunity. The tanks gave excellent fire support.[14]

Major Parziale describes the situation from the perspective of his position at the battalion CP on Objective White.

A heavy ground haze or fog limited visibility to such an extent that the platoons crossed the valley without enemy detection of the movement. The Company L platoon reached the first approach to Hill 383 before the enemy discovered its presence. The Company K platoon was not so successful. As soon as it started toward Hill 300, intense enemy small-arms and some mortar fire was received.

When the fog lifted, the TAC officer called air strikes on Hill 383 and on the ridge mass leading to Hill 380. The air strikes seemed to loosen up the attack, and the platoons were able to move after having been pinned down. Furthermore, the tanks were able to give supporting fire when the fog lifted.

The regimental commander visited the battalion CP on Objective White during the morning, and I requested permission to use the entire battalion strength to secure the high ground. I wished to do so because the enemy had begun to react violently to the attack by firing mortars and artillery on the assaulting troops and on the supply lines. I felt it was necessary to take Hills 383 and 380 to deny the enemy observation. The regimental commander granted permission to commit the battalion in strength.

I then instructed the commanding officers of Companies K and

L to commit their companies in the attack. Company I was to be prepared to take Hill 499 when Hill 383 was secure.[15]

The 3d Battalion Attack

Captain Lohela describes the movement forward of the rest of Company K and the continuation of the attack on Hill 380. The battalion commander wanted Objective E taken before night, and he ordered me to take the remainder of the company forward and secure Objective E. At 1345 I moved the company toward the bridge. I instructed my men to move forward quickly. This maneuver worked to good advantage, for after the company crossed the stream, enemy mortar rounds fell behind the company. At 1430 I moved to Objective D while the rest of the company searched out the ridges to that point. Lieutenant Barr and myself reconnoitered the forward area.

When the battalion commander asked me to hurry and take Objective E, I ordered a bayonet assault. The 3d Platoon was to envelop Objective E from the left, but it arrived too late to be of assistance. I moved with the 1st Platoon, under strength, over the rising ground and attacked Objective E.

The men received small-arms and automatic-weapons fire until they arrived at the base of Objective E. A small force, less than a squad, moved to the right along the ridge and killed two enemy soldiers with rifle fire. I had the communications sergeant throw me a grenade, and I neutralized an automatic-weapons nest at the base of Objective E. The 1st Platoon moved up the ridge and the hill in assault, making as much noise as possible because it was a small force. On the top of Objective E, I grenaded two more enemy, while the men on the right killed two more. At least eighty grenades had been thrown at the platoon from the top of Objective E. The Chinese on the machine-gun position to the left of Objective E retreated upon the approach of the platoon. This machine-gun nest had pinned down Lieutenant Barr's platoon on Objective D. Friendly mortars, 57mm rifles, machine guns, and two squads of riflemen had supported the 1st Platoon assault. The enemy had abandoned ammunition and some weapons on Objective E. Between 1630 and 1700, Company K consolidated on Objective E for the night.[16]

Major Parziale relates his observations of the attack from below. From my observation post I could see that the attack was progressing slowly. However, it was moving. There was no hesitation on the part of the companies on the hills, in spite of the mortar and small-arms fire being received. Maximum use of air, artillery, and mortars was effected to neutralize this enemy fire. A total of seven flights struck against Hill 383, including napalm, rockets, bombs, 20mm shells, and .50-caliber machine-gun fire. A total of six flights struck against Hill 380 and that ridgeline. The enemy continued to occupy his positions. In position to make its assault at 1600, Company K took Hill 300 [Objective C] using hand grenades and bayonets.[17]

Company K succeeded in capturing Hill 300 and pushed beyond it about 500 yards, but they were unable to take Hill 380. At the same time, to the west, Company L assaulted Hill 383. Captain Cook describes the commitment of the rest of Company L and the attack on Hill 383.

When the battalion commander asked me by radio if I wanted the remainder of my company committed, I said I did. At 1015 Lieutenant Kent [Company L executive officer], with the 2d, 3d, and Weapons Platoons, plus a section of light machine guns from Company M, jumped off from Objective White to join the 1st Platoon on Objective M.

Immediately after calling the remainder of the company forward from Objective White, I ordered Lt. Norman R. Nellis, 1st Platoon leader, to move forward and take Hill 383. I accompanied this platoon. I left a machine gun on Objective M to give supporting and overhead fire against Hill 383 and to fire against enemy machine guns on the right and left flanks.

Almost immediately upon leaving Objective M the platoon came under direct fire from the machine gun on the right flank as well as from small-arms fire. About halfway, or fifty yards, down the northern slopes of M, the platoon received heavy small-arms and machine-gun fire from the left.

The only approach to Hill 383, other than coming up directly from the valley floor, was across a sparsely wooded ridge so narrow that only three men could move along the ridgeline at one time.

The enemy fire was continuous and intense. It grew in intensity as the platoon moved farther. When the platoon reached within twenty yards from the crest of the hill, the entire defensive positions on Hill 383 opened up with small-arms and automatic-weapons fire and pinned down the 1st Platoon. Fortunately the saddle was wooded, and bushes and small trees interfered with the enemy line of fire. Between twenty and thirty grenades were thrown from Hill 383 on the platoon.

The platoon leader sent a squad to each side of Hill 383 in an attempt to flank and find the enemy. This was done under intense enemy fire. The squad on the left reached the top of Hill 383 but was driven back immediately below the crest. The platoon tried twice more to get on the hill. Each time, by sheer numbers of small arms and grenades, the enemy was able to keep the platoon from reaching the top. The enemy was so well camouflaged that his positions could be seen only by the flash of firing.

It was then about 1100, and I decided to pull back to Objective M and direct artillery on Hill 383. This was done. Artillery and heavy-mortar fire was placed on Hill 383. The heavy mortars had already been placing fire on Hill 380 and north of that hill in order to eliminate the enemy flanking fire being received by the Company L platoon. Since airpower was available only until noon (later airpower was prolonged past noontime), I asked battalion to place an air strike on Hill 383.

Considerable casualties had been received by the platoon. One aid man was with the platoon; litter bearers had remained with the company on Objective White. Casualties were being pulled into the deepest part of the saddle between Objective M and Hill 383 for cover. There they were collected and treated by the aid man. The walking wounded were sent back over the route to the valley where litter jeeps picked them up. One improvised litter was made, and two ROK soldiers carried a seriously wounded man to litter bearers who were already starting to come up the slope toward the platoon.

Ammunition was running low, and ammunition was taken from the casualties and redistributed. Some weapons were disabled by grenade fragments, and some redistribution of weapons had to be made.[18]

The Company L executive officer, 1st Lt. James W. Kent, describes how he brought the rest of the company forward to join Captain Cook in the attack.

At 1030 I received the call to bring the company up. The company was already prepared to move on orders. Because Captain Cook had said he was running low on ammunition, I had the men pick up an extra load. The company then moved out on foot with the 2d Platoon, company headquarters, the 3d Platoon, and the Weapons Platoon in that order. The same route was followed as had been taken by the 1st Platoon.

As soon as the company cleared the hill mass occupied by Company I, it began to receive automatic-weapons and small-arms fire from its left front and flank (Hill 252 and to the northwest for about 500 meters). At the same time enemy mortar and artillery fire came in on the company near the bridge and cut the company into two parts. The 2d Platoon followed the road past Objective K and arrived at a point on the road just west of Hill 383 in the valley. The company was unaware of this at the time because the radio operator and the platoon runner were hit by enemy fire, thereby cutting communications. The radio was also disabled by enemy fire.

I guided the 3d and 4th Platoons through Objectives K and L and joined the 1st Platoon on Objective M about 1230. First Sergeant Baker with the 2d Platoon picked up the SCR536 radio that had been disabled, and he followed the 2d Platoon up the road.[19]

Captain Cook picks up the story.

I had already called for an air strike, and this strike was imminent. I was therefore worried about the whereabouts of the 2d Platoon, since Lieutenant Kent had informed me by radio of the disappearance of the 2d Platoon up the road.

Some of the men of the 1st Platoon observed some activity to the left of Hill 383. This activity appeared to be friendly. When the men shouted, the unknown group answered, and thus I knew it was the 2d Platoon. I passed word up to shout to the 2d Platoon and tell them to get off Hill 383 as fast as possible because of the imminent air strike. To mark the location of the company I had a white phosphorus grenade set off. The 2d Platoon Leader later said that this grenade was not observed. Once the planes started on their strike, I felt it would be impossible to call them off.

In the meantime First Sergeant Baker, fiddling with the radio, which had a piece of shrapnel through the bottom, miraculously got on the air. Complete instructions were given the 2d Platoon to get off the hill and come back to Objective M. Several minutes later an air strike of four planes with napalm made passes and strafed and bombed Hill 383.[20]

The company first sergeant, George M. Baker, describes the situation in the 2d Platoon.

When the 1st Platoon was on Objective M the remainder of the company was called forward to join the 1st Platoon. The company moved with the 2d Platoon in the lead until small-arms, mortar, and artillery fire caused the company to be separated into two parts. The 2d Platoon moved up the road and passed to the left of the 1st Platoon. At this time the 2d Platoon suffered two killed and several wounded.

The 2d Platoon was moving up the road in two groups. I started to take the second group east across the ridge midway between Objectives L and M, but I began to receive additional enemy fire. Consequently I continued up the road and joined the forward platoon elements.

As I moved up the road I picked up the platoon radio, which had a shell fragment through the bottom of it. I gave it to the communications sergeant who threw the radio away. I instructed the communications sergeant to keep the radio so that it could be turned in for salvage. The communications sergeant carried the radio, banged it with his fist, shook it, and suddenly the radio worked. The company commander ordered the 2d Platoon to join the company.

The 2d Platoon was in the process of moving up the hill when the radio came on. The platoon was operating under support of tank guns and was under enemy fire until halfway up the hill, when steep wooded terrain afforded cover. The 2d Platoon had no idea of the situation or the condition of the company until radio contact was established.

I believe that the 2d Platoon, by approaching from the left, made the enemy withdraw from his positions west of the hill. This probably made it easier to take Hill 383.[21]

Captain Cook also felt that the 2d Platoon had managed to get into an excellent position, except for the air strike coming in on top of it. He describes the continuation of the attack after the air strike.

If the air strike had not already been called in, I believe that the 2d Platoon could have taken Hill 383 in its flanking movement. The platoon was in perfect position for a coordinated attack with the remainder of the company.

After the air strike lifted I ordered the 2d Platoon to jump off from Objective M and assault Hill 383 frontally, while the 3d Platoon was sent around to the position where the 2d Platoon had been. On my order both platoons closed on Hill 383. The 2d Platoon advanced about halfway to Hill 383 when it received fire from its front and left. Ten to fifteen yards from the crest the platoon met a barrage of hand grenades. Six casualties resulted, including the platoon sergeant and the radiomen of the platoon leader and me. Lieutenant Hurley led a group to the right, and First Sergeant Baker rallied a group to the left. Both groups assaulted the ridge. Grenades and bayonets had to be used to subdue the enemy.

In the meantime the squad of the 2d Platoon, which had been sent to the left, reached a position west of Hill 383 and made contact with the 3d Platoon, which had cleared the western nose and the northern portion of Hill 383, eliminating a machine-gun nest and clearing enemy fire trenches dug in on the nose. The Weapons Platoon with one 57mm rifle and its three mortars supported the attack from Company M. The 1st Platoon remained in support and reserve. Company L formed a perimeter on Hill 383, including a nose to the north and east and the high ground to the east. At 1600 the position was consolidated.[22]

Officers of the 3d Battalion describe the situation after the battalion attack ended and during the night of 16–17 March.

CAPTAIN MARSH, S-3: During the night Companies K and L sent patrols to the front. It was estimated that Hills 383, 300, and 380 were each occupied by a reinforced enemy company. Enemy mortar fire was received from the high ground east of Hill 499. At 1900 the battalion CP received about fifty rounds of enemy mortar fire.

CAPTAIN LOHELA, COMPANY K: That evening the Chinese on Hill 380 must have thought Company K was continuing its attack because enemy fire was directed on the area between that hill and Objective E.

CAPTAIN COOK, COMPANY L: I expected a counterattack that night, since there was an estimated company of enemy above Hill 383, and possibly as many as 300–400. Due to the fact that the closest vehicles could get to Hill 383 was 2,000 meters away, and because I could not spare twenty men as a carrying party for supplies and ammunition, I requested the battalion to form the P&A Platoon into a carrying party to supply the company with water, rations, and ammunition on Hill 383.[23]

The Advance Continues

On the next day, 17 March, when the 3d Battalion continued its attack to the north, the advance was much easier for Company K, but the enemy still held out on Hill 499. Members of the battalion describe the action.

CAPTAIN LOHELA, COMPANY K: It seemed to me that taking Objective E demoralized the enemy. Early the next day, Company K took Hill 380 without resistance and remained there. While Companies I and L moved toward Hill 499, Company K gave mortar support by firing on targets of opportunity.

CAPTAIN COOK, COMPANY L: On the following day, Company I passed through Company L to occupy Objective Y immediately south of Hill 499. By that time Company K was on Hill 380. Company L moved to cover the western slopes of the hill mass between Objectives M and Y, and remained there. The enemy threw a great amount of artillery from the northwest. Most of the artillery fell between the three companies.

CAPTAIN MARSH, 3D BATTALION S-3: On 17 March Company K reached Hill 380 at 1230 without encountering opposition. The company sent patrols northeast and northwest from there. Company L, remaining on Hill 383, sent patrols toward unnumbered Hill 400 [Objective Y]. These patrols drew fire from Hill 499. Company I passed through Company L, prepared to assault Hill 499, but at 1600 Company I buttoned up on Hill 400 for the night.

It was difficult to displace friendly mortars for direct support of the rifle companies because of the existence of the minefield in the blind valley north of Sanghwagye-ri. Although it was contemplated that the battalion CP would be established in this valley, the minefield prevented such action. During the night of 17 March, Companies L and K received enemy artillery and mortar fire. Much of this fire passed over Company I and fell into the blind valley where the CP had anticipated moving.

MAJOR PARZIALE, 3D BATTALION COMMANDER: On 17 March I ordered Company K to take Hill 380. Company I reached the hill just short of Hill 499, where it came under terrific enemy fire late in the afternoon. One air strike by Navy planes using rockets, VT, napalm, and machine-gun fire on Hill 499 for one hour failed to dislodge the enemy who still occupied Hill 499 in great strength. All the supporting weapons of the battalion were being displaced to the valley south of Hill 383. I ordered Captain Stevens [Commander of Company I] to hold and attack again in the morning.

At that time the 3d Battalion, 5th Cavalry Regiment, was 3,000–4,000 meters ahead of the Marines on the right; and the 2d Battalion on the left was not abreast.[24]

During the night of 17–18 March the 3d Battalion witnessed a most unusual event for UN forces during the Korean War. Captain Lohela of Company K explains.

During the night of 17 March, about 2000 hours, a strange plane bombed and strafed enemy positions on Hill 499. That night listening posts heard an attempted enemy attack gathering, but an estimated fifty enemy troops were dispersed by mortar and artillery fire.[25]

That night the 3d Battalion checked with its higher headquarters all the way to corps, but there were no reports of any friendly aircraft in the area. Apparently, the enemy had their own "friendly fire incident" involving one of their few airplanes attacking their position still holding on, or possibly in the process of withdrawing from, Hill 499. On the next day, 18 March, enemy resistance in front of the 3d Battalion largely disappeared as described by battalion officers.

MAJOR PARZIALE, 3D BATTALION COMMANDER: On 18 March, Company I attacked after an artillery concentration, and by 1300 it secured Hill 499. Most of the enemy troops had withdrawn, leaving only a strong outpost. With the securing of Hill 499, the 2d Battalion moved on Hill 426 [2,000 meters west of Hill 383], and the Marines moved up on the right against light opposition. The regiment then ordered the attack to continue northward toward Ch'unch'on. Progress was made slowly because of the terrain and the resulting problems of logistics rather than because of strong enemy resistance.

CAPTAIN STEVENS, COMPANY I COMMANDER: The company directed artillery fire against Hill 499, and on 18 March the company assaulted and took this objective. One casualty from enemy mortar fire was suffered.

Company L moved through Company I and assaulted Songch'i Mountain. Company I moved behind and assaulted the high ground to the west [about 1,000 meters north of Hill 499] without casualties, killing one Chinese. On this hill enemy emplacements for a pack 75mm artillery piece and a 4.2-inch mortar were found. There also the enemy had the most beautiful dug-in positions I have ever seen. Trenches were two to three feet wide and eight to ten feet deep, with bays for ammunition storage.[26]

The 3d Battalion's daily journal provides more details of Company I's discovery.

2120 HOURS, COMPANY I COMMANDER TO 3D BATTALION S-2: Minefield found using 60mm and 81mm shells as booby traps. Mortars placed nose down as AP mines along trail on Songch'i Mountain. Also 4.2-inch shells with trip wires. Seven cases of 82mm shells found on Hill 499 along with an estimated twenty-five cases of 60mm shells. Six-strand barbed wire fence strung with metal stakes, approximately two miles long, running southwest from Songch'i Mountain to the MSR. Very extensive fortifications and an estimated mile of trenches up to several feet deep and two feet wide with dug-in 4.2-inch mortar positions. Many positions and part of the trenches have overhead covering.[27]

Captain Cook, Company L commander, describes his advance on Songch'i Mountain.

On 18 March, Company I was to jump off between 0700 and 0800 to secure Hill 499 (Hwagum-Bong). When Hill 499 was secured, Company L was to move through Objective Y and Hill 499, then take Objective T, Songch'i Mountain, approximately 560 meters in height and rock-capped, with a very rugged ascent. Two intermediate objectives, A and B, were established.

Company I jumped off between 0730 and 0800, 18 March, and got to the top of Hill 499. Company L jumped off at 1000 after Company I had secured the hill, passed through Objective Y and passed through Company I, and jumped off to Objective A, the high round hill about 1,000 meters northeast of Hill 499. The company cleared Objective A without meeting enemy resistance. The 2d Platoon was in the lead to Objective A, with the 1st Platoon and the Weapons Platoon in support. The 1st Platoon was in the lead to Objective B [about 400 meters northeast of Objective A], with the 2d and 3d Platoons following on the ridgeline. The company passed through Objective B without meeting resistance. Prepared enemy positions were found. These consisted of short fire trenches, individual emplacements, and communications arrangements of very heavy wire on poles alongside the ridgeline from Objective A to Songch'i Mountain, where an elaborate CP was found. The company arrived at Songch'i Mountain between 1300 and 1330.

Company K was then to move to Hill 272 [about 1,800 meters

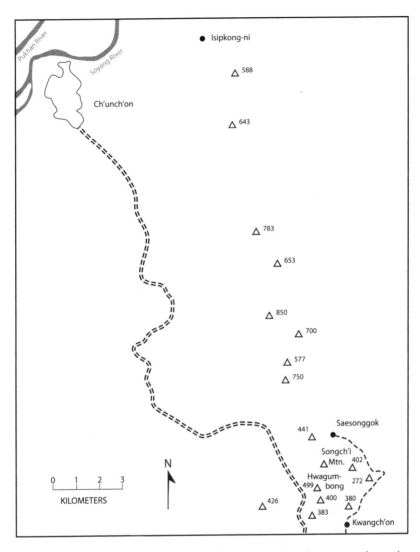

Advance on Ch'unch'on (original map by author, based on maps from the
Army Map Service).

northeast of Hill 380] and then to Hill 402 [about 800 meters
northwest of Hill 272], while Company L remained on Songch'i
Mountain and tied in defensively with Company K.

Songch'i Mountain was a solid granite rock formation. It looked
like soil but in reality was solid smooth rock covered with eroded

soil that had washed down on it. Some grass grew on this soil, cam-
ouflaging the cliff face. This earth, made muddy by melting snow,
would not hold when the men walked over it, and made the advance
slippery and perilous. There was no place to dig in. The eastern side
was sheer cliff, making physical contact with Company K impossible. I phoned the battalion and explained. I asked whether we should
stay on Songch'i Mountain, withdraw, or move forward. I was instructed to move the company 1,000 meters northeast from Songch'i
Mountain into the area of the three knolls. Company L started to
find a route off the mountain and located a ridge running generally
in the direction of the three knolls. The company formed a perimeter
there and stayed the night.

Resupplying the company with ammunition and rations, particularly from Hill 703 to the Hongch'on River, was a tremendous
problem. It was necessary to send twenty-five to thirty combat soldiers, as carrying parties, two or three miles to the rear for resupply.
This resulted in the following effects: (1) it decreased the number of
men on the lines available for line operation and reduced the general combat efficiency of the company; (2) the same route, which
had already necessitated strenuous efforts to advance over, had to
be retraversed by these men who formed the carrying party, both on
the return and forward trips to reach the company. Very little water
was found because of the necessity of remaining on the high ground.
It was impossible to descend into the valley for stream water to be
made potable with halazone tablets. The company tried at every
opportunity to secure Koreans for carrying parties, but rarely was
the company in the vicinity of villages. It was impossible to bring
vehicles close to the company.[28]

The advance was not without danger as Company I discovered.
Captain Stevens describes what happened.

On 19 March the company moved north, assaulted, and seized
Hill 750. Continuing north, the company crossed Hill 577, Hill
700, and cleared and outposted Hill 850 before buttoning up for the
night. That night seven of the eight men comprising the outpost
were captured, and the enemy moved on Hill 850 in force.

The next morning, 20 March, Company I attacked Hill 850. As

the 3d Platoon assaulted the rocky ledge at the top of the hill, the platoon was in turn assaulted by six enemy soldiers who were promptly killed. The company counted seven enemy dead on the hill. I think the enemy troops were North Korean rather than Chinese because they fought like North Koreans. The company suffered two killed and eight wounded in action.

When Hill 850 was taken, Company I moved to Hill 653, then northwest to Hill 783, and buttoned up for the night. On 21 March the company moved to Hill 643 and immediately dispatched a platoon-size patrol north over Hill 588 and down into the valley at Isipkong-ni. No enemy contact was made that day. Reports from civilians indicated that the enemy was retreating. Company I remained on Hill 643 until it was relieved by Company L, 7th Cavalry Regiment.[29]

An Assessment

This was the last major action of the advance. After reaching the outskirts of Ch'unch'on, the 5th Cavalry was relieved by units of the 7th Cavalry Regiment. Later, the officers of the 3d Battalion evaluated their experience.

CAPTAIN STEVENS, COMPANY I: This operation was the longest movement through mountain that I have ever experienced. From Songch'i Mountain to Hill 850 and beyond, the supply problems were overwhelming. Approximately thirty-five South Koreans who had been recruited were being used as a mule team to transport water, rations, and ammunition. A full C ration and a full canteen of water were delivered to each soldier per day. No hot meals were eaten from the time the company passed through Company L and went north.

I believe that the taking of Hills 383, 380, and 400 broke the enemy defense line in the Hongch'on area. The operation, which continued beyond these hills, was a matter of maintaining pressure against the enemy to keep him from reforming to make another stand. Indications were found that the enemy was suffering from exposure and frostbite. Due to the friendly advance and the threat of air and artillery, the enemy was living in damp trenches and bays where sunlight did not penetrate. I estimate that between 500 and 700 enemy troops occupied Hills 380 and 383. During this operation Company I lost three killed, seventeen wounded, and seven missing in action. There were six nonbattle casualties.

CAPTAIN LOHELA, COMPANY K: Company K walked at least thirty-five miles over the ridges from 13 March to 21 March. Casualties consisted of four killed, three officers wounded, two of whom continued fighting, and twelve enlisted men wounded. Four nonbattle casualties, nervous or shock cases, were evacuated, two to rear medical installations. These shock cases indicated how heavy the enemy fire was.

In my opinion, the importance of this operation was due to the fact that the enemy was apparently demoralized by the speed and shock of the action. As a result of quick initial success, the operation as far as Ch'unch'on was comparatively easy.

FIRST LIEUTENANT LONGSTROTH, 3D BATTALION S-2: It is suspected that the mission of the defenders was to hold and delay the advance of the UN forces as long as possible. When forced to withdraw, the plan seemed to be for the forward battalions to leapfrog in a series of delaying positions behind the first line. The enemy MLR was stubbornly defended until overrun by the 3d Battalion.

MAJOR PARZIALE, 3D BATTALION COMMANDER: I am of the opinion that the enemy had deployed a battalion in his defensive positions, with probably an enemy company each on Hills 380, 383, and 499. These positions appeared to have been built for a regiment. The enemy troops in defense seemed to have been supported by weapons normally in support of a regiment.

These positions comprised the main enemy defense position of the Hongch'on–Ch'unch'on road. This defense line was fixed generally east and west through Hills 426, 383, 380, and 399. When Companies K and L secured their objectives, penetration of the enemy main line of defense had been made, and the enemy continued to hold Hills 426, 499, and 399 in strength only to permit withdrawal of his heavy supporting weapons. When Hill 499 was taken, the entire defensive system collapsed.

The aggressive action of Companies K and L was important in capturing large amounts of all types of ammunition and weapons up to and including a medium-size artillery piece. By the number of enemy dead (approximately ninety-five), and the number of grenades, bandages, and other equipment found, it is estimated that the enemy suffered the loss of a greater part of a battalion in his holding operation on these positions.

Engineer troops removed over 200 mines in the valley between Hills 383 and 380. East of Hill 383, mines had been laid in the valley along the streambed. One tank was destroyed by a mine immediately after Objective White was taken. One tank was lost by mine action on the road due west of Hill 383. One was knocked out by a mine on the road due east of Hill 380.

On 18 March the battalion executive officer was moving the CP into the valley to facilitate communications. A jeep driving over the same trail used by the regimental commander, the division commander, and others was destroyed and completely demolished by an antitank mine.

I believe that the enemy commander allowed the 3d Battalion to cross the Hongch'on River because he chose to defend the high ground overlooking the main road rather than the flat valley floor. This choice was probably dictated by the fortifications already constructed and by the number of men at his disposal. Many more troops would have been needed to defend the valley floor. Quite probably he lacked antitank weapons, and since the river could be forded almost any place, tanks could have overrun his infantry positions.[30]

The 3d Battalion's higher headquarters agreed with the importance of this attack. Maj. Charles E. Harris, 5th Cavalry Regiment S-3, discusses the operation in more detail and evaluates the enemy's plan of defense.

The rapid advance of the 3d Battalion, 5th Cavalry Regiment, across the Hongch'on River, and its clearing of the critical terrain features, made the advance of the 1st and 2d Battalions much easier and aided the regiment in securing its objective, Phase Line Buffalo, just north of the Hongch'on River, more quickly.

At Phase Line Buffalo [located on the hill mass north of Hongch'on] all battalions of the regiment had to be slowed down to allow the 1st Marine Division elements on the right to come abreast.

The 7th Cavalry Regiment, on the left of the 5th Cavalry Regiment, encountered strong enemy resistance south of the Hongch'on River and was unable to advance abreast of the 5th Cavalry. This exposed the left flank of the 5th Cavalry and held up its advance.

When the 5th Cavalry Regiment arrived at the outskirts of Ch'unch'on, the 1st Cavalry Division held up the regimental advance while a 7th Cavalry Regiment task force proceeded to Ch'unch'on and patrolled north of the river at Ch'unch'on.

A marked increase in the enemy's use of mines, both antipersonnel and antitank, was noted in this operation. The enemy organized his halting action against friendly elements on key terrain features. He then planned a withdrawal, which was excellently executed, with the exception of his abandonment of certain equipment. The friendly advance was more aggressive than the enemy had expected it to be. Therefore, the enemy did not have enough time to evacuate all his equipment. Supplies in this area were undoubtedly left for the enemy holding forces who, according to information received from prisoners of war, were to hold several days, then withdraw. The enemy was without doubt forced to withdraw before he had planned to do so.

In my opinion the Hongch'on defense was a holding effort on the part of the enemy in order that he would have sufficient time to establish well his defenses farther north, and in order for him to be able to resupply his forces to the north in comparative security.

In this advance, the 3d Battalion was the most aggressive of the 5th Cavalry Regiment battalions. From the middle of January to the present, the advance north has been magnificently supported by artillery and air. Furthermore, no large enemy groups or units have been bypassed. Friendly forces have also employed organic supporting weapons to advantage. As a result of these factors, progress has been made with comparatively light casualties.

Enemy resistance during this period has been no less tenacious. But the use of supporting weapons by friendly forces has decreased the effect of the enemy's tenacity.[31]

The 3d Battalion's attack opened a hole in the enemy defense line astride the main road south from Ch'unch'on. Lt. Col. Robert

J. Natzel, chief of the G-3 Operations Section of IX Corps, notes the critical nature of this action.

The importance of this operation was opening the MSR from Hongch'on to Ch'unch'on, the road west of Hwagum-bong [Hill 499]. This road to the Ch'unch'on basin was important to the enemy.

Any action that caused the enemy to withdraw meant that pressure on units on a similar lateral front was eased. Friendly advance in this area decreased enemy pressure elsewhere. Enemy withdrawal here enabled a more rapid advance in other sectors. Each time the road was opened more, enemy ridgeline positions along the lateral front became untenable. The enemy defended the road to enable equipment to be withdrawn from the mountains. When the road was taken, the enemy had to withdraw back over the ridgeline.

The enemy did not choose to defend along the Hongch'on River because the river was fordable in several places and it would therefore have to be defended in its entirety. Better terrain for defense existed beyond the river.

The Hongch'on–Ch'unch'on highway was the most important point in the corps advance. The friendly advance along this main enemy axis eased enemy pressure all along the front.[32]

By 21 March the 1st Cavalry Division was on Line Cairo, just south of Ch'unch'on. That same day an armored task force entered the town, only to find it abandoned by the enemy with all supplies evacuated. The advance continued to the north, but it was obvious that the enemy, despite the best efforts of units such as the 3d Battalion, 5th Cavalry Regiment, once again had escaped Ridgway's efforts to destroy a sizable portion of its forces.

Chapter 4

SUPPORTING THE ATTACK

3d Battalion, 5th Cavalry Regiment, 13–18 March 1951

Effective logistical support was one of the key factors in the success of the 3d Battalion, 5th Cavalry, during its March advance in Operation Ripper. The battalion operations—the movement over extremely rugged terrain to the Hongch'on River, the successful attack on the main enemy defense line, and the sustained advance through a mountainous region to Ch'unch'on—depended on the ability of the battalion to keep its front line companies supplied with the essentials of food, water, and ammunition. Maj. Charles E. Harris, S-3 of the 5th Cavalry Regiment, notes the special problem of the 3d Battalion.

The regimental supply problem was not great, since the regiment was able to utilize the MSR. The supply problem existed on battalion level, for the battalions had difficulty bringing supplies to the companies. The 3d Battalion had the most difficult problem of supply, for it operated over more rugged terrain and in a zone where few roads existed. Hand carry of supplies was necessary.[1]

Maj. James M. Gibson, the 3d Battalion's executive officer, explains the supply problem during this operation and how it was solved.

Prior to relieving the Australians, the 3d Battalion reconnoitered the positions to be occupied and realized that the troops on the hilltop would have to be supplied by carrier parties. At a battalion staff meeting it was decided that carriers would have to be secured. I instructed Lieutenant Watcke, Battalion S-4, to recruit

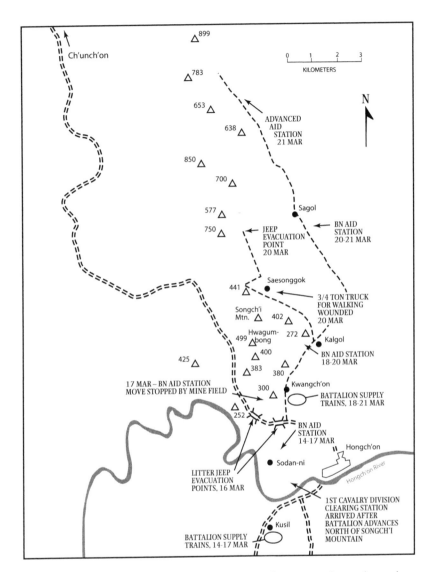

Supporting the advance, 3d Battalion, 5th Cavalry (original map by author, based on maps from the Army Map Service).

through the regimental civil affairs office approximately thirty healthy Korean males with A-frames.

Relief of the Australians was effected on 13 March 1951. That night the battalion commander, 1st Battalion, 7th Marine Regiment, visited the 3d Battalion CP. Logistical problems were discussed. I received the impression that the Marines solved the problem of transportation in mountainous terrain by having the individual Marine carry all his supplies. No attempt was made to feed hot meals. At that time, the Marines had been on C rations for twenty days. Standard operating procedure in the 3d Battalion, 5th Cavalry, was to serve at least one hot meal to the riflemen per day, regardless of the difficulties.

When the battalion advance began, the troops, with the exception of Companies I and M, proceeded cross-country from the line of departure. It soon became apparent that the thirty Koreans who had been procured to transport the battalion supply were not sufficient in number, particularly in view of the rapidity of the battalion movement and the fact that the battalion boundary had been changed so that no road net existed for battalion use. Between thirty and fifty Koreans were needed per company.

The unit administrative officer of each company was ordered to secure additional Koreans by the quickest means possible. To do this, it was necessary to recruit laborers from the native villages. By treating the Koreans well and by feeding them better food than they were accustomed to having, good relations were maintained. Such good relations resulted that it was difficult to separate the Korean carriers from the battalion at the end of the operation. They were turned over to the 1st Battalion, 7th Cavalry Regiment, which relieved the 3d Battalion, 5th Cavalry.

The rifle companies reached the Hongch'on River with little or no resistance, and I was able to bring the battalion organic vehicles around by road to meet the companies at the river. When I learned that the battalion was to cross the river, I set up the kitchens on the south side of the river in the vicinity of the regimental CP. I did this because the area north of the river was not cleared of the enemy. Kitchen tents are easily vulnerable to attack and to hostile fire. In order to feed the line troops two hot meals a day and a C ration for the noon meal, jeeps and trailers were used to ford the river and bring food to the companies.

When the battalion was ordered to attack north and secure the high ground, the 3d Battalion had no road net. However, a trail in the Marine zone had been designated as the boundary between the

Marines on the right and the 3d Battalion. The battalion requested permission for and was granted access to this route for supply and evacuation.

About 1400 each day, the company supply sergeant and unit administrative officer, who had made prior reconnaissance of the route and who had consulted me concerning the proposed location of the companies that night, led a carrying party as far forward by vehicle as possible. From there, the party hand-carried food, ammunition, and water to the company to give the troops one hot meal before dark. From the time the battalion entered the high ground north of the Hongch'on River to its arrival on Hill 499, the companies were fed two C ration meals and one B ration meal [a cooked meal without fresh vegetables, fruit, or meat; an A ration includes fresh ingredients] per day. From Hill 499 to Ch'unch'on, the battalion ate C rations only.

The Korean carrying party was divided into two sections. One group remained with the kitchen to carry supplies forward. The other remained on the hill with the company. When the company moved forward, the carriers with the company carried the bedrolls of at least the lead platoon, sometimes more, so that the company would not be encumbered in the event of enemy opposition. Often the two carrying groups rotated and exchanged places.

On several occasions the Korean carrying parties from the companies were utilized by the battalion medical personnel to carry wounded to the valley. From there the wounded were able to be transported by litter jeep to the aid station.

Particular precautions were taken during an advance and at night to protect carriers from enemy action. This was done by having them follow well in the rear of the lead elements of the company during a move, and by placing them in Korean houses in the valley, well behind the lead elements, at night. No battle casualties were sustained by the Korean carriers during this entire operation. Carrying parties were always accompanied by at least a squad of soldiers.

During this operation, the shortest carry was not under three hours. One carry took eleven hours for a one-way trip.

The difficulties of the carrying party were great. There was always the possibility of getting lost, or of losing contact with the battalion. Although it never occurred, there was always the possibility of encountering scattered enemy groups. Fatigue was an ever-present factor. The hillsides were muddy and extremely slippery due to spring thaws, and the ground was treacherous. Some areas lacked trails over the mountains. It was often necessary to give medical aid for minor cuts and bruises to carriers who slipped and fell over steep embankments.

After Hill 499 was secured, only scattered enemy resistance was encountered, with the exception of Hill 850. Had enemy resistance been strong, supply and evacuation problems, particularly the latter, would have been increased tremendously.

The battalion watched enviously while Marine helicopters across the valley, about 1,000 yards distant, brought supplies and evacuated the wounded.

During the entire operation there was no shortage of food, ammunition, or supply. In an attack, the battalion kept well forward, as close to the companies as the terrain would permit. This facilitated communications, such as wire laying, supply, and evacuation. Kitchens were moved as far forward as possible and still kept out of the actual battle zone. On 19 March, the kitchens were moved into the valley just east of Hill 300.

Korean carrying parties should be organized as a field expediency and made available to the line battalions. Except for difficulties of forage, the terrain would have been excellent for mule trains.[2]

The 3d Battalion's S-4, 1st Lt. Henry S. Watcke, provides more details about supply operations.

The battalion supply train gave as close support to the companies as possible, operating about three miles behind the rifle companies. Until enemy artillery shells began to be received, battalion supply was located in the vicinity of Kusil [on the main road about 1,000 meters south of the Hongch'on River]. It then moved 1,000 yards to the rear and into a cut, out of enemy observation. Regimental supply was operating very close to the battalion and rendered magnificent support.

During the first phase of the operation, two hot meals and one

C ration were served to the line companies per day. The food was carried from the kitchen area to the forward elements by jeep and trailer. When the troops arrived on Hills 383 and 380, rations were delivered to the base of the hills. Portions of the companies were sent to these points to be fed or to carry the food to the company.

From Hill 499 to the end of the operation, food was hand carried from the base of the hills by Koreans to designated positions on the hill. Distances involved were too great to pull the men in the line companies off the hill. Rations, ammunition resupply, and weapon replacement were carried out this way. Clothing resupply was held to a minimum, although some socks and a small quantity of web equipment were delivered.

After Hill 499 the carrying parties remained with the companies. When the companies moved forward the carriers brought bedrolls forward to the companies' objectives. At that time the company gave information to the carriers on how many rations and which items of supply were needed. In addition to those secured by the companies themselves, about 175 Korean carriers were recruited by the battalion.

When the battalion was operating in the Ch'unch'on area, six miles south of the 38th parallel, the terrain was so mountainous that carrying parties with food would leave the battalion area at 0600 hours and return during the afternoon. The normal carry from the base of the hill to the company position was four and a half hours. One carrying party walked for twelve hours before overtaking the company, which had moved out in attack.

For a period of five days no hot meals were served to the line companies. Hot soup, hot doughnuts, and hot coffee, however, were sent to supplement the C rations. Occasionally the companies were able to withdraw to the reverse slope of a hill to heat their C rations.

Three meals of C rations for one company weigh 1,400 pounds. Five 5-gallon cans of drinking water are needed by each company every day.

The roads were very bad. In some places the road was washed out by the drainage from the mountains. Streambeds were often used as roads by the vehicles. The road in the valley east of Hwagumbong, the Marine MSR, was particularly bad.

When the battalion CP displaced forward to the draw west of Kalgol, the battalion trains moved to a point southeast of Kwangch'on. No further displacement forward was done because the road in the northeast valley came to an end. Eventually the supply trains moved up the northwest road to the vicinity of Ch'unch'on.

All communication was performed by messenger. Wire was very critical, and there was a distance of between six and seven miles between the battalion CP and the battalion supply. At 1000 and 1700 hours every day I reported personally to the battalion commander for instructions.

I believe that helicopters are needed organically in the regiment for terrain such as this, in order to transport food and ammunition and evacuate the wounded. Even if the helicopters could not land because of the terrain, supplies could be dropped.[3]

Within the rifle companies, the executive officer, a unit administrative officer, a supply sergeant, and the first sergeant were all involved in supply matters. Some of these soldiers provide more detail about the problems of supply within their units and present a somewhat different perspective from that of the battalion officers.

WARRANT OFFICER, JUNIOR GRADE (WOJG) JIMMIE D. SPENCER, UNIT ADMINISTRATIVE OFFICER, COMPANY I: In order to supply 180 men over the type of terrain encountered in this operation, it was necessary to have fifty to sixty well-controlled carriers. It was necessary also to have communications between the supply point and the company in order to coordinate the carrying party's time of arrival at the company. The SCR300 radio was used for this purpose.

The C ration was the only type ration that could be carried. Water was constantly a problem. Four to five hours were necessary to evacuate wounded from Hill 850, a distance of 4,000 straight-line meters, with four to six men carrying the litter. A helicopter was required to evacuate the seriously wounded from Hill 850, but no helicopters were available. The company had hoped helicopters would also be able to bring ammunition and supplies on the up-trip.[4]

1ST SGT. ARNOLD E. MITCHELL, COMPANY I: Company I had approximately 190 men, including the attachments, on line during this operation. To supply the company, thirty-seven cases of C rations per day, ten to twelve cans of water per day, plus ammunition resupply, had to be carried on the backs of human beings.[5]

WOJG Thomas J. Sherman, unit administrative officer, Company K: Since a road net was lacking in this mountainous terrain, it was impossible to bring vehicles close to the base of the hills. This necessitated reconnaissance to locate the best overland supply route. After the supply route was reconnoitered, transportation in the form of civilian laborers had to be found. Not many Koreans lived in such mountainous areas. Refugee columns could not be touched because of the possibility of spies. Therefore, inhabitants of the area had to be used, and sometimes it was necessary to use coercion to obtain the number needed. Korean carriers were not paid. Usually they were fed, clothed, and returned to their area upon completion of their service. Feeding the carriers necessitated securing Korean food. ROK soldiers with the company were particularly useful in this operation.

When the company was on Hill 899, I loaded up a carrying party and took the most obvious, direct route to the company as shown on the map. Departing the kitchen area at about 1730, and without losing my way or deviating from the map course, the carrying party reached the company position at 2330. After delivering the rations, the party returned to the battalion area. On the following morning I arose early and reconnoitered a new route to the base of the hill, hoping to cut down the carrying time. Carrying a hot meal from the jeep point at 0800, the carrying party arrived at the company at 1130. But this route was too steep, and the carriers had to rest too often.

To overcome the problem of distance, a second carrying party was organized. One party brought C rations for the noon meal; the second party carried rations for the evening meal.

Since fires could not be built during the tactical operation, C rations were eaten cold. They were not very tasty. Hot meals, thus, were an important morale factor. The first jeep up the northeast valley road was carrying hot food to the company.

When the tactical situation permitted, the carrying party with the company carried ammunition and helped carry impedimenta.

Ordnance, signal, and quartermaster supplies were carried up to the company with the rations. In an emergency there were always enough people available at battalion to carry these supplies.[6]

1ST LT. JAMES W. KENT, EXECUTIVE OFFICER, COMPANY L: When the company is to move tactically over mountainous terrain, the men are exhausted if they must return over the same ground and transport supplies over the same route. On Hill 638 the men had to climb a sheer cliff of about twenty meters. In some places the trail was wide enough for only one man at a time. In addition, the trails were covered with snow and ice. Often the rocks were covered with a thin coating of mud. Getting the supplies in and the wounded out, consequently, was extremely hazardous. Carrying parties were allowed to operate only in areas that had been completely cleared of the enemy.

Due to the necessity of moving rapidly in tactical formation, it was necessary often to dispense with impedimenta. One evening the company had to choose between having chow or bedrolls. The company chose bedrolls.

The ridgeline the company followed to Hill 899 was easy traveling. The kitchens moved to the vicinity of Ch'unch'on so that the only problem was that of carrying the food uphill.

The Korean carriers were slow moving, but they were able to carry about a hundred pounds per man. Their difficulty lay in getting the supplies up to the ridgeline. Once there, the operation was comparatively easy.

Lack of roads added to the supply problems. The jeeps went anywhere an oxcart had been.[7]

CHIEF WARRANT OFFICER (CWO) CLARENCE J. UMBERGER, UNIT ADMINISTRATIVE OFFICER, COMPANY L: The most difficult problem during this operation was getting food to the company. It was necessary to have enough carriers to transport sufficient rations at one time for the entire company. Carrying trips took between five and nine hours (the usual trip was five hours; the longest was nine) to carry C rations sufficient for one or two meals for the company. The carrying parties of about twenty-five elderly South Koreans were very good. The carriers were transported on trucks or jeeps as far as the road or trail would permit. They worked voluntarily and received their meals in return.

During much of this operation, no road existed within two or three miles of the company. The Koreans carried company supplies for a distance of between one and a half and three miles. Carry was made over very rugged mountains. Very few Americans carried supplies. A Korean was able to carry about a hundred pounds, two C rations boxes, or one ration and one can of water. The trails were usually very steep inclines, and it was necessary to hang onto bushes and trees to ascend and descend.

The carriers were secured from the villages. It was impossible to keep records on these personnel, for the company needed the carriers and used them immediately. The carrying parties were indispensable. It would have been impossible to get supplies to the company without them.

In one case when the company needed ammunition, a carrying party brought ammunition at night to the company. This was unusual, for the company usually carried its own ammunition.

Koreans were also used to evacuate the wounded where there were not sufficient litter bearers. This operation was always supervised by an American soldier. It took hours to get a man on a litter off the hill. In some places it was necessary to inch along. Some trails on the ridgeline were wide enough for only one man.

I tried to get individually packed C rations to the company twice a day, once early in the morning, and once in the evening. If conditions permitted, hot meals in food containers were carried. Water always went with the C rations.

Twice during this operation hot food was brought to the base of the mountain, and carrying parties from the company descended and carried the food to the company. This was not feasible, however, because the men were too tired after a day of combat.

Koreans also carried bedrolls when necessary. Some socks were carried up by the supply sergeant. During combat, individuals who had lost or worn out equipment were resupplied. Torn shoes and steel helmets were replaced on an individual basis.[8]

SFC CARL P. MICHAEL, SUPPLY SERGEANT, COMPANY L: When

the company relieved the British, supply personnel started rounding up Koreans to transport C rations, ammunition, and radio batteries to the company on Hill 703. When the company advanced north the carriers followed.

At the Hongch'on River the carriers followed the company across and delivered rations between 2100 and 2130 that night. I led the carriers back, fed them, and gave them blankets, clothes, and cigarettes.

When the company was on Hill 638, carriers left the company supply point at 1800 hours. This party with bedrolls and rations reached the company at 2100 hours. The carrying party arrived back at the company supply point at 0400. It was necessary to walk about five miles from the 4.2-inch mortar positions (at the jeep point) to the company.

Sometimes after the carrying party started up toward the company, the company received orders to advance. The carrying party then had to follow the company advance.

I recommend that civilian carrying parties be organized and made available to divisions, regiments, battalions, and companies as needed. I believe that civilian carriers should be held in a work compound to keep them from giving information to the enemy.[9]

Medical support in combat operations is particularly difficult and becomes even more of a challenge in rugged terrain. Lieutenant Junior Grade (LtJG) Robert M. Adams, the 3d Battalion's surgeon, and his assistant, 1st Lt. Bill T. Wilson, explain the medical support system and the special problems during this operation. Lieutenant Adams was a U.S. Naval Reserve officer, assigned to the Army because of a shortage of Army Medical Corps officers at the outbreak of the Korean War.

The 3d Battalion medical section consisted of two officers and thirty-three enlisted men. This figure included the aid men and the litter bearers who operate with the rifle companies. Four aid men and four litter bearers work with each rifle company; three aid men, no litter bearers are with the Heavy Weapons Company. There are also six drivers, Medical Department personnel, who drive one ¾-

ton truck with trailer, three litter jeeps, and one headquarters jeep, which can become a litter jeep when needed.

The 3d Battalion relieved the Australians on 13 March 1951. At midnight, when Company L moved off Hill 703, a man broke his leg during the move. Because it was impossible to get a litter jeep to the patient, helicopter evacuation was requested. It was necessary to phone through regiment, division, and corps to the Mobile Army Surgical Hospital (MASH), which dispatched the helicopter.

On 14 March the medical section moved on its organic transportation across the Hongch'on River to a small village [Sodan-ni] in the valley. Enemy mortar and artillery fire was being received at that time.

Company I went into attack soon after crossing the Hongch'on River and suffered six wounded and one killed in action. There was no particular problem of evacuation because the medical aid station was close to the company at this time.

On 16 March the companies pushed off against the hills. Evacuation then required a hand-carry approximately one mile from the place where the man was wounded to the point where he could be picked up by litter jeep. The battalion's assistant surgeon selected litter jeep points, establishing one such point at one bridge, another near the other bridge. The litter jeep had a run of about one mile under enemy small-arms fire and through a minefield. One medical driver was hit by enemy fire that day.

On 16 March the battalion suffered thirty-four wounded in action and six killed in action. The aid men with the companies administered first aid and prepared the patient for evacuation to the aid station by litter bearer and litter jeep. At the aid station, blood plasma was given if necessary, dressings were changed, but no definitive treatment was administered. Then the wounded were carried to the collecting station by litter jeep. Litter jeep drivers, aid men, and litter bearers performed magnificently under enemy observation and fire. It took at least one and a half hours to two hours to evacuate wounded from the slopes of Hills 383 and 380 to the aid station.

This particular action seemed different in that most of the

wounds were from bullets (small arms and automatic weapons), rather than from mortars, as had been generally the case. More combat exhaustion cases came in than usual. Nine in three days was more than the total suffered from the middle of January to that time.

On 17 March, when the rifle companies pushed farther north, the evacuation hand-carry was increased to about two miles, for it was impossible to get litter jeeps up the roads because of mines. The aid station moved forward and almost set up in the minefield in the blind valley. But at that time a communications jeep was knocked out by a mine. There were two wounded and one killed. The wounded were handled by the 2d Battalion aid station because the 3d Battalion aid station was in the process of moving.

On 18 March the aid station moved into the draw to be in a better position to support the rifle companies, which were on Hills 499, 402, and 272. The collecting station [operated by the 5th Cavalry Regiment Medical Company] was then six miles to the rear. There were no casualties.

On 20 March, with Company I on Hill 850, the battalion suffered three killed in action and eighteen wounded in action. Litter bearers, with Korean civilian and prisoners of war to assist, carried patients from Hill 850, a litter haul of two hours and an estimated three-mile walking distance from Hill 850, to the jeep evacuation point near the end of the trail. As soon as one litter came to the jeep, the jeep departed immediately for the aid station, a trip of one hour and ten minutes. Two jeeps were operating that day. The ¾-ton truck used for walking wounded generally hauled litter squads to a point in the vicinity of the village of Saesonggok.

It was normal to set up the jeep point in the vicinity of the mortar platoon because of the aid to communications. Also, the mortar platoon had a litter jeep that could be utilized. The mortars were set up near the end of the trail.

On the afternoon of 20 March the aid station moved to a point south of Sagol. Company L had three casualties that day. These were evacuated by the Marines because the 3d Battalion aid station was not yet set up. The aid station was now about ten miles from the collecting station.

On 21 March, with the aid station proper at Sagol, the battalion surgeon's assistant, an enlisted technician, and three litter jeeps established an advance aid station near the end of the road. Between 1600 on 21 March and 1100 on 22 March there were no casualties. The road [northeast valley] came to an end, and had there been casualties on Hill 899, the worst evacuation problem of the Korean experience would have had to be faced. Hill 899 was a good six miles traveling distance from the advance aid station. From the advance aid station to the aid station was a distance of four miles. From the aid station to the collecting station was ten miles.

The regimental collecting station had moved up the northwest road [MSR from Hongch'on to Ch'unch'on] to evacuate the 2d Battalion, but part of its personnel remained for 3d Battalion patients. Then the division clearing station moved to a point across the Hongch'on River, and the 3d Battalion shuttled its casualties directly to the clearing station.

On 22 March the aid station moved to the vicinity of Ch'unch'on, and the problem of evacuation became comparatively simple.

The most important consideration in evacuation is the distance between the troops and the jeep evacuation point. As the hills increased in height to Hill 899, the problem became more severe. Often no trails suitable for litter evacuation existed. Often jeeps traveled over very rough terrain, in streambeds, over wagon trails, and this did not help a patient's condition. Lack of roads prevented the collecting station from moving close to the battalion aid station.

Company commanders and platoon leaders, when requesting medical aid, must report the number of casualties, the seriousness of the wounds, and the number of litters needed, so that medical personnel may make specific and adequate provision for aid and evacuation.[10]

Two aid men, PFCs J. C. Weston and Vern Tidwell, who provided medical support on Hill 850, describe their experience.

To evacuate patients by litter from Hill 850 it was often necessary, in order to keep the litter level, to let the back end of the litter drag on the ground, while the front end was carried at shoulder height. Often no trail existed. Many times the existing trail had turns that were too sharp for the litters. It was always necessary to be alert for sliding rock and for slick spots. In some places the narrow ridgeline made it necessary to have two men carry the litter instead of the normal four.

The litter haul on Hill 850 took two and a half hours.[11]

Despite the problems of supply and medical support, the 3d Battalion succeeded in its mission of driving the enemy from the Hongch'on defense line back over the ridges to Ch'unch'on. The determination, skill, and ingenuity of the soldiers of the unit overcame all obstacles presented by the enemy and the terrain. Nonetheless, the results were disappointing, and General Ridgway continued to search for ways to destroy part of the retreating enemy forces.

Chapter 5

OPERATION TOMAHAWK

187th Airborne Regimental Combat Team, 23–24 March 1951

One tool available to General Ridgway that could be used to trap and destroy part of the enemy forces was the 187th Airborne Regimental Combat Team (RCT). From its arrival in Korea in the fall of 1950, the 187th had performed exceptionally well in combat, although the results of its airborne operations, through no fault of the regiment, had been less than expected. The drop north of the North Korean capital of P'yongyang in October 1950 had failed to catch sizeable numbers of enemy troops, the bulk of which had already withdrawn. After fighting in January and February under X Corps in the central mountains, near Wonju and elsewhere, the regiment was withdrawn to Taegu airfield to train and prepare for future airborne operations. A planned jump north of Ch'unch'on was canceled because the ground advance during Operation Ripper overran the target area first. However, the preparations for this jump were helpful, as related by the deputy commander of the regiment and some of the regimental staff officers.

COL. GEORGE H. GERHART, DEPUTY COMMANDER: We were alerted on 16 March 1951 that we were to jump on 20 March. We only had four days notice. We prepared for a drop in the Ch'unch'on area. It was well planned. Too bad we couldn't have dropped there. But it didn't materialize. The troops got in there ahead of time.[1]

MAJ. RAYMOND H. ROSS, ASSISTANT S-2 OF THE REGIMENT: We had been planning and preparing for a jump on Ch'unch'on for approximately one week. So, as far as equipment was concerned, we were fully prepared.[2]

LT. COL. THOMAS H. LANE, REGIMENTAL SURGEON: Preparations for a jump were initially made during the first week of February 1951, at which time the 187th Airborne Regimental Combat Team was located at Wonju. Assisted by the S-2 and S-3 of the regiment, I prepared a list of minimum requirements in the form of medical supplies. On 19 February I directed my medical supply officer to fly to Taegu to complete necessary arrangements with the Eighth Army Medical Depot. Thus the drawing and storage of supplies was accomplished, with subsequent shipment of a number of litters to Japan for preparation and storage.

I received alert orders for a jump approximately one week in advance of the actual jump and began preparations. At this time the regiment's location was on the border of the K-2 airfield at Taegu. I immediately directed my medical supply officer to draw the required supplies, which included nine litter jeeps, and turn the items over to the Air Packaging Officer of the regiment for preparation and shipment to the packaging area in Japan. Those particular supplies were not handled thereafter by medical personnel until received on the drop zone.[3]

The escape of the enemy from Ch'unch'on led General Ridgway to look for another opportunity to use the 187th Airborne RCT. It appeared that the North Koreans and Chinese still held their lines north of Seoul in strength. Particularly vulnerable were North Korean forces directly above Seoul, who would have to cross the unfordable Imjin River near Munsan-ni if forced to withdraw. The new operation, code-named Courageous, would involve the U.S. I Corps, but a key element of the plan was the use of the 187th Airborne Regimental Combat Team to seize the area around Munsan-ni and trap the enemy frontline units, setting them up for destruction (code-named Operation Tomahawk). A combat historian, Capt. Edward C. Williamson, interviewed members of the 187th Airborne and prepared a summary of the operation. He describes the plan.

Operation Tomahawk [the airborne portion of Operation Courageous] was planned, in continuation of Operation Ripper, to block enemy movement north through the Munsan-ni area. The 187th

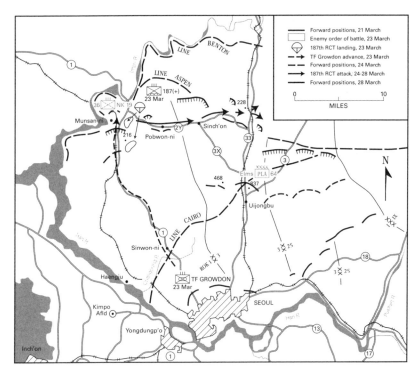

Operation Courageous, 22–28 March 1951 (based on map in CMH manuscript, U.S. Army).

Airborne Regimental Combat Team, reinforced by the 2d and 4th Ranger Companies, was to drop in the vicinity of Munsan-ni; at the same time U.S. I Corps continued its attack to the northwest from Seoul. Task Force Growdon, consisting of the 6th Medium Tank Battalion, 2d Battalion, 7th Infantry Regiment, 58th Armored Field Artillery Battalion, and Company A, 14th Engineer (C) Battalion, was ordered to link up with the 187th Airborne Regimental Combat Team in the Munsan-ni area within twenty-four hours after the drop was initiated.[4]

Preparations

Col. George H. Gerhart, deputy commander of the 187th Airborne, describes the receipt of the new orders.

We were alerted on 16 March that we were to jump on 20

March. We only had four days notice. We prepared for a drop in the Ch'unch'on area. On 20 March we received a message from Eighth Army on the change of target. We immediately instituted necessary measures in connection with the new target. This necessitated a complete change of plans. I was acting in the capacity of chief of staff. All plans and necessary changes were made, and on the afternoon before the jump, we checked over everything again to make certain we were in readiness.[5]

Preparations for an airborne drop are extensive and complicated. The last minute shift in drop zones from the Ch'unch'on area to Munsan-ni was an added problem, even though the 187th was already preparing for an airborne operation. Major Ross, the assistant S-2 of the regiment, explains.

I was given two days advance notice of the jump at Munsan-ni. The big problem, due to the change of target, involved preparing terrain analyses, engineering studies of roads, trails, bridges, fords, and stream conditions, as well as estimating enemy capabilities and probable courses of action, in sufficient time to brief the regimental and battalion staffs so that they might take full advantage of the information given prior to the drop. The sudden change in target meant that the troops could not study sand tables [three-dimensional terrain maps made of hardened sand, with the key geographical features, used for operational planning and orientation], aerial photos, or local land areas similar in nature to the actual drop zone. The troops had previously spent one week thoroughly preparing for the Ch'unch'on drop.

The S-2 was notified of the change of drop zones by General Bowen [187th Regiment commander] on the evening of 21 March, at which time he gave us the information verbally. About 0900 hours on 22 March, we received the top secret operation orders [from I Corps] showing that D-day H-hour would be 0900 hours on 23 March.

As a consequence of the time limitation, the individual soldier received only minimum information of the objective area. There was not sufficient time for actual unit problems, nor were aerial photos received in time for their study. However, technical information was in the hands of the battalion staffs by approximately 1200 hours, 22 March 1951. In general, the entire S-2 section worked until about 0100 hours on 23 March.[6]

Some information was available about the enemy in the area, as stated in the intelligence estimate for the operations plan.

Enemy Situation. The U.S. I Corps is opposed on the left flank by elements of the North Korean (NK) I Corps, which has an estimated 15,000 troops. The divisions of this corps are approximately 40 to 50 percent of full strength. These divisions are equipped with an unknown number of medium tanks, self-propelled (SP) guns, and automatic weapons. Some antiaircraft guns (75 and 85mm) have been reported in the NK I Corps sector in the last four days. The 8th and 47th NK Rifle Divisions and the 17th Mechanized Division are part of the NK I Corps. The NK 19th and 18th Rifle Divisions are elements of the NK VI Corps, located between Kaesong and the Imjin, near Munsan-ni. The 8th Rifle Division of the NK I Corps, with an estimated strength of 5,000 men, contains the 81st, 82d, and 83d Rifle Regiments. The 47th Rifle Division has an estimated strength of 4,000, as does the 17th Mechanized Division. The 18th and 19th Rifle Divisions of the NK VI Corps have estimated strengths respectively of 4,200 and 5,740.

Recent Significant Activity. In the last seven days the NK I Corps has defended Seoul and the high ground to the north with company- and battalion-size groups. Each day during this period, the enemy has placed tank, SP gun, artillery, and heavy-mortar fire on positions of the U.S. I Corps. Friendly aircraft flying over the NK I Corps sector have been fired on by small-arms, automatic-weapons, and antiaircraft-artillery fire. Before withdrawing from Seoul, the enemy set up many booby traps in the area. In the last few days an estimated enemy regiment has dug in astride the Seoul–Munsan-ni road about fifteen miles south of Munsan-ni. The NK I Corps is believed to be adequately supplied for offensive and defensive operations.

Reinforcements. The 8th and 47th NK Rifle Divisions are southeast of the objective area, about ten and fifteen miles respectively. An unknown number of troops of the Chinese Communist

Forces 50th and 27th Armies are in the valley north of Uijongbu [about fifteen miles east of Munsan-ni].

Enemy Capabilities. The enemy can (1) attack troop carrier aircraft with automatic-weapons and small-arms fire; (2) attack the objective area [Munsan-ni] with an estimated battalion by H plus 5 to 8 hours from the south, possibly supported by tanks; (3) attack the drop zone from the south with an estimated regiment, possibly supported by tanks by H plus 8 hours; (4) attack the drop zone and objective area with an unknown number of troops and tanks from the east or northeast at any time; (5) withdraw to the north around the east flank of the 187th RCT position; (6) defend in position about fifteen miles south of Munsan-ni with a reinforced regiment. There is insufficient information to indicate which capability the enemy is likely to pursue.

Effect of Enemy Courses of Action on Our Mission. An attack on the regiment's position by enemy forces presently available from the south or southeast is not sufficient to dislodge the regiment from planned positions. A strong defense by the enemy south of Munsan-ni could seriously delay the advance of the link-up group. Withdrawal of the enemy to the northeast would most adversely affect our mission.[7]

Despite the limited time, a detailed study of the terrain was conducted and published the day before the operation.

Topography. The principal streams in this area are the Imjin, which flows from northeast to southwest forming an unfordable water barrier north of the objective area, and the San-ch'on, which flows from south to north, forming the westernmost boundary of the objective area. In general, drainage is from east to west into the San-ch'on, which in turn converges with the Imjin at Munsan-ni. Hill 216 forms a long north–south ridge, extending from a point approximately 500 yards south of Munsan-ni, south to Pongam-ni, a distance of about two and a half miles. The village of P'aiu-ri (junction of three secondary roads) is located southeast of Hill 216 and is bordered by a paddy valley approximately two miles long (north–south) and three-quarters of a mile wide. North of P'aiu-ri are Hills 181 and 232, which form an irregular east–west hill mass,

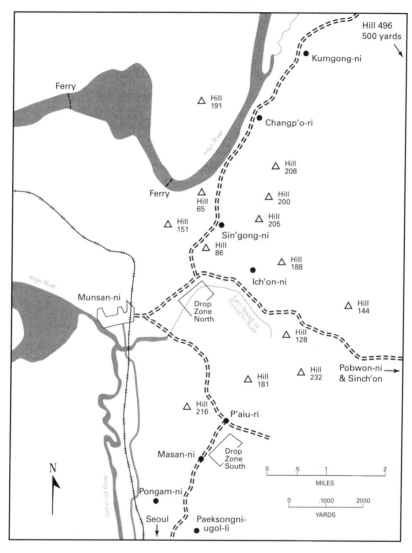

Munsan-ni area of operations (original map by author, based on maps from the Army Map Service).

which joins Hill 216. North of these connecting ridges, the east branch of the San-ch'on forms an irregular east–west paddy valley, interspersed with low finger-like hills and containing Munsan-ni. North of this valley and Munsan-ni, the Imjin River forms a large pocket approximately two and a half miles by two and a half miles, containing a large paddy field in the north, partly on two low, sub-divided hill masses running generally northwest–southeast, which join together at the mouth of the pocket containing the Munsan-ni–east San-ch'on River valley. Containing the pocket and east valley area from the east are Hills 188, 205, and 208, which form a fairly high north–south ridge that dominates the entire area. A series of low ridges and hills contain the north bank of the Imjin River and dominate the pocket from the north and west.

Vegetation. The flats are devoted mainly to rice. Small valleys between the hills are tilled for dry crops and some rice. Grass, weeds, scattered brush, and scrub evergreens will be found on the lower hills. In general, the high hill masses are sparsely covered with vegetation.

Cultural Features. (1) Munsan-ni is an important road junction and communication center. (2) A main line, standard gage, double-track railroad. (3) Railroad bridge over the east fork of the San-ch'on River, 700 yards south of Munsan-ni. (4) Sandbag and gravel bypass over the east fork of San-ch'on River 700 yards south of Munsan-ni and on the Munsan-ni–Seoul MSR. (5) Twelve known revetments capable of holding automatic weapons in a paddy field 200 yards south of Munsan-ni. (6) Irrigation canals bisecting most wide flat areas are more than fifteen feet wide and diked above the level of the flats.

Critical Terrain Features. (1) Munsan-ni controls railroads, road approaches, and communications in the pocket area. (2) Hills 151, 205, and 208 control observation of ferry crossing sites, road and water approaches, and inland areas in the pocket, sand island, terrain to the north, and road and valley approaches from the south. (3) Hill 191 [north of the Imjin] controls observation of the entire north and central pocket area as well as the Imjin road and water approach from the northeast. (4) The east–west ridge southeast of Munsan-ni formed by Hills 216, 181, 232, and 144 controls observation of road, railroad, and valley approaches from the west, south, and east. (5) Critical terrain includes the Imjin River, which presents a formidable obstacle to north–south movement in the Munsan-ni area. (6) P'aiu-ri controls the junction of the main roads between

Munsan-ni and towns to the south, and other small trail and road approaches from the south.

Military Aspects of the Terrain. (1) Observation and fields of fire in the flats will be almost ideal for small-arms fire. Dikes and scattered brush will offer some limitations. (2) The hills provide ideal observation and good opportunity for interdictory fire on targets in the flats or surrounding hills. (3) The Imjin River, affected by tides, is not fordable in this area. (4) Canals, some fifteen feet wide and ten to fifteen feet deep and dikes ten to fifteen feet high preclude armored cross-country movement in large paddy areas except on known roads. (5) Irregular paddy formations preclude light vehicular movement except on higher ground and graded roads. (6) Cover and concealment in the flats is spotty. Dikes and small drainage ditches may be used. (7) Cover in the lower hills is fair, with numerous valleys for protection. Trees and bushes provide fair concealment. (8) Cover and concealment in the high hills is good, with many deep ravines providing excellent protection.

Effect on Enemy Capabilities. (1) Except for the north and west, the terrain and road nets are ideal for rapid, concealed movements of armor and foot troops into the objective area. (2) The enemy's first strong defense line would probably be the high ground approximately five miles northeast of Munsan-ni, extending from the Imjin River near Kumgong-ni, southeast to Hill 496, as this presents a natural defensive barrier. (3) The Imjin River precludes arrival of enemy reinforcements from the north; however, Hill 191 provides ideal OPs overlooking the objective area. (4) The San-ch'on River and low paddy valley preclude armor attack from the west; however, the stream is fordable in many places, and foot movement of substantial enemy troops may be expected.

Effect on Friendly Capabilities. (1) The terrain requires swift action by all troops to clear the pocket and the area between P'aiu-ri and Munsan-ni of all enemy and to seize the high ground extending from Munsan-ni east to Hill 208 to block enemy movement and to withstand organized counterattacks. (2) Hills 188, 205, and 208 must be secured and held in order to defend the objective area from attacks from the east. (3) Control of many approaches from the west, south, and east requires immediate establishment of antitank defenses. (4) Since small guerrilla-type units may effect a crossing of the Imjin River from the north by small craft at night, provisions for defense of outposts must be made. (5) Emphasis should be placed on the fact that enemy units in the Munsan-ni area are predominantly North Korean and therefore excel in night attack and infiltration.[8]

It is doubtful if much of this information trickled down to individual soldiers and their leaders at company level and below. Luck played a part in the preparations, as related by Lt. Col. Harry F. Lambert, battalion commander of the 674th Airborne Field Artillery Battalion.

For the landing at Munsan-ni, I held a dress rehearsal for the 674th Airborne Field Artillery Battalion where the terrain was damn near identical, although the airdrop was originally planned for Ch'unch'on.[9]

Logistical preparations were extensive, both for those dropping near Munsan-ni as well as the so-called "land tail" that was to move by vehicle after the linkup with Task Force Growdon was accomplished. The regimental S-4, Maj. Joseph E. Jenkins, provides details.

The 187th Airborne Regimental Combat Team mission to assault the area in the vicinity of Ch'unch'on via parachutes on 22 March was changed at 1230 hours on 21 March to the mission of assaulting the area in the vicinity of Munsan-ni at 0900 hours on 23 March.

The G-4 section acted swiftly and efficiently in preparing for the action. In connection with the Class I [food] supplies, all units of the 187th Airborne RCT were issued six assault packets per individual in the assault wave. A total of 20,916 packets were distributed. The land tail personnel were issued three days of C rations, totaling 1,677 rations. Arrangements were completed for a resupply of 7,000 C rations at Ashiga Air Force Base, Japan.

Clothing and equipment (Class II and IV) required by the individual soldier was checked, and those shortages noted were immediately filled. Due to a shortage of parachute helmets, regular helmets were issued in lieu. There was, however, a critical shortage of the proper boots. The combat service boot was not found acceptable because the suspension lines of the parachutes sometimes caught in the buckle of the shoe, with consequent disastrous results.

With regard to Class III [fuel] supplies, airdrop vehicles were supplied with three-quarters of a tank and one five-gallon drum of gas. The basic load of Class III for the land tail was drawn and issued. In this connection, arrangements were made to resupply fuel at Taejon and Suwon. Other arrangements completed included resupply via airdrop of fuel for airdropped vehicles and fuel, if needed, for the 6th Tank Battalion, to be delivered by the combat cargo carriers.

Relative to Class V [ammunition] supplies, all units were issued more than basic loads, especially in caliber .30 machine-gun, BAR, and mortar ammunition. The 75mm-pack howitzer ammunition was drawn and issued to the 674th Field Artillery Battalion, and arrangements were made with the Japan Logistical Command for a resupply of 75mm ammunition by airdrop.

The Japan Logistical Command had modified twenty-four ¾-ton trucks for airdropping. However, only two were actually dropped. The remainder were not dropped due to lack of availability of heavy drop equipment platforms. Twenty-five ¼-ton trucks (jeeps) were airdropped. The land tail, consisting of 418 vehicles, departed Taegu before 0100 hours on 23 March.

Insofar as the light planes were concerned, arrangements were made to use the K-16 airfield [near Seoul] for their base of operations. The helicopter evacuation of wounded and injured from the drop zone was coordinated between the regimental surgeon, the I Corps surgeon, and the Eighth Army surgeon.

Loads of all class supplies were prearranged and established at Ashiga, Japan. Major items of equipment lost due to the drop or enemy action were ready on call at Ashiga Air Force Base.

Plans called for recovery of parachute equipment. Arrangements were completed with I Corps to furnish Korean laborers to police the drop zone and to have the equipment evacuated through the

Class I Depot at Yongdungp'o [near Seoul]. The parachute maintenance detachment dropped sixteen enlisted men and one officer to
supervise recovery of parachute equipment.[10]

*The special arrangements for medical evacuation are explained
by the regimental surgeon, Lt. Col. Thomas H. Lane.*
The evacuation plan envisaged the initial use of helicopter, until
ground linkup could be made. To this end, I contacted Col. C. E.
Dovell, Eighth Army surgeon, who gave clearance for the use of
helicopters and directed me to contact Major McClure of the Air
Sea Rescue Service, 5th Air Force, whose helicopters were evacuating in the I Corps zone. Major McClure advised me to contact the
helicopter pilots at Suwon, where they were located, at that time,
prior to the jump. This was done two days prior to the jump, in
conjunction with a regiment and I Corps staff conference that I attended for the purpose of discussing the medical plan with the corps
surgeon.

At the meeting with the helicopter pilots, the probable location
of the collecting station site was pointed out on their maps. Ground
recognition signals were agreed upon, both for "do" and "do not"
land. These consisted of a white parachute spread out with a super-
imposed red cross made of red cargo chutes, with green smoke
burning to indicate both wind direction and that it was considered
safe for them to land. Red smoke would be burned if conditions
were unfavorable for landing. The wavelength of the helicopter radio was also ascertained, so that medical communication personnel
could talk to the helicopters from the ground if necessary. It was
prearranged that the helicopters would hover over the drop zone,
commencing at fifteen minutes following the last person to drop,
and would come in or not and land by the marker in the vicinity of
the collecting station. Helicopters were to carry patients to the
8055th MASH, then located at Yongdungp'o. It took approximately
forty-five minutes to make the round trip, including the unloading
of the patients.[11]

*Although not authorized under organization tables, the regi-
ment decided that the subject of public relations had to be addressed.*

The "unauthorized" but essential public relations officer needed to have well-rounded experience and a suitable temperament. The Public Information Officer (PIO) for the 187th Airborne Regiment, Capt. Alvin Ash, describes his preparations for the operation.

The organization's past experience with newspaper correspondents and matters of public relations revealed the necessity for an officer and enlisted man to be detailed to cope with this situation. A man was required to act as a buffer and liaison officer between correspondents and the staff, as well as to perform routine PIO duties.

I was detailed from overstrength [in the artillery battalion]. I relieved the former PIO just a few days prior to the jump, in connection with Operation Tomahawk. Along with the title, I inherited the services of seven enlisted men. Included among these was a photographer, a cartoonist, and one enlisted correspondent per battalion.

Immediately upon assuming this responsibility, I was informed of the proposed operation. I checked with the Eighth Army PIO on security matters pertaining to the assault, then informed accredited correspondents at their Eighth Army billets on 19 March. I only released information that a jump was proposed and that accredited correspondents could accompany the 187th on their mission if they so desired. I further stated that I would be glad to assist correspondents in every way possible.

Arrangement for transportation of the correspondents was then coordinated with the Far East Air Forces Combat Cargo Command through Captain Thompson, their Public Information Officer.

On the night prior to the drop, the correspondents visited me in the PIO tent. I gave them brief instructions in jumping and assigned them to various units for the jump. Nine persons, including correspondents and personnel not within the command, elected to jump. Of these, I noted a few had experienced at least one jump. Other correspondents were promised transportation in planes that would circle over the drop zone and then return to the airfield at Taegu.

The correspondents who were to jump with the troops expressed concern over their possible inability to send "copy" back from the drop zone for transmission to its proper destination. I solved this problem with the promise to send copy back in canvas dispatch cases via evacuation helicopter. It was planned to have the helicopter take the copy to the 8055th MASH, where it would be received by Air Force personnel, who in turn would transport it to the censors at General Headquarters in Japan.[12]

Members of the staff, once their staff preparation responsibilities were completed, could turn their attention to packing and loading their individual and section equipment, along with the rest of the regiment. Several soldiers describe their activities.

MAJ. THOMAS P. MULVEY, REGIMENTAL S-1: The S-1 section finished work at about 0200 hours, 23 March, and went to bed until 0400 hours when they arose and finished packing their personal gear. The two officers and three enlisted men who were to go via airlift walked about 500 yards from their tent area to the airfield, where they waited until time to load. At 0725 hours personnel were split between two planes, because the section couldn't fit in one plane. They loaded with their equipment, consisting of cargo packs, horseshoe rolls (blankets and ponchos), individual weapons, and ammunition. Each man carried two grenades.[13]

CAPT. CHARLES E. WEDDLE, ASSISTANT S-3 OF THE REGIMENT: At about 0400 hours, 23 March, men of the section donned their gear and secured their weapons. Each man carried a carbine and a pistol, for which they had 90 and 21 rounds of ammunition respectively. In addition to the combat packs that all wore, the S-2, Operations Sergeant, and myself slung field cases containing situation overlays, message books, maps, grease pencils, and acetate. A sufficient quantity for operation of the entire section was enclosed in each case so that loss of one man would not entirely incapacitate the section.

About two hours later the group walked to the airfield, and in accordance with our prearranged plan, split up and loaded on different planes. The "split up" policy had been established to overcome the possibility of loss of all personnel of the section in the event one plane was downed during flight to the drop zone.

Planes were loaded and ready for takeoff by 0700 hours, with personnel of the section scattered as passengers on the planes as follows: the S-3 and one enlisted man as radio operator in the first plane of the first serial; two officers in the twelfth plane with some personnel of the 3d Battalion; one enlisted man in the twenty-fourth plane of the third serial with part of the 2d Ranger Company; one officer in the sixty-first plane of the fourth serial with part of the 674th Field Artillery Battalion.[14]

The Drop

The planes began taking off from the Taegu airfield about 0715 hours. After a rendezvous over an island in the Sea of Japan, the aircraft headed for the drop zones (DZs) in the Munsan-ni area and began their drop at 0900 hours. For most, the jump was routine, but for some there were complications. Several members of the regiment describe their experiences.

COL. GEORGE H. GERHART, DEPUTY REGIMENTAL COMMANDER: Station time was 0630 on 23 March, when I boarded the lead plane in the fourth serial. The fourth serial carried the 2d Battalion. The general wanted to spread the command group, so he told me to get on the fourth serial lead plane. Colonel Connor, commanding officer of the 2d Battalion, and his command group were also on this plane. I was number one man on the right stick, and Colonel Connor was number one man on the left stick. The general was to remain behind to see that everyone got off the ground alright.

We were in the air about an hour and twenty-five minutes when the four-minute red warning light came on. When the green light blinked I jumped; it was about 0900 hours. We were flying at an altitude of about 700 feet. I had to dodge bundles and parachutes most of the way down, so I didn't have much time for looking around. I was actually in the air about twenty-eight seconds.[15]

LT. COL. J. P. CONNOR, COMMANDING OFFICER, 2D BATTALION: I led my stick of paratroopers out of the plane. One of the paratroopers was shot in the foot on the way down, and one airplane clipped four parachutes. Fortunately, all four were able to open their reserve chutes and land safely.[16]

M. SGT. YEN CHIN CHOW, COMPANY K: I was the platoon sergeant of the 1st Platoon of Company K and rode in the seventh plane of my serial. A verbal warning was issued twenty minutes before a red light flashed on. We had a one-foot-wide space to climb out of the ship. I pushed the stick out of my airplane; that is, I jumped twenty-first out of twenty-one.[17]

CAPT. DORSEY B. ANDERSON, COMMANDING OFFICER OF THE 4TH RANGER COMPANY: At 0730 hours on 23 March, the Rangers were airlifted in four C-46 planes on the second serial. The scheduled drop time on the drop zone, vicinity Munsan-ni, was 0915. With the planes at an altitude of 700 feet, flying in a Vee of Vees formation at a speed of 120 miles per hour, the company unloaded its bundles containing heavy weapons and mortars, and three large regimental bundles containing communications equipment. These bundles were door loads, and had to be thrown from the jump door before the personnel jumped. Since the drop zone was approximately 1,400 yards long (the last 300 yards an orchard), it was necessary to get the bundles out of the plane and jump quickly in order to be out of the plane before the drop zone was passed.[18]

MAJ. MULVEY, S-1 OF THE 187TH AIRBORNE: Planes carrying personnel of the S-1 section took off at approximately 0805 hours and flew an angular course to the DZ area. We were given a twenty-minute warning to make final adjustments of equipment. Four minutes out from the DZ the red light went on, at which time each man stood up, hooked up, and checked the man's equipment in front of him. The planes were flying at an altitude of approximately 700 feet when the green light came on, and we began to jump. I was the number nine man, and two other men from the S-1 section on the same plane were numbers seventeen and twenty.[19]

SFC ADASIUS KARWASA, CHIEF OF THE 4TH HOWITZER SECTION OF BATTERY B, 674TH AIRBORNE FIELD ARTILLERY BATTALION: On 23 March, Battery B left Taegu at 0900 hours. While in flight, because of a leak of hydraulic brake fluid in the cabin, the crew chief ordered everyone to put out his cigarette. Four minutes before we hit the DZ, we stood up, hooked up, checked equipment, and sounded off. The stick leader gave the command, "Jump."

I jumped as number four, and when the time was due for the opening shock, I felt a jar that I thought was the parachute opening. I made a grab for the risers, looked up, and saw that the entire chute had been ripped off by a following plane. I then made a grab for the reserve chute. I missed it the first time, but grabbed it the second time. I estimate that while the entire incident took place, I fell 300–400 feet.[20]

Perhaps the greatest mishap involved mechanical problems in the aircraft carrying the command group of the only battalion destined for the southern drop zone. All other units of the 187th were to drop in the northern DZ. The 437th Troop Carrier Wing operations officer, Maj. Vernon W. Froelich, and the executive officer of the battalion, Maj. Charles M. Holland, describe what happened.

MAJ. FROELICH: Regarding the twenty-one ships in the serial [carrying the 1st Battalion, 187th Airborne, headed for the southern DZ]: about fifteen minutes after it had taken off, I learned that the lead aircraft had aborted. Both propellers died out. The pilot had no control over the props whatsoever, either manual or automatic. The crews had previously been briefed that if they had to abort, they were either to land at Taegu or, if they could maintain altitude, to drop their troops on the practice drop zone near Taegu. The pilot managed to retain enough altitude to allow them to land at Taegu. The lead of the formation was taken over by the deputy commander of the serial and continued on to the drop zone.

I had received word from the CP at Taegu that the lead plane had aborted, so after the runway at Taegu was cleared, I dispatched a spare C-46 to the airfield. By the time the load and the crew had changed, and a discussion with the battalion commander, who was with the original lead plane, had been accomplished, an hour had elapsed between the original takeoff and the second takeoff. It was my understanding that the formation missed the southern drop zone by one and a half to two miles. The spare aircraft, with the battalion commander aboard, dropped their load on the southern drop zone, thereby causing a small separation of about one and a half miles.[21]

MAJ. HOLLAND: I took off at 0730 hours from Taegu, flying in the plane with the 1st Battalion commander's party, which included also the S-3, the forward air controller, the artillery liaison officer, and the battalion medic. Engine trouble forced the plane from the 187th Airborne formation, and it returned to an airfield just outside Taegu where another C-46 picked up the party and attempted without success to catch up with the formation. As a result, the 1st Battalion commander's party was unaware that the entire 187th Airborne Regimental Combat Team had dropped on the northern DZ, instead of the 1st Battalion dropping on the southern DZ in accordance with prior planning. The southern DZ was three miles southeast of Munsan-ni.[22]

Members of the regiment explain the reasons the 1st Battalion dropped on the wrong DZ.

COLONEL GERHART, DEPUTY COMMANDER OF THE REGIMENT: The entire 1st Battalion, less one planeload, was dropped on the wrong drop zone. The pilots of the planes carrying that battalion were not sufficiently briefed so that when the lead plane aborted, which it did, the pilot of the second plane, who should have assumed command and delivered the battalion to the proper drop zone, was uncertain where to drop the 1st Battalion. Consequently, he followed the other serials and dropped the 1st Battalion where the others had dropped at the northern drop zone, which was incorrect by a distance of about five miles. Fortunately the tactical situation was such that this made little material difference. However, it could have had serious consequences.[23]

1ST LT. LEO R. GULICK, ASSISTANT S-3 OF THE 1ST BATTALION: I jumped about 0915 northeast of the northern DZ. In all the confusion, the northern DZ appeared similar to the southern DZ, about which I had been briefed at Taegu and where I was supposed to drop. There was a dike on both DZs, to add to the confusion.[24]

Despite these mishaps and the additional density of troops going into the northern DZ, the assembly of the units proceeded relatively smoothly. According to plan, the 3d Battalion was to be first to land on the northern DZ and secure the area for the other units that were supposed to land there. Members of the 3d Battalion describe the situation on the ground and their actions.

MAJ. RONALD C. SPEIRS, 3D BATTALION S-3: The northern DZ was initially saturated with personnel due to the 1st Battalion's accidental drop. This hampered the assembly of the 3d Battalion, as there were too many men at the assembly point, which was the northwest sector of the DZ. The initial mission of the 3d Battalion was to secure the DZ, and this was accomplished. Forty to fifty enemy were killed and wounded by the battalion.[25]

SGT. CHARLES P. MCDONALD, 3D BATTALION OPERATIONS SERGEANT: The 3d Battalion left our home station near Taegu at 0530 hours and completed loading in planes at 0630. From 0630 to 0700 the engines warmed up, and at 0715 hours we took off. The aircraft rendezvoused above an island in the Sea of Japan, and after a smooth flight the 3d Battalion dropped at 0904 hours on DZ North. At 0955 hours, 60 percent of the battalion had assembled; at 1005 hours 80 percent; and at 1215 hours 100 percent. Companies moved into position [with Company I north of the DZ, Company K on the eastern edge of the DZ, and Company L to the southwest of the DZ]. The 4th Ranger Company, which was attached, attacked to secure Hill 205. The Rangers were in contact with the enemy at 1200 hours. All during the period of assembly, the 3d Battalion received incoming mortar and artillery fire. Company M suffered five wounded, and the 4th Ranger Company suffered six, in the vicinity of Hill 205.[26]

2D LT. MELVIN C. STRAWSER, PLATOON LEADER, 1ST PLATOON, COMPANY I: I jumped at 0900 hours, leading the 1st Platoon. Two prisoners were captured immediately. Company I gathered at the predesignated assembly area and moved to attack the main objective at 0930 hours, killing eight enemy, capturing twenty-one, and securing one machine gun. At 1000 hours the company set up a defense, and the company commander sent one squad to secure Hill 86.[27]

2D LT. EVERETT MACKLEY, PLATOON LEADER, 2D PLATOON, COMPANY I: After landing on the northern DZ about 0905 hours, the 2d Platoon of Company I assembled in an apple orchard with only one jump casualty. At battalion order the platoon moved east, passing through the DZ and encountering four North Koreans who were running. The North Koreans were promptly killed. More North Koreans were encountered as the platoon moved to its initial objective. In all, six were killed and five captured.[28]

M. SGT. NEAL A. PERKINS, PLATOON SERGEANT, 1ST PLATOON, COMPANY I: I jumped at 0905 hours. Eight minutes after landing, my platoon had two prisoners. The platoon assembled in thirty minutes in a dry creek bed and moved out to the high ground that we were to secure north of the DZ. Because the enemy defensive position was dug in, it took one and a half hours to secure the high ground. The 1st Platoon of Company I took eleven prisoners, Company I taking thirty-four in all. Two men from Company I were hurt on the drop and one wounded.[29]

Capt. John E. Strever Jr., commander, Company K: Company K's original mission was to secure the east and north approaches to the DZ against enemy attack. Two men were injured in the drop; however, all equipment was recovered. Company K dropped in the first serial at 0900 hours. Because of a mix-up, the 1st and 2d Battalions did not jump in their assigned DZs, the 2d Battalion dropping in the artillery DZ [part of the northern DZ]. Moving to its first objective, Company K found enemy equipment, and in searching villages nearby, flushed eight enemy, killing five and taking three prisoners. There was no organized resistance met on the first objective.[30]

1st Lt. Edward F. Gernette, executive officer, Company L: There were six casualties in Company L on the drop. After dropping, Company L moved to high ground south of the DZ, finding enemy positions, weapons, and clothing. Company L acted as security for the southern half of the DZ.[31]

Capt. Thomas J. Watkins, commander, Company M: Before the jump, I decided to turn the 75mm recoilless-rifle section into a machine-gun platoon because the limited amount of ammunition that the section could carry would make the 75mm recoilless rifle ineffective. Company M jumped with four 81mm mortars, dropped in bundles with 220 rounds of ammunition. The machine-gun platoon, four light machine guns with 3,000 rounds per gun, and the provisional machine-gun platoon, with 2,000 rounds per gun, dropped with the men carrying the equipment. The provisional platoon did not carry as much ammunition as the regular section because it was short of men; machine-gun ammunition is dropped with two boxes per man. Six 3.5-inch bazookas with six rounds each were dropped on men.

One section of machine guns each was attached to Company I

and Company L, jumping with the companies. The provisional machine-gun platoon jumped under Company M control and was immediately attached to Company K after the drop. Forward observer parties from the 81mm Mortar Platoon, consisting of a forward observer and radioman, jumped with each of the three companies of the 3d Battalion. Company M dropped 126 men and one Korean interpreter, including the forty-four men attached to the rifle companies.

I left the home base at Taegu at 0430 hours, arrived at the airfield at 0455 hours, took off at 0755 hours, and dropped at 0900 hours. Planes under Company M control consisted of two C-119s, 17 and 18 in line, and one C-46. Five men from Company M dropped in the 2d serial. In the assembly phase, Company M headquarters assembled on the north end of the northern DZ near 3d Battalion headquarters. The mortar platoon assembled in Company K's area. The assembly was accomplished, without great difficulty, one-half hour after the drop. The only equipment lost was one radio, which was found and used by another company; five men were injured. During the assembly phase, five enemy were lightly wounded by hand grenades. Incoming mortar rounds wounded five men at 1100 hours, three of whom were evacuated. An estimated thirty mortar rounds and twenty to twenty-five rounds of 75mm artillery came in.[32]

The 1st Battalion, although it landed on the wrong DZ, quickly recovered. Members of the 1st Battalion describe their experiences in the assembly area.

CAPT. ROBERT A. CHABOT, EXECUTIVE OFFICER, COMPANY A: At 0908 on 23 March, the 1st Battalion dropped on the wrong DZ, landing on the northwest corner of the northern DZ instead of the southern DZ. Although the elements were scattered, it was a relatively short time before the battalion assembled. In landing, one man from Company A was killed in his chute by shrapnel; however Corporal Lutz killed two enemy before getting out of his chute. I assembled the company and joined forces with Captain Dessert, commanding Company D. While still on the assembly area, I was notified by a radio message that the Company A commander had been dropped on the southern DZ with the 1st Battalion commander's party. The 1st Battalion assembled first under the leadership of Captain Odum, the S-4, and Captain Pickel, the S-2; later Major Delameter, the battalion executive officer, took over.[33]

PFC WILLIAM COKER, MACHINE GUNNER, 3D PLATOON, COMPANY A: I dropped near the northern DZ about 0905 hours, landing on an adjacent hill. As I started to get out of my chute, I saw two North Korean soldiers coming at Corporal Lutz, also of Company A, with bayonets fixed at the end of long rifles. Corporal Lutz was about ten yards from me, and the North Koreans were in a ditch on the other side of a road from Corporal Lutz. Lutz shot both North Koreans with his M-1, causing a third North Korean, ten yards in back of the two, to drop his burp gun and run. This North Korean was also shot by three soldiers in the area. As I continued to cut myself out of my chute I heard a burp gun shooting, but was fortunately covered by PFC Barcello, also of Company A. Five or six enemy were killed in the nearby area. Free of my chute, I went to the top of the hill, saw the DZ at a distance, dropped my pack and, although sniped at, successfully joined up with Company A.[34]

1ST LT. JAMES E. HANLIN, PLATOON LEADER, 3D PLATOON, COMPANY B: I dropped at 0907 hours and landed in the wrong place. By 0930 hours the 3d Platoon had secured its equipment and assembled on its bundles, moving from there to the company assembly area. From 1015 to 1130 hours, the 3d Platoon secured the high ground around the assembly area.[35]

SGT. WALTER E. CHANEY, PLATOON SERGEANT, 3D PLATOON, COMPANY B: I got on the wrong DZ. There was a bit of small-arms firing on the DZ, and one man from Company C who had been shot was hanging in a tree. On the way down I tried to get oriented in accordance with the sand table, briefing, and maps, but the ground did not look familiar. As soon as I landed I took another check and knew I was in the wrong place. I assembled my platoon and moved east contacting Captain Miller, Company B commander, who was assembling the company.

SGT. ROBERT J. WOTHERSPOON, SQUAD LEADER, 1ST PLATOON, COMPANY B: Our platoon split up into two groups. I jumped with company headquarters, and as soon as we hit the ground, I organized my squad, looked around, and knew I was on the wrong DZ. We started out to where Lieutenant Berthall had the platoon assembled, short one squad which joined that evening, having attached itself to another company in the 1st Battalion. It took twenty minutes for the 1st Platoon to assemble.

SGT. PERCY L. MCDANIEL, SQUAD LEADER, 2D PLATOON, COMPANY B: There was confusion on the DZ after the jump. I succeeded in getting the squad together except for one man, a BAR man who had a leg cut from barbed wire. It took five to ten minutes to get the squad together.[36]

CAPT. DANIEL L. MELVIN, COMMANDER OF COMPANY C: Company C dropped at 0905 hours on some small hills near the northern DZ. Everyone near me was lost for the next few minutes, since we were supposed to drop on the southern DZ. I wore a big red patch for identification. Within fifteen to twenty minutes a small group was organized, and within an hour the company was pretty well organized. Company C was given the objective of patrolling into Munsan-ni, which it accomplished, killing seven enemy and capturing one.[37]

CPL. NORMAN I. FULLERTON, SCOUT, COMPANY C: I landed on top of a hill. I met the platoon sergeant and was told to go to the south end of the DZ and pick up a bundle, which I did. While on the DZ, about 0940 hours I saw an enemy soldier running. I shot at the soldier four times, and the soldier crawled into an irrigation ditch, wounded. I then sneaked up on him and jabbed him the full length of the bayonet in the ribs twice and once in the breast. Searching him, I found two books that I turned over to the company commander when I returned to the company area.[38]

CAPT. ROLLAND A. DESSERT, COMMANDER, COMPANY D: On 23 March, one section of machine guns from Company D was attached to Company A and one section was in general support. The 1st section dropped on the northern DZ because of pilot error. It assembled near the west end of the DZ, moved out in support of Company A, and occupied positions just north of Munsan-ni by 1400 hours. The 1st section recovered two heavy machine guns, one light machine gun, and 9,000 rounds of ammunition. No enemy were contacted. The 2d section also dropped on the northern DZ and assembled near the west end of the DZ. It moved out attached to Company C to high ground 1,000 yards east of Munsan-ni.[39]

The regimental command group quickly adjusted for the erroneous drop of the 1st Battalion and issued appropriate orders. In the midst of the activities on the DZ, General Ridgway arrived by light aircraft. Colonel Gerhart and Captain Weddle describe their actions.

COLONEL GERHART, DEPUTY REGIMENTAL COMMANDER: I landed in a muddy spot on the predetermined area. We were carrying packs, horseshoe roll, carbine and pistol, but no hand grenades. I had about forty rounds for my carbine and three clips for my pistol. Immediately upon landing I went to a road junction about 1,000 yards distance. There were three men hit that I saw on my trip to the road junction. On my way I stopped and saw Captain Mangle, the artillery officer. I had noticed that he was hurt; he had at least one broken leg and possibly two, so I dispatched a soldier to get a litter to carry him out of there. There were several other men who had sustained jump injuries due to landing on a dike.

I noticed a helicopter, so I signaled for him to come down, and I talked to the pilot. He didn't know just when they would set up the aid station or where, so I told him to fly around and pick up the casualties, as he could undoubtedly see them as well as I could.

I saw General Ridgway, who had come in on an L-19 between the two preceding serials. At first I thought he had jumped with us, but apparently he was there checking on the drop. I finally arrived at the road junction and saw General Bowen. He gave me some instructions that I proceeded to carry out.

We were in the process of assembling our CP and moving it up near a draw about 1,000 yards from a road junction. About fifteen minutes after my radio operator landed, he had set up at the road junction; so I contacted the S-3 and S-2 of the three battalions regarding what the situation was and how much resistance they were meeting. I found out that the Rangers were having a scrap to reach their objective. Then I got hold of the headquarters commandant and had him start organizing a CP. While this was going on I went on a reconnaissance to look over the terrain. I had tried but hadn't been able to contact the 2d Battalion on the radio.

When I came back we had to move the CP because we were getting mortar and small-arms fire pretty close, within a few feet. The command group that had been at the road junction had been dispersed. The entire CP moved up to the new location, and General Bowen left to inspect the 2d and 3d Battalions, while I stayed at the CP without incident. Upon the general's return I went to the 1st Battalion to inspect their dispositions. Meanwhile the general had dispatched one company to the southern drop zone to extricate the one planeload of people who had been dropped there and were pinned down by enemy fire.[40]

CAPTAIN WEDDLE, ASSISTANT S-3 OF THE REGIMENT: I landed with Company L of the 3d Battalion, whose initial mission was to secure the DZ for other units that were to follow. As I moved toward the designated CP assembly area, I observed elements of the 3d Battalion moving out to secure high ground north and east of the DZ. I saw and heard intermittent small-arms and automatic-weapons fire in the vicinity of that high ground. There seemed to be an absence of artillery and mortar fire at the time. Approaching the CP area I saw General Ridgway standing in the road at the point designated for the command post. He was observing the remaining units parachuting to the ground.

Subsequently, other members of the S-3 section arrived in the area. It took less than forty-five minutes for the section to become operational after personnel had dropped. The S-3's driver was operating an SCR300 radio, and the artillery liaison officer's assistant had an SCR619 radio.[41] These two, plus the remainder of the section, started checking on the status of units.

The 1st Battalion, less one planeload of thirty-two men, reported that they had dropped on the northern DZ in error and that the lead plane of their serial had aborted during flight to the drop zone with thirty-two of their men, whose whereabouts at that time was unknown. The 1st Battalion was immediately directed to proceed on their mission of securing the high ground north of Munsanni from their present location.

Lt. Col. Benjamin Keist, the S-3, continued checking on the

overall location and progress of units, while issuing additional instructions for adjustments in relation to the enemy. During this activity, the command post area came under sporadic mortar and artillery fire that started at 1030 hours and continued throughout the day.

At 1100 hours the 1st Battalion (less thirty-two men) reported that they had accomplished the initial phase of their mission. A few minutes later, the S-3 learned that the one aircraft that had aborted had returned and dropped the thirty-two men on the southern drop zone, where the entire battalion should originally have been dropped. It was further learned that among the thirty-two men were the battalion commander of the 1st Battalion, the Tactical Air Control Party, and the S-3, the absence of which personnel had left the remainder of the battalion under the control of the executive officer.

The 187th Airborne RCT S-3 ordered one company of the 1st Battalion to immediately proceed south to contact the stranded personnel. At approximately the same time, contact was established with the group of thirty-two men through the Tactical Air Control Party radio and by artillery liaison aircraft. With Lt. Col. Arthur H. Wilson in charge, the group reported that they were in a firefight but felt that they could cope with the situation.[42]

Action at Drop Zone South

The lone planeload of 1st Battalion troops had landed in the middle of a sizeable number of enemy troops and was quickly pinned down. Members of the group recall the action.

MAJ. CHARLES M. HOLLAND, EXECUTIVE OFFICER, 1ST BATTALION: At 1002 hours, the 1st Battalion command group dropped on DZ south and immediately came under fire from small arms and automatic weapons by enemy on Hill 216 and the nearby ridge. The 1st Battalion, on learning that the command group had landed on DZ south, dispatched Company B. A mosquito-type air strike was delivered on Hill 216. As a result of the air strike, the 1st Battalion command group, which had been pinned down in a dike, was able, at 1200 hours, to get off the drop zone. Two of the command group who dropped at P'aiu-ri couldn't move because of fire from the ridge.[43]

1ST LT. JESMOND D. BALMER, FORWARD OBSERVER, BATTERY A, 674TH AIRBORNE FIELD ARTILLERY BATTALION: I rode in the lead plane of the 1st Battalion with the 1st Battalion control group. This plane developed engine trouble, landed at Taegu, took off a second time at 0945 hours, and I finally jumped at 1030 hours on the DZ, 6,000 yards south of the main DZ. No one paid attention to the ground, since they were busy pushing bundles out and jumping. There were an estimated 200 to 300 Chinese soldiers on Hill 216 and in Masan-ni, between our command group and our main body.

The control group, with the exception of two who remained in a hole on the DZ, made its way into a gully. A radio was set up and contact with the main body established. General Ridgway sent Company B south to contact the control group, and the air observer called an air strike from 1050 to 1100 hours on Masan-ni and the ridge above the village. CCF soldiers were observed moving from Paeksongni-Ugol-li [a village about two kilometers south of DZ South], and at 1145 hours two Chinese scouts were captured. Lieutenant Colonel Wilson, commanding the 1st Battalion, told the members of the control group to drop their equipment, and the small party began skirting the south end of Masan-ni. Two men were discovered missing, and ten of the control group entered Masan-ni, returning to get the two missing.[44]

Company B made rapid progress in its mission of moving south to rescue the 1st Battalion command group. Members of the unit describe the action.

1ST LT. JAMES E. HANLIN, 3D PLATOON LEADER, COMPANY B: At 1130 hours the 3d Platoon moved south to secure the approaches to Hill 216. At 1230 hours the 2d Platoon passed through the 3d Platoon and secured Hill 216. Company B then moved around the east side of the hill about one and a half miles to pick up a planeload of people who had landed on the southern DZ near P'aiu-ri. After reaching the party from the plane, Company B moved to a position northwest of Munsan-ni.[45]

SGT. WALTER E. CHANEY, PLATOON SERGEANT, 3D PLATOON, COMPANY B: We moved out in company formation, the 2d Platoon leading about 2,000 yards out. Then the 3d Platoon passed through the 2d Platoon during the afternoon, attacking Hill 216. Three hundred yards from the peak it received fire. The 3d Platoon swung a squad to the right flank and was fired on by four to five enemy at 700 yards range.

SGT. PERCY L. MCDANIEL, SQUAD LEADER, 2D PLATOON, COMPANY B: Before we received this fire, I was with the lead squad that got up to the long ridgeline, a saddle behind sheer rock, and heard some firing. I then hollered back. Lieutenant Reith got information by radio, and I saw enemy on top of Hill 216. The enemy was not firing on the 2d Platoon. We continued to the plateau that extended from the edge of the hill, encountering ten to twelve enemy in rocks thirty yards straight up. Neither side fired. Lieutenant Reith came forward, conferred with me, and hollered to the enemy to surrender. Two or three got up to surrender, and one man in my squad started to fire. The 2d Platoon down the ridge laid 81mm mortar rounds on the hill. The air observer said the enemy had withdrawn. Six enemy were captured on the hill, eleven were caught on the ridgeline, and one killed. There were no friendly losses. Hill 216 was well fortified.

SGT. CHANEY, 3D PLATOON: One friendly casualty was incurred on our right flank. During the time the 81mm fire was landing on Hill 216, word was received that Lieutenant Colonel Wilson and the battalion staff had jumped on the southern DZ and were pinned down by enemy fire from the south side of Hill 216. The 1st, 3d, and 4th Platoons received orders to form on the road north of Hill 216. The 2d Platoon remained on Hill 216, and the entire company moved south to P'aiu-ri. No enemy fire was met on the way down; the 1st Platoon swung on the ridgeline 400 yards north of P'aiu-ri, passing through the 3d Platoon.

SGT. ROBERT J. WOTHERSPOON, SQUAD LEADER, 1ST PLATOON, COMPANY B: While the 2d and 3d Platoons were taking Hill 216, the 1st Platoon was in reserve. During this time the squad carried a wounded man to the helicopter. As we went down and passed through the 3d Platoon, one squad went over to the small foothills to the right and found barbed wire up on the hill. Shooting one "Gook" and moving forward, we contacted Major Holland, executive officer, and member of the 1st Battalion staff that had landed on the southern DZ. He said there were troops on the DZ pinned down by enemy fire. The 1st Platoon moved to high ground north of the DZ, got up on the foothills, and spotted an enemy machine-gun platoon. We fired on the enemy machine guns. Artillery was brought in by Major Holland's group. Two enemy and one machine gun were hit, and two enemy ran over the hill. One wounded man from the 1st Platoon was evacuated, and I was told that the group was off the DZ. We fell back to the rest of the company.

SGT. CHANEY, 3D PLATOON: We backed the 1st Platoon up, and held until the 1st Platoon pulled back through. The DZ party moved north with the company with the 3d Platoon acting as rear guard on the way north. Company B assembled and moved to Munsan-ni, arriving at 1900 hours.[46]

Maj. Holland describes the action from his perspective.

From 1200 to 1300 hours a firefight occurred as Company B, under Captain Miller, cleared Hill 216. At 1400 hours Company B had cleared the enemy, estimated at 150 North Koreans and Chinese Communists in full quilted uniforms, from Hill 216. The enemy retreated to the southwest. By 1500 hours, the two missing men had been extricated from the drop zone, and a linkup with the command group was effected by Company B. Twenty-five enemy were killed on Hill 216, five in P'aiu-ri, and three by the command group. I captured one North Korean policeman who had deserted. At 1715 hours, the 1st Battalion Command Group joined the rest of the 187th Airborne Regimental Combat Team.[47]

The 2d Battalion Action

Meanwhile, the 2d Battalion had assembled on the northern drop zone and moved quickly to capture its objective, the high ground north of the DZ. Members of the unit describe the action.

LT. COL. J. P. CONNOR, 2D BATTALION COMMANDER: The northern DZ was under mortar fire, causing three wounded in action in the 2d Battalion. The 2d Battalion, with the 2d Ranger Company attached, had as its objective the high ground north of the DZ, and by 1700 hours we had driven the enemy off the objective, killing thirty-five North Koreans, wounding eighty-three, and capturing twenty-two. Friendly losses were two killed and seventeen wounded.[48]

2D LT. EDWARD J. WHELAN, PLATOON LEADER OF THE 2D PLATOON, COMPANY E: The 2d Battalion was the second battalion to drop on DZ north, the 3d Battalion having secured the DZ. The 2d Battalion dropped at 0930 hours and Company E was 95 percent effective at 1000 hours. We moved out in the attack with the objective of the high ground overlooking a railroad tunnel [about 1,500 meters due north of Munsan-ni]. The 2d Platoon advanced across a rice paddy, laying down a base of fire; we reached the foot of the hill where the enemy was fortified. Apparently the top was not occupied. At 1000 hours the enemy, estimated as one platoon, withdrew down the road to the northwest, suffering six killed in action. At 1100 hours the objective was occupied. Several men broke the skyline on top of the hill, although I ordered them down. As a result, a high velocity enemy weapon fired on the hill.[49]

SFC GEORGE G. LANE, PLATOON SERGEANT, 1ST PLATOON, COMPANY E: At 1100 hours, in a draw between two hills, a squad of the 1st Platoon drew small-arms fire and withdrew. It built up a base of fire and fired into the high ground for thirty minutes with machine guns. At 1130 hours, when Lieutenant Whelan's platoon had advanced to the high ground, the 1st Platoon followed, capturing fifteen North Korean soldiers. They were young soldiers, fifteen years old and up, who had been drafted. Although the North Koreans had weapons, they were frightened and put up no fight. Three 82mm mortars were found in the area. Enemy artillery fire, said by the 2d Battalion commander to be from self-propelled guns, fell in the area. We took cover in holes the North Koreans had dug. There were no casualties.[50]

1ST LT. RUDY V. PARAISO, FORWARD OBSERVER, BATTERY B, 674TH AIRBORNE FIELD ARTILLERY BATTALION: I was the artillery forward observer with Company E and dropped with the 2d Platoon at 0915 hours. The platoon I was with rolled up its stick and proceeded to the designated assembly area. Subjected to mortar fire while moving, the platoon quickly moved into defilade. At 1015 hours I met Captain Shanahan, the Company E commander. The company was on its objective at 1600 hours, meeting light opposition with sixteen enemy killed and eleven prisoners.[51]

1ST LT. DONALD L. ROBERTS, 2D PLATOON LEADER, COMPANY F: Company F dropped at 0930 hours, and the entire company landed on the DZ with a good bundle dispersion. One man was hit by small-arms fire in the air while coming down. At 1030 hours, Company F was assembled and moved out toward its objective, high ground where small groups of North Koreans, four to five men in a group, were moving west. An air strike was called at 1100 hours, and the movement ceased. At 1130 hours the 2d and 3d Platoons moved on line across the open ground, contacting the enemy below the objective and taking the objective at 1230 hours. The enemy retreated to the west. A small holding force of the enemy on Hill 65 was dispersed, and the hill cleared by 1800 hours.

SFC ROSS C. DUNCAN, 2D PLATOON GUIDE, COMPANY F: Hill 65 had dugouts on top where troops could command the area with plunging fire.

SFC RAYMOND MORRIS, 2D PLATOON SERGEANT, COMPANY F: The jump went well. The stick assembled in good time with only one casualty. In the morning, an estimated twenty enemy were observed moving toward Hill 65 in groups of four to five.[52]

1ST LT. JACK W. VON STEIEGEL, FORWARD OBSERVER, BATTERY B, 674TH AIRBORNE FIELD ARTILLERY BATTALION: I was the artillery forward observer with Company F. The first OP that I established was on high ground north of the DZ where I had a commanding view of the terrain [about 1,000 meters northeast of Hill 151]. Among the first missions I fired while in this location was a platoon of enemy on Hill 65 and enemy soldiers moving northeast into Changp'o-ri. Company F suffered no casualties here.[53]

1ST LT. J. L. BEASLEY, 81MM MORTAR PLATOON LEADER, COMPANY H: I came in the second wave and dropped first in my stick, hitting the 2d Battalion assembly area located in the first draw northwest of Ich'on-ni. The assembly of the 81mm Mortar Platoon of Company H was without mishap. For the first two hours after the drop there were no requests for mortar fire. At 1130 hours the mortar platoon displaced forward one section at a time; I brought the 2d section. At 1200 hours the mortars fired sixty rounds in support of the Rangers on Hill 151 and also fired for Company E. At 1230 hours Company E captured three 82mm mortars, which I went for with an ox-train. One mortar was given to nearby ROK troops, one turned over to the 2d Battalion S-4, and one destroyed. Twenty-seven rounds of mortar ammunition found with the mortars were buried.[54]

Consolidation on the Drop Zone

While the infantry battalions went about their missions, there was a bustle of activity in the area of the drop zone to recover equipment and ammunition, care for casualties, establish normal command and control centers, and prepare for expected enemy counterattacks. Several staff officers describe their efforts.

MAJ. JOSEPH E. JENKINS, S-4 OF THE REGIMENT: The heavy equipment arrived at 0955 hours on the heavy drop zone. About 80 percent of the items were dropped on the actual DZ. From 8 to 10 percent of the material was destroyed. A 105mm howitzer became disengaged from its parachute after the opening shock (believed due to faulty connection links), and two 75mm-pack howitzers were destroyed by fire when the pack howitzer, with its ammunition, collided with a bundle in midair.

At 1000 hours S-4 personnel, with the parachute maintenance detail and the field artillery battalion, began the policing of equipment and ammunition from the drop zone. The attached Indian surgical team did an excellent job of recovery of their equipment. Later in the day, at approximately 1750 hours, resupply began to arrive over the drop zone. The first six planes made perfect drops. The remainder of the resupply planes were 80 percent off the marked drop zone. Five loads were jettisoned after passing the drop zone. In fact, one ¼-ton truck landed behind Hill 188.[55]

MAJ. BURNSIDE E. HOFFMAN, S-3 OF THE 674TH AIRBORNE FIELD ARTILLERY BATTALION: Because of the shortage of heavy drop equipment, only four 105mm howitzers were dropped; three were recovered, and one streamered because the disconnect on the streamer functioned prematurely. Eight 75mm howitzers were dropped on the assault. Two streamered and one was dropped approximately three miles from the DZ. This last was recovered by the enemy, who fired ten rounds at friendly troops; it was later recovered by our men. A total of 1,100 rounds of 105mm ammunition was heavy dropped, ten rounds with each howitzer and the remainder on pallets. A total of 4,400 rounds of 75mm were heavy dropped, 130 rounds with each howitzer and the remainder on pallets. Twelve jeeps and two ¾-ton trucks were dropped and recovered in serviceable condition. One jeep was dropped three miles from the DZ with the 75mm howitzer. It was hidden by the enemy, but later recovered. Ammunition for 3.5-inch rocket launchers on a howitzer platform streamered, exploded, and burned equipment that might have been salvaged. Of the 6,230 rounds of 75mm ammunition dropped on 23 March, approximately 3,500 rounds were recovered on that day. Of the 3,470 rounds of 105mm ammunition dropped on 23 March, approximately 1,000 rounds were recovered the same day. On 23 March, 284 rounds were fired in support of operations.[56]

LT. COL. THOMAS H. LANE, REGIMENTAL SURGEON: It was prearranged that helicopters would hover over the drop zone, commencing at fifteen minutes after the last person to drop, and come in, or not, and land by the marker in the vicinity of the collecting station. The helicopters actually came in before the prearranged time and before the panel could be set out. They landed on the drop zone near casualties, which they could observe from the air. At least eight casualties (four loads) went out this way before the marker signals were placed on the ground. As a result of their early landing, the helicopters subjected themselves to unnecessary hazards as the supplies were still being dropped. I saw at least one very near miss that could have put the helicopter out of action had it hit.

Copters were to carry patients to the 8055th MASH, then located at Yongdungp'o. It took approximately forty-five minutes to make the round trip including unloading the patients. Helicopter pilots were told to make a maximum effort, including all four of the copters in operation at the time, and to make continuous trips, weather and the enemy situation permitting, until all the casualties had been evacuated. When they were seen coming in, runners were sent to notify the pilots to land in the vicinity of the markers on their following trips.

Once this change had been accomplished, approximately forty-five minutes with the first load of casualties picked up on the drop zone, the flow of evacuation was smooth and according to plan. No injured men were being unnecessarily delayed due to helicopter evacuation facilities. The eventual landing area was about seventy-five yards from the collecting station, giving a minimum hand-litter haul. Hand-litter carry was being used because of the nature of the terrain. Due to the proximity of landing area, a dust nuisance was encountered. However, we had no occasion to operate or work on open wounds, so dust was tolerated for sake of short litter hauls.

In the collecting station, patients were given a priority for evacuation in proportion to the severity of their wounds. The letters "A," "B," and "C" were marked on the EMT [Emergency Medical Tag] tags. The letter "A" was for the most serious, and these patients were evacuated first, followed by "B" and "C" patients as space became available. Coordination in the evacuation was managed by Major Bethart, the regimental dental surgeon, who assumed the duty in addition to his regular dental duties. On the first day, 23 March, sixty-five patients were evacuated.

About noon, it was decided that the regimental headquarters would set up in a draw in the vicinity of the collecting station. In accordance with the Airborne SOP, once that decision had been made, the clearing station was established in a neighboring draw within the regimental security zone. The station was set up in a series of old gun emplacements that had recently been dug by the enemy and gave excellent defense in three directions.

The operating tent of the attached Indian para-surgical team was set up and put into operation in the same vicinity. This unit from the 60th Indian field ambulance was included in the medical personnel dropped at the suggestion of Colonel Dovell, the Eighth Army surgeon, and with the concurrence of General Bowen, to give additional surgical support to the regiment if necessary during the operation. They dropped and used their own medical equipment, with the exception of blankets and litters on loan from the regiment's medical company.

During the remainder of D-day, routine medical duties were performed by all personnel. Work continued until dusk. On the last trip, it was agreed that the helicopters would return at first light the next morning in spite of the fact that the ground linkup was expected. Serious battle casualties were expected for evacuation the next day. Continued use of the helicopter for evacuation on the next day was due to the questionable security of the roads. About noon of D-day, helicopters brought in sixteen units of whole blood according to prearranged plan.[57]

MAJ. THOMAS P. MULVEY, REGIMENTAL S-1: I tangled with two parachutes at different times on my way down but was able to free myself on both occasions. Approximately thirty feet off the ground, I landed on top of another man's chute, thus causing my own chute to collapse. I then fell twenty to twenty-five feet in an almost horizontal position. The shock of the landing caused the stock of the carbine to break across my left arm. I also had the wind knocked out of me. After a few minutes, with the help of another man, I was able to release myself from the parachute harness.

I didn't see the other men of the S-1 section immediately on landing because of the dispersion that is normal in this type of action. The assembly area was about 800 yards from the position where I landed. It took me and the others of the S-1 section about fifteen minutes to walk and gather there as a section. A temporary command post in the form of a little circular area about twenty-five yards from a Korean shack was immediately established.

After the first two or three hours, personnel of the S-1 section found no necessity to use their weapons and were able to carry on their normal routine duties, except for the periods of movement of the CP from one location to another. The commanding general, deputy commander, and the S-3 section joined the S-1 section within a few minutes, and radio contact was established with all units. These units reported in every fifteen minutes on the degree of completion of their assembly. I kept the commanding general and the S-3 informed of the facts as reported.

As the perimeter expanded east, a new CP was established about 500 yards to the east, which afforded better protection from the surrounding hills. The S-1 section moved to this position about 1130 hours. The perimeter of the CP was within a diameter of seventy-five yards. It was dug in on a small slope with surrounding flat terrain. That day [23 March], each man dug a foxhole with dimensions of two and a half feet in depth, two and a half feet in width, and six feet in length. Mortar fire could drop in on the men, but artillery fire could not, which was the reason for the selection of that particular position for the CP, and why the men dug in. Outposts were in position to the north, east, and south, while friendly troops provided protection on the west side of the CP.

I was evacuated by helicopter at 1430 hours and flew twenty minutes. I was then transferred to an ambulance for a two-mile ride to the 8055th MASH for x-rays on my arm. The reverse procedure was then made to get me back on duty by 1700 hours on the same day.[58]

The 674th Airborne Field Artillery Battalion quickly put its howitzers into service and prepared to provide fire support for the infantry units of the regimental combat team. The artillery battalion commander, Lt. Col. Harry F. Lambert, explains their actions.

The initial plan was to have two 75mm howitzers set up on the DZ where they landed, for the purpose of supporting the 1st, 2d, and 3d Battalions as they moved out to their objectives. In the heavy drop, the 75mm howitzers actually landed over a wide area, whereas three of Battery A's 105mm howitzers dropped close together, the fourth having streamered in. Battery A reported ready to fire at 1030 hours. Battery C with three guns (the fourth streamered) and Battery B with two guns (the 3d streamered, the 4th dropped several thousand yards east of the DZ) were ready to fire at 1100 hours. A few rounds of enemy mortar and artillery fell on the DZ, and a little ammunition that streamered in exploded.

The artillery went into position in a draw 300 yards north of the heavy drop zone, the 187th Antiaircraft Artillery setting up positions around the artillery. The L-5 aircraft, operating from the time of the drop, were based at the I Corps airstrip at Seoul. The first missions for the air OP were to search for the missing gun and jeep, which were located three miles east of the DZ, and for missing drop equipment west of the DZ.

Initially two batteries were laid in southern and southeastern directions to prevent the escape of North Koreans. However, the first mission, fired at 1215 hours on one enemy company for the Rangers, was on Hill 205, which lies northeast of the drop zone.

At 1300 hours, the battalion fired in support of the party of the commander of the 1st Battalion that had been dropped on the southern DZ and was moving north to rejoin the battalion that had erroneously dropped on the northern DZ. The air OP directed fire on scattered groups of enemy moving north throughout the afternoon. By 2000 hours the battalion had fired 284 rounds.[59]

Members of Battery B describe their efforts to recover the howitzer that had landed in enemy lines southeast of the northern DZ.

CAPT. BERTRAM K. GORWITZ, BATTERY B COMMANDER: Battery B jumped at 0930 hours with six officers and eighty-one enlisted men. Equipment dropped included four 75mm howitzers, four jeeps, four .30-caliber machine guns, two .50-caliber machine guns, six SCR619 radios, and 1,000 rounds of 75mm ammunition.

Of the four howitzers, two landed on the northern DZ, one streamered in, and the fourth, with its jeep, landed two and a half miles southeast of the northern DZ. This gun was loaded and fired by the enemy within thirty minutes after it dropped: ten rounds were fired, five of which hit the northern DZ. The gun was fired from the traveling position, which wrecked it. Then the gun with the jeep was hidden under a straw stack. At 1100 hours I took a driver and three sergeants and went after the gun. In the vicinity of Hill 128 I observed two hundred enemy withdrawing to the northeast. Because of the enemy being in the area, we returned without finding the gun, which was found on 24 March.[60]

SFC ADASIUS KARWASA, CHIEF OF 4TH HOWITZER SECTION, BATTERY B: After I made a successful landing, I went to secure equipment and, while doing so, talked to the Battery B commander. The heavy equipment drop occurred at 1100 hours, and included a

few streamers on howitzers and jeeps. The 2d section's howitzer
streamed in and burned. The 1st section's howitzer was located and
placed into position. I was detailed to pick up ammunition. I heard
that my howitzer was located two and a half miles east. Between
1300 and 1400 hours, the battery commander and I reconnoitered
by jeep in an attempt to recover the gun. About one and a half miles
east of the DZ, we discovered soldiers on a ridge. Approaching to
within 500–800 yards of the unidentified soldiers, the battery commander, with field glasses, counted sixteen enemy. After firing a few
shots, the jeep withdrew to the DZ.[61]

The drop of the 187th Airborne had met only scattered resis-
tance around the DZ, but intelligence before the jump indicated
that a strong counterattack could be expected within hours of land-
ing. The regimental S-2, Maj. Raymond H. Ross, immediately be-
gan work to determine the strength of the opposition.

Everyone in the S-2 section landed alright with the exception
of one enlisted man who fractured his ankle. The assembly of the
section was good. Within twenty minutes the section was gathered
around the CP at the road junction. I immediately set up a prisoner
of war (POW) collection point and began interrogation of prisoners. This was about 0930 hours on D-day. The first prisoner had
been picked up while personnel were assembling.

Information was revealed that approximately 300 enemy of the
36th Regiment, 19th North Korean Division, were in the objective
area, and that the 19th Division was moving north across the Imjin
River where they would take up defensive positions in conjunction
with the Chinese Communist Forces south of Kaesong. One of the
POWs intimated that the 19th Division had been alerted to our drop
in the Munsan-ni area and had therefore evacuated and pulled their
rear elements around to the northeast of Munsan-ni. Another POW
indicated that there were approximately 500 members of the 36th
Regiment, 19th North Korean Division, southeast of Munsan-ni at
the time of the drop, and when they saw the parachutes they fled to
the northeast across the Imjin River.

During the day inaccurate mortar fire, believed to be from
122mm mortars, dropped at various places on the DZ proper. At

frequent intervals during the day, what was believed to be high velocity 76mm self-propelled weapons fire dropped in and around the CP area. Generally about four to six rounds came in every half hour in the morning and about four to six round volleys at odd intervals during the afternoon.

Several Russian radios and numerous Japanese and Russian small arms were turned in to the ordnance collecting point. The G-2 of I Corps was immediately notified. New identification of enemy units, gleaned from the POW interrogation, was promptly dispatched by air evacuation helicopters to the G-2 of I Corps.

By nightfall of the first day there had been 136 enemy killed in action (counted on the field), and an estimated 489 enemy killed or wounded. Prisoners taken totaled 149. I spot-interrogated all of the prisoners and found out what unit they were from, but picked out the highest ranking and those who looked intelligent for detailed interrogation. Approximately thirty were thus interrogated in detail.

Several enlisted men of the S-2 section killed three or four enemy within 200 yards of the CP. The enemy in this area were dug in in L-type entrenchments with connecting trenches and bunkers, all well camouflaged. Most entrenchments had been dug several weeks, or longer, prior to the drop. There were North Korean direction signs spotted at the road junction in the vicinity of the CP and in the town of Munsan-ni, pointing to the route that the 36th Regiment was to take as they moved north.[62]

4th Ranger Company at Hill 205

While activity around the drop zone soon settled into routine operations, to the north the 4th Ranger Company had a major fight in securing its objective, Hill 205, overlooking the Imjin crossing sites used by the North Koreans in their withdrawal. The commander of the 4th Ranger Company, Capt. Dorsey B. Anderson, and his artillery forward observer, 1st Lt. George H. Lehmer, describe the fight.

CAPTAIN ANDERSON: The jump was made at 0917 on the drop zone, a rice paddy in the vicinity of Ich'on-ni, and the company assembled on the northwest side on the road that paralleled the drop zone. At 0945 hours, 90 percent of the personnel were accounted for. The company moved toward its objective, Hill 205, about 1,700 yards northeast of the drop zone. Four drop-zone casualties were evacuated by helicopter.

As the company secured its equipment from the bundles and assembled just off the drop zone, firefights took place on all sides of the drop zone and in the immediate vicinity. Enemy mortar fire fell on the drop zone, none, however, on the 4th Ranger Company assembly area.

When the company was formed, it moved to its objective with the 1st Platoon, company headquarters, 2d Platoon, and the 3d Platoon, in that order. Attached was a forward observer team from the 674th Airborne Field Artillery that had joined the company the day before.

The two Ranger companies participating in the drop, the 2d and the 4th, were given the mission of securing hills in the vicinity of the drop zone. The 4th Ranger Company was to secure Hill 205 northeast of the drop zone, the 2d Ranger Company Hill 151 northwest of the drop zone.

The 1st Platoon advanced to the long middle finger of Hill 205. The 3d Platoon was sent to clear the finger north or left of the advance. Both ridges were clear of enemy. The company then continued up the southwest fingers of Hill 205 until the lead elements came under enemy small-arms and automatic-weapons fire from the top of the hill.

The 1st Platoon went into position and returned the enemy fire. I moved the 2d Platoon into position to the left of the 1st Platoon. The 1st Platoon was then to proceed to the high ground directly to the front, southeast of Hill 205. Sporadic enemy mortar and heavy-weapons fire began to be received by the company. Under the cover of the 2d Platoon fire, their own automatic weapons, and the use of marching fire, the 1st Platoon attempted to move up the slope of the hill to assault positions. Due to the nature of the terrain, only one narrow approach was open to the top of Hill 205, which was a nearly concave sloped hill on two sides.

When the 1st Platoon reached an assault position, it went immediately into the assault, but, as the lead elements reached the top of the hill through the shower of concussion and fragmentation grenades, they found themselves out of ammunition. Two men on top of the hill used their BARs and carbines as clubs, but at 1200, the attack was beaten back with a loss of thirteen wounded in action.

Since the 1st Platoon had lost so many men and was low on ammunition, I pulled it back and put the 2d Platoon in its place. The 3d Platoon, in the meantime, had moved to the vicinity of Sin'gong-ni. There it received enemy fire from its front, right, and rear. The platoon was, therefore, unable to return the fire because of the necessity of remaining in defilade.

Artillery fire was ineffective, as the nature of the terrain caused the forward observer to lose his rounds. Furthermore, the forward observer stated that the ground had not been surveyed and one gun had not been calibrated. The forward observer of the 187th Airborne RCT 4.2-inch mortars reported to the company at this time and placed accurate fire on the target.

I then called in an air strike through the 3d Battalion. Four P-51 planes strafed and rocketed Hill 205, but the strike was premature because the 2d Platoon was not in position to attack when the air strike was over. I requested a second strike with napalm. This was delivered, but without napalm. The 2d Platoon moved to attack, but when one man was killed and one wounded before the platoon had moved thirty yards, I concluded that the air strike had been ineffective and called the platoon back.

The 1st Platoon was too short of ammunition to provide fire support, and the 3d Platoon was pinned down on the left where it was impossible to assist by fire. Only one narrow approach to Hill 205 existed. This limited maneuver room. In addition, if the company moved to the right, it received fire from Hills 200 and 208.

At that time, about 1545, the 3d Battalion instructed the 4th Ranger Company to consolidate with Company I, which had moved up on the right. This was done, security was posted, and the company remained there that night. At 2100 hours the company was instructed to send a squad to high ground about 1,000 yards southwest of Sin'gong-ni to contact friendly forces and fill a gap in the perimeter. Sergeant Robinson and his squad moved to that location, remained there during the night, and met no one.

Immediately after dawn on 24 March, the company resumed its attack on Hill 205. With no preparatory fires, and utilizing speed and stealth, the 2d Platoon took the hill. Seven enemy dead were found. Two heavy machine guns and two light machine guns that the enemy had abandoned were found, as well as a quantity of ammunition.[63]

1ST LT. LEHMER, ARTILLERY FORWARD OBSERVER: The mission of the 4th Ranger Company was to move out across the finger ridgeline, secure Hill 205, and observe the far side of the Imjin River and ferry crossings. I dropped at 0920 hours, assembled in the left drop zone on the north–south MSR at 0945 hours, and moved out to the ridgeline with the company CP. Between 1100 and 1300 hours two artillery missions were fired on Hill 205, and a patrol went up the left flank of the hill, withdrawing when, between 1400 and 1500 hours, an air strike was called for Hill 205. The 3d Battalion commander came forward, and it was decided between 1600 and 1700 hours that Captain Anderson would move his Rangers up on the hill at first light on 24 March. On the night of 23–24 March, the 4.2-inch mortars, the 674th Airborne Field Artillery Battalion, and a battery from the 999th Field Artillery Battalion [with Task Force Growdon] fired on Hill 205. At first light the artillery was ready to fire on call from me. The 4th Ranger Company met no resistance and took its objective.[64]

The capture of Hill 205 on 24 March ended the fighting around the drop zone. Meanwhile, at 1848 hours the previous evening, the leading elements of Task Force Growdon had met the 1st Battalion about 5,000 yards south of Munsan-ni. The task force continued to arrive through the night so that by morning the linkup was complete, bringing the airborne operation to a close. Casualties were light, one killed in action and eighteen wounded; there were eighty-four jump-related injuries. Operation Tomahawk was a success, except for one key aspect; the enemy had not been caught in the trap.

Chapter 6

TASK FORCE GROWDON

21–24 March 1951

The other part of Operation Tomahawk was an armor-infantry task force assembled in Seoul to advance ahead of the I Corps troops and achieve a linkup with the 187th Airborne Regiment at Munsan-ni. The task force was built around the 6th Medium Tank Battalion from the 24th Infantry Division of IX Corps and was called Task Force Growdon after the tank battalion commander, Lt. Col. John S. Growdon. Capt. Edward C. Williamson, a combat historian who interviewed members of the unit and prepared a narrative report of the operation, describes the organization of the task force.

At 1830 hours, 21 March 1951, Lieutenant Colonel Growdon, accompanied by his S-3, arrived at I Corps headquarters at Suwon. Here he was briefed concerning the operation by Colonel Johnson, G-3 of I Corps, and told that Task Force Growdon must join up with the 187th Airborne Regimental Combat Team within twenty-four hours after the drop. Johnson and Growdon at that time decided on the composition of the task force, and the following units were selected:

6th Medium Tank Battalion [from 24th Infantry Division of
  IX Corps]
2d Battalion, 7th Infantry Regiment [from 3d Infantry
  Division]
58th Armored Field Artillery Battalion [from 3d Infantry
  Division]

One battery from the 999th Field Artillery Battalion [I Corps Artillery]

Company A, 14th Engineer Combat Battalion with two bridge-laying tanks from the 29th British Independent Brigade attached

It was originally planned that all these units would ride in their organic transportation with the exception of the 2d Battalion, 7th Infantry Regiment, which would be furnished with M-39 personnel carriers. As it turned out only Company E, 7th Infantry Regiment, was furnished M-39s, the rest of the battalion riding in 2½-ton trucks.

Lieutenant Colonel Stelling, commanding officer of the 58th Armored Field Artillery Battalion, and Major Cleary, commanding the 2d Battalion of the 7th Infantry Regiment, joined Colonel Growdon at I Corps at 2000 hours. Operation Directive 51 for Operation Tomahawk [the name assigned to the airborne operation] was issued by I Corps at 0900 hours on 22 March forming Task Force Growdon, and ordering it to assemble in Seoul, attack at 0630 hours on 23 March to the northwest via the Seoul–Munsan-ni road, and link up with the 187th Airborne Regimental Combat Team.

At 0830 hours on 22 March, a meeting of commanders and key personnel was held at I Corps concerning the operation. General Bowen, Commanding General, 187th Airborne Regimental Combat Team, explained the part that the 187th Airborne would take in the operation, and Colonel Growdon went into plans for Task Force Growdon.

The unit commanders of Task Force Growdon met at 1400 hours on 22 March in Seoul at the CP of the 6th Medium Tank Battalion. At this time, Colonel Growdon issued his attack order orally. The spearhead of the task force was to be divided into four teams:

Team A (commanded by Captain Moss)

Company A, 6th Medium Tank Battalion

One infantry platoon from Company E, 7th Infantry Regiment

One engineer platoon from Company A, 14th Engineer Combat Battalion

Team B (commanded by Captain West)

Company B, 6th Medium Tank Battalion
One infantry platoon from Company E, 7th Infantry Regiment

Team C (commanded by Captain Plumley)

Company D, 6th Medium Tank Battalion
One infantry platoon from Company E, 7th Infantry Regiment

Team D (commanded by Major Cleary)

Company C, 6th Medium Tank Battalion
2d Battalion, 7th Infantry (minus Company E) mounted on 2½-ton trucks
One engineer platoon from Company A, 14th Engineer Combat Battalion TacAir Party

Following these teams would come the field artillery and the combat trains, the field artillery leapfrogging so as always to keep a battery in position to fire. The field trains would remain at Seoul.[1]

Preparations

SFC Daniel Crough, the armor operations chief of the 6th Medium Tank Battalion, describes the preparations within the battalion for the mission.

On 21 March Captain Landers, the battalion S-3, received a call from the 24th Division to alert the unit to move the next day to the vicinity of Seoul for attachment to I Corps. At 1500 that afternoon, another call came from the 24th Division ordering Colonel Growdon and Captain Landers to report to I Corps headquarters at Suwon. At first Colonel Growdon was going to drive down to Suwon, but because of the distance he changed his mind, went to the 24th Division, and caught a plane. At 1800 that night Captain

Landers phoned from I Corps. The phone connection was so faint at battalion headquarters that the executive officer, Major Kobbe, went to the 24th Division and called Captain Landers back. He received from him the boundary coordinates for the Checkpoint (CP) map and other necessary information, and returned to the battalion about 2000 hours. The 6th Tank Battalion started making preparations, and Major Kobbe sent a liaison officer to reconnoiter the route. The battalion passed the initial point (IP) on the route at 0700 hours on 22 March and got into Seoul completely closed at 1230 hours. Colonel Growdon and Captain Landers rejoined the battalion there, holding a meeting of the commanding officers of all attachments at 1330 hours. The S-3 had already attended to the march order, and Colonel Growdon briefed the meeting to the effect that there would be three teams heavy in armor and one heavy in infantry. One team heavy in tanks, Company A, 6th Tank Battalion, plus a platoon of engineers was to lead out, followed by Team B, which was Company B, 6th Tank Battalion and engineers, followed by the task force commanders' echelon with a control half-track containing Colonel Growdon, Captain Landers, and myself. Next came Team C with more armor, then Team D heavy with infantry with Company C, 6th Tank Battalion, attached, and, last, the combat trains.[2]

The battalion S-3, Captain Joseph F. Landers, describes the communication plan for the task force.
    The commanders again met at I Corps and got together on visual recognition signals and call signs. For communication within the 6th Tank Battalion, the SCR508 [short-range FM radio] was used. Half-tracks, with SCR506s [medium-range FM radios] mounted, maintained communications with I Corps and Team D. Team D could also be contacted by SCR508. A SCR506 was with the combat trains and an SCR193 [medium-range radio] with the field trains. A checkpoint map was set up with I Corps before the start of the operation. For air, one M-39 carried Team I VHF air observer, and a second team used a ¼-ton jeep.[3]

Logistical support preparations are described by Chief War-

rant Officer Michael Pineda, the assistant S-4 of the 6th Tank Battalion.

The battalion supply trains closed in at Seoul on 22 March at 1300 hours. At 1430 hours, Captain McIntosh and I visited Colonel Taylor, I Corps G-4, to discuss the logistical support of Task Force Growdon.

The I Corps surgeon was consulted on evacuation of wounded, and plans were made to support the task force with a clearing station consisting of personnel and equipment from the 6th Tank Battalion and the 3d Infantry Division Ambulance Company. Lieutenant Colonel Reagan, I Corps provost marshal, was consulted on processing and evacuation of prisoners of war. Telephone wire (forty miles) was released by the I Corps signal officer for issue to the 2d Battalion, 7th Infantry, and the 58th Armored Field Artillery Battalion. The I Corps Class I Dump issued 4,284 C rations to supply all elements of the task force with four days of combat rations in vehicles as prescribed in the field order. Arrangements were made for me to accompany Major Cook, assistant G-4 of I Corps, to an area about four miles northwest of Seoul to survey a site for quartering the task force field trains and establishing a supply point. Delivery of combat rations and wire to units was accomplished by 0030 hours on 23 March.

At 0600 hours on 23 March, Major Cook and I reconnoitered the area, and arrangements were made with the commanding officer of a British artillery unit, which was bivouacked in the same area, for field trains to move in. Field trains were ordered forward by Major Kobbe, after the combat trains, consisting of battalion supply vehicles commanded by me, closed into the area at 1800 hours. The supply point was set up and readied for operations. Major Cook closed in with this element and established liaison between Task Force Growdon field trains and headquarters I Corps. His primary duty was to assist and coordinate all supply functions pertaining to the task force. A radio set (SCR193) was furnished by I Corps for use by the battalion field trains commander. This radio was not in contact with the task force due to the lack of Signal Operating Instructions (SOI). Messages were relayed through the I Corps command and administrative nets.[4]

1st Lt. Arthur Keeley, supply platoon leader, headquarters and service company, 6th Tank Battalion, provides more details about logistical support for the operation.

After the battalion supply trains had closed in at Seoul on 22 March, the forming of the combat trains for Task Force Growdon was started with Major Kobbe commanding, and Captain McIntosh and me assisting.

The following units were included in the combat trains with their respective organization vehicles:

a. *6th Tank Battalion—forty-one vehicles*

nine ¼-ton
two ¾-ton
twenty-two 2½-ton
five half-tracks
two M-24s
one M-32

b. *2d Battalion, 7th Infantry—eight vehicles*

one ¾-ton
seven 2½-ton

c. *58th Armored Field Artillery Battalion—thirteen vehicles*

one ¾-ton
twelve 2½-ton

One platoon of thirty men under Lieutenant Galt from Company F, 7th Infantry Regiment, was sent for security of the column in the event the enemy closed the road after the main force had passed.

After the entire combat train had assembled at Seoul, the composition was as follows:

two M-24s	one communications half-track
one medical ¼-ton	one corps communications ¼-ton
one medical ¾-ton	eight ¼-ton

one communications ¾-ton   one message center 2½-ton
one maintenance ¾-ton   four maintenance half-tracks
twenty POL 2½-ton   eighteen ammo 2½-ton
two C rations 2½-ton

The order of march was light tanks, communications half-track, I Corps commo jeep, 6th Tank Battalion vehicles with infantry riding the first four trucks, 2d Battalion, 7th Infantry vehicles, 58th Armored Field Artillery Battalion vehicles, a 6th Tank Battalion maintenance half-track, and a radio jeep. The combat trains followed the last element of the task force.[5]

The Advance

Captain Williamson describes the route of Task Force Growdon.
It is twenty-four miles from Seoul to Munsan-ni. The road, a dirt graded highway, parallels the Han River as far as Togun-ni, the river running an average 8,000 yards to the southwest of the road. Along the route of the road lie the usual rice paddies and small villages. The terrain west of the road is low ground with small hills sloping away to the Han and the Imjin rivers. To the east of the road extending to the Uijongbu Corridor is a mountain range with heights ranging as high as 836 meters. The town of Munsan-ni lies at the mouth of the San-ch'on River where it flows into the Imjin.[6]

Preparations completed, the task force began moving from Seoul at 0530 hours 23 March and passed through the lines of the 1st ROK Infantry Division at 0630. Capt. Jack G. Moss, commander of Team A, in the lead, describes the beginning of the advance.
Seoul was left at 0530 and the Line of Departure (LD), approximately ten miles north of Seoul, was crossed at 0630. About eleven miles out of Seoul, at 0730, the lead tank came to a bypass around a blown bridge in the vicinity of Kumam-ni. The first four tanks were waved around the bypass, and I went forward to investigate the bypass. As I came out of the other side of the bypass, the tank following me hit a mine, blowing the left track off. The rest of

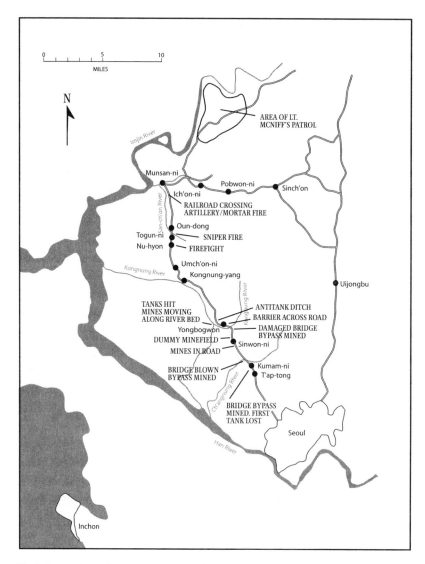

Task Force Growdon's route (original map by author, based on maps from the Army Map Service).

the column was waved through the alternate bypass that the four lead tanks had made.

The march continued until the crossing of the Ch'angnung River at 0800. Finding the bridge here blown, the column halted while several mines were removed from the bypass by the company of engineers. The advance then continued until Sinwon-ni was reached. At this time the task force discovered four belts of mortar shells in the road, laid two feet between shells and six feet between belts. These were removed by the engineers, and the column continued. In the next one hundred yards, four booby-trap box mines were removed, any one of which would have blown in the bottom of a M-46 tank.

From 0900 to 1000 the road sloped down to the Kongnung River for a straight stretch of about a mile, along which the mine detecting teams picked up such objects as beer cans, C ration cans, and cover for powder canisters, buried so as to appear to be mines. This deception by the enemy slowed the advance to practically a walk.

When the river crossing of the Kongnung was reached, the bypasses were found to be heavily mined. The bridge here had been weakened, but three tanks managed to cross before it caved in without any damage to a tank that was on it at the time. Immediately, a bypass was reconnoitered approximately 500 yards west of the bridge, and the column routed around.[7]

The engineers of Company A, 14th Engineer Combat Battalion, had the unenviable task of removing the mines from the road and bypasses around blown bridges. The company first sergeant, M. Sgt. Billy M. Skiles, describes the situation.

I rode with Captain Gass, the engineer company commander, in a jeep to the rear of Company B, 6th Tank Battalion. When the leading elements crossed the LD about five miles north of Seoul, nothing unusual had occurred.

At 0730 Lieutenant Colonel Growdon called Captain Gass forward of the convoy. Here I saw the lead tank, with its left tread blown off, in a bypass to the left of the detonated bridge. Colonel Growdon requested Captain Gass clear the bypass of mines, and at the same time ordered the tank dozer to doze a bypass to the right of the bridge, over which alternate route Colonel Growdon shot several tanks. While the left bypass was being cleared, I found a mine under the right track of a tank in the bypass. Twelve mines were found in the bypass. At 0745 a British vehicle hit a mine in the area. None of the mines were booby-trapped.

The convoy proceeded on at 0845, and the mine detector team found more mines in the vicinity of Sinwon-ni. At this point, an ROK soldier was seriously injured pulling a mine, and the task force held up for forty-five minutes due to the large number of booby-trapped mines, about fourteen. From Sinwon-ni north about five miles, dummy mines containing C ration and beer cans laid out in standard mine pattern in the road were encountered.[8]

SFC Laverne Cordry, squad leader of the 2d Squad, 2d Platoon, of Company A, 14th Engineers, was in charge of the mine clearing operation. He provides more details.

At 0400 hours my squad joined Company A, 6th Tank Battalion, commanded by Captain Moss. This company was to lead Task Force Growdon in the operation from Seoul to Munsan-ni. The squad, mounted in a 2½-ton truck, started out behind the third tank in line. Five miles north of Seoul, a call came for a mine detector crew on the lead tank. A three-man team, armed with a mine detector and composed of Corporal Holiday, Private Vigo Pesante, and Private Hammond, went forward. Corporal Holiday operated the mine detector, while Private Pesante and Private Hammond probed with bayonets on the end of M-1 rifles. After a Korean had an accident with a booby-trapped mine [a mine clearing detail from the 1st ROK Division was working in this area also], Corporal Forlenza and I started pulling mines with grappling hooks. After the five pairs of grappling hooks that the squad possessed were blown up, communication wire was used. Private Pesante and Private Hammond marked the mines for Corporal Forlenza and me to pull. Corporal Holiday was able to pick up U.S. M-6 block mines on his mine detector. Upon digging, we would at times discover a wooden mine on top of the M-6 mine.

At the first bypass the column came to, Colonel Growdon said to the engineers, "Taking too long, let's hurry it up." Shortly thereafter a tank, a British vehicle, and an ROK jeep ran into mines at this bypass. Old C ration cans with a piece of board, mounds of dirt in orderly fashion, and "bouncing betties" booby-trapped to land mines slowed the column up.[9]

Captain Moss continues his description of the slow advance.
At 1030 the lead tanks approached the railroad pass in the vicinity of Yongbogwon. Here the enemy had placed five brush barriers across the road at hundred-yard intervals. Several dummy mines and a few live ones were found and removed from the barrier area. I sent the 1st Platoon under Lieutenant Busey up the Kongnung riverbed to find a route that would bypass the barriers. Lieutenant Busey went up the riverbed to the north, passing a point where the third tank in the column had hit a mine without any casualties, and continuing to a position where he halted and waited for the column.

In the meantime Lieutenant Wilcox, with the lead platoon, had advanced to an antitank ditch six feet deep and ten feet wide. Here, since sheer cliffs overlooked each side of the road, preventing bypassing, the tank dozer came forward and filled in the ditch, thus enabling the column to continue.[10]

Master Sergeant Skiles of the engineers provides more detail.
Near Yongbogwon at 1100, an abatis across the road, consisting of entwined barbed wire, halted the column. About 1,000 yards farther north, the column hit another abatis of the same type. I noticed AP mines, consisting of U.S. block mines and enemy hand grenades, not in a minefield pattern, off to the sides of the road in rice paddies.

At 1300 Colonel Growdon sent five tanks down the riverbed of the Kongnung with orders to independently reach the objective. One hit a mine in the riverbed. Meanwhile, Task Force Growdon ran into an AT ditch made by blasting six feet of the road the width of the roadway. At 1330 Colonel Growdon and Captain Gass, having surveyed the ditch, called the tank dozer to fill it in. The tank dozer began work around 1400 hours, and at 1430 the ditch was filled. The column encountered holes from there to Kongnungyang [a distance of about five miles]. I noticed that live minefields had telephone wire across the road marking one end of the field, but dummy mine areas did not have this marking.[11]

Colonel Growdon became increasingly frustrated and con-

*cerned as the frequent encounters with mines slowed the column to
a crawl and cast doubt on a quick junction with the 187th Airborne.
A report prepared by the 6th Tank Battalion after the operation
highlights the situation.*

At 0645 hours, while bypassing a blown bridge, one of the lead
tanks struck a mine, which disabled the tank but caused no casualties. The road and bypasses from this bridge on were so thoroughly
mined and booby-trapped that it took the column four hours to
reach a point 5.2 miles from the Line of Departure. Brigadier General Harrold, assistant corps commander, I Corps, joined Colonel
Growdon at the head of the column at 1050 and remained with the
column for three hours. The column proceeded very slowly, encountering hundreds of mines and buried mortar shells. Ninety percent
of all mines lifted were booby-trapped, necessitating pulling all of
them with grappling hooks on the end of long cords or destroying
them by demolition. Because of the delay of the column by mines,
Colonel Growdon ordered a tank platoon from the lead company to
leave the road and to proceed north using the riverbed. This platoon
advanced to the north approximately 2,000 yards, when the lead
tank hit a mine and had a track blown off. This route could not be
used by wheeled traffic due to loose sand and, as it was faster to
sweep the road for mines than the river, the platoon was ordered to
return to the road and rejoin the column. Another attempt to bypass
was made at 1148 hours, when Colonel Growdon ordered Team D
to find another route to the west of the main axis and advance to
Munsan-ni as soon as possible.[12]

*Major Thomas Cleary, the commander of Team D, recalls his
unsuccessful attempt to find an alternate route.*

At 1310 hours, Colonel Growdon radioed me to find an alternate route and move to the final objective with Task Group B [Team
D]. I reconnoitered the road, which forks to the west on the MSR
about 800 yards northwest of T'ap-tong, encountering on the first
hundred yards twenty mines, and turned around. I spent until 1430
searching for an alternate route without success until Task Group A
[Team A] notified me that they were through.[13]

Captain Moss continues his description of the movement.

At 1200 the air OP reported what appeared to be mine belts about 200 yards apart for the next two miles in front of the column. Checking these belts, I found every other one to have live mines in it. Some of the dummies were square pieces of wood the same size as the top of the small box mine. The task force passed through this mine-belt zone at 1630.

Since it was late in the afternoon, Colonel Growdon desired to speed up the column, taking advantage of the remaining hours of daylight. From there to Munsan-ni the engineers on the first three tanks moved out, checking only suspicious areas.[14]

1st Lt. Robert H. Turner, commander of Company E, 7th Infantry Regiment, had the mission of accompanying the armor-heavy teams with his men loaded on M-39 personnel carriers. For most of the journey the pace was slow and, for the infantry, uneventful. However, toward the end of the route the situation changed, as Lieutenant Turner relates.

The M-39 personnel carriers were interspersed with the tanks in the column; Lieutenant Haefli with the 1st Platoon was with Company A, the leading tank company. Reinforcing Company E were one 75mm recoilless-rifle section and one heavy-machine-gun section, both from Company H. The only casualty was one man from Company H wounded by a piece of shrapnel.

Mines held up the column from Seoul north. Most of the towns passed were on fire or had been burned by the Air Force. Two-thirds of the way to Munsan-ni, at Oun-dong and on the high ground nearby, enemy snipers were harassing the column with small arms and automatic weapons. At 1630 the column began to receive mortar and artillery fire, with fifteen to twenty rounds falling in the next two hours. Patrols of the 187th Airborne were seen operating on the high ground south of Munsan-ni.[15]

Captain Moss describes the end of the journey for Company A at the head of the column.

At about 1730, Task Force Growdon made radio contact with

the 187th Airborne Regimental Combat Team. As the head of the column reached a bridge on the south edge of Munsan-ni, a bracketing salvo of field artillery rounds, estimated to be 150mm, straddled the column. Without checking the bypass, Task Force Growdon continued on into Munsan-ni and set up a perimeter. As the rest of Company A came through the bypass, the 3d Platoon had two tanks hit by the artillery fire, damaging one beyond repair, the other being recovered at 1830 hours. Company A moved into a perimeter at Ich'on-ni and remained there for the night.[16]

The engineers with Captain Moss at the head of Task Force Growdon's column of vehicles located and removed 153 live mines and 150 dummy mines. The rear of Task Force Growdon, composed of the combat trains, did not reach Munsan-ni until early the next day. Lieutenant Keeley, the supply platoon leader of headquarters and service company of the 6th Tank Battalion, describes the end of the journey.

The combat trains followed the last element of the task force, moving slowly in a leap-bound fashion. All went well until approximately four miles out of Munsan-ni, where a halt was required to await the clearing of a bypass up ahead. At approximately 0200 hours on 24 March, intense enemy small-arms and mortar activity took place about 500 yards to the left of the column with some rounds directed at the convoy. The tanks were readied, and the infantry platoon placed out about fifty yards. No action directed at the trains occurred, so the trains moved on to Munsan-ni, joining the main task force at 0500 hours. The vehicles of the various units then broke up and proceeded to their organizations to supply them. During the hours of resupply, the trains were under sporadic fire from an enemy SP gun.[17]

The combat historian, Captain Williamson, provides more details about the firefight south of Munsan-ni and summarizes the vehicle losses for Task Force Growdon.

At 1630 Team D discovered a firefight between a platoon from the 1st ROK Division and an estimated two platoons of enemy in the vicinity of Nu-hyon. This firefight caused small-arms fire to fall on the column until 0400 hours, 24 March.

A total of four M-46 tanks, one ¼-ton truck, and one British armored car were disabled by mines; two M-46 tanks were disabled by artillery fire.[18]

A Day of Patrols, 24 March

Upon arrival in the Munsan-ni area, Task Force Growdon came under the control of the 187th Airborne Regimental Combat Team and received new instructions. The 6th Tank Battalion's After Action Report provides details.

Task Force Growdon effected juncture with the 187th Regimental Combat Team at 1830 hours, 23 March. Colonel Growdon reported to the Commanding General, 187th Regimental Combat Team, and was directed to keep Task Force Growdon as a unit. An assembly area was designated, and Task Force Growdon completely closed into the area at 0650 hours, 24 March.

On 24 March Team A, Team B, and Team C conducted patrols to the northwest, east, and northeast, respectively. Team A reached the Imjin with no enemy contact and returned to the area at 1640 hours. Team B advanced to the east, capturing one 57mm gun with no enemy contact. They halted and formed blocking positions to the east.[19]

The first two patrols were relatively uneventful, as was the beginning of Team C's reconnaissance to the northeast. This situation quickly changed, however, as described by 1st Lt. James McNiff, 3d Platoon leader of Company E, 7th Infantry Regiment.

At 0630 on 24 March, I was ordered to take out a combat patrol consisting of fourteen tanks from Company D (3d and 4th Platoons) of the 6th Tank Battalion, and the 3d Platoon from Company E, mounted on M-39s. From 0800 to 1000, enemy artillery fire fell in the perimeter of Task Force Growdon, a volley coming in each time the helicopter landed.

At 1000, three combat patrols moved out of the perimeter, my patrol going up the Imjin River to Changi-wa-ri, which was reached

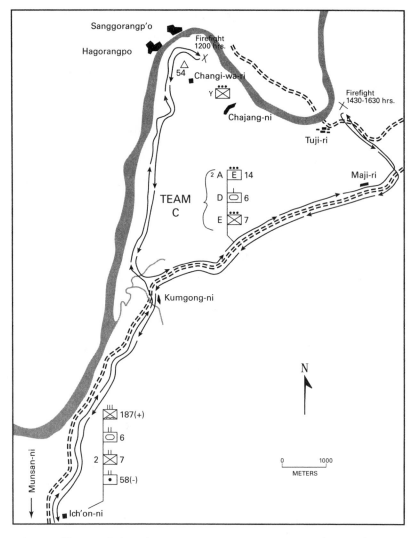

Lt. McNiff's patrol (based on map in CMH manuscript and maps from the
Army Map Service).

at 1200. As we approached the village, an estimated forty enemy in
the houses ran to dug-in positions. We took the enemy under fire,
and at about 1230 two enemy soldiers sneaked over Hill 54, made
gestures to surrender, and appeared eager to give up. These were
young boys. After they surrendered, I noticed that two of the enemy

were haranguing the others, and soon twenty-eight more came
down and surrendered. All these prisoners were North Koreans. In
the firefight the North Koreans had not fired back, and there were
no American casualties.

The patrol then investigated the ford across the Imjin to
Sanggorangp'o on the north bank to determine whether it could be
crossed. At the ford we found a sandbag-and-log bridge and determined that the river could be crossed there. The tanks brought the
enemy in Sanggorangp'o under fire.

At 1300 the patrol moved out of Changi-wa-ri, finding the trail
that ran east by the river impassable, forcing a return to Kumgong-
ni, which was virtually destroyed by an air strike. A new route was
chosen. This time the road to Maji-ri was used, and the patrol continued northwest to the river, about 800 yards northeast of the town
of Tuji-ri, losing one tank, which hit a mine at a stream crossing
nine hundred yards east of Tuji-ri.

The position east of Tuji-ri was reached at about 1430, and four
or five enemy were observed in the village by a wall. The tanks were
brought into position, and the town taken under fire. At 1530 an
ammunition dump in the village blew up as a result of a direct hit
from a tank's 90mm gun. The enemy attempted to flank the patrol
by moving northeast in trenches along the river from Tuji-ri, and it
was decided to call an air strike on the village. When the air strike
came at 1630 the patrol took cover in the streambed by the knocked-
out tank. After the strike, the patrol moved up the river and found
it from three to four feet deep at the ford.

The patrol had accomplished its mission of checking the stream
crossings north of Munsan-ni, and I decided to leave a platoon of
tanks and one squad of riflemen with the disabled tank and to return to the perimeter. At 1900, since there was no heavy equipment
available to haul the disabled tank back, it was destroyed, and the
remainder of the patrol pulled into the perimeter at 2100 hours.[20]

*The unit After Action Report provides more details of the at-
tempts to recover the disabled tank of Lieutenant McNiff's patrol.*

At this point, the lead tank was disabled by a mine, and the
column began receiving small-arms and mortar fire from positions

across the river. Tank fire and air strikes were called, and every effort was made to repair the tank and tow it back to the assembly area. Because the road wheels were blown, the track could not be replaced, and although one tank retriever and three other tanks were used as tow vehicles, the disabled tank could not be moved. Darkness was approaching and, as the patrol was eight miles ahead of friendly troops, Colonel Growdon ordered the tank completely destroyed. This was accomplished by pouring gasoline over the engine and transmission, using thermite grenades, and firing two rounds of 90mm armor piercing ammunition into the hull. All sights, tools, and guns were removed. The tank burned for three hours and was completely destroyed.[21]

The Resupply Effort

While patrols were investigating river-crossing sites on 24 March, a major resupply effort was underway for both Task Force Growdon and the 187th Airborne Regimental Combat Team. After the vehicles of Task Force Growdon's combat trains delivered their supplies to the units of the task force, they were formed again into combat trains. Lieutenant Keeley describes their return to the supply point north of Seoul.

At 1000 hours the combat trains reformed with the following vehicles: two light tanks, one communications half-track, two jeeps, and nineteen 2½-ton trucks; the breakdown was fifteen trucks from the 6th Tank Battalion, three trucks from the 58th Armored Field Artillery Battalion, and one truck from the 7th Infantry Regiment. The trucks, with the exception of five, were loaded with empty gas drums. Two empty trucks carried an infantry platoon [for security], one truck bore the five American bodies [killed in the airborne operation the previous day], one truck was loaded with thirty-two wounded prisoners of war, and the last truck contained twelve war correspondents. At 1100, the combat trains moved out of Munsan-ni and headed for the supply point, arriving at 1330 hours. The trip was uneventful.

Having been resupplied with 19,000 gallons of gasoline, the combat trains were integrated with the field trains, which had been ordered up, and moved toward Munsan-ni at 1700. About one mile from Munsan-ni the 6th Tank Battalion field trains were ordered to return to the former area due to a change in plans, but the combat trains and the 58th Armored Field Artillery Battalion and 7th Infantry Regimental field trains proceeded on to Munsan-ni. There the vehicles were regassed, and the two light tanks, communication half-track, and fifteen POL trucks returned to the resupply point, loaded up, and proceeded to Seoul to await the return of the tanks.[22]

Task Force Growdon's opening of the land route to Munsan-ni also permitted the expansion of resupply efforts in the 187th Airborne Regimental Combat Team, which was dependent on the arrival of its "land tail." Although the airborne unit also received aerial resupply, it was still hampered in its ability to conduct future operations. Members of the 187th Airborne RCT explain the difficulties.

MAJ. JOSEPH E. JENKINS, REGIMENTAL S-4: That night [23 March] at 2100 hours, the I Corps G-4 telephoned regarding the resupply for 24 March. In effect, the Corps G-4 desired to call off the airdrop because he thought the RCT could be supplied by road. But there was the question of trucks. I reiterated that resupply by air had been called for by Eighth Army, and that the time element involved plus the unknown security of the Munsan-ni to Seoul road did not warrant the risk of calling off the resupply by air.

At 0816 hours on 24 March the first flight of resupply was dropped. Ninety percent of the supplies were off the marked drop zone. Further, there was 15 to 20 percent damage to supplies because the useful life of the chutes had been exceeded. Thus chutes did not open; also the Japanese rope used for bundles was found to be faulty and unsuitable.

Problems arose with the arrival of a hundred Korean laborers, twenty military policemen, and seventeen Korean army trucks at Munsan-ni to assist in the police of the drop zone at 1930 hours the night of 24 March. No food had been provided for the laborers by higher headquarters. This fact was immediately reported to the corps G-4.[23]

LT. COL. THOMAS H. LANE, REGIMENTAL SURGEON: The night of 23 March it became apparent that there would be both water and water-container shortages in the area, and an airdrop of 400 five-gallon field cans was arranged. The drop was made about noon on 24 March. The drop was faulty because the bundles were dropped in the regimental CP area, medical area, and task force CP area. One man, a corporal of the 6th Tank Battalion task force, was killed when, realizing the drop was falling among personnel, he leaped from his hole to warn the people in the different tents to take cover. One of the bundles, containing five filled water cans, hit him in the back. He died of his injuries shortly thereafter.[24]

Before the resupply vehicles of Task Force Growdon returned to Munsan-ni, and before the scheduled arrival of the 187th Airborne RCT's "land tail" at 1800 hours, the entire force received a new mission.

Chapter 7

THE ADVANCE EAST

187th Airborne Regimental Combat Team, 24–25 March 1951

Operation Courageous, begun on 22 March, was the continuation in the U.S. I Corps area of the Operation Ripper advance that was taking place farther east. The Courageous plan was to sweep north almost to the 38th parallel, with the objective of destroying major North Korean and Chinese units. However, after two days it appeared that the operation was another failure. The airborne drop and armored linkup at Munsan-ni (Operation Tomahawk) came too late to prevent the North Koreans from withdrawing across the Imjin River. To the east, the 3d Infantry Division advancing north from Seoul hit stiff resistance from Chinese forces near Uijongbu. Commanders believed that the only hope for UN success was a rapid move east by the 187th Airborne RCT to hit the rear of the Chinese in front of the 3d Division. However, the 187th Airborne with its attached Task Force Growdon was in the midst of resupply activities, and would be hard pressed to move fast enough to catch the enemy before they pulled back.

Capt. Charles E. Weddle of the 187th Airborne RCT's S-3 section describes the receipt of the order.

Word was received from I Corps at 1110 hours ordering the 187th to move immediately to the vicinity of Sinch'on. The S-3 alerted all units and directed them to recall their patrols, move into a tight bivouac, and prepare to move to new positions by foot. The 674th Airborne Field Artillery Battalion was notified to carry all ammunition possible with what transportation was available. At this time, transportation was critically short due to the fact the land tail had not as yet accomplished their linkup. The land tail was not late in arriving, however. The move was ordered prior to their scheduled arrival. The move entailed travel without basic transportation over a distance of approximately thirty miles with both flanks exposed.

The commanding general of the 187th Airborne RCT called a meeting of all unit commanders of the organization at 1200 hours, at which time a warning order in connection with the proposed move was verbally issued. At a later meeting at 1530 hours, the commanding general again assembled all unit commanders at the command post and verbally issued the movement order. During this meeting, while the commanding general was speaking, the command post area was subjected to several rounds of enemy artillery fire. Shells landed within seventy-five to a hundred yards, which disrupted the meeting momentarily.[1]

The After Action Report of Task Force Growdon provides additional details.

At 1530 hours, a meeting was held at the 187th Regimental Combat Team command post of all unit commanders. General Bowen stated that the 187th Regiment plus attachments was to attack east, seizing the hill mass north of Uijongbu. Colonel Growdon explained that POL had not arrived from Seoul and that it was not possible for his entire Task Force to accompany the 187th Regimental Combat Team until it did arrive. However, he stated that he could send the tank company that had not gone on patrol, as that company had full gas tanks. During this meeting, General Bowen received orders from I Corps that the 2d Battalion, 7th Infantry Regiment, was released from control of the 187th Regiment and would return to Seoul immediately.

It was then decided that a task force of Company C, 6th Medium Tank Battalion, Battery C, 58th Armored Field Artillery, a platoon of engineers from Company A, 14th Engineer Combat Battalion, and the 2d Ranger Company would be made up to lead the attack to the east. This force was commanded by Major Kobbe, executive officer of the 6th Medium Tank Battalion, and was named Task

Force Kobbe. The 187th Regimental Combat Team, followed by the 6th Medium Tank Battalion (minus Company C) with the 4th Ranger Company attached, was to follow the entire force when POL arrived. The 4th Ranger Company was attached to Company B, 6th Medium Tank Battalion, which was still blocking to the east, to replace the infantry detachment of the 2d Battalion, 7th Infantry Regiment, who was with them. Company B, with 4th Ranger Company attached, was to remain in position blocking to the east, and the entire attacking force was to pass through them on the attack east. Company B was then to join the rest of the 6th Medium Tank Battalion when it passed their position.[2]

Capt. John Wahl, commander of the support company of the 187th Airborne, provides details of the airborne regiment's movement plan.

At 1230 hours I went to the 187th Airborne Regimental CP, where a fragmentary order for a move eastward was issued. The S-3 announced that the regiment would move in the following order: 3d Battalion, 2d Battalion, headquarters company, medics, support company, and, finally, the 1st Battalion mounted on field artillery vehicles. Every ten miles the battalions were to rotate. The mission of the regiment was to move eastward, contacting an enemy holding force and linking up with forces moving north from Uijongbu.[3]

The Move Begins

About the time that the move to the east started, the resupply vehicles of Task Force Growdon and the "land tail" of the 187th Airborne RCT began to arrive. The After Action Report of Task Force Growdon describes the advance through a rainy night.

Task Force Kobbe began its move at 1800 hours, followed at 1820 hours by the 187th Regiment. Passage through Company B, 6th Tank Battalion, was without enemy contact. The force moved by bounds, staying approximately two miles ahead of the main body. In a defile seven and one-half miles from the starting point, the road caved away behind the lead tank; ahead, the road was too narrow to proceed. Reconnaissance was immediately initiated for a bypass, and the wall of the defile was prepared for demolition to widen it. A bypass was found, and three tanks were pushed through before the bypass became impassable due to marshy land. The three tanks proceeded one more mile along the route of advance, when the road again caved. No bypass was available. The three tanks were able to extract themselves and assemble off the road awaiting instructions. Demolition work at the first bypass to widen the road was completed at 0200 hours, 25 March, and the point tank was extracted.

At this time Major Kobbe informed Colonel Growdon that Task Force Kobbe was hindering the advance of the 187th Regimental Combat Team by blocking the road, and that the road was not passable to tanks. Major Kobbe recommended that the Task Force assemble off the road, and that the 187th Regiment pass through and continue on its mission. It was further recommended that the Task Force proceed to the objective of the 187th Regiment by a route from Seoul to Uijongbu. Colonel Growdon concurred, and directed Major Kobbe to inform General Bowen. General Bowen concurred and directed Task Force Kobbe to withdraw to the 6th Tank Battalion assembly area when the 187th Regiment had cleared. The 58th Armored Field Artillery Battalion was to continue in support of the 187th Regiment, and the battery of 999th Field Artillery remained attached to the 6th Tank Battalion. The 2d and 4th Ranger Companies were relieved from attachment to the 6th Tank Battalion and went forward with the 58th Armored Field Artillery at 0400.[4]

On 25 March, Task Force Kobbe returned to Munsan-ni with the 999th Field Artillery battery. There the battalion was refueled by the trains that had arrived from Seoul. Later the same day, the remaining elements of Task Force Growdon moved to Seoul, where the task force was dissolved. The next day the 6th Tank Battalion returned to the 24th Infantry Division, taking with them the memory of hoped-for armored thrusts, frustrated by enemy mines, rainy weather, and poor roads. In two days of operations the task force had lost two killed and fourteen wounded in action.

After Task Force Growdon left the Sinch'on road the night of

24–25 March, the 187th Airborne continued pushing to the east in its attempt to overcome miserable weather, harsh terrain, and stiff enemy resistance in order to trap the Chinese before they could retreat from the Uijongbu area. Almost from the beginning, it appeared that this attempt would also fail. Although supply vehicles and the 187th Airborne "land tail" arrived just as the force was assembling, in the haste and confusion of the move some units did not receive their vehicles and were not resupplied. The subsequent withdrawal of Task Force Growdon/Kobbe added to the problems. Soldiers of the 187th Airborne RCT describe what happened on the march.

LT. COL. HARRY F. LAMBERT, COMMANDER OF THE 674TH AIRBORNE FIELD ARTILLERY BATTALION: At noon 24 March, a warning order was received to move east across the I Corps front to the vicinity of the north–south road from Uijongbu, a distance of approximately fifteen miles. At 1500 hours a company of tanks, one battery of field artillery, and one company of Rangers moved halfway and took up blocking positions. The 674th Field Artillery Battalion, with the 58th Armored Field Artillery Battalion and Battery A, 999th Field Artillery Battalion, started to move at dusk. That afternoon the land tail had brought up eight additional 105mm howitzers and 2,300 rounds of 105mm ammunition.

The tanks in the security column blocked the road, and the artillery was halted five miles east of the DZ at Munsan-ni from 2200 hours on 24 March to 0400 hours on 25 March.[5]

CAPT. DORSEY B. ANDERSON, COMMANDER OF THE 4TH RANGER COMPANY, IN THE REGIMENTAL CP AREA: [I] was instructed to mount my company on trucks that had arrived with Task Force Growdon. The company was to join Company B, 6th Tank Battalion, west of Pobwon-ni, form a tank-infantry team, and continue the attack to the east to link up with units of the 3d Infantry Division. At the tank company headquarters, while waiting for orders to mount the tanks, the Ranger Company formed a security perimeter around the tanks. Between 0300 and 0400 on 25 March, Colonel Gearhart [deputy 187th Airborne RCT commander] instructed me to mount trucks belonging to the [58th Armored] Field Artillery Battalion as they passed the tank company. The Ranger

Company had mounted the trucks in darkness and moved out slowly for a distance of about three miles, to the base of a large hill, when word came via radio for the 4th Ranger Company to dismount and continue on foot. The 2d Platoon of the Ranger Company had been instructed, unknown to me, to dismount from the trucks and mount others. It was raining, and the road was muddy.[6]

1ST LT. WARD C. GOESSLING JR., ARTILLERY LIAISON OFFICER WITH THE 3D BATTALION: At 1800 hours the 3d Battalion began the march. Company L had one day's rations, the other companies none, since the land tail did not come up until the next day. Civilians had reported to the advance guard, 4th Ranger Company and tanks, that North Koreans were entrenched in the road. When the 3d Battalion passed through this area, however, there was no evidence of the enemy. On the march, smoking and fires were not permitted. After the first and second hours, there were ten-minute halts. It had been planned to load the 3d Battalion on trucks after six miles. The battalion waited from 2000 to 2400 hours to be loaded, only to find out that 25 percent of the unit could not be loaded. Lieutenant Colonel Munson, the 3d Battalion commander, gave the order to unload, and the battalion continued on the march.[7]

CAPT. JOHN E. STREVER, COMMANDER OF COMPANY K: On 24 March at 1500 hours I was told that the ROKs were coming in to take over the area, and Company K pulled into an assembly area to await orders to move out. Without drawing rations, as a result of which four meals were missed, Company K dropped its extra ammunition at the starting point for the march and moved out. It was a mistake to drop the extra ammunition. At 2030 hours, after walking six miles, Company K was told to mount on trucks. Unfortunately the men became scattered out on the trucks, which were also being used for logistical support. To retain control of them, the battalion commander ordered them to dismount and walk.[8]

CAPT. THOMAS J. WATKINS, COMMANDER OF COMPANY M: At 1800 hours on 24 March, Company M moved out on foot since the land tail had not yet arrived. Equipment included eight machine guns with 2,000 rounds per gun for the machine-gun platoon and

1,250 rounds per gun for the provisional machine-gun platoon. Each man carried one box of ammunition. The four mortars had 72 rounds.[9]

1ST LT. J. L. BEASLEY, 81MM MORTAR PLATOON LEADER, COM-PANY H: At 1930 hours on 24 March, Company H assembled for the road march east. Fifteen to twenty Korean laborers, twenty oxen, and one cart were recruited for the move. Just as Company H moved from its assembly area, it was joined by its vehicles. At around 2400 hours there was a brief firefight with some ROKs before the column was properly identified.[10]

1ST LT. DONALD L. ROBERTS, 2D PLATOON LEADER, COMPANY F: The 187th Airborne Regimental Combat Team moved out in route march at 1900 hours, an armored spearhead moving ahead, followed by the 3d Battalion, the 2d Battalion, and the 1st Battalion in that order. Because of the wet weather and the condition of the road, the armored vehicles bogged down near Pobwon-ni. At 2100 hours the 2d Battalion passed through the 3d Battalion, moving in the following order: Companies G, F, E, H, and headquarters. The approach march continued with no activity, Company F stopping at 0345 hours on 25 March at a road junction [near Sinch'on where the main road to Munsan-ni intersected a road running southeast to Uijongbu].[11]

Actions Near Parun-ni, 25 March

Soon the enemy joined with the weather to further delay the advance. Members of Company F describe the beginning of the action.

1ST LT. DONALD L. ROBERTS, 2D PLATOON LEADER: At dawn around 0545 hours Company F, with the 2d Platoon leading as the point, moved out, contacting an enemy roadblock [about 2,000 meters west of Parun-ni] at 0700 hours. The enemy was about one company strong and was on each side of the road, pinning Company F in a ditch.

SFC ROSS C. DUNCAN, 2D PLATOON GUIDE: Around 0730 hours a jeep from the regimental I&R Platoon detonated a box-type mine while passing the 1st Platoon of Company F, which was bring-

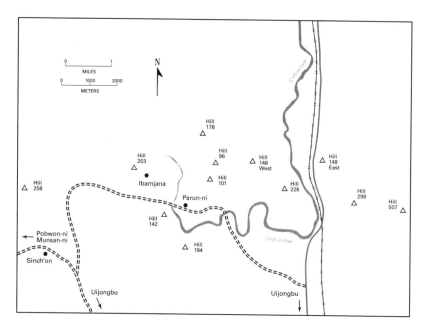

Area east of Sinch'on attacked by 187th Airborne (original map by author, based on maps from the Army Map Service).

ing up the rear of the company. Two men from the I&R Platoon were killed and one wounded; six men from Company F were wounded. Five more mines were discovered in the vicinity. The enemy on the high ground were prepared to defend from the south rather than the west, but were able to bring heavy small-arms fire and inaccurate mortar fire on Company F.

LIEUTENANT ROBERTS: As the fire slackened, Company F formed a skirmish line. At 0800 hours a bugle was heard, and the enemy began to withdraw. I think the enemy was surprised and expected an attack from the south rather than the west. Company E then passed through Company F and made contact with the enemy 1,000 yards farther east around 1000 hours.[12]

1ST LT. DANIEL L. BALDWIN, 3D PLATOON LEADER, COMPANY F: Moving out on 25 March, Company F led the 2d Battalion. At 0630 hours an I&R jeep, moving up and passing the 1st Platoon of Company F, hit a land mine, killing two, wounding eleven, and throwing the jeep twenty-five yards. At 0700 hours the column was fired on. The 3d Platoon moved up, and the 2d Platoon went to the high ground. Between 0830 and 0900 hours, Company E passed through in the area 500 yards west of Parun-ni.[13]

The 2d Battalion commander, Lt. Col. J. P. Connor, describes the fight that ensued.
On 24 March the 2d Battalion was ordered to make a night march through enemy country, acting as advance guard for the 187th Airborne Regimental Combat Team. After marching on the night of 24–25 March, the 78th CCF Division was contacted on the morning of 25 March at 0730 hours. Company F, leading the advance guard, forced the Chinese to withdraw, and the battalion continued on to Parun-ni, which was reached at 0900 hours. Here the enemy, estimated at two battalions, was again encountered. Captain Shanahan, the commander of Company E, now in the lead, was killed at 0915 hours in the firefight that followed. I was with him when he fell. The executive officer of Company E was killed five minutes later, and the battalion adjutant took over the company. The enemy had observation of the advance of the 2d Battalion, but had not been able to identify the column as American until it made contact. Artillery radios were not working because of heavy rain.[14]

An officer and a sergeant from Company E and the artillery forward observer provide more details of the action.
2D LT. EDWARD J. WHELAN, 2D PLATOON LEADER, COMPANY E: The whole 2d Battalion assembled and marched east starting at 1800 hours on 24 March. At 0400 hours on the 25th the 2d Battalion halted for two hours. Between 0700 and 0730 hours an I&R jeep hit a wooden box-type land mine while a rifle platoon was walking beside the jeep, inflicting many casualties. At 0800 hours, Company F ran into light resistance coming from machine-gun and rifle fire. Company E pulled up using ditches alongside the road as a covered route, passing through Company F at 1100 hours. At this time, as the 1st Platoon went around a curve in the road, it ran into a CCF concentration, and the advance was held up. The 2d Platoon laid a base of fire to the right of the 1st Platoon, then I led the 2d Platoon 400 yards up a creek bed and across an open rice paddy.

After organizing behind the rice paddy dike, we jumped off and moved 300 yards up to Parun-ni. Two squads on the left swept the town, but the squad on the right was held up. The weapons squad of the 2d Platoon cleared Parun-ni, killing four enemy and receiving grenades thrown by enemy behind a large dike outside. At this time I was told to take over the company. I committed the 3d Platoon, which attacked at 1200 hours; the 2d Platoon jumped off up a hill, killing fifteen to twenty Chinese. The M-1 rifles, because of weather, mud, and the fact that the M-1 doesn't work on semi-automatic half the time, were not functioning. The men used hand grenades and pistols. Seven Chinese on the reverse slope were causing trouble. The hill was stormed, and the new company commander, Captain Case, came up.[15]

SFC George G. Lane, 1st Platoon sergeant, Company E: On 25 March at 1100 hours, as the 1st Platoon was deployed to the left of a creek bed about sixty yards west of Parun-ni, it ran into small-arms and automatic-weapons fire from the enemy. A sniper on the left flank was causing considerable trouble. Captain Shanahan, Company E commander, was killed. The terrain back to the rest of Company E was swept by sniper fire, and two men from the 1st Platoon were hit while trying to make contact. Finally a runner got through with the message to send a machine gun to the right flank and place machine-gun fire on the snipers' position. At 1200 hours the sniper fire lifted, and the 1st Platoon pulled back to the road. The 2d Platoon forced the enemy to withdraw, and Company E entered Parun-ni.[16]

1st Lt. Rudy V. Paraiso, artillery forward observer with Company E, Battery B, 674th Airborne Field Artillery Battalion: On the morning of 25 March, Company E reached Parun-ni with Captain Shanahan marching at the head of the column. I checked with the 2d Battalion artillery liaison officer on enemy observed along ridges and on the artillery battalion's readiness to fire. The 674th Airborne Field Artillery Battalion was emplaced along the Munsan-ni–Parun-ni road. I fired my first fire mission at an estimated one hundred enemy dug in on the ridgeline of Hill 194 [about 1,500 yards south of Parun-ni]. Batteries B and C fired 252 rounds of fuze quick and inflicted an estimated 150 casualties.

Company E had trouble entering Parun-ni, and I kept artillery fire 1,000 yards ahead of the advance. Company E finally entered Parun-ni from the south. They halted and waited for the rest of the 2d Battalion to move up. The village had been burned, with only a few houses remaining standing.[17]

While Company E cleared the enemy from the village of Parun-ni, the rest of the 2d Battalion moved forward for the attack. Members of the 2d Battalion describe the approach to Parun-ni and the subsequent fighting.

M. SGT. OTHON VALENT, 1ST PLATOON SERGEANT, COMPANY G: During the night a slight rain started to fall, increasing to a heavy downpour by 0800 hours. Early in the morning Company E passed Company G and, in a firefight, secured high ground. Company F now passed Company E, and Company E went to the right flank. During Company E's firefight its commander, Captain Shanahan, was killed. Between 0830 and 0900 hours Company G came up to the rear of Company E and set up a base of fire for Company E's attack on Parun-ni from the west. When Company E had advanced 400 yards, Company G began to move forward, continuing through Parun-ni to high ground east of the village. The 1st Platoon, Company G, secured high ground to the front and saw fifteen Chinese at 1030 hours. Rain had caused the malfunctioning of 50 percent of the 1st Platoon's firepower, forcing men to rely on their .45s. Guns out of action included one machine gun, two BARs, and ten M-1 rifles. The 1st Platoon ran into trouble from a machine gun on high ground and from grenades. Although at 1050 hours the 1st Squad of the 2d Platoon of Company G moved up to help, at 1130 the 1st Platoon had to withdraw. At this time, PFC Morrison saw one Chinese soldier jump over the back of a grave and hit Sergeant Morris over the head with a tripod. At this time Sergeant Morris lacked arms, ammunition, and hand grenades. No trace of Sergeant Morris was found later.

Between 1130 and 1200 hours Company G built up a fire line, and the 3d Platoon advanced ahead of the fire line and then returned. At 1230 hours a platoon of at least forty Chinese attacked the left flank of Company G and were repulsed by hand grenades.

Twenty Chinese were killed; Company G lost two killed, three wounded, and one missing. At 1300 hours the platoon leader was hit, and I took over the 1st Platoon. Company G remained in position the remainder of the day and worked on weapons. It was raining, and the majority of the men did not have raincoats. During the night, the 2d Battalion set up a perimeter with Company E on the left, Company G on the right, and Company F in the rear.[18]

1ST LT. LEO F. SIEFERT, 1ST PLATOON LEADER, COMPANY G: The 2d Battalion moved east to approximately 1,000 yards west of Parun-ni. Company F in the lead was passed through here by Company E, which proceeded to attack a small village 500 yards west of Parun-ni. The 1st Platoon of Company G patrolled a ridge [southwest of Hill 101] to the wood line. We met opposition, and about a hundred enemy came out of prepared positions at 1500 hours and attacked. The 1st Platoon fell back, and Captain Milley, the company commander, sent the 2d and 3d Platoons to help. The Weapons Platoon went into action with the 57mm recoilless rifles and the 60mm mortars, shooting the mortars so as to get tree bursts. Because of the inclement weather, many of the infantry small arms (M-1s, BARs, machine guns, and carbines) were not functioning. The infantry was forced to use grenades and .45s.[19]

SFC GEORGE G. LANE, 1ST PLATOON SERGEANT, COMPANY E: In Parun-ni, Captain Case assumed command of the company. The 1st and 2d Platoons went into the attack with Company G on the left flank. The attack was started with only a small percentage of the weapons working due to sand, water, and rain. The 1st Platoon advanced a hundred yards to a defiladed position. The attack continued from 1400–1500 hours with the 2d Platoon on the right. At 1500 hours, Company E withdrew because of malfunctioning weapons, enemy fire, and casualties. Company G, for an unknown reason, did not receive the same intense fire.[20]

2D LT. EDWARD J. WHELAN, 2D PLATOON LEADER, COMPANY E: Captain Case thought that the 1st Platoon was still in trouble, and so he took the 3d Platoon and, at 1200 hours, went back to the 1st Platoon. I looked to the rear and saw a column of troops, about two companies, on Hill 203. At first they appeared to be Americans with packs on their backs. The troops were Chinese and went into defensive positions due east on Hills 178, 96, 101, and 148 West. The advance guard lacked numbers to attack the enemy at this time. At 1400 hours, Company E occupied high ground east of Parun-ni, and Company G got into trouble over toward Hill 101. The 1st and 2d Platoons of Company E went to help Company G, but at 1500 hours as they were crossing a rice paddy on a finger of high ground east of Parun-ni, an officer in the village hollered, "They're counterattacking in force." This caused the platoons to return. When they did so, Captain Case ordered them to continue on their original mission, saying that the 3d Platoon could hold the hill. Back went the 1st and 2d Platoons across the rice paddy, moving through CCF observed enfilading fire. Around me men were screeching and hollering. Lieutenant Dolan and I decided to fall back fifty yards to a knoll where we could build up a firing line. Meanwhile, the 3d Platoon knocked out the enemy machine gun that was causing a great deal of the trouble. The 1st and 2d Platoons then attacked and took the objective. After this, Company E passed through Company G, and between 1630 and 1700 hours captured Hill 101.[21]

1ST LT. RUDY V. PARAISO, FORWARD OBSERVER WITH COMPANY E, BATTERY B, 674TH AIRBORNE FIELD ARTILLERY BATTALION: At 1200 hours Company E formed on the line of departure to assault Hill 194, where there was an estimated Chinese battalion along the ridges. At the wall east of Parun-ni Company E was held up. Because of the close contact with the enemy, I fired way out and crept the fire in.[22]

1ST LT. DONALD L. ROBERTS, 2D PLATOON LEADER, COMPANY F: Company G moved up on the left flank of Company E; Company F moved up on the right flank, attacking down a long ridge shaped like a finger, then withdrew 200 yards and supported Company E and Company G. All day large groups of the enemy broke the skyline on Hill 228 where an enemy battalion was reported entrenched. Mortar fire fell in the Parun-ni area, one mortar operating from Hill 228. Company F gained cover from the former Chinese positions on the ridge.

SFC RAYMOND MORRIS, 2D PLATOON SERGEANT, COMPANY F: During the day Company F had one killed and six wounded in action. The wounded included the company commander, Captain

Agee; the 1st Platoon leader, Lieutenant Hammock; and a machine gunner from the 2d Platoon. Another machine gunner from the 2d Platoon was killed. At 1700 hours the 3d Platoon leader, Lieutenant Baldwin, was hit by sniper fire.[23]

1ST LT. J. L. BEASLEY, 81MM MORTAR PLATOON LEADER, COMPANY H: When the 2d Battalion made its initial contact, the mortars moved into position. The mortars did not fire. All but two radios were drowned out, and no wire was in. However, the platoon had radio communication with the mortar observer with Company F. At 1130 hours the mortar platoon was ordered to move to Parun-ni. We went into position and fired for Company F on the right, Company E in the center, and Company G on the left as they attacked east. Company E was in a hot firefight. On 25 March, the 81mm mortars fired 256 rounds: twenty white phosphorous, seventy heavy, and the remainder light. The platoon CP was located in a house in Parun-ni.[24]

1ST LT. DONALD L. ROBERTS, 2D PLATOON LEADER, COMPANY F: On the night of 25 March, Lieutenant Muse became the company commander, and I became the executive officer. We were the only officers remaining in Company F.[25]

LT. COL. J. P. CONNOR, 2D BATTALION COMMANDER: At dusk the enemy had been driven south of Parun-ni, and the battalion dug in for the night. Friendly losses were thirteen killed and forty-eight wounded. Patrols the next morning disclosed 150 CCF killed and evidence that many had been wounded.[26]

During the confused fighting east of Parun-ni on the afternoon of 25 March, the enemy launched a strong counterattack against Company G. Machine guns from the 2d Battalion's weapons company, Company H, played a key role in repulsing the assault. Two soldiers manning the machine guns were later posthumously awarded the Distinguished Service Cross for their actions. Eyewitnesses describe their heroism.[27]

SFC EARL B. DAVIS, COMPANY H: On 25 March at approximately 1300 hours the 2d section of Company H, attached to Company F, placed its machine guns in firing position immediately east of the town of Parun-ni. At that time, Company F was attacking eastward to drive the defending Chinese Communist Forces out of their heavily entrenched positions. M. Sgt. Ervin L. Muldoon, the machine-gun platoon sergeant, was with the second section at the time of its attachment and during the ensuing engagement. Shortly after Company F moved out in the attack, it was found that there was no opposition in their sector; however, Company G, which at that time was to the north, was in a heavy firefight. We could see this firefight as it took place, and because of the overwhelming superiority of the enemy, it was apparent that the position could not be held unless help was received. Sergeant Muldoon made the command decision to move this section to Company G's aid, for he reasoned that if Company G was pushed from its position, then Company F would be, for all practical purposes, surrounded.

The section of machine guns was moved across an exposed area under intense small-arms fire. During this time Sergeant Muldoon repeatedly exposed himself to enemy fire to insure that the section moved with a minimum loss of time. When the guns were placed in position, Sergeant Muldoon directed fire at the attacking CCF, which at that time was staging a fanatic "banzai" attack. I estimated the attacking force to be of battalion size, and their direction of attack came from the front and from both flanks. They never stopped attacking until some two hours later, and during this period of time they continually probed our front for weak points. Throughout this entire period, Sergeant Muldoon continually exposed himself while directing fire.

SGT. EARL D. HINEBAUGH, COMPANY H: When we got into position we found the situation to be precarious, to say the least. Many of the riflemen near one position had rifles that would not fire, and as we moved into position, I noticed several men firing their .45-caliber pistols. Some had only an entrenching tool or a bayonet, and they were preparing to use them. Sergeant Muldoon took command of the situation, directed the fire where it was needed the most, and continually exposed himself to make sure that the right thing was done at the right time. He did this for some two hours, for that was the length of the enemy attack.

After we moved into position to support Company G the machine guns came under heavy small-arms fire. The enemy threw several "banzai" attacks into our lines with a particular effort to knock out all of our automatic weapons. It was during this period of intense combat action that I observed the heroic efforts of one of the machine gunners, PFC Eugene Estep of Company H. PFC Estep took over a machine gun after two of its gunners had been wounded. He single-handedly moved the gun to a new position and then opened fire on the enemy. His fire was destructive because he caught the enemy completely by surprise. He inflicted many casualties on the enemy even though he was exposed to heavy enemy small-arms fire. He remained at that gun until he was mortally wounded, and I personally know that he exposed himself in manning this machine gun with little regard for his own personal safety. He exhibited an unusual amount of heroism in this action.

PFC Louis Villa, Company H: While we were engaged with the enemy on 25 March, I was a member of the 3d Squad of the Machine Gun Platoon. We were helping Company G, who was engaged in a hot firefight with the Chinese. In the firefight the Chinese "banzaied" us time after time, and the whole attack must have lasted two hours. During this whole time, PFC Eugene Estep was manning a .30-caliber machine gun on my right. I was about six feet from him throughout the entire action, and I saw the effects of the volume of fire that he delivered. Although in an extremely exposed position (he had to expose himself to gain a good field of fire), he continued firing a heavy concentration of machine-gun fire on the enemy, inflicting many enemy casualties. He did this without any regard for his personal well-being. His coolness under fire and his precise marksmanship did a great part in forcing the enemy to abandon their attack. We were under very heavy enemy small-arms fire the entire time, and it was his gun that put an enemy machine gun out of action.

PFC Tony R. Canales, Company H: Company G was engaged in a stiff fight, and we thought that they couldn't hold, so we went over to help them. When we got into position, the enemy opened up on us. One machine gun fired constantly and drew much enemy fire.

I was about twenty yards from one of the guns manned by PFC Estep. His gun was set up in an exposed area, and it was actually doing most of the damage, so the enemy concentrated their fire on him. PFC Estep could have pulled back, but the Chinese were "banzaing" us, and if he had they might have succeeded. He stayed at that gun until he was killed, and he inflicted terrible casualties on the enemy. I would estimate that he personally killed from thirty to forty Chinese from this one position in a forty-five-minute period. It was one of the bravest things I have ever seen, and I know that few other men would have exposed themselves to such tremendous small-arms fire so that the position could be held.

SFC EARL B. DAVIS, COMPANY H: On several occasions he [Sergeant Muldoon] took over the machine gun when the gunners were wounded. On one specific occasion he emplaced and fired the machine gun from a particularly exposed position so that he could gain better fields of fire and repel the enemy's frontal charges. It was while he was firing the machine gun from this exposed position that he was killed. The volume of fire that he delivered was done with a complete disregard for his own safety and undoubtedly was a decisive factor in repelling the enemy attack. The thing that impressed me most was the way Sergeant Muldoon handled this entire situation. In all of my thirty-five months in combat in the last war, I never saw a situation so much in need of leadership, and this is the intangible that Sergeant Muldoon provided. In all of the chaos and confusion, he was the "Rock of Gibraltar" on which everyone seemed to lean. If he hadn't been there, and done as he did, I doubt if the position would have been held; in fact, I'm sure of it.

SGT. EARL D. HINEBAUGH, COMPANY H: Continually, and with complete disregard for his own safety, he [Sergeant Muldoon] took over the machine guns when the gunners were wounded. His coolness under fire was an inspiration to those who were around him. In spite of the overwhelming superiority of the enemy, we all knew we were going to hold and fight (and win), and Sergeant Muldoon was the reason. It wasn't just the fact that he personally killed a lot of the enemy while risking his own life, nor was it the fact that he directed the fire in such a way as to "break the back" of the Chinese attack.

Rather it was the leadership that he displayed that made the difference. When he was killed he was firing the machine gun from an extremely exposed position. Sergeant Muldoon knew his position was exposed, and he still maintained a heavy volume of fire in spite of the heavy small-arms fire that engaged his machine gun. In disregarding his own personal well-being, Sergeant Muldoon upheld the highest tradition of the service. The valor and leadership he displayed are something of which the Army might well be proud.

PFC ROBERT L. COVILLE, COMPANY H: When we got into position, Company G was having a hard time holding the hill. I noticed that a lot of men in the rifle company had weapons which wouldn't work, and I kind of thought they would be run off because there were so many of the enemy attacking us. They "banzaied" us again and again, and many times we had to throw hand grenades at them. During the entire fight, the machine guns continually chattered away, and they took a terrible toll on the enemy. Sergeant Muldoon was constantly exposing himself to find targets and direct our fire. I would say that he was continually risking his life by doing this. Also, whenever a gunner got wounded (we had two killed and two wounded), Sergeant Muldoon would take over the gun and continue to fire. When Sergeant Muldoon got killed he was on a little hill on which the enemy was firing heavily. He went to this exposed gun and fired in spite of the fact that he knew his life would be seriously endangered. That's how he got it. The way Sergeant Muldoon fought and the way he led us was probably the big reason why the Chinese didn't take the hill. He was exceptionally cool under fire and he had the situation under control at all times.

When the 2d Battalion made contact with the enemy near Parun-ni early the morning of 25 March, the 187th Airborne ordered the battalion to attack east to seize the high ground of Hill 228. The 3d Battalion was to support the 2d Battalion's attack, while the 1st Battalion remained in reserve. The 2d Battalion spent the day clearing the enemy from the ridges near Parun-ni and from Hill 101 and beating off counterattacks. As a result, the 2d Battalion was unable to reach its objective some 2,000 yards to the east. The 3d Battalion was also drawn into the fighting to clear Chinese forces from hills in the rear of the 2d Battalion.

The 3d Battalion's operations sergeant, Sgt. Charles P. McDonald, describes his battalion's arrival and commitment to the fight.
The battalion marched all night and closed in the assembly area at 0400 hours on 25 March. At daylight the 3d Battalion moved through Sinch'on following the 2d Battalion and reaching Parun-ni at 1120 hours. We received sniper fire from Hill 142. Company I was ordered to attack Hill 142 and clear the area. Heavy-mortar fire was received in the battalion area throughout the day.[28]

Company I's capture of Hill 142 is described by members of the unit.
2D LT. MELVIN C. STRAWSER, 1ST PLATOON LEADER, COMPANY I: On Hill 142, enemy were observed digging in. The 1st and 2d Platoons of Company I moved to clear the ridgeline of Hill 142 and had almost reached the top at dusk when three interlocking enemy machine guns held up the advance. Company I killed eleven enemy and suffered one killed and four wounded.[29]

M. SGT. NEAL A. PERKINS, PLATOON SERGEANT, COMPANY I: On 25 March, Company I moved up to the Sinch'on River in the vicinity of a large dike. The 2d Battalion was attacking high ground to the north. Company I moved south across the Sinch'on to attack the hill with the 2d and 3d Platoons spearheading. I estimate one company of enemy occupied the hill. After a firefight in which Company I lost one man killed and four wounded, Company I withdrew and artillery fire was directed on the hill.[30]

2D LT. EVERETT MACKLEY, 2D PLATOON LEADER, COMPANY I: On the morning of 25 March, Company I was in the vicinity of Parun-ni. At 1600 hours the hill south of the village was cleared. Company I charged with fixed bayonets and killed eleven enemy and wounded five. The company then withdrew from the hill, which the enemy reoccupied on 26 March.[31]

1ST LT. JAMES J. COGHLAN, ARTILLERY FORWARD OBSERVER WITH COMPANY I, BATTERY C, 674TH AIRBORNE FIELD ARTILLERY

BATTALION: At 1600 hours on 25 March, Company I reached Parun-ni. Captain Garcia, the company commander, sent one platoon, led by Lieutenant Strawser, to clear the high ground immediately south of the town. At 1600 hours, Lieutenant Strawser's platoon contacted forty enemy, killing, in the firefight that lasted until 1700 hours, fifteen and dispersing the remainder. I was unable to bring artillery fire on the enemy because of the proximity of friendly troops.[32]

CAPT. NICK GARCIA, COMPANY I COMMANDER: On 25 March, Company I's main action was a small hill near Parun-ni. The attack on the hill swept from the base to the top and down the left side. Lieutenant Radcliffe, Company I's executive officer, took two Chinese officers prisoner on the hill. Eleven enemy were killed, mostly with the bayonet.[33]

Other members of the 3d Battalion describe their actions during the fight.

1ST LT. WARD C. GOESSLING, ARTILLERY LIAISON OFFICER WITH THE 3D BATTALION, 674TH AIRBORNE FIELD ARTILLERY BATTALION: At 0500 hours the 3d Battalion arrived in the vicinity of Sinch'on, and at 0600 hours we moved out behind the 2d Battalion. The order of march was Companies L, K, M, and headquarters last. As we moved up, an I&R Platoon jeep hit a road mine. Some small-arms fire was heard. At 0700 hours I returned to the rear to look for the 674th Airborne Field Artillery Battalion. I found Sergeant Lyles [artillery forward observer for Company K] beside the road sound asleep. I awakened him, and sent him to rejoin Company K. I replenished my supply of radio batteries from the artillery. I returned and rejoined the battalion at a bend in the road, where it had halted. We remained there until 1230 hours when the column again moved. The 2d Battalion ahead was to attack and secure the ground east of Parun-ni, and the 3d Battalion would then pass through the 2d Battalion. Between 1600 and 1700 hours the 3d Battalion tied in with the 2d Battalion. The 3d Battalion CP was in a house by the crossroads [on the west side of Parun-ni]. At 1600 hours one mortar round blew in its roof.[34]

CAPT. JOHN E. STREVER, COMPANY K COMMANDER: On 25 March at 0700 hours, as daylight was breaking, the 2d Battalion passed through the 3d Battalion, which then followed the 2d Battalion. Coming into Parun-ni at 1500 hours, the column underwent mortar fire without casualties. The mission of Company K was to secure the left flank of the 2d Battalion in the attack. Company K suffered one killed and three wounded while supporting, by fire, the assault of one company of the 2d Battalion for one hour.

At 1600 hours, Lieutenant Colonel Munson, the 3d Battalion commander, gave areas for the night perimeter. A reconnaissance was then made for the next day's attack. Company K now had 140 men remaining out of the 197 full strength. On the night of 25–26 March, sniper fire was received from Hill 194.[35]

SFC JAMES E. HOEH, COMPANY M MORTAR OBSERVER WITH COMPANY K: The 3d Battalion halted approximately two miles west of Parun-ni, a village in which the 2d Battalion was having trouble. At 0830 hours I assisted a platoon of Company K in sweeping the rear area for enemy. At 1000 hours, an enemy mortar round fell on the rear of the platoon, killing two and wounding three. At 1030 hours my radio stopped working, and I returned to Parun-ni and the 81mm Mortar Platoon. At 1130 hours enemy mortar rounds fell in Parun-ni.[36]

CAPT. THOMAS J. WATKINS, COMPANY M COMMANDER: At dawn on 25 March, Company M was at a crossroads just east of Sinch'on. The machine guns were still attached to the companies. At 1000 hours an enemy mortar round fell on the provisional machine-gun platoon, killing one and wounding four. Between 1000 and 1100 hours, Company M arrived at Parun-ni. The 3d Battalion set up a perimeter on the south side of the town, with the 2d Battalion on the north side of Parun-ni. Mortars and small-arms fire were falling in the western part of the town, and a firefight was going on to the northeast. Company M had left a detail at the DZ [near Munsan-ni] to load a basic load of 4,500 rounds per machine gun and 90 rounds per mortar, but the road was not yet passable for the ammunition train to come up. Therefore, with only 200 rounds, the mortars did not register or shoot.[37]

The 1st Battalion was to remain in reserve, but it too was drawn into the fighting to clear the enemy from hills in the rear. The battalion executive officer and the commander of Company A describe the unit's actions on 25 March.

MAJ. CHARLES M. HOLLAND, EXECUTIVE OFFICER, IST BATTALION: The 1st Battalion moved by motor and on foot through a dark night, cold with rain, down a muddy road. Sinch'on was reached, and the 1st Battalion was placed in regimental reserve as the 2d and 3d Battalions proceeded with the assault to the east. At Sinch'on, the 1st Battalion was in charge of local security to the north and east. The weather was wet, cold, dark, and dreary, and the 187th Airborne RCT lacked air support. The 1st Battalion CP was in a Korean house in Sinch'on. At 1400 hours on 25 March, the 1st Battalion commander and the company commanders made a reconnaissance of the proposed route of advance for the following day. The 3d Battalion, from whose position the 1st Battalion would jump off, was contacted, and the battalion assembly area was designated. At 1630 hours the battalion commander, Lieutenant Colonel Wilson, alerted Company A to secure Hill 203. Company A pushed up Hill 203 and at darkness requested permission to withdraw. Permission was granted, and Company A withdrew back to secure the area of the 674th Airborne Field Artillery Battalion, withholding the attack on Hill 203 to dawn.[38]

CAPT. ROBERT A. CHABOT, COMPANY A COMMANDER: Later on the morning of 25 March, Company A came into a valley near Sinch'on. The 2d Platoon was sent to Hill 258 [2,000 meters north of Sinch'on], and the remainder of the company remained in the 1st Battalion perimeter astride the road. At 1630 hours, Company A moved out to secure Hill 203 for the battalion jump-off. We passed through Ibamjana, and made contact with the 674th Airborne Field Artillery Battalion. Leading elements received fire from Hill 203 two hundred yards before they entered the town. Hill 203 was next approached with the 2d Platoon leading and the 3d Platoon slightly behind. Lieutenant Knight climbed the ridgeline with the 2d Platoon to hit the enemy on the flank. The 1st Platoon was to pass through the 2d Platoon. As it was growing dark, I decided to wait until morning before taking the hill. There had been no friendly casualties, and the enemy casualties were unknown. That night Company A tied into the artillery defense perimeter, and Lieutenant Balmer, the artillery forward observer, placed fire on Hill 203.[39]

Support Operations

The 674th Airborne Field Artillery Battalion received its vehicles and additional howitzers from the "land tail" before starting the night move. The next morning they were able to provide fire support for the regiment, as described by Capt. Edward C. Williamson, a combat historian who prepared a report of the operation.

At 0910 hours 25 March, after an unopposed night motor march, Battery B, 674th Airborne Field Artillery Battalion, went into position off the road 1,000 yards west of Sinch'on. Batteries A and C went into positions just west of Battery B. Later in the day, the artillery moved by echelon and occupied a position one mile west of Parun-ni. There, the AAA Battery established a perimeter around the artillery. The mission of the artillery was to provide support for the 2d Battalion, which was attacking troops entrenched on the low ridge running north to south through Parun-ni. Fire missions were directed especially on ridges north and east of Parun-ni, including Hills 178 and 148 West, where the enemy was entrenched. The 674th Field Artillery Battalion fired fourteen missions on enemy entrenchments, mortars, and assembly areas, killing an estimated seventy enemy soldiers, wounding an estimated 160, and neutralizing four mortar positions. 25 March was a cold, rainy, miserable day. Because of the bad weather, the air OPs did not fly. Communication, however, was established with the 3d Division Artillery.[40]

The heavy rain through the day made resupply difficult. The engineers were kept busy repairing roads and clearing mines. Capt. Billy P. Pendergrass of the regiment's engineer company and the engineer company's daily journal tell the story.

CAPTAIN PENDERGRASS: During the march [night of 24–25 March], rain made the road difficult to traverse. A jeep from the I&R Platoon struck a wooden box mine, killing two, wounding nine, and holding the convoy up. I went forward and cleared the road. I found three mines, including one the jeep had passed over. From that time on, teams of probers moved ahead of the convoy using bayonets and checking especially the easy-to-see soft spots. No other vehicles hit mines, and the column arrived in the vicinity of Parun-ni at 1400 hours. During the march, all engineer platoons were under engineer company control.

The 2d Battalion hit stiff resistance in the vicinity of Parun-ni, and the engineer company, moving immediately behind the 2d Battalion, had two men wounded by mortars. In the attack on enemy positions around Parun-ni, the 3d Battalion requested the 3d Engineer Platoon to remove booby traps and to destroy bangalore torpedoes, which had been placed thirty feet in front of bunkers with pull wires to bunkers so that the torpedoes could be fired. The 1st Battalion requested that the 1st Engineer Platoon find or make a jeep trail to Hill 228.[41]

Engineer Company Daily Journal, Summaries for 24 and 25 March 1951. During movement, the company engaged in expedient road repair. Tanks and rain had made the road impassable in places, and much emergency repair was necessary. The company was initially back in the column, but one platoon had to be moved to the head of the column to facilitate movement of vehicles. The company located four wooden box mines after an I&R jeep was destroyed by hitting a mine; placed a team to search and probe for mines ahead of column and found no other mines; stopped at Parun-ni where the infantry was stopped by enemy resistance; and maintained the regimental MSR, a difficult job because of rain, heavy traffic, and the fact that only hand tools were available. Much road difficulty was caused by poor driver technique. Drivers should be taught to use six-wheel drive and low gear ranges, maintain a constant speed, and not follow in ruts. A long column of traffic, stopping and spinning wheels in the same place, makes a wet earthen road impassable very quickly. Two enlisted men were wounded (one seriously) by enemy mortar fire.[42]

Road conditions and weather made resupply and medical support extremely difficult. The deputy commander and staff officers of the regiment describe the problems.

Capt. Charles E. Weddle, assistant S-3, 187th Airborne RCT: The 2d and 3d Battalions reported that a critical shortage existed in their ammunition and rations. Rain had prevented vehicles from obtaining these supplies. The S-3 immediately requested that an airdrop be made the next day to resupply the RCT with all types of small-arms and 105mm ammunition, as well as rations.[43]

Col. George H. Gerhart, deputy commander, 187th Airborne RCT: During the night, we were moving to the east toward our objective in the vicinity of Hill 299. About 1830 we made a linkup with our land tail. It rained like hell all night, making movement of vehicles to the forward assembly area most difficult. I personally brought up the CP rear on this move. Next morning [25 March] at daybreak the leading battalions established contact with the enemy. The CP was set up at Sinch'on, and operations continued throughout the day to capture the high ground west of the Uijongbu road. By nightfall we had run out of many types of ammunition and only had one-third rations remaining. Our supply trains were believed to be in Uijongbu, so I headed south in an attempt to make contact with them and get them up to our position prior to resumption of attack the next morning.[44]

Lt. Col. Thomas H. Lane, surgeon, 187th Airborne RCT: We had a long, slow twenty-mile move that took the entire night. The march was uneventful medically, as there were no casualties to handle. At 0800 hours the next morning (Easter Sunday), the clearing station opened in conjunction with the regimental CP in the vicinity of Sinch'on and immediately began receiving a heavy flow of battle casualties from the infantry battalion. Due presumably to inclement weather, the helicopters didn't show as prearranged the prior night. Consequently, the seriously wounded were forced to accumulate in the clearing station, as the road the regiment had moved over the night before was impassable to vehicular traffic. The road ahead was blocked by the enemy, and the road behind by mud and mired vehicles. This situation prevailed until approximately 1500 hours when a two-place liaison helicopter arrived with a G-3 representative from 3d Division. I explained the situation regarding the medical evacuation helicopters to this officer, and he instructed his pilot to take out a seriously wounded head case, and to contact the helicopters at the Seoul airfield, telling them that, in his opinion, the weather situation was such that they could make the flight, and that due to the number of wounded, immediate action on their part was imperative. The response was gratifying, in that at approximately 1615 hours helicopters began arriving and resumed evacuation of the more seriously wounded cases.

It would have been desirable to evacuate direct from the battalion aid station at this time, as road conditions made the carry from them to the clearing station a matter of two hours. However, due to the proximity of small-arms fire, the helicopter pilots felt that they couldn't risk their aircraft. That night the Indians operated on two or three patients, probably saving their lives. Otherwise the night was routine.[45]

Some sense of the confusion during the move the night of 24–25 March and its effect the next day is obtained from the 4th Ranger Company commander, Capt. Dorsey B. Anderson.

It was raining, and the road was muddy. I walked into the regimental CP and received the mission of securing the CP area. At 1400 hours [25 March] my executive officer, Lieutenant Warren, arrived with the 3d Platoon. I then learned that the 1st Platoon had been dropped off with the 674th Field Artillery Battalion to secure their area. I also learned that the 2d Platoon had mounted, then dismounted from the trucks by order of the field artillery battalion commander. That platoon was completely out of contact with the company. I tried my own radio communications to contact the platoon; then I tried the regiment's radio channel, and finally the artillery channel. No one knew where the platoon was. I then sent my runner to locate the 2d Platoon. One hour later the platoon leader came looking for me.

In the meantime I put my 3d Platoon in the most likely avenue of enemy approach. When the 2d Platoon rejoined the company about 1730, I placed it in a reserve position for the perimeter in conjunction with the 2d Ranger Company. The 3d Platoon was issued flares and ordered to watch for flares from link-up forces of the 3d Infantry Division, due to arrive at any time. Two amber flares were seen at a great distance by the platoon, which fired two in return.

At that time the regiment was deep in enemy territory, strung out in a line along the road, and open on both flanks. The regiment was in front; the field artillery was in the rear. Two battalions were in contact with the enemy; the third was in blocking and reserve positions.[46]

Despite the precarious position of the regiment, the 187th Airborne prepared to continue its attacks the next morning, hoping to cut the main road to Uijongbu and trap the enemy.

Chapter 8

CUTTING THE UIJONGBU ROAD

187th Airborne Regimental Combat Team, 26–28 March 1951

The plan to quickly move the 187th Airborne RCT fifteen miles to the east to block the retreat of the Chinese facing the U.S. 3d Infantry Division near Uijongbu was frustrated by rain and poor roads, which slowed the advance. By the end of 25 March enemy resistance in front of the 187th had stiffened. The airborne soldiers were still almost three miles from the Uijongbu road, but there remained a chance to catch the Chinese, who continued to fight the 3d Division to the south. On 26 March the 187th Airborne RCT resumed its attack to cut the enemy escape route.

Action on Hill 228, 26 March 1951

Hill 228, the regiment's objective for 26 March, was some 3,000 yards east of Parun-ni and overlooked the Uijongbu road, along which the Chinese were withdrawing in front of the 3d Division. The plan called for the 1st Battalion in the north and the 3d Battalion in the south to pass through the 2d Battalion and attack to the east to seize Hill 228. The 2d Battalion in reserve would protect the northern flank of the attack as it moved east.

The day began on a promising note, as clear skies indicated needed air support would be possible, both for attacks on enemy positions and resupply of the 187th. A small force from Company A easily occupied Hill 203, but from this point forward, enemy resistance was stiff. Members of the 1st Battalion describe the action as it unfolded.

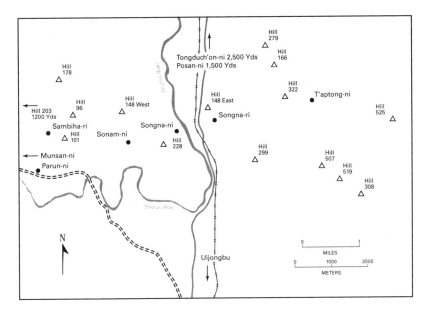

187th Airborne attack area, 26–28 March 1951 (original map by author, based on maps from the Army Map Service).

MAJ. CHARLES M. HOLLAND, EXECUTIVE OFFICER, 1ST BAT-TALION: On 26 March at 0700 hours the 1st Battalion, under supporting fires from the 674th Airborne Field Artillery Battalion and the 81mm and 60mm mortars of the 1st Battalion, jumped off in the attack. Two reinforced squads from the 3d Platoon of Company A took Hill 203 unopposed. The 3d Platoon of Company A remained on the hill to secure the left flank of the battalion attack. The 1st Battalion fought an all day firefight from 0700 to 1500 for Hill 178. Companies B and C attacked, and the remainder of Company A was in reserve.[1]

CAPT. DANIEL L. MELVIN, COMPANY C COMMANDER: At 0500 hours the morning of 26 March, Company C moved out to the 1st Battalion assembly area in the vicinity of Hill 203. The 1st Battalion attacked east with Company C on the left flank. The 2d Platoon sent a combat patrol to a knob just east of Hill 203. The final objective of the company was Hill 96 and a knoll [about 400 meters to the north]. At 1000 hours, using the knob for setting up a base of fire, one platoon moved across a rice paddy. They encountered small-arms fire from enemy on Hill 178, and one man was killed. The platoon continued to the knoll and got a toehold. The 2d Platoon, on the right, requested a base of fire on the final objective. At 1130 hours they charged the ridge, killing three enemy, two by hand grenades and one by bayoneting.[2]

MAJOR HOLLAND: Company C received mortar and small-arms fire from Hill 178 and from the spur between Hill 96 and Hill 178. On Hill 96, the company was led by Master Sergeant Kropka in a bayonet charge on fifty to sixty enemy armed with automatic rifles, carbines, U.S. light machine guns, and hand grenades. Twenty enemy were killed. Company C was supported by air and artillery that fired on the enemy on Hill 178, who stubbornly refused to leave the hill. I estimate that two battalions of Chinese held Hill 178 and the adjacent terrain.[3]

CAPT. ROLLAND A. DESSERT, COMPANY D COMMANDER: The 1st section [of machine guns] started 26 March in general support of the battalion attack on the north and northwest approaches to Hill 228. At 1200, the section was attached to Company C in close support of its attack. The resistance was moderate to determined, with an estimated thirty enemy killed and fifteen wounded. Fifteen thousand rounds were fired. Two men in the 1st section were wounded.[4]

PFC MILTON EISENHAUER, RIFLEMAN, 1ST PLATOON, COMPANY C: On 26 March, Company C was ordered to take Hill 148 West. At 1630 hours the platoon was pinned down. The 2d and 3d Squads, with two machine guns from the heavy-weapons squad, were to take the hill by going around the flank. The enemy on top of the hill were throwing grenades, and when I saw one enemy soldier stand up twenty-five feet away, I shot him with my M-1. The wounded enemy tried to crawl away. This was noticed by my squad leader, Sergeant Fox, who pointed his thumb downward and said, "Stick 'im." I bayoneted him in the shoulder blades, took out the bayonet, pushed the still moaning enemy over, and bayoneted him twice in the stomach, killing him.[5]

With enemy fire from Hill 178 hitting the flank of the 1st Battalion, the 2d Battalion was directed to attack and clear the enemy from this sector. Meanwhile, the 1st Battalion continued its attack to the east with Company B taking up the lead in an attack on Hill 148 West, some 1,200 meters east of Hill 96. Members of Company B and the 1st Battalion describe the action.

SGT. WALTER E. CHANEY, 3D PLATOON SERGEANT, COMPANY B: We moved out at 0600 hours to the northeast with the objective of Hill 148 West. There was little resistance in the attack, with five or six rounds of 105mm SP fire but no casualties. Company C to the left was having a rough go; Company A was in reserve.

SGT. ROBERT J. WOTHERSPOON, SQUAD LEADER, 1ST PLATOON, COMPANY B: The 1st Platoon took two prisoners, one of whom was wounded, in a small town; the platoon also killed three enemy as we moved toward Hill 148 West. In the foothills we discovered two more who got away.

MAJ. HOLLAND, EXECUTIVE OFFICER, 1ST BATTALION: Company B jumped off, moving to Hill 148 West. They received scattered enemy fire and killed twelve enemy. They drove the remainder from Hill 148 West and secured it during the afternoon.[6]

CAPT. ROLLAND A. DESSERT, COMPANY D COMMANDER:The 2d section [of machine guns] became attached to Company B at 1230 hours with the mission of closely supporting Company B. Resistance was light to moderate, with five enemy killed, ten wounded, and nine thousand rounds fired. No friendly casualties were incurred by the 2d section.[7]

Although opposition was light and Company B did not suffer greatly from flanking fire from Hill 178, Hill 148 West was not secured until 1530 hours. While Company B attacked to the east, Company F of the 2d Battalion moved north from its reserve position and began its attack on Hill 178. Members of the 2d Battalion and of Company F describe the action.

1ST LT. SAMUEL P. MUSE, COMPANY F COMMANDER: On 26 March, Company F was in position about 600 yards northeast of Parun-ni. At 1200 hours we were ordered to move out and occupy Hill 178. Enemy strength on the hill was unknown. At 1330 hours Company F moved north to the south finger of Hill 178. Upon arrival on the finger, the company deployed to the left, the 2d and 3d

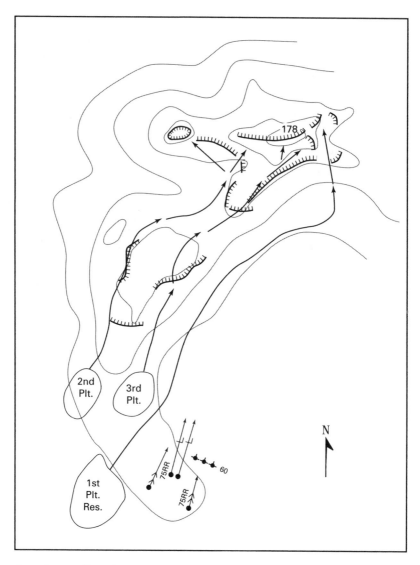

Assault on Hill 178 by Company F, 187th Airborne Regimental Combat Team, 26 March 1951 (sketch based on 1st Lt. Roberts interview in CMH manuscript, U. S. Army; not to scale).

Platoons abreast with a 57mm recoilless rifle with each platoon. The 60mm mortars were in position with the 1st Platoon near the finger. Lieutenant Von Steigel, the artillery observer, was only able to fire one battery concentration, since the 2d and 3d Battalions had priority of fire. The 81mm-mortar observer, however, was with the company and prepared to fire.

The first bunkers were hit by the 3d Platoon. The 2d Platoon moved a little farther up the hill, and the 1st Platoon came up alongside the 3d Platoon. A message from a liaison plane informed me that the enemy was digging in on the reverse slope of Hill 178. At 1715 hours, a platoon of Company G led by Lieutenant Epps came over and moved up a draw. It helped mop up the top. By 1730 hours the top of Hill 178 was controlled, and the hill was cleared by 1830 hours.[8]

1ST LT. DONALD L. ROBERTS, COMPANY F: On the night of 25 March Lieutenant Muse became company commander, and I became executive officer. We were the only two officers remaining in the company. At 1200 hours on 26 March, Company F was alerted to attack Hill 178 and was reinforced with the 75mm recoilless-rifle section and a machine-gun section, both from Company H. At 1230 the approach march to Hill 178 began; the company moved north from Parun-ni and deployed. A base of fire was set up on a line about 1,000 meters southwest of Hill 178. Two platoons made the assault, with one in reserve with the 60mm mortars. At 1330 the enemy was contacted about 800 meters southwest of Hill 178, in strength estimated as a reinforced company and well dug in. Company F advanced using hand grenades and bayonets. At 1500 hours, about halfway up the hill, we ran out of hand grenades. A heavy enemy fire came in on the left. The 1st Platoon that was in reserve was now committed on the right flank; the 3d Platoon was now in the center, and the 2d Platoon was on the left. At 1600 hours a resupply of ammunition and hand grenades came up, and the liaison plane dropped a message that an estimated hundred enemy were dug in on the reverse slope of Hill 178. Despite grenades that were hurled over the crest by the enemy, Company F continued the attack. At 1730 hours a bayonet assault cleared the left flank.[9]

SFC MANUEL M. GARZA, ASSISTANT PLATOON SERGEANT, 1ST PLATOON, COMPANY F: During Company F's attack on Hill 178, I was back with the 60mm mortars, which were moved forward to the right knoll when the 1st and 3d Platoons assaulted the high knoll. The 1st Platoon moved up on the right of the 2d Platoon, reaching the high ground and observing the enemy moving back. At 1245 hours the enemy counterattacked with hand grenades, forcing the 1st Platoon, lacking sufficient manpower, to withdraw. At 1315 hours the 1st Platoon reorganized and was resupplied with ammunition. At this time the Chinese sounded horns and began a banzai attack. The 1st Platoon then hollered, "airborne," and counterattacked.[10]

M. SGT. ELBERT V. RITCH, 3D PLATOON SERGEANT, COMPANY F: The 3d Platoon on the right hit the first bunkers, moving up to the right of the draw and drawing fire from the draw and ridgeline. At 1600 hours an estimated fifty to a hundred well-dug-in enemy were encountered, and the 3d Platoon pulled up ahead of the 2d Platoon. The 1st Platoon with Sergeant Lindsey was coming up on the east side of the hill. By direct assault, the 3d Platoon rooted the enemy out of their holes, overrunning their position. Between 1700 and 1730 hours the horseshoe-shaped top was secured.[11]

SFC TROY U. GILLEY, ASSISTANT PLATOON SERGEANT, 3D PLATOON, COMPANY F: As Master Sergeant Ritch moved up Hill 178, I moved back and brought up a machine gun into the draw where enemy were still left. On the first knoll I set up the machine gun and placed fire on Hill 178.[12]

SFC RAYMOND MORRIS, 2D PLATOON SERGEANT, COMPANY F: At 1730 hours the 2d Platoon made a bayonet charge on the enemy. The 1st and 3d Squads gained the saddle to the next ridgeline that was the top of the hill. Here I pulled out a machine gun and, with the 2d Squad, lay down a base of fire and started to move up in the rear of the 1st and 3d Squads. An enemy machine gun that had been bypassed opened up on my men and me and scattered us over the slope. I reorganized the squad, and three men from it knocked out the machine-gun nest, killing six, one of whom was bayoneted. In the meantime, the men were running low on ammunition and hand grenades. I set up supporting machine-gun and small-arms fire on the first ridge and sent the 57mm recoilless rifle, with ammunition and hand grenades carried by the weapons platoon, up to the 1st and 3d Squads. A defensive perimeter was then organized on the hill, and the friendly wounded and killed were evacuated. The rest of the platoon assaulted the left half of the high nose and gained the crest by means of hand grenades.[13]

1ST LT. RUDY V. PARAISO, ARTILLERY FORWARD OBSERVER WITH COMPANY E, BATTERY B, 674TH AIRBORNE FIELD ARTILLERY BATTALION: In the afternoon of 26 March the 2d Battalion assaulted Hill 178, and I fired on the ridges and reverse slope of the hill. At 1600 hours P-51s hit the hill in an air strike. Company F then went up the hill, facing light opposition until enemy fire caused a withdrawal. The artillery forward observer with Company F fired on the slope at 1600 hours. At 1830 hours Company F secured the hill.[14]

1ST LT. DONALD L. ROBERTS, COMPANY F: By 1800 hours Company F had reached the crest; mopping up continued until 1930 hours. The position was then consolidated using enemy entrenchments, tying in with Company G on the left [west]. On the right [southeast] there was a 1,000-yard gap covered by artillery and mortar fire. On the other side of the gap was Company E. Casualties for Company F were one killed and six wounded in action. I estimate we killed 150 enemy and wounded another 100.[15]

About the same time that Company F moved north to attack Hill 178, the 3d Battalion moved up on line south of the 1st Battalion and began its attack on Hill 228. Members of the 3d Battalion describe the initial advance and the beginning of the attack.

1ST LT. WARD C. GOESSLING, ARTILLERY LIAISON OFFICER FROM THE 3D BATTALION, 674TH AIRBORNE FIELD ARTILLERY BATTALION: At 0800 hours on 26 March, Companies I and L moved to ridges 500 yards east of Parun-ni to support the attack of the 1st Battalion. Between 1030 and 1100 hours, Companies I and L moved again and discovered that the enemy to their front had fled. Patrols were sent out. Hill 228 was now being approached. It was the original plan for the 1st Battalion to attack up the north side while the 3d Battalion stormed the south side. Unfortunately Lieutenant Colonel Munson, the 3d Battalion commander, found the southern approaches to Hill 228 too steep. He received permission to follow the 1st Battalion on the north side.[16]

SGT. CHARLES P. MCDONALD, 3D BATTALION OPERATIONS SERGEANT: On 26 March I went with the 3d Battalion command group to observe the attack, leaving the CP at 0900 hours and arriving at Company I on the LD at 1100 hours. The command group consisted of Colonel Munson; Major Speirs, the S-3; the sergeant major; the Company M commander; the artillery liaison officer; the FAC party; and myself. Between 0900 and 1100 hours two air strikes occurred on Hill 228. Company I pushed east from the ridge, and Company L pushed off just north of the road leading east from Parun-ni. The battalion command group moved through Sambihari to a little knoll just east of the town where we could observe the battalion reach the initial objective, which was a ridgeline about 1,200 yards to the east. The attack jumped off at 1200 hours. Company I moved up and was halted because of an air strike 150 yards to their front. Company L was not fired on and moved to the right position of the objective. At 1230 hours the command group moved forward. Company I came under fire but reached the ridgeline at 1300 hours and reorganized in order to be able to attack Hill 228. At 1415 hours the command group joined Company I. Company A took up positions on the ridgeline in Company I's area to support the Company I attack. Company L remained in the same location.[17]

As mentioned, elements of the 1st Battalion moved forward to support Company I's attack on Hill 228. Members of the unit describe their actions.

CAPT. ROBERT A. CHABOT, COMPANY A COMMANDER: The rest of Company A [one platoon was left on Hill 203] moved out at 0930 as 1st Battalion reserve. We moved to the vicinity of Hill 148 West, and at 1330 hours received the mission of securing the northern finger ridge of Hill 228 facing toward Sonam-ni. This ridge was taken despite enemy small-arms fire, automatic-weapons fire, and a few mortar rounds. At 1630 hours Company I passed through Company A and assaulted Hill 228 with Company A furnishing a base of fire.[18]

CAPT. ROLLAND A. DESSERT, COMPANY D COMMANDER: The 75mm recoilless rifle section, besides firing in support of the battalion attack, three times marked the extremities of air strike targets for friendly aircraft; it was a matter of two to three minutes to mark a target. At 1400 hours the section fired on point targets on the northern slopes of Hill 228 in support of the 3d Battalion. A total of 75 rounds was expended for the day. The 81mm Mortar Platoon was in general support of the 1st Battalion assault on Hill 228. It displaced later in the day by sections to the vicinity of Hill 148 West, closing at 1500 hours. One section was attached to Company B; the other section remained in general support. The estimated enemy casualties were twenty-five killed and forty wounded in action; 395 rounds were fired.[19]

1ST LT. JESMOND D. BALMER, ARTILLERY FORWARD OBSERVER, BATTERY A, 674TH AIRBORNE FIELD ARTILLERY BATTALION: On 26 March Company A occupied Hill 203, and the 1st Battalion moved in the early afternoon onto Hill 101; the regimental objective was Hill 228, which was attacked at 1500 hours. Air strikes occurred all during the day. The 3d Battalion was to attack Hill 228 from the south with the 2d Battalion in reserve. I could observe enemy activity throughout the day. While the 3d Battalion went up Hill 228, a company attacked Hill 178, and Company B fought its way up Hill 148 West. I fired 500 rounds, fuze delay and quick, WP, while working with Company I's artillery observer on Hill 228. At 1600 hours a 105mm shell hit a trench on Hill 228 in which there were ten to twelve enemy. I saw arms and legs flying into the air. Company A gave a cheer.[20]

After air strikes had softened up the enemy positions, and with fire support in place from the 1st Battalion, Company I began its attack on Hill 228. The executive officer of Company I, 1st Lt. Edward C. Radcliff, who prepared a report on the action, describes what happened.

The company commander received verbal orders about 1400 hours from the battalion commander regarding the mission to secure Hill 228. The 3d Battalion was so engaged or deployed that Company I was the nearest and most logical company to go. The best approach was pointed out to the company commander; air observation reported 400 or more enemy troops dug in on Hill 228. Company I moved about 1500 hours to a position near the base of Hill 228 being held by Company A. This position was on the west of Hill 228 and had very good observation and good potential for use of supporting fire. As we reached Company A's position, we were notified that an air strike had just been called, and we had to wait. The company commander used the time to make a reconnaissance and estimate of the situation. The decision was as follows: to make use of a ridgeline running north and south parallel to and about a hundred yards from the base of Hill 228 as the line of departure. Deploying the 3d Platoon along this ridge, the 1st Platoon was to move directly to the north base of Hill 228.

As expected, when the 1st Platoon started across the rice paddies they received small-arms fire. The 3d Platoon on the ridgeline was immediately ordered to fire covering fire on the enemy in support of the 1st Platoon. The 2d Platoon was ordered to deploy in place of the 3d Platoon as the 1st Platoon reached a defilade position at the base of Hill 228. The procedure was repeated while the 3d Platoon crossed over to Hill 228. By this time the 1st Platoon was in the process of clearing out their assigned sector on Hill 228. The 3d Platoon deployed abreast of and to the right of the 1st Platoon. Both platoons were ordered to move toward the top of Hill 228. The 2d Platoon was instructed to follow the two leading platoons by about 100 to 150 yards, checking each and every foxhole or dug-in position to ascertain that no enemy had been bypassed.

The leading platoons encountered well-dug-in enemy determined to hold their positions. The enemy were well armed with large numbers of hand grenades, which they used freely, at times causing the platoons to halt the advance. It was found that by mutual support and the use of enveloping moves the enemy positions could be outflanked individually and neutralized. It was further noted that by having one platoon fire across the front of the other, an almost continuous though slow advance could be maintained. Where the terrain demanded, all three platoons were deployed on line, though not often. It was also noted that the enemy was reluctant to hold when our men moved in aggressively with bayonets fixed. Due to the difficulty in routing the enemy and the steepness of the hillside, the men tired considerably. At times the platoons had to be leapfrogged.

Because of the type of dug-in positions, it was found that the air strikes had not bothered the enemy at all, and unless the enemy was caught in the open, our supporting weapons were of little use. The machine-gun section attached to Company I from Company M was left at the jump-off place to cover with fire the area to the front and right of the company as they moved in. Their fire was to cease when the company reached a point just short of the top. The 4.2-inch mortars were called on to fire on the reverse side of Hill 228, as the company was receiving mortar fire from that side. Not being able to actually see the enemy mortar position, our 4.2-inch mortar fire could not be properly adjusted and was of little or no avail.

As the clearing of the hill progressed, the company's ammunition dwindled to almost nothing, and we had to rely more and more on the bayonet. Just short of the top, at approximately 1800 hours, the ammunition was all expended, and the company was finally forced to halt the advance. At approximately 1815 hours, Company K moved into the rear of Company I, and a perimeter was set up by the two companies for the night. In this attack at least eighty enemy were killed and ten captured. Company I suffered seven killed and thirty-nine wounded.[21]

Members of Company I provide more details of the attack.
CAPT. NICK GARCIA, COMPANY I COMMANDER: On 26 March, Company I attacked Hill 228. Because of the failure of radios I was forced to run from platoon to platoon in directing the action. The Chinese made good use of reverse-slope defense and holes in draws and on each of the succeeding ridges. Company I used a maneuver of two teams in the attack, one attacking frontally while the other enveloped the holes. WP hand grenades were found to be more effective than fragmentation because the L-type opening of the Chinese holes protected them from fragmentation.[22]

2D LT. MELVIN C. STRAWSER, 1ST PLATOON LEADER, COMPANY I: The company jumped off across level ground at 1630 hours and captured three enemy in the first two hundred yards. An air strike on Hill 228 delayed the attack, which finally started with the 1st Platoon on the left supporting the 3d Platoon and crossing rice paddies. The 1st Platoon, moving on the flank, killed twenty enemy, captured ten, and made contact with the 3d Platoon. While I awaited the return of Sergeant Charles from clearing the ridge to the left, one enemy who was supposedly dead raised up to throw a hand grenade. I shot him in the head. He again attempted to rise up, and Master Sergeant Perkins shot him with his automatic carbine. Captain Garcia, the company commander, then ordered the 1st Platoon to pass through the 3d Platoon and attack the next ridge. Here the 1st and 2d Platoons became engaged in a hand-grenade duel with forty to fifty enemy. When the enemy counterattacked, the platoon was short of ammunition so it withdrew to the next ridge to the rear. Shortly after the withdrawal we noticed that Master Sergeant Peterson, who had been wounded, was left behind. Sergeant Perkins and Sergeant Hutton went back and got him. That night at 1900 hours Company K came up and joined Company I, replenishing Company I's ammunition. On the hill the 1st Platoon lost two killed and three wounded in action.[23]

M. SGT. NEAL A. PERKINS, 1ST PLATOON SERGEANT, COMPANY I: On 26 March, Company I proceeded into Sambiha-ri at 1400 hours and took as prisoner fifteen to twenty men wearing civilian clothes. At 1600 hours, with two hours of daylight left, Company I attacked Hill 228. The Air Force had reported five hundred enemy on the reverse (east) slope of Hill 228. At a whistle signal, with the 1st Platoon on the left, the 3d Platoon on the right, and the 2d Platoon in reserve, Company I attacked. Sergeant Charles led out for the 1st Platoon, and Sergeant Wisenbacker led out for the 3d Platoon. We crossed two hundred yards of open ground to the base of Hill 228. Minimum resistance was met for forty-five minutes until dug-in positions were hit. Here C-2 was used to blow in holes, and the company continued steadily to advance. Just before dark a hand-grenade fight ensued, with Lieutenant Strawser firing on the hand grenade–throwing enemy. One enemy was killed, one withdrew, and three were captured. I took an interpreter to nearby holes and came back with four prisoners. While guarding the prisoners, Lieutenant Strawser saw one reach for a hand grenade. Strawser shot him through the left ear. The prisoner fell forward, but five minutes later he rose up again to throw another grenade. I then fired ten rounds into the prisoner's head with my automatic carbine. The prisoner continued to live for ten minutes.

Continuing the advance to the next ridge, we met stiff resistance. Sergeant Peterson of the 2d Platoon was wounded. The firefight continued for forty-five minutes until finally Company I ran low on ammunition. All during the firefight hand grenades were thrown back and forth in a twenty-yard radius. The 1st Platoon had half a belt of machine-gun bullets, one to four clips of ammunition per rifleman, and little BAR ammunition when, at dusk, about 150 enemy counterattacked. The ammunition was fired and hand grenades were thrown. In the melee I lost contact with Lieutenant Strawser for a time. I then got together with the lieutenant and Sergeant Wisenbacker and we planned a withdrawal to the next ridge behind us. At this time we saw Company K moving up. Later, a lieutenant from Company K said that a defense would be set up on the next ridge back. Under a smoke screen of WP and smoke, Company I withdrew. The withdrawal was covered by Lieutenant Strawser with a machine-gun squad. An enemy mortar, which was an American 81mm, fired from the top of the hill on us during the withdrawal. Company K took over the defense, and Company I reorganized for the night.[24]

1st Lt. James J. Coghlan, artillery forward observer with Company I, Battery C, 674th Airborne Field Artillery Battalion: At 1600 hours Company I began an attack up the northeast slope of Hill 228, where the forward air controller estimated there were 400 enemy. The 1st Platoon entered a wooden draw where thirty well-dug-in Chinese soldiers were drawn up like a human minefield. At 1700 hours Captain Garcia sent platoons to the left and right sides of the draw to flank them. From my position I lacked observation, so Lieutenant Balmer with Company A fired in support of the attack, bringing rounds in as close as thirty-five yards to friendly troops. One platoon of Company I was stopped by Chinese throwing grenades in volleys. Company K passed through Company I and established a perimeter on the northern slope.[25]

SFC James E. Hoeh, mortar observer with Company I, Company M: On 26 March, I was assigned to Company I. We moved out at 1000 hours and attacked a ridgeline with no opposition. I moved later to a ridge where Company I awaited orders to begin the assault on Hill 228. Air strikes early that afternoon softened up the hill for the attack that began at 1600 hours. I remained behind with a machine-gun section and set up an OP. I fired 120 rounds of 81mm mortar. Targets included bunkers, trenches, and thirty to forty enemy moving on top of Hill 228. At 1930 hours I went forward at the request of the Company I commander. During the night the 4.2-inch mortars supported Company I. Company K joined Company I in a night perimeter on the northwest side of Hill 228.[26]

During the attack of Company I on Hill 228, one soldier, M. Sgt. Clarence A. Peterson, the platoon sergeant of the 2d Platoon, was conspicuous in his heroic leadership. Eyewitnesses describe his actions in their recommendations for award of the Distinguished Service Cross.[27]

CAPTAIN GARCIA, COMPANY I COMMANDER: On 26 March, Company I began an assault on Hill 228. There was an estimated enemy battalion emplaced in well-concealed bunkers, trenches, and foxholes, delivering an intense volume of small-arms, automatic-weapons, and mortar fire. As the 2d Platoon, of which Master Sergeant Peterson was a member, began the assault across open terrain, the platoon leader and four key NCOs were wounded and rendered helpless. The platoon was already one squad understrength due to previous casualties, and Sergeant Peterson, realizing the dire predicament of the platoon, immediately moved to a commanding position in the front, reorganized his men, and continued the assault. As the platoon advanced they were constantly within grenade range of the enemy, and friendly casualties mounted. But Sergeant Peterson showed such heroic courage that the men followed his orders without question. During the entire attack, Sergeant Peterson was continuously exposed to intense enemy fire, but disdained the thought of safety in favor of helping his comrades. He had been wounded the previous day but refused to be evacuated because his platoon was already understrength. At one point in the assault an enemy machine gun, manned by five Chinese soldiers, opened fire and pinned the platoon down. Disregarding his own personal safety, Sergeant Peterson crawled to a position twenty yards from the machine gun, and from that point, armed only with a carbine and a trench knife, he assaulted the enemy position, killing the five enemy soldiers. This act permitted his platoon and the platoon on the left flank to continue the assault with a minimum of casualties. Just after knocking out the enemy machine gun, Sergeant Peterson was fatally wounded by enemy small-arms fire and died one hour later.

LIEUTENANT MACKLEY, 2D PLATOON LEADER, COMPANY I: At approximately 1600 hours on 26 March, Company I jumped off in the attack on Hill 228. As my platoon moved forward across open terrain to the base of the hill, we received an intense amount of small-arms and mortar fire from a deeply entrenched enemy force of battalion size. My platoon was already one rifle squad understrength due to previous casualties. On the initial burst of fire from the enemy, four key NCOs and I were hit and rendered helpless. Sergeant Peterson, realizing the grave situation, moved forward in front of the remainder of the platoon and directed the attack so skillfully that the platoon moved forward as if they had not suffered any casualties. At one point in the attack the platoon was held up by a machine-gun nest, which pinned everybody down. Sergeant Peterson maneuvered within twenty yards of the emplacement and then charged it armed only with a carbine and a trench knife. He destroyed the machine gun and killed the five Chinese soldiers operating the gun. Though Sergeant Peterson had been wounded the previous day he refused to be evacuated due to the fact that his platoon was so much understrength. Throughout this attack and all previous missions that I have worked with Master Sergeant Peterson, he has always been an inspiration to the men by performing extraordinary acts of heroism above and beyond the call of duty.

PVT. JOHN C. MARTIN, WEAPONS SQUAD LEADER, COMPANY A: On 26 March, I was squad leader of the weapons squad, 1st Platoon, Able Company, and we were on the reverse slope of the hill mass 700 yards west of Hill 228. Our mission was to give supporting fire to Company I as they moved around the base of the hill on our left flank and thence into the assault. At approximately 1600 hours, Company I moved into the attack, and I started designating targets for my men. The enemy was emplaced in bunkers, trenches, and well-concealed foxholes and was practically invisible to the men of Company I until they were within hand grenade range. From the beginning of the assault all the way to the top of the hill, the battle was a visible duel of hand grenades. I realized that if we could keep the enemy pinned down, Company I would attain their objective with a minimum of casualties. To obtain that result I used field glasses, spotting and firing on heavy enemy troop concentrations. Eventually the enemy remained completely under cover until Company I came within hand grenade range of each individual soldier.

I ordered my men to continue their firing at a safe distance to the front of our own troops and procured a rifle with a scope. I began systematically picking off enemy soldiers who were within grenade range of Company I, and while doing this I noticed one friendly soldier who was constantly in front of the rest of the men. I could tell by his arm motions that he was leading the platoon. I later learned that it was Master Sergeant Peterson. During the continuing attack, I gave Sergeant Peterson individual support as close as ten yards, because in some cases cover was good and he could not see the enemy soldiers lying in wait for him. I particularly noticed that he always remained to the extreme front of his platoon and grenades were constantly exploding near him. Time after time I saw him expose himself to enemy fire when I could see the bullets kicking up dirt around him. At one time he went behind cover and did not reappear, so I knew that he had been hit. I have never seen such a gallant display of courage and devotion to duty, and his show of leadership was something that few men have the courage or initiative to attain.

Other members of the 3d Battalion describe Company I's fight as they observed it, and the advance of Company K.

SGT. CHARLES P. MCDONALD, 3D BATTALION OPERATIONS SERGEANT: At 1620 hours, Company I started up the northwest slope of Hill 228, taking advantage of the hill mask and following the ridgeline. The 3d Battalion control group joined the 81mm Mortar Platoon of Company M. I saw Chinese firing from Hill 228; mortar rounds were bursting on the hill; friendly and enemy soldiers were throwing hand grenades, and friendly soldiers were using the bayonet. At 1800 hours, Company I stopped near the top, and the battalion commander ordered Company K forward. At dark the battalion commander ordered Company K to make a perimeter with Company I, button up, and spend the night. During the night Company A shot 60mm illuminating shell on Hill 228, and Company L moved north of Company K.[28]

CAPT. JOHN E. STREVER, COMPANY K COMMANDER: On 26 March Companies I and L supported the 1st Battalion's attack with Company K in reserve. Company K was to go on line at the regimental intermediate objective. Company L took up positions on the high ground; Company I moved off in the attack, and Company K followed behind Company I. Company I got into a battle for Hill 228, and at 1730 hours I received the order to advance and assist Company I. Company K advanced to the northwest slope of Hill 228. At that time Company I was suffering quite a few casualties, and therefore, after a conference with Captain Garcia, the Company I commander, it was decided to move Company K up. Company I at the same time withdrew and reorganized, having its ammunition replenished by Company K. Both companies jointly set up a perimeter and combined their 60mm mortars. Intense enemy small-arms and light-mortar rounds fell in the perimeter, killing one man. Radio reception was very difficult on Hill 228. Control of the left flank was maintained by hollering. On the night of 26 March, patrols were sent out, and although enemy movement was heard, no contact was made.[29]

Lieutenant Radcliff, the executive officer of Company I, evaluates his company's attack.

In this action, the following points were found to hamper the success of the attack: (a) the attack was delayed too long, and darkness closed in too quickly; (b) communications went out between the company commander and the platoons due to dead batteries and badly jarred radios from the jump; (c) there were incorrect reports from friendly forces—the base of the hill was reported cleared of the enemy; (d) resupply of ammunition was not quick enough; when it did arrive it was dropped at the base of the hill, and nobody was notified of its location.

The following points were executed by the attacking unit to aid the success of accomplishing their mission: (a) use of basic principles of fire and maneuver, down to and including the rifle squad; (b) use of supporting fire as much as possible; (c) aggressiveness on the part of each individual, especially with the bayonet.[30]

On 26 March determined enemy resistance had again prevented the 187th Airborne RCT from cutting the Uijongbu road and trapping the Chinese. Elements of the 187th and the 3d Infantry Division made contact in the afternoon, and the supply situation brightened considerably, as described by the artillery battalion commander, Lt. Col. Harry F. Lambert.

Because of the rainfall of 25 March, the road back to the DZ [near Munsan-ni] was impassable for the ammunition train. A heavy drop on the west end of the battalion position brought the ammunition at 1700 hours. The commanding general of the 3d Division loaned the 674th Airborne Field Artillery Battalion 2,000 rounds of ammunition, and the heavy drop supplied 1,000 more. Fire missions on the west side of the Uijongbu road included Hills 299, 322, and 507.[31]

That night the Chinese struck back with an attempt to recapture Hill 178, which had caused so many problems during the attack to the east against Hill 228. Company F had ended the day in possession of Hill 178, and members of the unit describe the enemy night attack.

1ST LT. DONALD L. ROBERTS, 2D PLATOON LEADER, COMPANY F: At 0130 hours on 27 March the enemy counterattacked Hill 178, slipping up to within ten feet of the Company F perimeter without being discovered. The enemy used hand grenades and a 150mm mortar for firepower. The 1st and 3d Platoons on the right flank of Hill 178 were forced to withdraw to the crest at 0200 hours. Company F held at the crest, and was reinforced by a platoon from Company G at 0230 hours. A platoon from Company E, which had come to help, was returned without being used. At 0300 the enemy started to withdraw, and at 0330 hours the lost ground was secured. Company F's casualties were one killed and ten wounded in action; Company H had four wounded in action. The enemy lost fifty killed and an estimated fifty wounded, which were removed by the enemy.[32]

M. Sgt. Elbert V. Ritch, 3d Platoon sergeant, Company F: At 0045 hours on 27 March the enemy counterattacked Hill 178 and overran a Company H machine gun. At 0200 hours the 3d Platoon withdrew to the south side of the top of the hill. Between 0400 and 0415 Company F, with the 1st Platoon on the right and the 3d Platoon on the left, counterattacked and restored the original position. During the fighting the artillery observer fired defensive concentrations, with the 155mm howitzers firing; the 81mm mortars from Company H fired close in.[33]

1st Lt. Rudy V. Paraiso, artillery forward observer with Company E, Battery B, 674th Airborne Field Artillery Battalion: At 0200 hours in the morning of 27 March the enemy counterattacked on the east side of the knoll, cutting along the draw. I fired a fire mission of 205 rounds on the draw at 0220 hours and reported the enemy neutralized. From the draw I heard sounds of bugles, and I saw one red, one green, and three white flares. A platoon was sent from Company E to help out Company F, and the enemy was repulsed. At daylight I accompanied a patrol under Lieutenant Dolan, 1st Platoon, Company E, which moved to observe the ridgeline to the north. Civilians reported that just before daybreak an estimated 500 enemy, carrying 250 killed and wounded in action, withdrew to the north. The dead bodies were carried on sticks.[34]

Cutting the Uijongbu Road, 27 March

On the morning of 27 March, patrols from the 2d Battalion indicated that the enemy threat on the northern flank was reduced. The attack to the east was to continue. Soon after dawn, the 3d Battalion, with Company K in the lead, resumed its advance up Hill 228. Members of the battalion describe what happened.

Capt. John E. Strever, Company K commander: At 0715 hours on 27 March, a fifteen-minute artillery preparation was fired. Company K jumped off with two platoons abreast. The left platoon moved forward and set up a base of fire; the reserve platoon leapfrogged through. No enemy were found on the hill, although a WP booby trap exploded, injuring one friendly soldier seriously and five lightly. One wounded enemy soldier was taken prisoner and interrogated. He told me that the enemy officers left Hill 228 on the night of 26 March. The men then buried the dead, hauled off the wounded, and abandoned the hill. Company L then came up and occupied the north slope of Hill 228. Company K occupied the south slope. After I looked at the terrain, I believe it would have been impossible to have successfully assaulted the south slope of Hill 228.[35]

SGT. CHARLES P. McDONALD, 3D BATTALION OPERATIONS SERGEANT: At 0810 hours, Company K moved up Hill 228 without resistance, finding that the Chinese had pulled out during the night. Hill 228 was honeycombed with tunnels and trenches. At 0835 hours Company L moved to consolidate with Company K, while Company I remained in reserve. I stayed on Hill 228 throughout the day.[36]

An aerial resupply of small-arms ammunition was received at 0830 hours, and the rifle companies were replenished. Meanwhile, reports of enemy activity were received. 1st Lt. William L. Clark, air observer for the 674th Airborne Field Artillery Battalion, describes what he saw.

At 0900 hours on 27 March my L-5 flew the ridgelines of Hills 299, 507, and 519. Here, enemy soldiers were occupying foxholes, and heavy small-arms fire was directed at the airplane. At 1100 hours Colonel Lambert [the artillery battalion commander] reported enemy artillery fire landing on Hill 228 and coming from an area near Tongduch'on-ni [on the Uijongbu road about 6,000 yards north of Hill 228]. At 1600 hours I observed gun flashes and saw one gun between railroad cars and another gun inside a building. I collaborated with Sergeant Lyles, the Company K forward observer, in firing, and we got a direct hit on the gun between the two railroad cars and caved in the building. When the building caved in, I saw two men come out and lay on the ground. Later in the day I fired missions on Hills 507, 519, and 279.[37]

The 1st Battalion was ordered to continue the attack to the east across the Sinch'on River and Uijongbu road to capture Hill 148 East. Members of the battalion describe the action.

Maj. Charles M. Holland, 1st Battalion executive officer: On the morning of 27 March, Company B jumped off at 0930 hours for Hill 148 East under supporting artillery and mortar fire. They had secured the objective by 1200 hours. Two enemy mortars were destroyed, about twenty enemy were killed, and three were captured. Company B lost six wounded and one killed by small-arms and automatic-weapons fire. During the fighting the battalion commander and I were on an OP on Hill 148 West. At 1000 hours I was given charge of the Sinch'on River crossing. I dispatched the engineer officer to reconnoiter the road. At 1100 hours the battalion commander received the order for the rest of the battalion to cross the Sinch'on. Company A moved from Hill 228 to a spur of Hill 299, taking over that position at 1200 hours. The battalion CP remained west of the river. At 1600 hours the engineer road was completed.[38]

Sgt. Robert J. Wotherspoon, squad leader, 1st Platoon, Company B: The 1st Platoon started toward the hill between 0900 and 1000 hours. Halfway out in the Sinch'on River valley, with support from Company D's heavy machine guns, a line was built up about two hundred yards from the hill. A small amount of small-arms fire came in. The company assaulted the hill and consolidated its position. Heavy enemy mortar fire, twenty to thirty rounds, killed one man and wounded two others. Then the company pushed off for the next hill, a twin hill. We received small-arms fire from the foothills. Three men were wounded, one by mortar fire and two by small arms. The company remained there.[39]

Sgt. Walter E. Chaney, 3d Platoon sergeant, Company B: The artillery forward observer was wounded on the second hill. Four 105mm SP guns were picked up north in the valley. The guns fired twenty to thirty rounds at most, scattering their fire at moving targets. Company A followed at 1030 hours across rice paddies in the valley. Five shots from SP guns resulted in no hits. Company A attacked the hill from the south. A section of heavy machine guns from Company D laid down a base of fire for Company A as they moved on their objective.[40]

Sgt. Frederick Conrad, 4.2-inch mortar forward observer with Company B, Support Company: Although there was a small bridge across the Sinch'on, I waded through the waist-deep water at 0920 hours and continued across an open rice paddy. Company B received slight small-arms fire. At 0950 hours I fired a concentration of ten rounds of mixed WP and HE on Hill 148 East. Company B went up the hill at 1000 hours, forcing the enemy to withdraw to high ground to the east. The 1st Mortar Platoon fired about thirty rounds into a hill southeast of Hill 148 East, scoring two hits. I noticed two T-34 tanks firing down the valley from Posan-ni.[41]

CAPT. ROBERT A. CHABOT, COMPANY A COMMANDER: At noon, Company A moved east across the Sinch'on River valley and then south toward Hill 299. At 1530 hours we became engaged with the enemy on a ridgeline leading from Hill 299. At 1730, from positions on Hill 148 East, the 3d Platoon assaulted the ridgeline with the 2d Platoon on the left. The result was a heavy firefight. The enemy had twenty-four killed in action. Company A had three killed and ten wounded in action.[42]

1ST LT. JESMOND D. BALMER, ARTILLERY FORWARD OBSERVER WITH COMPANY A, BATTERY A, 674TH AIRBORNE FIELD ARTILLERY BATTALION: At 0930 hours the order came to secure Hill 299. The 1st Battalion, with Company B leading, forded the Sinch'on at 1000 hours. An SP gun bracketed Company C. Company B headed straight for Hill 148 East. Some artillery rounds fell near the battalion while crossing the stream, but no small-arms fire. As the battalion approached Hill 148 East, it received small-arms fire from the ridgeline. Company A, in attempting to secure the knoll on the south side of Hill 148 East, was halted 500 yards short. Enemy artillery fire came in from the vicinity of Tongduch'on-ni. The knoll was charged at 1400 hours by men of the 1st Battalion with fixed bayonets, screaming and yelling.[43]

CAPT. ROLLAND A. DESSERT, COMPANY D COMMANDER: On 27 March, both machine-gun sections were in general support of the battalion assault across the Sinch'on River spearheaded by Companies A and B. The 2d section displaced across the river at 1130 hours, and from a position on Hill 148 East, it fired support missions for Company A's attack on the high ground southeast of Hill 148 East, killing an estimated forty enemy, wounding fifty-five, and firing 12,000 rounds. The 1st section, attached to Company C, crossed the river with the company at 1730 hours and closed in the Company C perimeter in the vicinity of Hill 148 East at 1830 hours.

At 1000 hours the recoilless-rifle section displaced to a position southeast of Hill 148 West, where it supported the attacks of Companies A and B on Hill 148 East. The section displaced across the Sinch'on River at 1500 hours. In position on Hill 148 East, it went into action against an SP gun, one of a group of four, 6,000 yards to the north. It possibly scored a hit; all four ceased firing and displaced. Two targets were marked for the Air Force.

At 1000 hours the mortar platoon displaced to the southeast side of Hill 148 West and fired on targets in support of the 1st Battalion assault on Hill 148 East. Later, one section displaced to Hill 148 East, closing by 1500 hours; it was attached to Company B. The other section remained in general support. The estimated enemy casualties from mortar fire were forty-five killed and seventy wounded; 595 rounds were fired.[44]

CAPT. THOMAS J. WATKINS, COMPANY M COMMANDER: The 1st Battalion attacked across the Sinch'on River to a ridgeline. In support of the attack, the mortar platoon of Company M fired on enemy emplacements south of the 1st Battalion. After the 1st Battalion secured its objective and attacked south, the mortar platoon continued its support. In the late afternoon the 4.2-inch mortars from the Support Company and the 81mm mortars from Company M worked over the western slope of Hill 299 in preparation for the attack that would occur early on the following morning.[45]

The day's fighting ended with the enemy still holding the hills overlooking the Uijongbu road. Preparations were made to continue the attack on the next day.

Clearing the High Ground, 28 March

The plan of attack for 28 March called for the 1st and 3d Battalions to seize Hills 322 and 299. After these objectives were secured, the regiment would continue the attack to Hills 507 and 519.

The 1st Battalion was to begin the assault. Members of the 1st Battalion describe the action.

MAJ. CHARLES M. HOLLAND, 1ST BATTALION EXECUTIVE OFFICER: On the night of 27–28 March, the order was received that at 0600 hours on 28 March the 1st Battalion would attack from Hill 148 East to Hill 322, and the 3d Battalion would attack from Hill 228 to Hill 299. The 4th Ranger Company was attached, with the mission of protecting the 1st Battalion aid station [about 500 yards northeast of Hill 148 West].

At 0545 hours I joined the 1st Battalion commander. The 1st Battalion, with Company B leading, jumped off at 0600 hours for Hill 322. Seven tanks from the 65th Regimental Combat Team [3d Infantry Division] fired in support from a draw [about 500 yards northeast of Hill 148 East]. Company B encountered strong resistance from small arms, automatic weapons, and mortars from the left flank and left rear as it closed in hand-to-hand combat. Company C attacked the ridge to the right of Company B and assisted Company B in a nip-and-tuck fight. With assistance from air strikes and artillery from the 3d Division and the 674th Airborne Field Artillery Battalion, Company B secured Hill 322. There was much enemy small-arms and mortar fire coming from Hills 279 and 166.[46]

SGT. HOWARD HOUSTON, 1ST BATTALION INTELLIGENCE SERGEANT: On 28 March the 1st Battalion commander and S-2 estimated there were between 100 and 150 enemy on Hill 299. A former ROK army captain, who had been bypassed in the breakthrough and was hiding out at Songna-ri [just south of Hill 148 East], reported through an interpreter that approximately a regiment was on Hill 299. The enemy were only 25 percent armed, having a varied assortment of Russian, Japanese, and American weapons, and a large number of them were wounded. For messing, the enemy came off the hill at night to a village at the base of the hill where they cooked and ate their meals.[47]

1ST LT. JESMOND D. BALMER, ARTILLERY FORWARD OBSERVER WITH COMPANY A, BATTERY A, 674TH AIRBORNE FIELD ARTILLERY BATTALION: On the night of 27 March the base of Hill 299 was lit up every thirty minutes by 155mm illuminating shell. This lit up an enemy counterattack at 2000 hours, which was broken up by the 81mm mortars and artillery fire. At 0500 hours on 28 March an artillery preparation of 3,000 rounds, including support from the 3d Division, was fired on Hills 299, 507, 519, and 322. After the preparation, Company A climbed Hill 299, after which it went into reserve.[48]

1ST LT. JAMES E. HANLIN, 3D PLATOON LEADER, COMPANY B: At 0600 hours on 28 March the 2d Platoon of Company B, supported by the 3d Platoon, moved to the northeast, to the approaches to Hill 322, where they attacked. At 1115 hours the 3d Platoon attacked around the right flank of the 2d Platoon. We moved to the crest and tied in with Company C.[49]

SFC WILLIAM L. DUMAS, ASSISTANT PLATOON SERGEANT, 2D PLATOON, COMPANY B: On 28 March Company B attacked Hill 322. On a spur leading up the hill an enemy machine gun was giving considerable trouble, having wounded five men. Sergeant Tainpeah and I gained cover behind a small knoll. About 1100 hours, Tainpeah discovered the location of the machine gun and fixed his bayonet. When he did so, I asked him, "Are you fixing to get yourself some Chink ass?" Sergeant Tainpeah grinned and replied, "Yeah, I am going to get that machine gun." The assault jumped off, and Tainpeah headed for the machine gun. After the hill was secured, I went back to the machine gun and found one Chinese killed by a bayonet, one by a hand grenade. Six or eight feet farther up the hill Sergeant Tainpeah lay dead.[50]

SGT. PERCY L. MCDANIEL, SQUAD LEADER, 2D PLATOON, COMPANY B: Company B moved out across a valley and through a village to the objective. A series of ridgelines looked to the north and northeast, with enemy on the ridgelines. Captain Miller was making attack plans. We got on the ridgeline; small-arms and machine-gun fire was coming in. The 2d Platoon leading out took the next peak, losing three men wounded.[51]

SGT. WALTER E. CHANEY, PLATOON SERGEANT, 3D PLATOON, COMPANY B: Two squads then moved forward; my squad to the rear went ahead, took the next peak, and got to the top. Company B lost two squad leaders, two assistant squad leaders, and also three more men, two killed and one wounded, after taking Hill 322. I went to the edge of the hill and set up a perimeter. I counted fourteen Chinese dead, one machine gun and two mortars knocked out. The 3d Platoon knocked out two positions on the next peak with fire from both sides and the front. In the middle of the morning the 3d Platoon passed through the 2d Platoon on the second peak with five peaks to go. Enemy was on every peak except the fifth one. One man was killed and two were wounded; about fourteen enemy were killed. Company B moved on, contacting Company C on the right. The company commander broke the platoon sectors, set up the company defense, and tied in with Company C. Company B dug in.[52]

SGT. ROBERT J. WOTHERSPOON, SQUAD LEADER, 1ST PLATOON, COMPANY B: While the 2d and 3d Platoons were on Hill 322, the 1st Platoon carried ammunition. The 1st Platoon lost the platoon sergeant, two riflemen, and a medic to mortar fire.[53]

SGT. CLARK J. TANNER, 4.2-INCH MORTAR FORWARD OBSERVER WITH COMPANY B, SUPPORT COMPANY: Company B pushed off to attack Hill 322 with the two leading platoons moving up against enemy small-arms and mortar fire. They were pinned down by two machine guns and small arms. Artillery fire was directed on the machine guns, followed by an air strike at 1000 hours. The enemy machine guns, however, stayed in action. Captain Miller, commanding Company B, then directed that I fire on the machine guns. Between 1030 and 1100 hours I fired a fire mission on the machine guns, succeeding in the third round in scoring a direct hit and blowing one machine gun out of its hole. The company proceeded to take the hill. Captain Miller then ordered T'aptong-ni [about 500 yards east of Hill 322] burned. I set the fires by dropping fifteen rounds of WP at 1130 hours. Later in the day I fired concentrations on enemy troops to the north on Hill 166.[54]

MAJOR HOLLAND, 1ST BATTALION EXECUTIVE OFFICER: Company C moved up to jump off with the 2d Battalion and secure Hill 507. The 2d Battalion moved from Hill 299 to Hill 507, supported by 1st Battalion fire. Company B took its objective at 1230 hours, Company C its objective at 1300 hours, and the 2d Battalion its objective at 1700 hours. Company A moved into position back of Companies B and C and carried ammunition for those two companies.[55]

CAPT. DANIEL L. MELVIN, COMPANY C COMMANDER: On 28

March Company B attacked along the ridgeline of Hill 322. Company C, to the right of Company B, secured a knoll [about 1,400 yards east of Hill 148 East], losing only one man by sniper fire. The attack continued along the ridgeline, resulting in seventeen enemy dead by 1400 hours.[56]

PVT. ROLAND J. LEMAY, ASSISTANT MACHINE GUNNER, COMPANY C: On 18 March, between 1300 and 1500 hours, Company C attacked two knobs with a little saddle between on a large hill that was its objective. Attacking up the hill, I killed two enemy in three-to-four-feet-deep holes using grenades. After this I saw a Chinese soldier crouching in a hole, either wounded or hiding. I bayoneted the Chinese in the right shoulder, and when he gave a jump, I hit him in the center of the back and heart. I then moved across to the next knob.[57]

CAPT. ROLLAND A. DESSERT, COMPANY D COMMANDER: On 28 March both machine-gun sections closely supported the attacks of Companies B and C on Hill 322, inflicting an estimated 95 enemy killed and 135 wounded. Resistance throughout the day was heavy, and 18,000 rounds were fired. The recoilless-rifle section operated from Hill 148 East, firing 114 rounds in general support of the 1st Battalion and the 4th Ranger Company. Targets hit were dug-in troops and machine-gun emplacements. One mission was marked for the Air Force. Beginning at 0730 hours, the 81mm mortar platoon fired close support missions for the 1st Battalion's assault on Hill 322 and the Rangers' assault on high ground north of Hill 148 East. Fire missions included ten enemy OPs, three mortars, two machine guns, an estimated 200 troops dug in, and an estimated 300 troops in the open. The estimated enemy casualties from mortar fire were 70 killed and 125 wounded; 720 mortar rounds were fired.[58]

The 4th Ranger Company was drawn into the fighting to protect the northern flank of the 1st Battalion. Major Holland and Captain Anderson describe what happened.

MAJOR HOLLAND, 1ST BATTALION EXECUTIVE OFFICER: At 0700 hours the bridge was ready, and at 0800 hours I brought the 4th Ranger Company across the Sinch'on to secure the high ground on the battalion left flank and tie in with Company B. The 4th

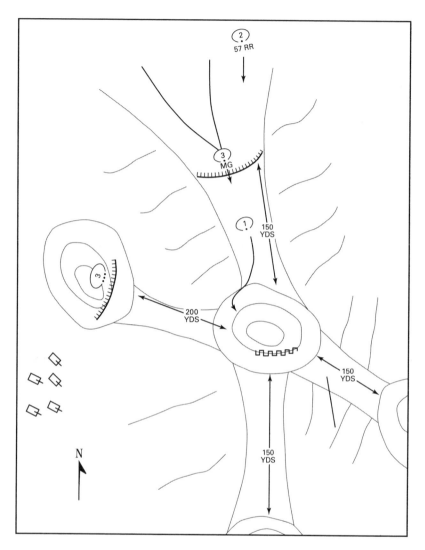

4th Ranger Company assault, 28 March 1951 (sketch based on Capt. Anderson interview in CMH manuscript, U.S. Army; not to scale).

Ranger Company took the brunt of the fire from Hill 279, thus
taking pressure from Company B. The 4th Ranger Company had
one killed and four wounded.[59]

CAPT. DORSEY B. ANDERSON, 4TH RANGER COMPANY COM-
MANDER: At 0900 hours on 28 March, the company (minus the 1st

Platoon) received orders to cross the river and move up to the 1st Battalion area. The 2d Ranger Company was acting as security for a company of tanks supporting the attack from the left. The 4th Ranger Company was ordered by the commander of the 1st Battalion to seize and secure an unnumbered hill mass to the left of the tanks, a finger of Hill 279. The battalion suspected the enemy of massing there for a counterattack. I believe that all combat elements of the regiment were committed in attack at that time.

I instructed the 2d Platoon to move up the approach finger. The 3d Platoon was to clear a low wooded knoll on the right [west] and furnish a base of fire for the attack on the hill mass. I made arrangements with the tank company to receive tank support fire if needed.

Company headquarters moved with the 3d Platoon on the hill, killing six enemy with small arms and grenades and capturing one prisoner. The 2d Platoon moved up the base of the hill without incident, until a liaison plane dropped the platoon leader a message saying that between twenty and thirty enemy troops were dug in on the top. Lieutenant Waterbury, the platoon leader, deployed his forces. The terrain limited maneuver room, and he could attack only with squads in line. He placed two squads as a base of fire and moved forward in a southeasterly direction with the remaining squad, covered by a machine gun and a 57mm rifle attached from the 3d Platoon. Waterbury crossed the first knoll under enemy fire from a range of 300 yards on the left flank and took cover in a ravine. He then moved the base of fire on the knoll and prepared to assault the high ground 150 yards directly to the front, up a very high and steep incline.

Lieutenant Waterbury and one squad began the assault under the support fires of the 3d Platoon, one 57mm rifle, a machine gun, and the small arms of two squads. The assault squad started up the hill on the double. The intense covering fires kept the enemy from firing small arms, but they stayed in their holes and showered the assault group with grenades. I estimate 200 grenades were thrown. The squad was moving through the grenades, when Lieutenant Waterbury was wounded and knocked down. The slope was so steep that he rolled to the bottom. When his men saw this, they wavered in the attack. The assistant platoon sergeant, Sergeant Atkins, continued, with First Sergeant Way, and Corporal Wolf. Lieutenant Waterbury got to his feet and, although wounded, resumed the attack with the remainder of his squad. Wolf and Sergeant McClellan rounded the right edge of the knoll and ran across the top of the hill. Out of ammunition, throwing grenades, using their bayonets and pistols against the enemy who was entrenched on the reverse slope of the hill, they killed eight or ten. These enemy troops were prepared for a reverse-slope defense, and they were completely surprised by the flank attack executed by Wolf and McClellan. The rest of the squad closed in on the foxholes on the forward slope with grenades and bayonets and killed five or six. Lieutenant Waterbury by that time had lost so much blood and was so weak that the medical aid man directed he be moved off the slope to a covered position for medical aid. Four others were wounded in this assault.

Sergeant Atkins immediately consolidated the captured position against an expected counterattack. Heavy small-arms and automatic-weapons fire from two ridges, directly to the front and from the left front, was received. The remaining two squads under the platoon sergeant moved up and assisted in the consolidation. Enemy mortar rounds began to fall on the platoon.

At this time the regiment was attacking eastward while the Ranger company attacked in a southeasterly direction. Instructed to prepare to continue my attack to the front, I made a visual reconnaissance of the area. I decided it would be impossible, due to lack of maneuver room, to attack across the saddle, as the enemy had frontal and flanking fire on this ground. At that time the 1st Platoon joined the company.

I pulled back the 2d Platoon and put the 1st Platoon in its position. The 2d Platoon then replenished its ammunition at the company ammunition point established by the executive officer and the first sergeant. The 2d Platoon was then sent to secure the hill directly southwest of the hill to be attacked in order to cover the attacking force with fire. The 1st Platoon was on the first objective where it could cover the 2d Platoon by fire. The 3d Platoon was sent through a covered cut and through a small village, which it cleared, to the base of the hill. A forward observer from the 674th Airborne Field Artillery Battalion reported to the company to call preparatory fire on the objective. While waiting about an hour for that fire, the battalion S-3 changed the mission of the 4th Ranger Company to that of seizing and securing the hill directly south of the hill the 2d Platoon was on. At the same time, the hill already taken was to be held.

I withdrew the 3d Platoon from its attack positions and sent it through and behind the 2d Platoon, leaving the 1st Platoon on the objective just taken. The 3d Platoon met no enemy on the objective, a narrow finger 850 yards long.

At that time the 1st Platoon began receiving a counterattack across a narrow neck of land. Its own small-arms fire stopped the enemy lead elements, and artillery directed by Lieutenant Allen, the forward observer, and an air strike using napalm, rockets, and machine-gun fire broke up a reported 200 enemy massing to attack. I then received word to consolidate and tie in with Company B for the night. I physically contacted the company, then moved the 4th Ranger Company 1,000 yards in darkness, through rain and mud, and tied in on the left of Company B with one open flank at 2230 hours.[60]

Meanwhile the 3d Battalion to the south was assaulting Hill 299. Members of the unit describe the action.

SGT. CHARLES P. MCDONALD, 3D BATTALION OPERATIONS SERGEANT: On the morning of 28 March, at 0500 hours, Companies I and K moved up to the Sinch'on River, which was the line of departure. They crossed the river at 0600 hours, and in a well-dispersed formation, continued through the rice paddies and attacked Hill 299. They moved up the slope of the hill and encountered fire from the draw. At 0815 hours the hill was secured, and the 3d Battalion command group moved to the summit in order to observe the regimental objectives of Hills 507 and 519.[61]

CAPT. JOHN E. STREVER, COMPANY K COMMANDER: On 28 March, the 3d Battalion moved across the Sinch'on River with Company K on the left and Company L on the right with the objective of the hill mass Hills 299, 507, and 519. We crossed the LD at 0600 hours. Company K moved through the 1st Battalion and continued the attack, tying in with Company L on Hill 299 within forty-five minutes. During the advance, some inaccurate long-range fire came in. The 3d Battalion assaulted Hill 299 with Company K on the north slope and Company L on the south slope. Company L secured the hill at 0930 hours with Company K supporting. Company K suffered one casualty.[62]

SFC JAMES E. HOEH, 81MM MORTAR OBSERVER WITH COMPANY K, COMPANY M: On the morning of 28 March at 0430 I came down Hill 228 and, with Company K, crossed the Sinch'on River at 0600 hours and proceeded to Hill 299, which was reached at 0730 hours. I fired one hundred HE mortar rounds at the ridgeline of Hill 299 to Hill 507, firing at enemy bunkers and personnel. Incoming mortar rounds, about fifty to sixty, caused three casualties in Company K.[63]

M. SGT. YEN CHIN CHOW, PLATOON SERGEANT, 1ST PLATOON, COMPANY K: On 28 March I was told Company K would cross the Sinch'on River, pass through the 1st Battalion, and continue the regimental attack. No enemy opposition was met until within a hundred yards of Hill 299. Then some mortar and small-arms fire came in. The 2d Battalion consolidated its position and set up a perimeter.[64]

1ST LT. EDWARD F. GERNETTE, COMPANY L EXECUTIVE OFFICER: On 28 March the 3d Battalion attacked Hill 299 with Company L on the right. The company moved across the valley of the Sinch'on River in company column, ten yards between men, and crossed the LD at 0600 hours. The river, which the men forded, was knee deep and thirty to fifty yards wide. Company K, crossing farther north, used a footbridge. A one-hour artillery barrage preceded the attack. At 0715 hours, the 3d Platoon of Company L, in the lead on the western slope of Hill 299, noticed movement of enemy among rocks on high ground above them. The enemy began to lay mortar fire and automatic-weapons fire in on the 3d Platoon. They dropped packs and started toward the high ground with the 2d Platoon behind and Company K on the left. Company L continued the attack to the summit, which was reached at 0830 hours. Fifteen enemy were killed, one was taken prisoner, and the remainder moved back toward Hill 507. I estimate that a reinforced enemy company had defended Hill 299. Company L had two wounded.[65]

CPL. JAMES T. PITTS, RIFLEMAN, COMPANY L: At 0400 hours

on 28 March the 3d Squad left the hill, proceeded through Songna-ri to the Sinch'on River, and held up on the bank until the order came to cross. After the order came, the river was crossed, and the company started up the high ground to Hill 299 around 0600 hours. The company reached the third ridgeline just at daylight without being fired on. I was acting as second scout, and on the second ridge I saw two Chinese on top of the hill. On the fourth ridgeline, Company L dropped packs in squad piles and went to the left behind the ridge. Company K was to the left rear. Some Chinese, nearly protected by a reverse slope, began throwing grenades. A grenade wounded the first scout. With the protection of covering fire, I threw grenades in the Chinese holes and killed seven enemy. The platoon continued to the next ridge then moved at 1000 hours to bunkers 500 yards south. We returned later to Hill 299 where a perimeter was set up.[66]

CAPT. THOMAS J. WATKINS, COMPANY M COMMANDER: At 0600 hours on 28 March, Companies K and L moved through the 1st Battalion and attacked Hill 299. The land tail reached the Company M position that morning, bringing the 75mm recoilless rifles and heavy machine guns. Two heavy-machine-gun sections and the 75mm recoilless-rifle section were set up at 0500 hours on the southeast ridge of Hill 228. These sections particularly supported Company L in the attack, the 75mm fire being effective on dug-in positions. The fire was masked by friendly troops at 0730 hours, and one light- and one heavy-machine-gun section displaced to the top of Hill 299. Two light-machine-gun sections and the mortars followed across the Sinch'on to the north slope of Hill 299. The 75mm recoilless-rifle section again took machine guns since Hill 299 was too steep to carry the 75mm recoilless rifle up. I joined the 3d Battalion commander on Hill 299 and ordered the provisional mortar platoon to an assembly area where they could be utilized as ammunition and litter bearers. Company M supported Company L in the attack with the 81mm mortar platoon and two machine-gun sections on Hill 299. I estimate that 200 rounds of mortar were fired. Six rounds of incoming mortar on the mortar platoon position did no damage. The enemy fired an estimated 200 rounds at Hill 299 during the afternoon.[67]

Sgt. Charles P. McDonald, 3d Battalion operations sergeant: At 1200 hours the 2d Battalion passed through Company L in accordance with the plan that the 2d Battalion would now seize the regimental objective. The rest of the day the 3d Battalion fired in support of the 2d Battalion attack. The FAC called air strikes on Hills 507 and 519. The 2d Battalion took their objective in the afternoon.[68]

While the attacks of the 1st and 3d Battalion continued, the regimental commander decided to maintain momentum by committing his reserve to capture Hill 507. The 2d Battalion commander, Lt. Col. J. P. Connor, describes the situation.

I reported to General Bowen, the 187th Airborne Regimental Combat Team commander, on Hill 228 at 0820 hours on 28 March and received orders to pass through the 3d Battalion, attack, and seize Hill 507. The 1st and 3d Battalions had driven an estimated enemy battalion up onto Hill 507. This enemy force was holding up the advance using mortars, small arms, and machine guns. Hill 507 was shaped like the back of a cone, thus preventing more than one company going up at a time. At 1145 hours the 2d Battalion passed through the 3d Battalion and started up the hill. Because the enemy were well dug in, napalm and artillery had not been able to dislodge them from their foxholes, and they had to be dug out with hand grenades and small arms.[69]

Members of the battalion provide details of the assault.

1st Lt. Samuel P. Muse, Company F commander: The 2d Battalion commander informed me on the morning of 28 March about the attack plan on Hills 507 and 519. The 2d Battalion was to attack through the 3d Battalion, whose objective was Hill 299. At 1000 hours the 2d Battalion moved out with Company E in front, passing through the 3d Battalion on Hill 299 at 1300 hours. Company E attacked a knoll on the first ridgeline, seized it, and moved out to the next knoll.[70]

SFC George G. Lane, 1st Platoon sergeant, Company E: Moving up at 0900 hours on 28 March, Company E contacted the 3d Battalion on Hill 299 and at 1145 hours jumped off with the 3d Platoon first securing 300 yards of ground. Then the 1st Platoon and the

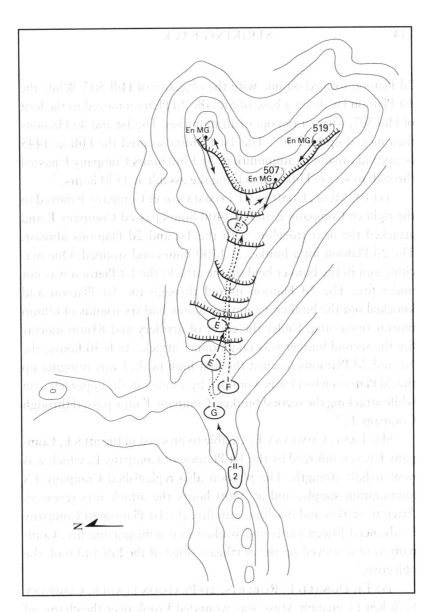

En MG

519
En MG

507
En MG

F

E

E

F

G

II
2

Z

Assault on Hills 507 and 519, 28 March 1951 (sketch based on narrative summary and 1st Lt. Roberts interview in CMH manuscript, U.S. Army; not to scale).

2d Platoon formed on line with the objective of Hill 507. While the 1st Platoon lay down a base of fire, the 2d Platoon moved to the foot of Hill 507, where it ran out of ammunition. The 1st and 3d Platoons then moved up Hill 507. The 1st Platoon secured the Hill at 1445 hours and ran out of ammunition. At 1500 hours Company F passed through to secure Hill 519, making the assault at 1530 hours.[71]

1ST LT. MUSE, COMPANY F COMMANDER: Company F moved to the right of Company E and at 1400 hours passed Company E and attacked the next ridgeline with the 1st and 2d Platoons abreast. The 2d Platoon hit a bunker at 1500 hours and stopped. One machine gun in the bunker held up the attack; the 1st Platoon was not under fire. The 3d Platoon moved through the 1st Platoon and knocked out the bunker. Company F now had six rounds of 60mm mortar remaining. Under the cover of artillery and 81mm mortar fire the second bunker was taken under attack. At 1630 hours, the 1st and 3d Platoons reached the first high peak. I was bringing up the 2d Platoon when I was wounded by a bullet in the upper left arm while attacking the second bunker. Company E now passed through Company F.[72]

SFC LANE, COMPANY E: Unable to proceed in the attack, Company F was reinforced by the 1st Platoon of Company E, which was now at half strength. The platoon also replenished Company F's ammunition supply, and at 1600 hours the attack was renewed. After air strikes and machine-gun fire, the 1st Platoon of Company E advanced fifteen yards and walked into semi-grazing fire. Company G now moved up the northeast slope of the hill and took the objective.[73]

1ST LT. DONALD L. ROBERTS, 2D PLATOON LEADER, COMPANY F: When Lieutenant Muse was wounded I took over the charge of the company. I was at the base of Hill 507. At 1700 hours Company F tried to get over the top by infiltrating to the left, but without success. The assault continued, and three enemy machine guns converged on Company F, two from Hill 507 and the third from Hill 519. One gun was a .303 British Bren gun. Company F was now running out of ammunition and was low on grenades. At 1715 hours Lieutenant Dolan arrived with the 1st Platoon to attack through Company F. Dolan and I made a reconnaissance and called for an 81mm mortar concentration. The 1st Platoon of Company E was to attack following the preparation. The mortar rounds came in, and at 1730 hours Lieutenant Dolan and his platoon stood up, yelled "airborne," and went forward twenty yards. There the three enemy machine guns cut them down, killing Lieutenant Dolan and his runner, wounding nine, and stopping the platoon. Colonel Connor then came up and said that Company G would make the attack through Company F. Between 1745 and 1800 hours an air strike hit Hills 507 and 519. Company G then moved up and secured Hill 507. Company G then sent two platoons to Hill 519, keeping one platoon on the north side of Hill 507.[74]

1ST LT. LEO F. SIEFERT, 1ST PLATOON LEADER, COMPANY G: At 1600 hours on 28 March Company G was committed in the attack on the north side of Hill 507. Company F had suffered severe casualties. In a coordinated attack four F80s first strafed with machine guns. Companies E and F were halted 150 yards from the top of the hill. Lieutenant Epps, the Company G commander, requested fire on the northeast spur by the automatic weapons. The 1st Squad of the 1st Platoon led off and had two killed and seven wounded of the eleven men in the squad in the first twenty-five yards. The 2d Squad moved forward, and Lieutenant Epps committed the 2d Platoon under Lieutenant Woolley for a front assault. Under close artillery and mortar support the 2d Platoon reached the summit at 1620 hours. I then displayed a panel from the summit.

At that time the 3d Platoon was going down the lower side of Hill 519 on the forward slope. Lieutenant Epps yelled at me to take off and catch the 3d Platoon with the panel. The 1st Platoon reached the crest of Hill 519 at 1700 hours, did not display a panel, and was strafed by a flight of F-51s attempting to strafe Chinese just in front of the company. Two were killed, one wounded, and the 1st and 3d Platoons were disorganized. Reorganizing, both platoons pushed over the east side of Hill 519 and advanced into intense automatic-weapons fire. The 3d Platoon consolidated, and Sergeant Doule, the platoon guide, and I took charge of the reorganization.[75]

SFC ROBERT E. MILLER, 3D PLATOON, COMPANY G: About 1600 hours on 28 March the 3d Platoon of Company G was in a grenade duel with stubborn, well-dug-in Chinese Communist Forces.

During the fight, Corporal Gardner threw two live enemy grenades back onto the enemy position. As he attempted to pick up the third enemy grenade it exploded, killing him instantly. Due to the limited terrain the men were close together in the attack; therefore the throwing back of enemy grenades saved the lives of several men. His actions reflect great courage in endangering his own life in order to save others and to inflict casualties on the enemy.[76]

PFC RICHARD D. FEHLNER, 3D PLATOON, COMPANY G: The enemy put up particularly strong resistance on the ridge in the form of hand grenades. I saw Corporal Gardner pick up two enemy hand grenades and throw them back at the enemy. He attempted to throw the third grenade but was killed when it exploded in his hand. I believe his outstanding bravery and complete disregard of his personal safety helped the company take its objective. Corporal Gardner was in the 3d Platoon and about twenty-five yards to my front when the engagement took place.[77]

M. SGT. OTHON VALENT, 1ST PLATOON SERGEANT, COMPANY G: The 2d Battalion crossed the Sinch'on River at 0900 hours, dropped packs at 1000 hours, and moved to the top of the ridgeline. At 1100 hours Company L was passed, climbing Hill 299. During the move Captain Milley was hit, and Lieutenant Epps took over the company. Mortar fire killed two and wounded two. At the base of Hill 507, Company G made contact with Company F; we were committed at 1500 hours. The steep slope made maneuvering impossible. Heavy enemy machine-gun fire from the east and northeast raked the slope. A Company F machine gunner saw Company G being held up; he brought his gun to bear on the forward slope of Hill 507 and covered a knoll and the ridgeline. Company G had at this time lost three wounded and two killed. The 3d Platoon managed to move up and bring fire on the reverse slope of Hill 507, causing the CCF to begin to withdraw amidst hand-grenade fighting. I saw as many as sixty Chinese withdrawing at 1600 hours. At 1630 hours Company G reorganized. The 2d Platoon was to remain in position; the 3d Platoon was to move to the southeast to Hill 519, and the 1st Platoon to move to higher ground.

Moving to Hill 519, the 3d Platoon had an air strike of P-51s hit them. I ran to their position and found them disorganized. I told PFC Dennis to get a panel from Lieutenant Siefert. Dennis placed the panel on the western saddle of Hill 519. As he displayed the panel, a Chinese machine gun on the north slope of the hill killed him. The time was 1730 hours. The last plane in the air strike saw the panel and did not fire. The machine gun on the north slope prevented a further advance since we were unable to knock it out and could not see it.[78]

1ST LT. JACK W. VON STEIEGEL, ARTILLERY FORWARD OBSERVER WITH COMPANY F, BATTERY B, 674TH AIRBORNE FIELD ARTILLERY BATTALION: On the morning of 28 March, Company F, in reserve at first, moved out in the attack on Hills 507 and 519. The 2d Battalion used leapfrog tactics with good progress resulting. I followed the ridgeline of Hill 299 with Company F. Company E was already in the attack. Lieutenant Paraiso [artillery forward observer with Company E] had an OP, which he left as Company F came up and Company E moved forward. I took over the OP. In the rest of the action the leapfrogging continued. The enemy was dug in using two-man foxholes, which I fired delay fuze on. At 1530 hours an enemy machine gun held up the attack and was able to inflict considerable casualties on the attacking troops. An air strike resulted in a direct hit on the dugout next to the machine gun with napalm; however, the machine gun went back into action after the air strike. I then fired on the machine gun with a battalion, two volleys, one of WP and the other with HE (quick and delay fuses) without silencing the gun. Finally a recoilless-rifle team got a direct hit, and the gun was silenced. At 1815 hours the objective was secured, and I established an OP. Defensive fires were fired, and after that fog set in. The expected counterattack never occurred.[79]

LT. COL. CONNOR, 2D BATTALION COMMANDER: The 2d Battalion losses were one officer and twenty enlisted men killed and eighty wounded. Enemy losses were 237 killed and twenty captured. During the night Lieutenant Von Steigel, the artillery forward observer, marked with two rounds of WP a night air strike that resulted in blood and dead men the next day. On 29 March at 1300, the Belgian Battalion relieved the 2d Battalion.[80]

Operation Tomahawk: An Assessment

This action ended Operation Tomahawk for the 187th Airborne Regimental Combat Team. On 29 March they were relieved and were moved to the rear for refitting. Operation Tomahawk was their last combat parachute operation during the Korean War. Maj. Raymond H. Ross, the assistant S-2 of the regiment, provides an assessment of the operation.

During the period of 25–29 March 1951, the 187th Airborne RCT attacked east from Munsan-ni to Hill 519 overlooking the Uijongbu road against the 232d and 234th Regiments of the 78th Division, 26th CCF Field Army. The two CCF regiments had well-prepared positions, consisting of foxholes and bunkers with connecting trenches, and utilized small arms, automatic weapons, 82mm, and many 122mm mortars (which caused all the trouble) in the same manner as UN forces (i.e., grazing, interlocking fire with mortars and artillery covering gaps and exposed areas).

No extensive minefields were encountered; however, the enemy used mines on almost all roads, trails, and fords without any definite pattern. A mine might be planted on the shoulder of a road, in a streambed, or on a foot trail. All mines encountered were the small wooden box types with plastic detonators, which in some cases were stacked three deep. These were difficult to locate with mine detectors. Vehicles hit mines on roads that had been well traveled for two or three days. One never knew where or when to expect mines. In view of mines not being detectable by mine detectors, it was considered advisable to probe for them with bayonets.

The CCF tactic was to fight a tenacious forward-slope defense, and then to quickly move to well-prepared reverse-slope defensive positions when friendly artillery barrages were placed on them and when friendly infantry moved into position for bayonet assault as our artillery was lifted. The most critical time for the assault troops was when they reached the crest of an objective. At this time the enemy would throw many hand grenades over the crest of the hill, or counterattack. The enemy's reverse-slope defenses would be covered by small-arms and automatic-weapons fire from the forward slopes of adjacent hills. Because of the L-type foxholes, fragmentation grenades were often inefficient, as fragments did not reach the inner chambers. White phosphorus and concussion grenades were highly successful. The sight of cold steel had a definite psychological effect on the North Korean soldiers and would cause them to break and run. However, most of the Chinese had to be bayoneted or shot from foxhole to foxhole.

From 25 to 29 March, the S-2 had tabulated a total of 511 enemy killed in action and an estimated 2,668 killed or wounded. These consisted of Chinese only. We also took fifty-two prisoners of war and interrogated them. The grand total for our operation from 23 March [D-day for the airborne drop] to 29 March, the day we were relieved, was 4,208 known or estimated killed or wounded in action, plus the prisoners captured.[81]

Chapter 9

OPERATION SWING—THE PUSH TO THE EAST

23d Infantry Regiment, 4–8 April 1951

Before Operation Courageous ended, General Ridgway ordered a further advance. Intelligence reports indicated the enemy was preparing for a general offensive but was not yet ready to attack. Ridgway decided that a continuation of the movement forward to Line Kansas, a phase line north of the 38th parallel that ran generally east from the Imjin River through the Hwach'on Reservoir to the east coast, would destroy additional enemy forces and supplies, position UN troops on defensible terrain, and facilitate, if desired, a further advance in the center to threaten the enemy's key logistical area in the so-called Iron Triangle bounded by the towns of Ch'orwon, P'yonggang, and Kumhwa. These actions might seriously disrupt Chinese preparations for their offensive. The advance to Line Kansas, scheduled to begin 3 April, was named Operation Rugged; the subsequent limited movement toward the Iron Triangle was designated Operation Dauntless.

The U.S. I and IX Corps began Operation Rugged on 3 April against mixed opposition. In the west, the advance reached the heights south of the Hant'an River on 6 April, but the IX Corps in the center was slowed by strong delaying forces three miles short of the Hwach'on Reservoir. In X Corps, for Operation Rugged, the corps' western boundary was shifted to the left, and the U.S. 2d Infantry Division was ordered to extend to the west and relieve the IX Corps' 1st Marine Division. The 2d Division's 23d Infantry Regimental Combat Team (RCT) played a key role in the ensuing operations.

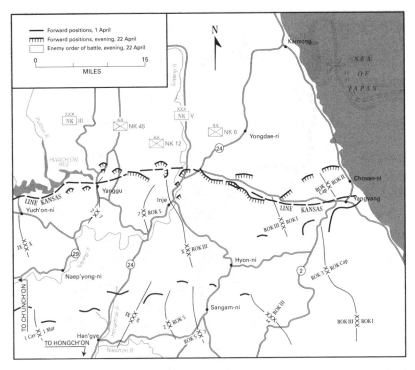

Operations Rugged and Dauntless, eastern front, 1–22 April 1951 (based on map in CMH manuscript, U.S. Army).

The receipt of orders for the 23d Infantry RCT and the general nature of the operation are described in the unit's After Action Report.

On 30 March, after eighteen days of training, reorganizing, and reequipping, the 23d Infantry was released from X Corps reserve and reverted to 2d Division control. The following day, orders were received directing the regiment to move to the vicinity of Hongch'on and prepare to relieve the 5th Marine Regiment on position. Later orders directed that this relief be completed by 1800 hours on 4 April. The original task force was composed of the following units: 23d Infantry Regiment, 37th Field Artillery Battalion, and Company B, 2d Engineer Battalion with one platoon of Company A, 2d Engineer Battalion, attached. With the development of the operation, the 2d Division Reconnaissance Company and the Netherlands Detachment from the 38th Infantry joined the task force. The 503d

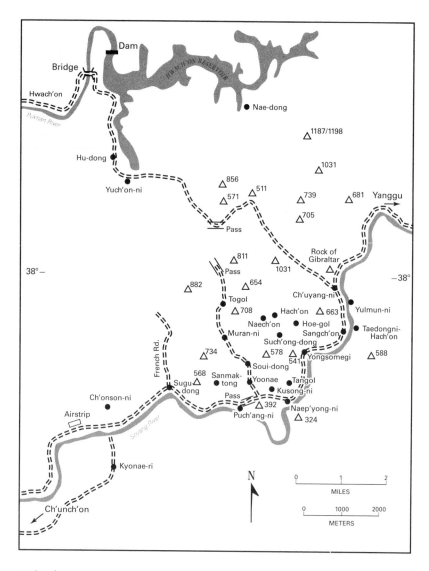

23d Infantry area of operations (original map by author, based on maps from the Army Map Service).

and 15th Field Artillery Battalions were also brought to the area to reinforce the fires of the 37th Field Artillery Battalion.

This operation was fought over an area immediately south of the Hwach'on Reservoir called the Whitehead Mountains. These mountains are a series of precipitous, spiny ridges that rise sharply from narrow, inaccessible valley floors. The tallest peak rises to a height of 1,187 meters, and there are many others between 500 and 1,000 meters high. The enemy, from prepared bunkers on these terrain features, had maximum observation for the many supporting arms they employed, including artillery and mortars of all calibers.

Because the southern boundary of the area was the unfordable Soyang River, it was necessary to first attack east to secure the east–west lateral road along the north bank of the river. Then the attack swung generally north. With the rapid advance of the units in the western portion of the sector the attack, hinging at the 3d Battalion, swung again to the east. This "S" like movement was the reason the operation was given the name "Swing." Mines and craters in the few usable roads of the inadequate road net increased the difficulty of supply. It was necessary to utilize approximately 900 Korean laborers as carriers to keep a steady flow of food and ammunition over the mountains to the fighting troops. The use of these carriers freed a comparable number of U.S. soldiers to fight.[1]

1st Lt. John Mewha, a combat historian in Korea, conducted a special study of this operation of the 23d Infantry. He describes the unit's missions and initial movements.

This combat team was given the dual mission of relieving the 5th Marine Regiment, 1st U.S. Marine Division, and striking north to Line Kansas (an imaginary line extending east and west through the Hwach'on Reservoir) to inflict maximum casualties on the enemy. Prior to the actual relief, the 23d Regiment's commander and the Marine commander met to coordinate movements. It was agreed that the Marines would move northward across the Soyang River to positions approximately nine miles south of the Hwach'on Reservoir. This was agreed upon because of the lack of a suitable road net in the area south of the river then occupied by the Marines. The 23d RCT used the road net in the 1st U.S. Cavalry Division sector and went into an assembly area near Ch'unch'on prior to relieving the Marines.[2]

Because of the lack of roads in the new area of operations, engineer teams were dispatched to find routes that could be im-

proved for movement and supply. Lieutenant Mewha describes this effort.

In April, the X Corps zone of advance was shifted westward, necessitating the shift of the American divisions in the corps sector. It was necessary for the 2d U.S. Infantry Division to assume responsibility for the sector formerly occupied by the 1st U.S. Marine Division. In anticipation of a move through the Marine sector, the 2d Engineer Combat Battalion ordered two reconnaissance teams to reconnoiter the roads to Ch'unch'on and any parallel roads leading eastward into the 2d Division sector. No roads existed in front of the 23d Infantry Regiment's route of advance to relieve elements of the 5th Marine Regiment. Two teams, commanded by M. Sgt. Warren Dailey and Sgt. James G. Sulzer, were given the assignment. The two teams left the 2d Engineer Battalion CP at 0930 hours on 2 April and went northward from Hongch'on toward Ch'unch'on. Two roads previously constructed for use by Marine artillery were checked, but the roads extended only to the base of high ground. The teams reached Ch'unch'on at 1530 and immediately reconnoitered the roads to the east. Sulzer's team checked the southernmost road, and Dailey's the northernmost. The roads ran into hillsides where they dwindled into trails. This was reported, and the teams remained in Ch'unch'on for the night with the 8th Engineer Battalion, 1st Cavalry Division.

On 3 April the two teams reconnoitered the roads to the north and northeast. Sulzer's team went north to the Soyang River to check the possibility of vehicles and engineering equipment fording the river, but the river was too deep and swift. Dailey's team checked the roads to the east and southeast, but again the roads ended in trails against high hills. At 1200 hours the two teams met and were joined by a third team under 1st Lt. Henry P. Leighton. Leighton received the teams' reports and told them to recheck the first two roads reconnoitered, as the battalion commander was not satisfied with the previous report. The map showed a power line extending over the mountain, and it was thought a jeep should be able to follow the power line through the hills. The two teams returned to the first roads checked and walked the entire length of the trails shown on the map. It was impossible for a jeep to negotiate the trails. Evidently mules had been used to drag the electrical towers into position. The teams returned to Ch'unch'on for the night. They were informed by the 8th Battalion S-3 that enemy troops were to the east along the Soyang River, and some enemy troops were south of it.[3]

Although the engineers were unsuccessful in locating trails that could be improved for vehicular movement, there was one existing road that followed the Soyang River from Ch'unch'on through Naep'yong-ni. However, there were problems with this road, as Capt. John H. King relates.

On 4 April the 1st Battalion, 23d Infantry Regiment, moved into the high ground east of Kyonae-ri and relieved elements of the 5th Marine Regiment. The French Battalion and the 2d and 3d Battalions, 23d Infantry Regiment, advanced into new positions over the Ch'unch'on–Naep'yong-ni road, passing through elements of the 1st Cavalry Division. The entire road, as well as the riverbed, draws, and some rice paddies in the area were extensively mined by the enemy. Thirteen tanks ran over one portion of the road safely, but when the fourteenth ran over it the mine exploded, destroying the tank. The mines were placed so deep that mine detectors and probing were useless. The road north of Sugu-dong formed the boundary between the 1st Cavalry Division on the left and the 23d RCT on the right.[4]

Capt. Stanley W. Selander, the S-3 of the 23d Infantry, provides more details of the operations plan.

The regiment was to relieve the 1st Marine Division, which was then to shift to the west. The Marines were south of the Soyang River at the time, and Colonel Chiles, 23d Infantry Regimental commander, and the Marine commander got together to coordinate movements. The Marines agreed to move north of the Soyang before being relieved. There were no road nets in the area, and the 23d Infantry Regiment received permission to use the road in the 1st U.S. Cavalry Division zone. The regiment moved out in the order: 3d Battalion, 2d Battalion, and the attached French Battalion. We came up from Hongch'on, through Ch'unch'on, and over to the vicinity of Sugu-dong.

The regimental zone extended southward from each finger of the Hwach'on Reservoir and was divided roughly into three zones: the French on the left, the 2d Battalion in the center, and the 3d Battalion on the right.

One Marine battalion advanced without opposition about 2,000 meters north of Sugu-dong where they were relieved by the French Battalion. The 3d Battalion was to go east on the road to Naep'yong-ni to make a junction with elements of the Marines, which were to cross the river at that point. The 3d Battalion encountered many mines and craters in the advance down the road, but finally a pass about 2,000 meters west of Naep'yong-ni was reached. The Marines had to fight north across the river but finally made the junction. The 3d Battalion still had to fight its way into the assigned zone.[5]

Relief of the Marines: 3d Battalion, 23d Infantry, 4 April

Lt. Col. Beverly T. Richardson, the 3d Battalion commander, describes the movement to reach the Marines.

The 3d Battalion, 23d Infantry Regiment, was assembled near the airfield about four miles northeast of Ch'unch'on when we received the mission of contacting elements of the 5th U.S. Marine Regiment on Hill 392 about one mile west of Naep'yong-ni. The 3d Battalion was then to turn north to a predetermined ready line near Hill 541 [about a mile and a half north of Naep'yong-ni], and from there it was to attack north to the Kansas line, an imaginary line extending east and west through the center of the Hwach'on Reservoir.

I ordered the battalion to move along the MSR (the Ch'unch'on–Naep'yong-ni road), paralleling the Soyang River, in a column of companies: K, battalion forward echelon, L, M, and I. A strong tank-infantry patrol, consisting of one platoon of Company I and one platoon of the 23d Regimental Tank Company, was to precede the column, clear the route of any possible enemy resistance, make a reconnaissance of the road, and contact the Marines. The battalion trains were to remain in the vicinity of Ch'unch'on.

On 4 April the tank-infantry patrol started down the MSR to

the east and soon found many obstacles—mines, craters, and boulders—blocking any possible vehicular movement. The infantry
platoon dismounted and proceeded on foot. The remainder of the
battalion followed on foot. At approximately 1415 hours, the infantry patrol reported that it was held up by enemy machine-gun and
82mm and 60mm mortar fire coming from the direction of Hill
392. The opposition was reported as being of platoon size and well
dug in. The evident mission of the enemy group was to defend the
pass on the MSR. The pass ran through a hill mass and afforded the
enemy a good defensive location.

I immediately ordered Company K to envelop the hill from the
north. The company approached to within 800 yards of the objective and was pinned down by heavy enemy machine-gun and mortar
fire. I then ordered Company L into action, and it moved to the left
between Company K and the road. Contact was finally made with
the patrol. By late afternoon, the tanks had found a bypass and rejoined the battalion approximately 1,400 yards west of Hill 392.
Due to the approaching darkness, the battalion held up for the
night.

Elements of the 2d Battalion, 5th U.S. Marine Regiment, could
be seen fighting for Hill 392. The 3d Battalion had been moving on
the enemy from the west, and the Marines had crossed the river and
were advancing on the south flank of the hill.[6]

*2d Lt. Walter E. Rodgers, 4th Platoon Leader of Company I,
describes the situation in Company I as it received word from its
platoon patrol.*

On 4 April, the 2d Platoon of Company I was given the mission
of accompanying a platoon of tanks to meet elements of the 5th U.S.
Marine Regiment. The armored patrol moved out at 1030, and a
short time later radioed back that the road was blown. The platoon
dropped their packs, left the tanks, and continued down the road.
At 1430 the remainder of the 3d Battalion moved out down the road
in a column of companies.

After going a short distance, Lieutenant McCoy, Company I
commander, received word from Lieutenant Rampendahl, the 2d
Platoon leader, that the 2d Platoon was receiving heavy mortar fire

at a pass. The remainder of Company I went up a small ridge on the left of the road and continued forward. The battalion commander, Lt. Col. Richardson, deployed Companies K and L on the ridges to the left. The companies held there for approximately an hour until engineers filled craters on the road to enable vehicular movement forward. The 2d Platoon of Company I was 500 yards to the front on a small ridge, and Marines could be seen trying to gain the high ground on the right of the Soyang River.[7]

Other members of the 3d Battalion recall the action.

1ST LT. VIVIOUS M. HALL, 1ST PLATOON LEADER OF COMPANY K: On 4 April the 1st Platoon, Company K, led out as the connecting file between the 3d Battalion, 23d Infantry, and a tank-infantry patrol from Company I. My platoon was approximately a half-mile behind the patrol. At 1600 hours I received orders from Lieutenant Waples, acting Company K commander, to move on the high ground to the left of the road. I could see Company I's patrol moving up toward a pass. We dug in on the hill and tied in with Company L on the right. Company I remained on the road with the tanks.[8]

SGT. JACK P. BROWN, SFC GEORGE H. GLASSMAN, SFC ROBERT G. BURGI, COMPANY K: On 4 April, the 3d Battalion assembled in the 1st Cavalry Division's area near Ch'unch'on and moved eastward on the Ch'unch'on–Naep'yong-ni road. A tank-infantry patrol from Company I preceding Company K was pinned down on the road by automatic-weapons fire from high ground. Artillery and 4.2-inch mortar forward observers were with Company K, and the FOs called for artillery on the hill in front of the Company I patrol. The tanks deployed to the flats near the river and placed fire on the hill. Company K held in the hills near Ch'onson-ni, and Company L came up the road and went on the higher ground behind Company I and in front of Company K. Three men in the 2d Platoon of Company K were hit that day by incoming enemy 120mm mortar rounds, and the company area received sporadic mortar fire during the night. The companies remained in position until the next day. The 2d Battalion, 23d Infantry Regiment, had advanced on the left of the 3d Battalion during the day, and Lieutenant Anderson, the artillery FO, called for a fire mission on the hill from which it was thought the mortar fire was coming. Permission was refused because elements of the 2d Battalion were moving down the suspected ridgeline.[9]

1ST LT. WILLIAM P. BARENKAMP, EXECUTIVE OFFICER OF COMPANY L, AND 1ST LT. RICHARD A. PALMER, 2D PLATOON LEADER, COMPANY L: Company I sent a platoon-size patrol ahead of the battalion on tanks, but the tanks were stopped by enemy mines. The patrol continued on foot to the vicinity of Puch'ang-ni where it was held up by enemy mortar and small-arms fire from Hill 392. We heard over the radio that Company K was moving up on the high ground north of the road about 2,000 yards west of Puch'ang-ni, but we continued on to the high ground just east of Company K. Our company started up a ridgeline and passed to the left of the Company I patrol. We received enemy small-arms fire from Hill 392 and from a ridge to the left. Elements of the 5th Marine Regiment had to fight for hill 392, but they finally secured it by dark. Company L moved about 900 yards north of Puch'ang-ni and tied in with Company I. We received sporadic small-arms fire through the night.[10]

The Initial Attack: 3d Battalion, 23d Infantry, 5 April

The Marines continued to fight through the night to secure Hill 392. The next day, 5 April, the 3d Battalion assumed the attack role. The battalion commander, Lt. Col. Richardson, describes the plan of action and events of the day.

The plan of attack for the next day was for Company L, along with the platoon from Company I, to move around to the north and then to turn south, enveloping the enemy's positions. The tanks were ordered to support Company L's attack on Hill 392 at daylight.

At 0800 on 5 April the effectiveness of the tank fire reduced the enemy position, and by 0930 troops were moving through the pass. Company I moved into the valley east of Hill 392 without difficulty, other than encountering several wooden box-type mines. However, when Company K, which was following Company I, crossed the pass, the enemy registered in with 60mm and 82mm mortar fire, killing one and wounding eight.

In the meantime, Company L moved northward and was told to take Hill 578 from the west, while Company I was to swing north up the hill's southern slope. Company L proceeded across toward Hill 578, generally abreast with Company I's advance eastward up the valley. While crossing a valley floor about 1,000 yards north of Hill 392, Company L received sniper and machine-gun fire from the approaches to Hill 578. In spite of the harassing fire, the company had gained a foothold on the forward slope of the hill by 1130 and was using all its supporting weapons—57mm recoilless rifles, 81mm mortars, and artillery—to the maximum.

Company I was delayed in its approach to the hill by brush fires and American-type antipersonnel mines (bouncing betties). I believe that the mines had been emplaced by ROK forces during the summer and early fall of 1950. The mines were rusty, the dirt around them had been washed away by rain, and there was no attempt at camouflage. At 1330, Company I encountered an enemy group of undetermined size on the southern slope of Hill 578 and were subjected to heavy enemy automatic-weapons, machine-gun, small-arms, and mortar fire. Company I immediately attacked the hostile positions in an attempt to neutralize the fire but was unable to make any headway. I then ordered Company K up between Company L on the west slope of Hill 578 and Company I on the road, to clear the ground between the two. The terrain was extremely difficult, even for dismounted troops, and the gains were limited.

By 1800 hours, Company L approached to within 400 yards of the summit, but Companies I and K were unable to advance. Due to the late hour and the tactical situation, I ordered Company L to withdraw. I then redisposed the battalion into a defensive perimeter for the night. Company L disengaged with the enemy at approximately 2030 hours and closed into the battalion perimeter. The remainder of the night was quiet. During the night, the 3d Battalion was ordered by regimental headquarters to proceed through Naep'yong-ni to Hill 541, which was situated on the restraining line initially designated.[11]

Lieutenant Rodgers of Company I describes the actions of his company on 5 April.

(Above) Col. Marcel Crombez, commanding officer, 5th Cavalry Regiment. (Below) Maj. Charles Parziale, commanding officer, 3d Battalion, 5th Cavalry Regiment.

Ford across the Hongch'on River, looking south at the terrain over which the 1st Cavalry and 1st Marine Divisions moved in their advance on Hongch'on. The 3d Battalion, 5th Cavalry, crossed the river at this ford.

Looking northeast toward the CP area of the 3d Battalion, 5th Cavalry, from the streambed of the Hongch'on River. The high ground behind the CP is Objective White.

Looking north toward Hills 400, 383, and 499, all part of the Songch'i Mountain hill mass. This photo was taken from the streambed of the Hongch'on River.

Looking south from the enemy outpost line on the ridges leading to Hill 300. The Hongch'on River can be seen at the base of the hills in the distance.

This trench was part of the main defenses of the enemy.

Enemy light-machine-gun position covering the main approach to Hill 380.

An enemy bunker with a roof reinforced with a double layer of logs and dirt.

Hill 300 from the finger ridge approach looking north. The 1st Platoon of Company K attacked in this area and captured Hill 300 in the late morning of 16 March 1951.

Looking southwest from Hill 380 at the valley between Hill 300 on the left and Hill 383 on the right. While the 1st Platoon of Company K was assaulting Hill 300, the 1st Platoon of Company L moved up the finger ridge against Hill 383. Later, after these hills were captured, elements of the 3d Battalion, 5th Cavalry, attempted to move into this valley only to discover extensive minefields.

Looking west from Hill 300 at enemy trenches on the finger ridge. Enemy fire from these trenches and from Hill 300 hit Company L in the flank as it advanced up the ridges against Hill 360 across the valley.

Looking west from Hill 300 at the ridge approaches to Hill 360. The 1st Platoon of Company L attacked over this ground the morning of 16 March to capture Hill 360.

Hill 380 as seen looking north from Hill 300. The 1st Platoon of Company K was only able to advance a short distance north of Hill 300 before being stalled by heavy enemy resistance from Hill 380. The remainder of Company K was committed to the fight to capture Hill 380.

The enemy view from Hill 380. Hill 300, captured by the 1st Platoon of Company K, is on the right. The valley from which tanks were firing is on the left.

Looking south from Hill 380 at the knob approach used by Company K in their attack. Note the steep incline. In the afternoon of 16 March 1951, Company K was able to advance only part of the way to Hill 380. During the night the enemy abandoned Hill 380, which was occupied by Company K, the morning of 17 March without resistance.

Hill 499 as seen from Hill 380 looking northwest. The enemy still held Hill 499 on 17 March 1951, although several air strikes were put in against enemy positions and Company I, committed to the fight, reached within a few hundred yards of the top. During the night, an enemy plane attacked enemy positions on Hill 499, and the next morning Company I occupied it after a stiff fight.

Looking north at Hill 300 from the valley of the Hongch'on. Enemy observation from the high ground of movements in the valley put support elements at risk. Supply parties struggled to climb the hills.

The supply trail looking south along the ridgeline between Hills 300 and 380. Once supply parties reached the top of the ridge, they were able to move much faster along the top of the ridgeline.

The valley east of Hill 300. The trains of the 3d Battalion, 5th Cavalry, operated from this area between 18 and 21 March 1951 in support of the rifle companies advancing north of the Hill 300–383–499 area.

A bridge where a litter jeep evacuation point was established on 16 March 1951. When soldiers were wounded in the fighting in the hills in the background, they were hand carried by litter approximately one mile to this area. From here, they were evacuated by jeep to the battalion aid station another mile away. The entire area of the evacuation was under enemy fire and sown with mines. Only one medical driver was wounded during the day, but there were several near misses.

Northern drop zone of the 187th Airborne Regimental Combat Team. The "drop zone," "heavy drop zone," and two enemy positions are marked on the photo.

(Above) Looking north across the edge of the Hwach'on Reservoir. Beyond the dam the Pukhan River can be seen as it flows north and then west before curving back to the south. (Below) Looking west across the Hwach'on Reservoir. The dam is on the right. The high ground is the area over which the 2d Battalion, 7th Cavalry Regiment, attempted to advance toward the dam.

Looking toward the south over the Hwach'on Dam. The Rangers landed on the tip of the peninsula to the left of the dam. Their objective (Objective 77) was the tallest peak directly to the left of the dam. The boat launch site was in the inlet across the reservoir from the peninsula.

On the night of 9 April 1951, Battery A, 937th Field Artillery, fired 155mm "Long Toms" on enemy positions near Ch'orwon as part of the artillery preparation before the 24th Infantry Regiment's attack. Artillery was moved forward to within 300 yards of the front line to range the enemy supply center.

Hill 642, the key to the enemy defenses along the Hant'an River and the objective of the 24th Infantry Regiment's attack.

Terrain on the north bank of the Hant'an River at the site of the crossing of the 1st Battalion, 24th Infantry, on 11 April 1951.

Valley of the Hant'an River at the crossing site of the 1st Battalion on 11 April 1951. The pontoon bridge was erected on 12 April. The Chinese bridge is to the left of the pontoon bridge.

The Chinese mud and branch cart bridge across the Hant'an River over which part of the 1st Battalion, 24th Infantry, crossed on 11 April 1951.

V cut in the north bank of the Hant'an River from which an enemy machine gun fired on the crossing of the 1st Battalion on 11 April 1951.

Pine grove where the 1st Battalion reassembled after crossing the Hant'an River on 11 April 1951.

Flat ground between the pine grove and Hill 642 across which Company B attacked on 11 April 1951.

Finger ridge, which was the initial objective of Company A on 11 April 1951.

Soldiers of the 3d Battalion forward CP attempting to relay information to line companies north of the Hant'an River.

Soldiers of the 3d Battalion under enemy mortar fire along the Hant'an River.

Soldiers of the 77th Engineer Company wait for Chinese troops to come out of their hiding places along the Hant'an River, 11 April 1951.

Men of Company B, 65th Engineer Battalion, and the 77th Engineer Company begin construction of a crossing over the Hant'an River on 11 April 1951. The 77th Engineers built the approaches while Company B erected the pontoon bridge.

Completed pontoon bridge over the Hant'an River.

Main supply route used by the 24th Infantry Regiment near the Hant'an River.

GIs and Korean civilians bringing supplies up a steep hill to men of the 24th Infantry north of the Hant'an River.

Heavy mortars fire in support of the 24th Infantry soldiers north of the Hant'an River.

The 75mm recoilless rifle fires on enemy positions north of the Hant'an River. The recoilless rifle was also used to mark targets for air and artillery strikes.

Enemy troops were well protected in dugouts such as this one, which held five soldiers and was located at the base of Company A's initial objective.

The southern side of Hill 642 as viewed from the 1st Battalion's attack positions.

The southern slope of Hill 642 showing the ground over which elements of the 1st Battalion attacked as viewed from Chinese defensive positions.

At 0800 5 April, Company I moved down the road with two quad 50s and one twin 40 as support. A short distance away, the road was blown in two places and heavily mined. The vehicles were halted and the company continued on to a small village. The company commander received orders from the battalion commander personally to take a high ridge to the left. The company commander wanted to clear the high ground leading to the ridge first, but the battalion commander advised the company to move up through a saddle which was part of the high ground and through a valley to the next ridgeline.

The 2d Platoon was given the mission of securing the high ground to the right of the saddle, and the 1st Platoon was to go over the saddle. The 4th Platoon was to be in support along with the 3d Platoon. As the 1st Platoon started up the saddle, it received enemy machine-gun fire from the left. The 4th Platoon then placed 60mm mortar, 57mm recoilless-rifle, and small-arms fire on the enemy positions. Lieutenant McCoy notified the 1st Platoon to deploy to the left and to work up toward the enemy. The platoon worked up to an open space near the enemy positions and then deployed lower along the slopes to take advantage of cover. As they were deploying, enemy machine-gun and small-arms fire came from the ridge in front.

Colonel Richardson, who was with Company I at the time, gave the company commander permission to clear the ridge. The 3d Platoon was given the mission and was to be supported by the 4th Platoon. The platoons were told that Company K would be attacking on the left.

The 4th Platoon found a level place three-fourths of the way up the ridge spur on the left, set up mortars, and placed fire on enemy positions that were holding up the advance of the forward elements of the 3d Platoon. The enemy returned with 82mm mortar fire, and one dud landed between Colonel Richardson and Lieutenant McCoy. The 3d Platoon also reported booby traps and antipersonnel mines (bouncing betties) on the trails. The 4th Platoon kept placing mortar fire on the ridge, and Lieutenant McCoy instructed the 3d Platoon to link up with Company K. A call came in just then from Lieutenant Waples, Company K commander, that the two had

joined and were going on to the higher ground. The ridgeline leading to the higher ground was so narrow that only one squad could
be deployed. Sergeant Sobolsky took a squad and secured the hill by
1630. The enemy had withdrawn to the northeast.

In the meantime, the 1st Platoon had engaged twenty-five to
thirty enemy and had advanced very slowly. When Company K and
the 3d Platoon met, the enemy in front of the 1st Platoon withdrew.
Lieutenant McCoy then instructed all the platoons to move up on
the objective. The battalion commander notified Companies K and
I to coordinate defenses and to secure the hill for the night. At 1730
both companies received a heavy five-minute barrage of 60mm and
82mm mortar fire that killed and wounded several men. From the
objective, enemy movement could be seen on Hill 541, and fire from
mortars and a battalion of 105mm howitzers was placed on them.
There was no further enemy contact that night.[12]

*Members of Company K describe the fighting involving their
company on 5 April.*

1ST LT. VIVIOUS M. HALL, 1ST PLATOON LEADER, COMPANY
K: At 0800 5 April, Company K moved down to the road and advanced to the pass while Companies I and L were attacking a hill to
the left of the road. Company K, with my platoon leading, pushed
through the pass and came to a blown place in the road. Here the
company received twenty-five to thirty rounds of enemy 60mm
mortar fire that killed one man and wounded eight others. Company
K continued a mile farther. My platoon moved on the left of the
road and established a base of fire for the 3d Platoon, which attacked up the left of the hill in support of Company I.

Company I took the hill ahead of the 3d Platoon and the remainder of Company K moved up. The acting company commander,
along with the platoon leaders, went forward to consolidate positions with Company I for the night. At approximately 1700 hours
the hill received enemy small-arms fire from the ridgeline to the
front, forcing the men to the reverse slope. Eight more rounds of
enemy 82mm mortar fire fell on the slope and killed Lieutenant
Waples and wounded four others. Captain Perry took over command

of the company that night. The company consolidated their positions and dug in after dark. There was no further enemy contact.[13]

M. Sgt. George D. Chamberlain, platoon sergeant, 1st Platoon, Company K: At about noon on 5 April, Company K moved back down on the road and continued eastward through a pass and up a high hill just north of the road and about 800 yards north of Hill 392. The 3d Platoon led the advance, and the 1st Platoon deployed on a little knoll and covered the advance of the 3d Platoon up the hill. The 3d Platoon received some small-arms fire from their immediate front and also received heavy enemy 82mm and 120mm mortar fire. Lieutenant Waples, commander of Company K, was killed, and Lieutenant Hulett, 3d Platoon leader, was wounded at the time Company K was trying to tie in on the left flank of Company I. Because of the casualties and lack of officers, the company was confused for a few minutes. Then Lieutenant Swarthout assumed command of the company and organized the defense. While digging in, the company received enemy effective machine-gun fire from the right front.

After dark, Captain Perry from Company H, 23d Infantry, took over the company. During the night an enemy automatic weapon could be heard to the front. I think the enemy was trying to draw fire.[14]

Sgt. Jack P. Brown, 1st Platoon; SFC George H. Glassman, 2d Platoon; and SFC Robert G. Burgi, 3d Platoon, Company K: At 0800 5 April, Company K went down to the road and pushed through elements of the 5th Marine Regiment for approximately three or four miles in a column of platoons—1, 3, 2, and 4. At 1000 hours the company came up to some tanks supporting Company I, which were pinned down in a pass. Company M's 75mm recoilless rifles, commanded by Lieutenant Scott, were firing directly at enemy dugout positions 700 to 900 yards to the front; they succeeded in eliminating the enemy positions. Company K moved down the road, passed the tanks, and continued for approximately one and a half miles. Company I had turned into the hills on the right. From the time Company K had left the pass until turning left into the hills for an assault on the high ground, it was subjected to heavy enemy mortar fire.

The company's first objective was high ground about 700 yards north of the village of Kusong-ni. Company I had moved up on the right about 500 yards away, and Company L was on the left on the ridgelines. The 3d Platoon moved up on a ridge finger to take the high ground and had traveled about 200 yards before an enemy machine gun from the left, in front of Company L, opened fire. The platoon deployed and moved forward on the reverse slope until contact was made with Company I, which had secured the high ground. The remainder of Company K moved up with Company I.

After the 3d Platoon had tied in with Company I, an enemy mortar round came into the area and killed Lieutenant Waples and wounded Lieutenant Hulett. Lieutenant McCoy, the Company I commander, escaped injury. The platoon started to receive small-arms fire from the hill 150 yards to the front and, being in an exposed position, had to dig in after dark. Harassing enemy machine-gun fire came in on the 1st Platoon's positions all night, but there were no casualties. All night, 4.2-inch mortars fired in close support, trying to eliminate the enemy position. They finally used white phosphorous rounds, which succeeded in quieting the machine gun by burning brush on the side of the hill.[15]

While Companies I and K were clearing the high ground north of the road and east of the pass, Company L moved against Hill 578 to the north. Members of the company describe the action.

1ST LT. WILLIAM P. BARENKAMP, EXECUTIVE OFFICER, AND 1ST LT. RICHARD A. PALMER, 2D PLATOON LEADER, COMPANY L: At 0800 hours on 5 April, the 1st Platoon of Company L moved out to a pimple 200 yards to the front and encountered no enemy opposition. At the same time the 3d Platoon went about 1,000 yards and cleared the high ground to the left. After the 1st Platoon had secured the pimple, the 2d Platoon pushed on through and went to the left, passed through the 3d Platoon, and went into position to move up to Hill 578. The 3d Platoon remained in position to give any necessary supporting fire. The 1st Platoon worked to Yoonae, a little village in the flats, and swung north to Hill 578. The 2d Platoon approached up a ridgeline to the left to within 500 yards of the top of Hill 578 before a squad leader, Corporal Sperondio, hit a bouncing betty AP mine and was killed. The 2d Platoon then with-drew and followed the 1st Platoon on up their ridge. Approximately 300 yards from the top, the company saw a North Korean soldier coming down the ridge and killed him. There were others on the top, and four more came down to investigate. These were also killed by the 1st Platoon. The platoon started to work forward again, but the enemy placed small-arms fire and threw grenades on the leading elements. In the meantime, the 3d Platoon followed behind on the foothills and placed 60mm mortar and machine-gun fire on the enemy. About one-half hour later the 1st Platoon moved forward approximately 200 yards and again received small-arms fire from Hill 578 and its ridgelines to the right and left. Lieutenant Palmer brought the 2d Platoon on line and placed machine-gun fire on the enemy. Company E, 23d Infantry, also had Hill 578 as their objective, and the enemy were fleeing from in front of them over toward Company L's positions.

About 1630 hours Captain Jackson, the Company L commander, received permission from the battalion commander to withdraw. We withdrew in a leapfrog manner, with one platoon covering another, and reassembled at Yoonae. We then moved down to the southeast to the village of Kusong-ni. At this time, Company I was about 800 yards north of Kusong-ni, and Company K was on their left flank on a small hill. At 2400 hours Company L tied in with Company I. There was no enemy contact that night.[16]

PFC David E. Russell, machine gunner, 1st Platoon of Company L: At 0600 hours 5 April, the platoon saw six or seven enemy running around on the top of a knoll to the front. We thought it might be a patrol from the 2d Platoon and held fire. Our platoon leader checked with the company commander and was informed that no patrols had been sent out. We immediately opened fire but could not tell if any of the enemy soldiers were hit. At 0800 the 2d Platoon attacked the knoll and secured it without resistance. The remainder of the company moved up and then followed a trench down the ridgeline. Approximately 1,800 yards away, six North Koreans were seen coming down out of a village [Yoonae] and heading to the right along a small stream. The company opened fire, and the enemy disappeared.

The company crossed the stream, went through the village, and prepared to attack a hill to the front. The hill had two ridge fingers separated by a draw. The 2d Platoon went up the right finger, and the 1st Platoon on the left finger. The 2d Platoon approached halfway to the crest of the ridge finger, and one of the leading scouts stepped on a bouncing betty booby trap and was killed. Booby traps were spotted all over the ridge approximately ten feet apart. The 2d Platoon was then ordered to cross the draw and join the 1st Platoon.

After four hours of climbing, the 2d Platoon got three-fourths of the way up the hill. The 1st Platoon had encountered small enemy groups and had dispersed them. One squad of 1st Platoon was sent on up to the top of the hill, and after going 500 yards they encountered automatic-weapons fire from a pillbox. The squad withdrew back to the company. The 1st Platoon stormed the pillbox and met no resistance. One prisoner was captured.

The 1st Platoon led off again up the hill supported by the 2d Platoon. The two leading squads were immediately pinned down by a heavy machine gun and small-arms fire from the front. I engaged the enemy machine gun with fire, which enabled the platoon to withdraw to the company. The company immediately disengaged with the enemy, withdrew down the ridge to the river, and followed the river to the road. Company L then rejoined the 3d Battalion forward CP and dug in for the night.[17]

CPL. HARRY N. NISHIDA, 1ST PLATOON RUNNER, AND PFC EDWARD L. VICKERS, 1ST SQUAD SCOUT, 2D PLATOON, COMPANY L: At 0630 hours on 5 April the company withdrew to the reverse slope behind the ridgeline and started to receive enemy sniper fire. The 2d Platoon had three men pinned down on the forward slope by enemy machine-gun fire, and Lieutenant Palmer called for a base of fire from all the 2d Platoon's weapons in order to get the men out. After the three men returned, one squad from the 1st Platoon advanced to the enemy machine-gun position, but the enemy had withdrawn. The rest of the 1st Platoon joined the squad on the high ground. The 1st Platoon moved out in a leapfrog manner, one squad at a time, and the 3d Platoon moved out on the left flank of the 1st Platoon in a separate operation. The 1st Platoon went down to a village and saw abandoned burp gun ammunition. The 2d Platoon went around and approached the village on the left of the 1st Platoon. The 1st Platoon started up the hill behind the village on the right slope, and the 2d Platoon took another ridgeline. Both platoons met on the hill, and the 1st Platoon cut to the right to another ridgeline. The 2d Platoon moved east up the original ridgeline. There were brush fires all the way up the ridges.

At 1200 hours the 3d Squad of the 2d Platoon hit a bouncing betty booby trap, killing the squad leader. The platoon withdrew and brought the squad leader's body with them. The platoon cut across and followed the 1st Platoon. The 1st Platoon advanced forward about 500 yards, stopped, and set up a perimeter. A brush fire started up the ridge to the 2d Platoon's right front, toward an enemy pillbox, and a North Korean "gook" came out and brushed away the fire. The 1st Platoon and one squad of the 2d Platoon opened fire on him. The machine gunner saw four other enemy come down with new uniforms that looked like Chinese Communists, and he placed fire on them. The platoons held there about an hour while radio contact was made with the company commander.

The 1st Platoon was ordered to send out a squad patrol to the pillbox. The patrol advanced a short way and was pinned down by machine-gun and small-arms fire from the direct front near the pillbox. The patrol returned fire and then returned to the platoon area. Captain Jackson, the Company L commander, had artillery and 81mm mortar fire placed on the enemy positions. When the fire lifted, the 1st Platoon sent out another patrol. Fifteen minutes later, a man from the patrol returned with a North Korean prisoner, who was sent back to the company CP. After the 1st Platoon secured the pillbox, the 2d Platoon followed the 1st Platoon patrol and moved up past the pillbox. The 1st Platoon then sent out a two-man patrol, which was pinned down by machine-gun fire from another small ridge to the front. The 2d Platoon and attached elements from Company M placed fire on the enemy. After ten minutes of firing, the 1st Platoon patrols were still unable to advance. In the meantime the 2d Battalion on the left was forcing the enemy toward Company L.

Lieutenant Palmer, the 2d Platoon leader, contacted the 1st Platoon leader, Master Sergeant Aguayo, and Captain Jackson in an effort to find out the situation. The company commander then ordered the 1st and 2d Platoons to withdraw. The platoons went back to the village where the company regrouped and went back to the main road. About 1900 hours the company passed the battalion CP and went into an assembly area for the night.[18]

The 3d Battalion's After Action Report summarizes the events of 5 April.

The MSR was closed to vehicular traffic due to mines and craters. Supplies were brought forward by native carrying parties. At 0800 on 5 April the battalion began their attack with Companies K and L abreast with Company K on the right; Company I moved along the road with the tanks as the road was cleared. Companies K and L moved forward to take Hill 578. Light opposition was met initially. Considerable enemy mortar fire was received, killing the commanding officer of Company K. At 1715 hours Company L was still meeting opposition just short of Hill 578. Company I was ordered to move up on the left of Company K to a position on a ridge leading to Hill 578. Company L was ordered to withdraw and tie in on the right of Company K for the night. During the day a considerable number of enemy soldiers were killed by small-arms fire. The woods were on fire, driving the enemy from their foxholes and making them an excellent target for riflemen. Orders were received from the 23d Infantry Regiment at 2130 to attack at 0800 hours on 6 April to seize Hill 541 and to continue on order to seize Hill 663.[19]

Clearing the High Ground: 3d Battalion, 23d Infantry, 6–7 April

Orders from the 23d Infantry Regiment called for continuing attacks to clear the high ground to the left of the Soyang River road. Lieutenant Colonel Richardson describes the operations of the next day, 6 April.

During the night the 3d Battalion was ordered by regimental headquarters to proceed through Naep'yong-ni to Hill 541, which was situated on the restraining line initially designated. At 0800 hours on 6 April the battalion moved out in attack with Company L on the right and Company I on the left. Company K followed

Company I. While closing in on the objective, the battalion received approximately twelve to fifteen rounds of enemy 60mm mortar fire and occasional enemy long-range small-arms fire from the vicinity of Hill 578. Hill 541 was secured by 1400 hours. That night the battalion was disposed with Company I on the west slope of the hill, Company L on the objective, and Company K on the right, tied in with the 1st Battalion, 23d Infantry Regiment. This was the initial contact with other elements of the 23d Infantry since leaving Ch'unch'on.[20]

Members of Company L provide additional details of the fighting on 6 April.

LIEUTENANTS BARENKAMP, EXECUTIVE OFFICER, AND PALMER, 2D PLATOON LEADER, COMPANY L: At 0800 hours on 6 April, Company L received orders to secure the high ground east of Tangol. The 2d Platoon was to stay in position and support the attack of the 1st and 3d Platoons, but fog limited visibility. At 0930 the 2d Platoon pulled off and rejoined the other two platoons. Company I had remained in position but moved out at this time to secure their objective about 500 yards southwest of Hill 541. This was supposed to have been done after Company L had secured their objective.

In the meantime the 3d Platoon of Company L had received heavy enemy automatic-weapons fire, and tanks and quad 50s on the Ch'unch'on–Naep'yong-ni road placed supporting fire on the company's objective. The 3d Platoon managed to secure a little knoll. As the 1st Platoon passed through in attack, it received enemy 60mm mortar fire. Company L finally reached its initial objective southwest of Hill 541, and Company I pushed on through and secured Hill 541. The 3d Battalion formed a line of companies on the hill for the night with Company I on the left, Company L in the center, and Company K on the right extending down to the road. About 2200 hours, Company L received a few rounds of enemy 60mm mortar fire, and at 0300 the battalion CP received some long-range enemy artillery and 120mm mortar fire.[21]

CORPORAL NISHIDA, 1ST PLATOON, AND PRIVATE FIRST CLASS VICKERS, 2D PLATOON, COMPANY L: On 6 April the company moved out up the road to the east with four tanks, two twin 40s, and six quad 50s. After passing through a village, the company swung left and started up a hill. The company took the hill with no enemy opposition. The 3d Platoon then pushed through the 1st Platoon and secured the high ground to the front against light automatic-weapons fire from a hill to the right. Twin 40 and artillery fire was placed on the enemy positions. Company I on the left came up on the next ridgeline. While advancing we saw many old and rusted booby traps.

The 1st Platoon secured the next higher ground and was joined by the remainder of the company. Several enemy 60mm mortar rounds came in, wounding several men. Company I, working up the left side, also received enemy mortar fire. Artillery was placed on the hill where the mortar fire was thought to be coming from. Company I sent out a patrol, and Company L followed and went down a ridgeline to the right where they tied in for the night. Company K tied in on the right of Company L.[22]

Colonel Richardson relates the plan of attack and ensuing operations on 7 April to capture Hill 663.

The 3d Battalion objective for 7 April was designated as Hill 663. The plan of maneuver was for Company I to lead the attack, followed by Companies L and K. Company I crossed the line of departure at 0800 hours and by 0900 reported enemy small-arms and mortar fire coming from pillboxes on Hill 663. I then directed Company L to select the most practical route to the left of Company I and to outflank the pillboxes and trenches on the hill. Artillery and mortar fire was placed on the target in the meantime. When Company L was in a position generally abreast with Company I, it was also engaged by an unknown enemy group. After another artillery barrage, approaches to the objective were occupied by 1830 hours. The battalion organized in a line running generally northwest to southeast, with Company K on the right, Company I in the center, and Company L on the left, facing north.[23]

Capt. Gerald W. Barnitz, the new commander of Company I, describes his company's attack on Hill 663.

I assumed command of Company I on 6 April during an attack

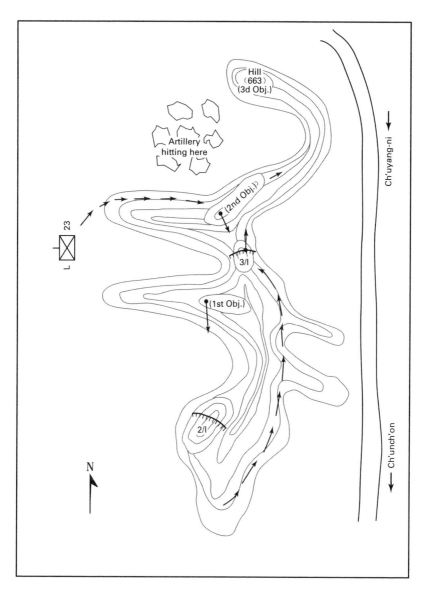

Assault on Hill 663, 7 April 1951 (sketch based on Capt. Barnitz interview in CMH manuscript, U.S. Army; not to scale).

by the company on Hill 541. At the time, 1st Lt. Robert J. Griffith was in command of the company. When I joined the company the 1st Platoon had already taken Hill 541, which screened the rest of the company's approach to the three assigned objectives. The objectives were Nan (about two-thirds of the distance between Hills 541 and 663), Peter (halfway between Objective Nan and Hill 663), and Victor (Hill 663). The battalion commander, Lt. Col. Beverly Richardson, had an OP overlooking the first two objectives and directed mortar and artillery concentrations on the objectives as the company moved out. Company L was to follow my company and secure Hill 541, releasing the 1st Platoon back to the control of Company I.

Company I moved out in a column of platoons—2d, 3d, 4th, and 1st—and took what was thought to be the first objective without any enemy opposition. However, there was a slight mix-up on intermediate objectives, and the advance continued on to Nan, the first objective. The 2d Platoon scouts received enemy automatic-weapons fire from well-dug-in enemy on a ridgeline to the right. The bunker-type emplacements were forty yards below the crest of Objective Peter. Very accurate machine-gun fire was received from the enemy to the left.

The 2d Platoon deployed along the ridge and returned fire on the objective. The 3d Platoon moved up one squad to support the 2d Platoon, and the other two squads covered a finger to the right to protect against a possible enemy flanking attack. Lieutenant Griffith was with the 2d Platoon at the time, along with the mortar and artillery forward observers, and was having mortar and artillery concentrations placed on the enemy positions. Lieutenant Griffith notified me that the platoon could not advance. I notified the battalion commander, who in turn ordered Company L to move up through Hoe-gol and down the ridge to hit the enemy's left flank.

When I saw Company L moving up the ridgeline, I sent the 3d Platoon to the right to contact them. By this time the firing from the first objective (Nan) had ceased. As the 3d Platoon reached the peak of the first objective, it received enemy automatic-weapons and 2.36-inch bazooka fire from the ridgeline to the northeast, to the right of the second objective (Peter). Lieutenant Dieter W. Rampendahl, the 2d Platoon leader, who had advanced up with the 3d Platoon, grabbed a machine gun and killed four or five North Koreans on the ridgeline.

From his OP, the battalion commander could see men around a pillbox on the first objective but couldn't see the air panel. Mistaking them for enemy forces, he called for mortar fire on the objective, which forced the men to take shelter in the pillbox. I immediately informed the battalion commander and had the fire placed on the ridge to the left and right of the second objective (Peter). The enemy fled to the north to Hill 663, which was the third objective (Victor); and the 3d Platoon continued on to the second objective unopposed.

Captain Jackson, Company L commander, noticed several hundred enemy on the trail about 500 yards west of Hill 663 and called for artillery fire. As the remainder of Company I closed on the second objective, artillery fire was observed combing the road and draws.

The Company I OP, with the artillery and mortar forward observers, moved to the second objective where a clear view of Hill 663 could be seen. A huge pillbox, approximately thirty feet across and with a stone wall around it, could be seen directly on the top. I think that this was part of the original South Korean defense line on the 38th parallel. Mortar and artillery fire was placed on the hill covering the forward and reverse slopes. After the barrage lifted, the 1st Platoon went forward following the ridgeline on the reverse slope. No opposition was encountered, and the hill was taken by 1800 hours. No enemy dead were found, although traces of fresh blood could be seen. Company L moved up to the ridge on the left of the trail and tied in on Company I's left flank.

The battalion commander and Captain Jackson, Company L commander, came over to Hill 663. At this time a friendly 155mm shell exploded over the hill, killing Lieutenant Rampendahl and wounding several others. Because of darkness, a battalion defense line was established with Company K on the right extending to the river, Company I in the center, and Company L on the left flank. During the early morning hours, Company L repulsed a light enemy probing attack. Company I had no enemy contact.[24]

Other members of Company I provide additional information about the capture of Hill 663 on 7 April.

LIEUTENANT RODGERS, 4TH PLATOON LEADER OF COMPANY I:
On 6 April, Captain Barnitz took over the company from Lieutenant McCoy who was to be rotated. Company I was given the mission of securing Objectives Nan, Peter, and Victor. The company
moved out in a column of platoons—2d, 4th, 1st, and 3d—and was
supported by overhead fire from tanks and quad 50s on the
Ch'unch'on–Naep'yong-ni road.

The 2d Platoon got on a small peak, which was thought to be
Objective Nan, but was ordered on to the next crest, which was re-
ally the first objective. The 2d Platoon spotted thirty to forty enemy
soldiers on Nan and engaged them with machine-gun fire. The platoon assaulted the position and forced the enemy to flee in a disorganized state toward a little knoll between Nan and Peter. The
entire ridgeline had well-prepared defensive positions. I estimate
that one-third of the enemy soldiers were killed by the 2d Platoon.

Captain Barnitz ordered the 3d Platoon around the right side of
Nan below the ridgeline to attack the right side of the knoll that the
enemy was on. The 2d and 4th Platoons laid down a base of fire
covering the attack. The enemy withdrew to Peter, and the 3d Platoon was ordered to seize it. Approximately seventy-five yards from
the objective, the platoon received enemy machine-gun, mortar, and
small-arms fire. The 1st Platoon had followed the 3d Platoon up the
ridgeline and had received enemy machine-gun fire from a ridge
finger to the right front, where eight to ten enemy could be seen. The
1st Platoon deployed its automatic weapons and returned fire to
their right front and on Objective Peter. The firefight lasted twenty
minutes. At 1600 hours, the 3d Platoon took Peter without further
opposition. One short friendly 155mm round landed in the area and
killed Lieutenant Rampendahl.

The remainder of the company rejoined the 3d Platoon on Peter
and prepared to support the 1st Platoon in an attack on Victor [Hill
663]. Artillery, 4.2-inch, and 81mm mortar fire was placed on Victor, which was very ineffective. The mortar crews claimed the range
was too great. Company L was approaching Peter from the left up a
ridgeline and was ordered to support Company I's attack on Victor.
Company K was to follow Company I to Victor.

No enemy opposition was encountered, and Victor was secured

by 1715 hours. The remainder of the battalion joined Company I on the objective, as sporadic sniper fire came into the battalion area from the high ground to the right of the Ch'unch'on–Naep'yong-ni road. The battalion commander came up to Victor and assigned the defensive positions for the night.

From Victor many of the former South Korean defense positions on the 38th parallel could be seen. Some of the ridge fingers had old enemy dead dressed in winter clothes lying around. They were evidently killed by air strikes.[25]

1ST LT. JOSE L. PERDOMO, 2D PLATOON LEADER, COMPANY I: The 3d Platoon was told to move up a ridgeline leading into a higher ridge to the front. Company L was pushing up another ridge on the left paralleling the approach of the 3d Platoon. Company L ran into some resistance and displayed their panel. The enemy withdrew from in front of Company L and came over to the right and placed small-arms and automatic-weapons fire on the 3d Platoon.

The 1st Platoon, following the 3d Platoon, immediately laid down a base of fire with BARs and machine guns, forcing the enemy to withdraw. The 3d Platoon then took the objective against no further resistance. No enemy dead were found, but evidence of fresh blood could be seen. The 1st and 2d Platoons, led by Lieutenant Craig, passed through the 3d Platoon's positions and took the next objective against no resistance. On the next objective, Lieutenant Rampendahl was killed by a short artillery round.[26]

Members of Company L describe their role in the attack on Hill 663.

LIEUTENANTS BARENKAMP, EXECUTIVE OFFICER, AND PALMER, 2D PLATOON LEADER, COMPANY L: On 7 April, Company I had the mission of taking Hill 663 and was to be followed by Company K. Company L was in reserve and could observe Company I moving up on the right to three small peaks. When it reached the vicinity of Objective Nan it received heavy enemy small-arms and automatic-weapons fire. Company L was then ordered to go up and support Company I. The company moved out in a column of platoons—2d, 1st, 4th, and 3d—and moved down through a rice paddy, swung left of Hoe-gol, and from there went up on a high ridge to the left of

Company I. When Company L reached the top, the 2d Platoon swung down to help Company I. During this time, friendly 155mm and 105mm howitzers were shelling Hill 663. The 2d Platoon, approaching to within 50 yards of Company I, observed thirty enemy soldiers fleeing down a ridgeline to the northwest of Hill 663. The platoon placed machine-gun and 75mm recoilless-rifle fire on the enemy. Approximately 400 rounds of 81mm mortar and artillery were also placed on the fleeing enemy. At 1430, Company I moved out and secured Hill 663 with no further enemy opposition. The hill was the battalion objective, and plans were made for setting up a perimeter on it for the night. The companies formed a line of defense, and the men occupied former ROK defense positions overlooking the 38th parallel.[27]

Cpl. Nishida, 1st Platoon, and PFC Vickers, 2d Platoon, Company L: At 0800 hours on 7 April, Company I led off in the attack to seize Hill 663. The 2d Platoon of Company L followed Company I, leading the company. The 2d Platoon of Company L advanced up the road about a fourth of a mile and started down a ridge to the left of Company I. The 1st Platoon went up the valley to the right of the 2d Platoon and met the 1st Platoon on top of the ridge, and a junction was made with Company I. Company L was hit by nine short rounds of friendly artillery during the advance, and one man, Master Sergeant Aguayo, was killed. The men were told that Company I had sent a nine-man patrol to the next pillbox, and the company was to move on down and contact the patrol. The company arrived there at 1615 hours. The 2d Squad started over toward Company I's objective and received enemy machine-gun fire from the right front. Friendly machine-gun fire from the 2d Platoon was placed on the enemy, forcing the enemy to lift their fire from the squad and return fire on the friendly machine gun. The squad was forced to take cover in a trench, and, about dark, fifteen North Koreans moved from a hill to the right and opened fire on the trench with burp guns. The squad withdrew under the cover of darkness back to the reverse slope of the ridge and returned to the company. A company perimeter was established on high ground for the night. There was no enemy contact.[28]

PFC David E. Russell, machine gunner, 1st Platoon, Company L: At 0800 hours Company L came off the hill, followed the road [to Hoe-gol] for approximately one mile, and then turned right up a draw to attack Hill 663. There were two ridge fingers, which led to the crest of Hill 663, and these joined approximately halfway up the slope. The 2d Platoon advanced up the finger to the left, and the 1st Platoon up the one on the right. The two platoons met at 0930 and had not encountered any enemy fire. The 2d Platoon then moved out toward the peak followed by the 1st Platoon. About halfway up the ridgeline, the 2d Platoon received sporadic small-arms fire but continued to advance. During the advance, eight 105mm howitzer rounds landed in the 1st Platoon's area but inflicted no casualties. When the fire was lifted, the remainder of the company joined the 2d Platoon. While moving up, we could hear 155mm howitzer rounds hitting Company I's objective.

As the 1st Platoon neared the crest of the ridge, it could see the enemy caught in a cross fire between Companies I and L. The 2d Platoon of Company L pressed the attack, supported by the 1st Platoon. At this time a single 155mm round exploded in the 1st Platoon's positions, killed Master Sergeant Aguayo and an unknown lieutenant [Rampendahl], and wounded an entire squad of riflemen. After an hour's firefight, Companies I and L dug in on their ridges with the enemy in between, thus keeping the enemy in the trap. The companies did not fire during the night, and the enemy kept up harassing fire throughout the night. During the night the enemy withdrew.[29]

M. Sgt. George D. Chamberlain, platoon sergeant of the 1st Platoon in Company K, watched the fighting from his position in reserve.

On 7 April, Company K was ordered to the hill patrolled by the 1st Platoon the day before. The battalion commander went with the company. Company L was attacking a very high hill to the front of Company K, and Company I was attacking up a ridgeline toward the right flank of Company L. Approximately an enemy company was opposing Companies I and L. Friendly mortar and artillery fire was falling on the enemy's positions.

A South Korean interpreter with Company K heard a radio transmission by the enemy ordering his forces to withdraw. The information was passed on to the battalion commander, who quickly notified Companies I and L to attack and secure the positions. Heavy casualties were inflicted on the enemy, and the hill was secured at 1600 hours.

After the hill was secured, the 1st Platoon of Company K was ordered to join Company I. The remainder of Company K was ordered to go with tanks up the road to clear the small village of Ch'uyang-ni. The 1st Platoon joined Company I and was ordered to tie in with their defenses near the road. At the time, Company I was receiving long-range enemy small-arms fire from their front. The remainder of Company K was supposed to tie in from the road up to the ridge, but never did, leaving a gap of 500 yards to the road. When the 1st Platoon went into position, a friendly artillery shell fell short into the platoon area and killed several men. The platoon secured the right flank by making a strong point with a machine gun. The platoon leader, Lieutenant Hall, ordered the assistant platoon sergeant to go to battalion headquarters to see whether Company K would tie in and to see what the next day's orders were. All this was after dark, and it was difficult to maintain control. The sergeant reported back and said the platoon was to rejoin the company at the road near the tanks of the 72d Tank Battalion in the morning. The rest of the night was quiet.[30]

Sgt. Brown, 1st Platoon; SFC Glassman, 2d Platoon; and SFC Burgi, 3d Platoon, all Company K, provide their observations of the action along the river on 7 April.

On the morning of 7 April the 2d Platoon moved out with five tanks and two quad 50s to cross the 38th parallel and shoot up the village of Ch'uyang-ni. The patrol moved up the riverbed, but the tanks drowned out. The patrol started to receive enemy mortar fire from a hill overlooking the road junction, the "Rock of Gibraltar." The quad 50s returned fire on the hill. At 1500 hours the tanks came abreast with the infantry platoon, and together they advanced to the 38th parallel. Word was received for the patrol to hold until the remainder of Company K moved up. In the meantime Company

A, 23d Infantry Regiment, called over to the patrol and pointed out an enemy machine gun in front of Company A's positions. The patrol from Company K succeeded in capturing the machine gun and four or five prisoners.

The 1st, 3d, and 4th Platoons moved up the ridgeline through Company L, supposedly to tie in with the tanks and 2d Platoon on the right on the low ground. When the company, minus the 2d Platoon, had moved into position, a short friendly artillery round fell in the area, killing one man and wounding two others. The Company I commanding officer ordered Company K off the ridgeline back to the right flank of Company I. It was dark at the time, and Lieutenant Hall sent Sergeant Brown to the battalion CP, where he was told that a gap of 400 yards existed on the right flank. Colonel Richardson, the battalion commander, said for Company K not to close the gap but to remain in position until the next morning.[31]

The "Rock of Gibraltar": 3d Battalion, 23d Infantry, 8 April

With the capture of Hill 663 and the old South Korean defenses overlooking the 38th parallel, the 3d Battalion faced North Korea's border fortifications. Lieutenant Colonel Richardson describes the 3d Battalion's advance on 8 April.

The battalion was ordered to send a strong company-size tank-infantry patrol east along the MSR to the vicinity of Ch'uyang-ni with the mission of reconnoitering the road and securing the road junction on the 38th parallel. Company K was assigned the mission.

At 0800 hours on 8 April the patrol moved out and, after traveling approximately 1,000 yards, encountered mines and craters. The road paralleled the river so closely that there was no room for the tanks to bypass, and efforts to ford the river failed. Company K dismounted and continued. They met bitter enemy resistance on the high ground overlooking the road junction. The enemy was so strongly entrenched that the ground was called the "Rock of Gibraltar."

The rest of the battalion also moved out at 0800 hours toward the southern extremity of Hill mass 1198, Whitehead Mountain [about 8,000 yards north of Ch'uyang-ni]. Company L moved out to clear Hill 663 before turning directly north and crossing the 38th parallel. The company had to fight for three hours before taking the hill, and air strikes supported the attack. At 1100 hours the commanding officer of Company L reported enemy vehicular traffic moving to the northwest along the Hwach'on–Ch'uyang-ni (northwest–southeast) road. Companies I and L swung across the road, but the enemy could no longer be seen. Company I was on a ridge finger to the left of Company L and had approached to within 800 to 1,000 yards of the 3d Battalion objective [an unnumbered hill about 2,500 yards northwest of Ch'uyang-ni] by 1700 hours. Due to darkness, the companies were ordered to organize separate perimeters for the night.

During the afternoon, Company K battled to within 100 yards of the hillcrest at the road junction. From my OP on Hill 663 I could see its air panel and knew the company could not reach the objective. Company K was ordered back to the battalion OP for the night.

The enemy defense positions on Hill 663 were former ROK defense lines placed along the 38th parallel prior to the outbreak of hostilities in June 1950. The ridgeline of Hill 663 was littered with enemy bodies that had been dead two months or longer.[32]

Members of Company K describe the fighting to capture the "Rock of Gibraltar" overlooking Ch'uyang-ni.

1ST LT. VIVIOUS M. HALL, 1ST PLATOON LEADER, COMPANY K: At 0700 hours on 8 April my platoon moved down to the road and rejoined the company. The company moved eastward on the MSR with the 2d Platoon in the lead followed by the 3d Platoon. The 1st and 4th Platoons brought up the rear. The company approached the "Rock of Gibraltar" and was held up by enemy small-arms and mortar fire coming from the right of the hill. Tanks were deployed across the river, and the 1st Battalion, 23d Infantry Regiment, came up on the right.

Captain Perry dispatched the 3d Platoon to take the "Rock of Gibraltar," and at 1400 hours the platoon moved out in the attack. After going 200 yards, the platoon ran into barbed wire entanglements and was pinned down by small-arms fire. Captain Perry then ordered me to attack the hill. I moved my platoon to the left of the 3d Platoon, traversed a ridge covered with trees and bushes, and then crossed an open field to the base of the hill. No enemy fire was encountered en route to the ridge fingers, but one man was wounded by a bouncing betty AP mine. I sent two squads forward in a skirmish line, and set up the platoon machine gun in support of the attacking elements. The two attacking squads reached the first ridgeline and found unmanned enemy emplacements. I brought the platoon machine gun up to cover an attack on a second ridgeline. The attacking elements received enemy small-arms and automatic-weapons fire from the direct front and right front. I grouped my three rifle squads on line and prepared to attack forward. About the same time, a friendly plane with a loud speaker flew over and broadcasted: "If any groups of enemy want to surrender, don't shoot them." The enemy ceased firing, and the plane flew around the hill for about ten minutes broadcasting in Korean. A Korean interpreter with my platoon called and asked the enemy to surrender and told them that the platoon was going to attack. One of the enemy soldiers told the interpreter that he was hit in the leg and couldn't surrender. The interpreter said the enemy soldier was lying. So, the platoon opened fire, launched the attack, and killed four of the enemy. Two of the enemy did surrender to the platoon. My platoon still had to take the higher ground, and there were 200 yards of open ridgeline in between us and the summit.

The platoon was low on ammunition, and I organized the platoon and had one squad cover each slope. The platoon then withdrew back down to the bottom of the ridge and did not receive any enemy fire in the withdrawal. During the attack, we lost the platoon sergeant and five men. I contacted Captain Perry and moved back to the vicinity of the tanks for the night.[33]

M. SGT. CHAMBERLAIN, PLATOON SERGEANT, 1ST PLATOON, COMPANY K: On 8 April the 1st Platoon rejoined the company and started out, with the 3d Platoon leading. The company was divided along each side of the road until terrain forced them back on the road. Tanks were following behind along the edge of the river. Later, quad 50s and twin 40s came up and supported the advance from the road. After the company moved about half a mile it started to re-

ceive enemy 120mm mortar and artillery fire, limiting the movement. The 1st Platoon to the rear received orders that the 3d Platoon
was halted and that we were to swing around and attack a small hill
to the left of the road. Long-range bursts of enemy machine-gun fire
were coming in from a high hill to the north. Artillery, mortar,
tank, and AAA fire was placed on both hills prior to the attack
launch.

The 1st Platoon leader, Lieutenant Hall, decided to move the
platoon across a field in a single file to approach the hill. This was
fortunate because we discovered the field had many antipersonnel
mines, and none were exploded. The men were ordered to proceed
to the hill as fast as possible and to form a skirmish line at the base.
The platoon then moved up cautiously, one knoll at a time. As the
platoon got about three-fourths of the way up, a friendly loudspeaker came on suddenly and scared the platoon. We had no previous
notice that this would take place. The speaker said to allow the enemy groups to surrender. The platoon then continued to move up,
and the lead scouts spotted five or six enemy soldiers on the high
ground fifty yards to the north. The platoon leader had the South
Korean interpreter call to the enemy asking them to surrender. The
platoon received no reply, so we assaulted the hill. The enemy
started throwing hand grenades down on the attacking platoon. I
was hit at this time and evacuated.[34]

SGT. BROWN, 1ST PLATOON; SFC GLASSMAN, 2D PLATOON;
AND SFC BURGI, 3D PLATOON, ALL COMPANY K: At 0600 hours on
8 April, Company K moved off the ridgeline to the road and joined
with the 2d Platoon. At 0830 the company came abreast with tanks
along the riverbed, and by 1100 hours had pushed to within 500
yards of the road junction at the 38th parallel. Enemy small-arms
and machine-gun fire was placed on the advancing troops from the
"Rock of Gibraltar." The enemy had spiral trenches and pillboxes
about seventy-five yards from the bottom of the hill, and pillboxes
extending down the ridgelines. Two big pillboxes were on the very
top. In the meantime, Company A, on the right across the river on
the high ground, was placing fire on the hill.

By 1300 hours the tanks moved up into the river flats and fired directly on the hill. Company K was receiving enemy 60mm and 120mm mortar fire at this time, but held their positions until Company C, 23d Infantry Regiment, came up on the left flank. Companies L and I also moved up on the left of Company K. At 1500 hours the 3d Platoon, Company K, moved out through a booby-trapped field to assault the "Rock of Gibraltar" and was followed by the remainder of the company. Small-arms and mortar fire was received from the hill behind the "Rock of Gibraltar" and forced the 3d Platoon to halt their attack. The 1st Platoon managed to reach the base of the hill, and while the company's 57mm recoilless-rifle crews laid a base of fire, the platoon moved up the hill in an assault formation. Small-arms fire from the top of the hill and from the hill to the rear harassed the platoon during their advance.

Upon reaching the top of the hill, a South Korean interpreter tried to get the enemy to surrender, but the enemy would not reply. When the platoon was ready to carry on the assault, a friendly loudspeaker in the valley called for the enemy to surrender. The friendly loudspeaker took the platoon by complete surprise, and everything halted for a moment. During the moment of silence, an enemy soldier threw a hand grenade, and the platoon assaulted the enemy's position. The enemy (approximately a hundred) withdrew to higher ground to the rear and placed fire on the platoon. In the meantime the 3d Platoon had withdrawn and followed the 1st Platoon up the hill. Due to the approaching darkness and the need for resupply of ammunition, the platoons withdrew back to the road and joined the tanks. The enemy did not fire at the platoons during the withdrawal. The 1st Platoon and the tanks crossed the river and tied in with Company A, 1st Battalion, 23d Infantry Regiment. The night was uneventful.[35]

Securing the Flank and Rear

While the 3d Battalion of the 23d Infantry pushed east, clearing the high ground along the road to Ch'uyang-ni, the regiment's 1st Battalion secured its rear and protected its right flank, while engineers worked to clear the main supply route from Ch'unch'on to

Naep'yong-ni and other roads running north from the river into the hills. M. Sgt. Warren F. Dailey, a reconnaissance sergeant in the 2d Engineer Battalion, describes these efforts.

On 4 April we knew the enemy was along the Soyang River and some were still south of the river. The engineer reconnaissance teams left Ch'unch'on about 0730 hours and took notes of roads and bridge information. We ran a detailed reconnaissance (culverts, roads, dimensions of bridges, etc.) out to where the enemy had placed a minefield on the road about 500 yards west of Sugu-dong. A tank from the 72d Tank Battalion of the 2d Infantry Division had hit a mine and was destroyed. Behind it was a destroyed 2½-ton truck. When we saw the destroyed tank we assumed the MSR was mined from then on out. Friendly troops were around the area, and someone had built a temporary bypass around the mined area in the road. We drove along the road between marching Marines and 23d Infantry soldiers, which had come out of the high ground south of the river. At 1530 hours, about 300 yards west of Sugu-dong, we reached a huge hand-dug crater, twenty feet long, from the roadbed to the creek bed, and thirty feet deep. The high ground to the northeast of the crater was in enemy hands, and infantry were fighting all along the hills, especially around Hill 568.

We walked with the infantry along the road and found wooden box AP mines (twenty-three were later taken out of the road). Trees were cut down across the road, and along a little narrow spot, tons of rock had been dislodged onto the road. While walking along the road, we received scattered bursts of ineffective small-arms fire. When we reached the bridge about halfway between Sugu-dong and Puch'ang-ni, an enemy machine gun opened up on the infantry on the road, and I saw three men fall. The infantry took cover in the hills and started to withdraw. We ran back along the road until protected by a hill from machine-gun fire. We then walked carefully down the road. We saw spots where dirt in the road had been disturbed, and when we put bayonets on our carbines and probed, we found mines. I removed detonator caps from two of the mines. We returned to the jeep at the crater, where we wrote up the day's work. By that time the roads were jammed with vehicles from the 23d Infantry. At 1730 we managed to bypass the vehicles near the crater and returned by jeep to the engineer company CP. A detailed report of everything was sent back, including the number of sand-bags required to fill the crater, and maps.

At 0630 hours on 5 April my recon team went back to the site of the crater. During the night the 8th Engineer Battalion of the 1st Cavalry Division had fixed the crater so a jeep could cross it with difficulty. We reached the road junction at Sugu-dong, where a 1½-ton trailer had hit a mine and was torn up. An officer from the 23d Infantry told me that the road due north, called the French Road, was heavily mined. My driver and I dismounted, went up the road about 600 yards, and saw several mangled bodies blown up by mines. I saw box mines along the road; they had been removed by the French. As we went up the road, about three to eight rounds of 60mm or 81mm mortar rounds fell on the road. The first three rounds fell about 150 to 200 yards north of where we were. Enemy small-arms fire hit at our heels as we ran back toward the jeep. When we went up the road we saw an abandoned empty ¼-ton trailer near the first ford. No friendly vehicles had been up the road before, and we thought the trailer had been captured by the enemy and abandoned. The tires were flat. French soldiers were around the road guarding two or three prisoners. During this time we heard heavy firing around Hill 568, and six air strikes hit the hill.

At 0900 we came back to the jeep and continued eastward on the MSR. The 23d Infantry Regiment's Antitank and Mine Platoon was sweeping the road for mines and blasting the boulders and trees out of the road. We drove cautiously. Harassing mortar fire hit the road approximately 500 yards in front of the jeep. I was hoping the day would end so I could go back to the engineer company, eat, and sleep. We proceeded to the pass east of Puch'ang-ni where we went around a curve and met a 2d Engineer jeep with a flat tire. Lt. Russell Blosser was with the vehicle. We stopped and helped repair the tire. About twenty rounds of 81mm mortar fire landed at the top of the pass about 250 yards to the east. We took cover in the ditch and under the jeep. After we saw where the rounds were landing and that there was no danger, we continued to change the tire. Lieutenant Blosser and I walked on up the pass when the mortar fire ceased, while the drivers moved the jeeps out of sight of any enemy observation. We walked to the top of the hill and saw reconnaissance teams from the 23d Infantry with some forward observers. Two or three tanks were in the defile where the pass started to descend and were in plain view of the enemy. The enemy dropped about fifteen rounds of WP and HE mortar fire around the tanks and the top of the pass. We scattered and took cover as best we could. When the enemy fire lifted, we walked down the hill and found three hand-dug craters, twenty feet by fifteen feet by twelve feet deep. As we got the information on the last crater, enemy mortar fire began again, and we ran up the hill and took cover. Lieutenant Blosser told me to radio the engineer company to send up a bulldozer, four truckloads of sandbags, and one platoon of men to the pass. After I sent the message, my team got in our jeep, went to the foot of the pass, and checked the river. It was deep and swift; fording was impossible. At about 1200 hours we returned to the engineer company and radioed to the 2d Engineer Battalion the information on both roads.

At about 1230 hours we drove to the top of the pass again, and all mortar fire had ceased. I left one man (Sgt. Earl J. Cayemberg) with the jeep to watch the radio; Cpl. Elmer L. Bartley and I walked along the MSR to within 300 yards of Naep'yong-ni. At that point we received heavy small-arms fire from an undetermined enemy position. We withdrew about 1630 hours and went up a northern trail to Hach'on. During this time the 23d Infantry's AT&M Platoon was removing mines from the road. They had taken about thirty-one American and Communist antitank and antipersonnel mines out of a five-hundred-yard stretch. Sniper fire hit the ground around the minesweepers. The men in the AT&M Platoon said they had been getting sniper fire all day long. They also warned us it was not safe to walk along the road. In the meantime, the craters had been filled and the MSR made passable for jeeps.

About 0830 hours on 6 April, Company B of the 2d Engineer Battalion moved up the MSR to Kusong-ni, and my reconnaissance team went with them. After the company closed in the area, my team made a quick hurried reconnaissance to where the line troops were fighting. We found the road mined and we returned. On the way back I met Lieutenant William Anderson on the road, and together we drove up a trail to the northeast [from Kusong-ni to

Muran-ni] where we met an infantry captain. We asked him where the front lines were, and he told us that the enemy was on Hill 578 and extended over to Hill 734. He said that friendly troops were up the trail to the northwest. Lieutenant Anderson and I dismounted and walked up the trail to Muran-ni. When we reached the village, we saw soldiers' pants and shirts hanging on the lines around the houses. We also spotted a woman and child near the huts. Small-arms fire was heard on the high ground northeast of the village. Other houses in the village were destroyed. No enemy soldiers were seen, but the hill to the right showed evidence of WP fire. We returned and met Brig. Gen. George C. Stewart, who wanted to know how far we had gone. When we showed him on the map, he told us that we had been in enemy territory. He asked us if we would guide tanks and infantrymen up the road. Lieutenant Anderson took a platoon of infantry up the road later that afternoon.

We returned at 1200 hours and ate chow with Company B. At 1230 my team moved to Naep'yong-ni. While I was checking a bridge in the village, a Korean child about a hundred feet away stepped off the road to let another jeep go by and struck an AP mine. The child was killed instantly. Three mines were later found underneath where my reconnaissance jeep was parked. We found some hand grenades and abandoned enemy equipment under the bridge. About 1330 hours we went to where six or seven tanks with some quad 50s were off the road in the riverbed and rice paddies to the east. We parked near the tanks, and Bartley and I dismounted and walked to a small bridge in Yongsomegi. When we reached the bridge, we received some scattered rifle fire from the high ground southeast of the river. Friendly artillery was hitting around the high ground. I started up the road to get information on the bridge and came to three craters in the road. As I was getting dimensions on the three craters, Bartley shouted, "There's a gook; I'm going to shoot him." I told him not to shoot but to take him prisoner. Bartley told the North Korean to wade across the river. The enemy soldier took his clothes off and waded out up to his chin. The river washed his clothes away, and he went back to the opposite side. I continued down to the bridge and got the desired information. I was fired upon three times and returned to where Bartley was. The North

Korean was still across the river. We made him walk southward along the opposite side of the river about 1,000 meters to a point across from the tanks. A man from the 82d AAA went across and got him, and turned him over to the S-2 of the 3d Battalion, 23d Infantry. About 1730 hours we returned to Company B.

At 0630 hours on 7 April we went back up to the tanks, which had not moved from the day before, and left the jeep there. The 1st Platoon of Company B was working on craters, sandbagging and filling them. Mine sweepers were working to the bridge at Yong-somegi. My driver and I went up to the bridge, and tanks from the 72d Tank Battalion and the 82d AAA started firing on the hill mass north of Yongsomegi and on Hill 663. The fire grazed the road and pinned down the engineer platoon working on the craters. We crawled and ran back to the craters and remained twenty minutes until the fire lifted. The infantry started moving up to Hill 663, and so Bartley and I walked up the trail to the northwest. We were near Hoe-gol and received small-arms fire from the vicinity of Hill 663. We withdrew to Naep'yong-ni. In the afternoon we headed to Hach'on. On the way to the village I disarmed six box mines in the road and put up a sign saying the road was mined. I walked on to the 38th parallel where the road petered out. On the way I received small-arms and machine-gun fire from enemy bunkers on Hill 811. About 2100 hours we returned to Company B.

On 8 April my reconnaissance team drove up to Sangch'on and started northward along the trail to see how much damage friendly tanks had caused. I warned an artillery colonel from the 37th Field Artillery Battalion not to take tanks or artillery up the road because it was too narrow and had high, unmortared rock shoulders. We found the road torn to hell and saw a disabled tank that had thrown a track on the road. At 1730 we returned to Company B. During the night Maj. Clair Farley, executive officer of the 2d Engineer Battalion, told me he wanted information on the bridge at Ch'uyang-ni as quickly as possible the next day.

On 9 April an infantry platoon and a platoon of tanks supported my reconnaissance team. About 0800 hours we moved out with an AT&M Platoon sweeping the road for mines in front of the tanks. Everything was quiet, and the tanks approached Ch'uyang-ni. They stopped and deployed in the fields on the left of the road. Tank fire was placed on the hill north of Ch'uyang-ni, and infantry deployed along the ditches on each side of the road. Lieutenant Anderson and I walked forward with the AT&M Platoon about 500 to 600 yards, to within ten yards of the bridge. We saw that one span of the bridge was dropped and no bypass was available. I had just lit a cigarette when hell broke loose. Burp guns or machine guns shot the dirt out from under our feet. I jumped down a twenty-five-foot embankment, and when I hit bottom a machine gun burst hit about three or four feet from my head. I jumped up and ran back to a minefield south of Ch'uyang-ni. I jumped into a foxhole with three men from the AT&M Platoon. We were pinned down in the foxhole for about one hour. Lieutenant Anderson went to the tanks and had them fire on the hill. Finally when the enemy fire quieted down, I got out of the hole amidst intermittent enemy mortar fire and went down the road past the tanks to my jeep. Lt. Col. Edmund Leavy and Major Farley were there, and I gave them the information on the bridge.[36]

Capt. John N. Botkin, the assistant division engineer of the 2d Infantry Division, explains the significance of Sergeant Dailey's reconnaissance efforts.

The value of the reconnaissance performed by the S-2 reconnaissance team was that it operated several hours ahead of the infantry advance and found where the existing roads were cratered or blocked by landslides. This was important to determine the effort needed to open the route of advance. As a result of the continuing reconnaissance by Sergeant Dailey's team, the 2d Division eventually tripled the engineering effort usually allocated to a regimental combat team. Three engineer companies were assigned to the roads in the 23d Infantry Regiment's sector instead of one.[37]

The 1st Battalion, 23d Infantry, was the reserve for the regiment. Members of the 1st Battalion describe their operations.

CAPT. KERMIT H. SELVIG, COMPANY B COMMANDER: On 5 April Company B moved to the vicinity of Puch'ang-ni from the high ground south of the river. The 2d Platoon occupied low ground north of the village, and the 3d Platoon had the mission of establishing a roadblock east of town to block any enemy movement eastward along the Ch'unch'on–Naep'yong-ni road. The 1st Platoon was on high ground south of the river.

On 6 April the company moved into a blocking position at the pass over to Company C on Hill 392. About 1300 hours the 1st Battalion said that the 2d Battalion was receiving mortar fire, and Company B was ordered out on a company-size patrol. The company moved out on the ridgeline about 1,000 meters, until the village of Sanmak-tong could be seen. Six male civilians were observed sitting around an opening in a straw stack. I ordered a 57mm recoilless rifle to fire a WP round at them. The shell landed in the middle, ignited the straw, and mortar and small-arms ammunition started to explode in the stack. Two more houses in the village were fired upon with the same results. One was a definite bunker, camouflaged with new straw too thick to be realistic. I think the company had neutralized an enemy mortar position, because the enemy started throwing cases of ammunition out of one house. We killed about ten North Koreans in the village. The 2d Platoon deployed down the ridge to Yoonae and did not find anything. At 1700 hours the company withdrew to our old positions and remained there the rest of the night.

On 7 April Company A was at Naep'yong-ni trying to cross the river, and Company B remained in the same blocking positions. During the night the 1st Platoon was sent to a high point south of the river. At 0600 hours on 8 April my company moved down the road through Naep'yong-ni to Yongsomegi, turned north up a draw, and followed the ridgelines up to Hill 663. There we relieved Company I and remained for the night.[38]

1ST LT. JAMES B. SCHRYVER, 2D PLATOON LEADER, COMPANY A: On 4 April Company A was located near Kyonae-ri. The 2d and 3d Battalions of the 23d Infantry, along with the French Battalion, were in attack north of the Soyang River, and the 1st Battalion was in regimental reserve. The 2d Platoon of Company A was attached to the 3d Battalion to assist in carrying wire to the attacking companies. The platoon went into a perimeter defense at the 3d Battalion headquarters for the night. On 5 April, the 1st Battalion moved north of the river and went into blocking positions. At this time the platoon rejoined the company. The 1st Battalion remained in regimental reserve.

On 6 April Company A, with attachments from Company D, was assigned the mission of being a screening force for the 3d Battalion's attack. At 0530 the Company moved to Naep'yong-ni and waited while preparatory fire was placed on Hill 324, which was to be the company's immediate objective. At 0730 the company crossed the river, occupied the high ground, and then followed the ridgelines to the northeast to a hill overlooking the village of Yongsomegi. The area covered had apparently been occupied by friendly troops prior to Company A's movement, because some GI equipment and empty ration cans were found. Civilians in the area were interrogated and said that the enemy had moved to the west side of the river on 3 April. During the daylight hours fighting could be heard in the 3d Battalion's sector, but our company had no enemy contact.

The following day, 7 April, we continued advancing up the ridgelines overlooking the river. At 1500 hours we arrived on the high ground north of the village of Taedongni-Hach'on. Contact was made at noon with a friendly patrol from the 7th U.S. Infantry Division on Hill 663, and a company water detail received small-arms fire from that vicinity while they were at the river. The night was quiet.

The 1st Platoon, with an artillery FO, patrolled to the high ground about 1,000 yards northeast of Ch'uyang-ni. From the hill, enemy ammunition bearers on the road and enemy positions on the hill across the river could be seen. The platoon fired on these with BARs, machine guns, and 60mm mortars. At this time, tanks from the 72d Tank Battalion crossed the river and were in the vicinity of the patrol. They were firing directly on the enemy's positions. During the day the patrol had an 82mm mortar barrage for approximately one hour. There were no friendly casualties. The area had extensive entrenchments and pillboxes, and the patrol found the old barbed wire boundary at the 38th parallel. The area also had many crude enemy booby traps. The patrol returned to the company at 1800 hours and remained in position during the night with no enemy activity except a little inaccurate mortar fire.[39]

M. Sgt. Fillman B. Leaphart, 3d Platoon sergeant, Company A: On 8 April, Company A moved forward to the high ground east of Ch'uyang-ni. At the junction of the road on the opposite side of the river, tanks could be seen getting mortar fire. The tanks crossed over to the opposite side of the river to the vicinity of Yul-mun-ni and started to receive enemy self-propelled weapons fire from a hill to the north. One of the rounds landed in Company A's area and killed one man. The company then started to receive mortar fire. The 3d Battalion could be seen fighting for the "Rock of Gibraltar."[40]

The efforts of the 1st Battalion to secure the open right flank and of the engineers to clear the supply route to the 3d Battalion were successful. However, the 3d Battalion, after clearing the high ground along the river road, had now come upon the main enemy defenses. Overcoming the North Korean fortifications atop the "Rock of Gibraltar" and the surrounding high ground would require something more than a direct assault.

Chapter 10

OPERATION SWING— THE THRUST NORTH AND THE "SWING"

23d Infantry Regiment, 4–14 April 1951

While the 3d Battalion pushed east along the road paralleling the Soyang River and the 1st Battalion guarded the rear and right flank, the French Battalion on the left and the 2d Battalion in the center moved north toward the Hwach'on Reservoir. The thrust to the north initially met some opposition, but it soon appeared to promise better results than the 3d Battalion's attacks along the Soyang River.

The Initial Attack: 2d Battalion, 23d Infantry, 4–7 April

Members of the 2d Battalion, 23d Infantry Regiment, describe their move into position to relieve the Marines and their initial contact with the enemy.

MAJ. LLOYD K. JENSEN, COMMANDING OFFICER OF THE 2D BATTALION: Prior to crossing the 38th parallel, the 2d Battalion, 23d Infantry, relieved elements of the 3d Battalion, 5th Marine Regiment, on Hill 734. The hill was the objective of the Marines, and the 2d Battalion was to take over at 1800 hours. The Marines were still fighting for the objective when the leading elements of my battalion arrived at 1600 hours. By 1800, however, the hill had been secured.[1]

1ST. LT. CHESTER C. BRUMET, EXECUTIVE OFFICER OF COMPANY E: The 2d Battalion was in an assembly area near Ch'unch'on, and on 4 April we were given the mission of relieving the 5th Marine

Regiment on Hill 734. At 1230 hours the battalion moved eastward
on the Ch'unch'on–Naep'yong-ni road. Companies E and F were the
attacking elements. Company F led, followed by Company E, with
Company G in support. The machine-gun sections from Company
H were attached to each rifle company. The attack companies continued down the road behind the Marines, who had not taken the
objective. The companies cut off the road about 1,200 yards west of
the pass, and Company F started north through a draw. The Marines had 81mm mortars set up and were firing on Hill 734. Companies E and F moved up to Sanmak-tong and held up for thirty
minutes until the Marines had advanced farther. The 2d Battalion
actually relieved the Marines on Hill 734 at 2000 hours. During the
night, Company E had several probing attacks by an estimated enemy platoon, and Company F received mortar fire. From the light of
friendly flares, Company E saw the enemy and called for friendly
mortar fire. The fire silenced the enemy mortar and killed ten North
Koreans.[2]

1ST LT. MARVIN L. NANCE, COMMANDING OFFICER OF COM-
PANY F: Company F was on the airstrip east of Ch'unch'on, and at
1800 hours on 4 April relieved Company H, 5th Marine Regiment,
on Hill 734. When Company F arrived on the objective at 1600
hours the Marines were fighting for the ground, and the company
held up. I had the 1st Platoon, which was the lead platoon, deployed
along the ridgeline to support the Marines if necessary. I went forward to the Marines' CP, contacted their commanding officer,
Lieutenant Pritchard, and stayed with him until the hill was secured.
My orders were to relieve the Marines after they had secured the
hill. When Company F arrived, I had harassing fires placed on Hill
708, Hill 547, and the village of Muran-ni.

Company E followed Company F on the hill and relieved Company G, 5th Marines, at 2000 hours. A two-company perimeter
was set up for the night with Company E on a ridge to the left.
Company F had a section of heavy machine guns from Company H,
23d Infantry Regiment, set up to cover draws and noses of the ridge.
During the night, intermittent automatic-weapons fire could be
heard to the left in the French Battalion's sector. Company E repulsed a small enemy patrol during the night.[3]

1st Lt. Donald O. Miller, executive officer of Company G: On 4 April, Company G relieved elements of the 5th Marine Regiment on Hill 734 and tied in the battalion's perimeter for the night. The French Battalion was moving up to the company's left flank, and Company F of the 23d Infantry was on the right. Company G moved out at 1230 and reached its positions at 1700 hours. About 2330 hours, a man in the 2d Platoon noticed twenty-five to thirty enemy troops on the skyline to the front of the hill. The night was clear and visibility was about twenty yards. About the same time, a 60mm mortar flare revealed four men in the valley approaching the company's positions. They were taken under fire by BARs and machine guns, and mortar concentrations were fired by the company's 4th Platoon. The enemy returned automatic-weapons and small-arms fire. The firefight lasted off and on for about two hours, and then the rest of the night was quiet. The next morning, three known enemy dead were seen in front of the 2d Platoon's positions.[4]

The next day, 5 April, the 2d Battalion began its advance against the enemy. Major Jensen describes the mission for his battalion and the ensuing operations.

Hill 734 overlooked the village of Muran-ni and the battalion objective for the next day, a flat tabletop mountain about 2,000 yards east of Hill 734 and almost due north of Soui-dong. The French Battalion was to relieve the 2d Battalion on Hill 734 at 1200 hours on 5 April. The 3d Battalion was meeting heavy resistance at a pass on the Ch'unch'on–Naep'yong-ni road. Colonel Chiles, the 23d Regimental commander, ordered my battalion to cut the north–south road just north of Yoonae and to secure the high ground overlooking the 3d Battalion sector. The 3d Battalion had advanced to the ridgeline just north of Kusong-ni. I ordered Company G to remain on Hill 734 as cover and moved Companies E and F southeast down the valley to ridge fingers leading up to the objective. Company F was to go up the left finger [to the tabletop hill] and Company E up the right approach [to Hill 578] from the valley road. Company E ran into heavy automatic-weapons fire and was unable to advance. Company F was able to push up to the tabletop hill [west of Hill 578] against light enemy resistance and reached the top

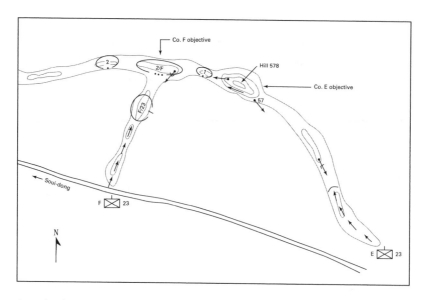

Attack of Companies E and F, 5 April 1951 (sketch based on 1st Lt. Engberg interview in CMH manuscript, U.S. Army; not to scale).

by 1700. Company E withdrew down the slope and went up behind Company F. The enemy placed flanking fire on Company F from the vicinity of Hill 578, and I ordered the company to tie in with Company E for the night. The 3d Battalion had withdrawn, and I thought it unwise to take Hill 578 and have my right flank exposed. At the same time, by holding, it protected the 3d Battalion's left flank. In the meantime, I moved my CP to Soui-dong. Tanks were able to close in the village, and Companies G and H formed the Battalion CP defense perimeter.[5]

Members of Company F provide details of the action.

1ST LT. NANCE, COMMANDER OF COMPANY F: On 5 April at daylight, Company F sent patrols out about 400–500 yards in front of its positions. The patrols returned at 0800 encountering no enemy. At 0930 Major Jensen, the battalion commander, and Captain Saeger, the battalion S-3, came up and set up a battalion OP with the Company F OP. It was very hazy, and observation was poor. By 1000 the haze lifted enough that terrain features could be distinguished, and the battalion commander gave Company F a hill to secure. He told me to take my company southeast, as that was the easiest route to a rice paddy near Soui-dong. We were to drop bedding there and attack the tabletop hill to the north. We moved out at 1030 hours and arrived at the rice paddy at 1245. In the meantime, Company E followed my company and set up an OP and had preparatory artillery fire placed on the hill in front of Company F. At 1330 hours my company advanced due north up a very steep slope toward the tabletop hill. This was a very unlikely route of approach as far as the enemy was concerned. The 2d Platoon under Lieutenant Engberg assaulted the ridge and found it unoccupied. Lieutenant Engberg then sent a squad-size patrol down the ridgelines to the left and right. Two squads remained as a base of fire. The squad on the ridge to the right proceeded about 200 yards to another knob and was counterattacked by a squad of North Koreans. The enemy set up a machine gun and fired on the rest of the company as they came up the hill. The company deployed, set up machine guns, and returned the enemy fire. Company E was advancing up a ridge on the right and was getting enemy fire from the northeast. While the company machine guns were giving covering fire, the 1st Platoon attacked and secured the ground by 1800 hours. Company E failed to take its objective [Hill 578], being hindered by many pillboxes and bunkers in the wooded area to its front. Company F placed supporting fire on these, but could not dislodge the enemy. At 1830 hours, Captain Tait, Company E's company commander, came over to Company F and told me that they were unable to take their objective. Company E then moved off the covered side of the ridge they were attacking and pulled behind Company F and tied in to the south and west. Company F called for harassing fires through the night on enemy positions to the front.[6]

1ST LT. ROBERT W. ENGBERG, 2D PLATOON LEADER, COMPANY F: The next morning, Company F moved down the ridgelines about five or six miles to seize a high hill in conjunction with Company E. Company E was to attack up a ridgeline, and Company F was to attack on their left. The 2d Platoon, my platoon, was to lead the company's attack. At 1430 my platoon reached the ridgeline, and I immediately deployed squads to the left and right as flank security. The remainder of the company was approximately 200 yards to the rear at a lower elevation. I radioed back that the objective was secured, and that the remainder of the company could move up.

About this time the squad that deployed to the right toward Company E's objective (Company E couldn't advance up their ridge due to heavy enemy resistance) started to receive automatic-weapons, machine-gun, and small-arms fire from the right flank. I estimate that the enemy had two machine guns firing at that time. About fifteen North Koreans then attacked the squad under cover of machine-gun fire. The attacking enemy troops were firing burp guns and throwing grenades. The right flank squad was forced to withdraw approximately one hundred yards, and the enemy followed close behind. The 2d Platoon's machine gun, which was set up on a high knob near the center of the company's positions, forced the enemy to withdraw to cover.

The company commander, Lieutenant Nance, sent the 1st Platoon to protect the 2d Platoon's left flank. I then led a counterattack against the enemy. At about 1730 the platoon retook the original position, and the enemy withdrew to the north. Mortar fire, both 60mm and 81mm, was placed on the enemy's positions. My platoon dug in under small-arms fire from Company E's sector. A section of heavy machine guns moved up to add support to the position just retaken.

After dark, I was informed that Company E had withdrawn and was coming up the same route of approach as did Company F to tie in for the night. A short time later a platoon from Company E came to reinforce my platoon. I used one of its squads to secure the platoon's perimeter on the right, and I told another squad to dig in on the reverse slope to protect against an attack from the rear.[7]

SFC James T. Laster, 3d Platoon leader, Company F: Around 0800 hours on 5 April, Company F moved out about three or four miles without enemy contact. The company commander said that he did not know what was out in front, whether it was enemy or friendly troops. The company came off the mountain and turned north on a road, went approximately 300 yards, and turned right toward a big hill, which was to be the company objective. Artillery blasted the hill before the company jumped off in the attack. About 1600, the 1st Platoon secured the objective and sent out a squad patrol down a ridgeline to the right. The patrol went approximately 200 yards and was pinned down by small-arms fire from ten to twenty North Koreans. The company commander called me on the SCR536 (walkie-talkie) and ordered me to set up my machine guns and place fire on the enemy so the squad could withdraw. The 4th Platoon was at the base of the hill and was firing 60mm mortars at the enemy's positions. The firefight lasted forty-five minutes, and the enemy withdrew to the north. The company went into a perimeter defense with my platoon (3d) on the left, the 2d Platoon in the center, and the 1st Platoon on the right. The 4th Platoon was in the center of the three. Company E tied in the perimeter for the night.[8]

Members of Company E describe their part in the actions on 5 April.

CAPT. LAWRENCE TAIT, COMMANDING OFFICER OF COMPANY E: On 5 April Company F followed the ridgeline, circling from the southeast back to the northeast to secure their objective, a tabletop hill about 2,000 yards east of Hill 734 and due north of Soui-dong. Company F reached their objective about 1500, and at about that time Company E was ordered to take Hill 578. I moved the company up the nose that leads from Yoonae northeast to the hill. Approximately halfway to the objective, a squad of enemy placed sniper fire on the company's right flank. The company deployed to the left of the ridge and continued toward the objective. No artillery or mortar fire was placed on the enemy because Company L of the 23d Infantry Regiment was attacking up the ridgeline to the right.

About a hundred yards from the objective the 2d Platoon, which was the assault platoon, was brought under enemy mortar and rifle-grenade fire. The terrain was very rugged, and it was difficult to deploy the platoon, so an order was given for it to hold and return the enemy fire. An effort was made by radio to coordinate fire with Company F on the enemy, but the radio batteries were dead, and communication was impossible.

About 1800, Company F was approaching Hill 578 from the west and had reached the top at the time Company E came under enemy fire. I thought that with a coordinated attack, the two companies could have easily secured the two objectives, but the enemy attacked Company F, forcing it to withdraw back to its original objective. When my company attempted to move forward, we were subjected to automatic-weapons and small-arms fire from the front and right front, and it was impossible to alleviate pressure on Company F. I was ordered by the battalion commander to move my company back from Hill 578 and to tie in for the night with Company F. We closed in the perimeter about 2130 and dug in. During the night a very strong probing attack came from the direction of Hill 578 but was driven off by machine-gun fire.[9]

2D LT. RALSTON K. DENNIS, 2D PLATOON LEADER OF COMPANY E: The next afternoon [5 April] the company tried to take Hill 578. My platoon started up a ridge finger toward the hill and had approached two-thirds of the way toward the objective before the enemy opened fire on us with small arms from the right flank of the platoon. Some of the enemy threw hand grenades at the lead scouts. We quickly set up our machine gun on the reverse slope of a little knoll and returned the fire. I was ordered by the company commander, Captain Tait, to hold and return fire. In my opinion, the approach of the 2d Platoon caught the enemy by surprise because most of the enemy's activity was directed against Company F advancing up another ridge finger on the left. The firefight lasted twenty minutes. I was ordered to withdraw my platoon back down the ridge finger and then up behind Company F for the night.[10]

1ST LT. WILLIAM T. LIFFITON, 3D PLATOON LEADER OF COMPANY E: Company E was given the mission of securing the high ground to the east of Hill 734 and north of Soui-dong. About 1330 hours, Company F was attacking a large tabletop hill on the left and was receiving small-arms and automatic-weapons fire. The 2d Platoon of Company E was going up Hill 578, a small hill to the right of Company F. The 3d Battalion was supposed to be taking the high ground to the right of Company E. My platoon, the 3d Platoon of Company E, was advancing behind the 2d Platoon, but we could not see them due to the length and steepness of the hill. However, small-arms fire could be heard to the front in the 2d Platoon's sector. When my platoon finally reached the 2d Platoon, I heard over the SCR300 radio that Company F had received a small enemy banzai attack. One squad from my platoon placed small-arms fire on the enemy positions on top of the hill. After a short firefight the company was ordered to withdraw at 1600 hours. The company moved halfway down the hill and then swung left and moved in with Company F on their objective for the night.[11]

The night was unsettled as Companies E and F manned their perimeter. Members of the units describe the events.

LIEUTENANT ENGBERG, 2D PLATOON, COMPANY F: At approximately 2130–2200 hours, the enemy tried to probe my platoon's perimeter by firing automatic weapons and throwing grenades. The attacks came from the hill to the right, and each attack was repulsed by small-arms fire and grenades. At various times during the night, enemy troops could be heard scrambling among the rocks. Flares were sent up, and each flare revealed small groups of five to six men. Machine-gun and BAR fire was placed on the enemy each time, and the attacks were finally stopped around 0600. At daylight, five enemy dead were counted in front of the machine-gun position.[12]

SFC LASTER, 3D PLATOON, COMPANY F: During the night many short friendly 4.2-inch mortar and artillery rounds fell around the company's position, but there were no casualties. On 6 April at 0630 hours approximately six or eight enemy 82mm mortar rounds came into the 3d Platoon's positions and wounded three men. I got out of my foxhole to get to the wounded, and eight more rounds came in. About twenty minutes later, about ten more rounds came in.[13]

LIEUTENANT NANCE, COMMANDING OFFICER, COMPANY F: At 0300 hours on 6 April a platoon of enemy attacked from the east using burp guns and grenades and approached to within fifty yards of the 1st and 2d Platoons without being detected. The enemy was finally driven off by machine guns and grenade fire after a firefight that lasted an hour. The enemy then worked down to the ridgeline to the rear of Company F and attempted to storm the position, but were repulsed by BAR fire. Company E reported hearing enemy movement to their rear but had no contact. Mortar fire was placed in the reported enemy vicinity. At daylight no trace of the enemy could be found. Patrols sent to the west and south reported no enemy contact. The enemy was thought to be in force in the east, but no patrols were sent in that direction. At 0700 hours the enemy laid thirty-five or forty rounds of 82mm mortar fire on Company F's CP and on the 3d Platoon's positions, inflicting eleven casualties.[14]

LIEUTENANT BRUMET, EXECUTIVE OFFICER OF COMPANY E: At 0330 hours on 6 April, Company F was hit on the left flank by a small enemy probing attack and also received thirteen to fourteen rounds of enemy 82mm mortar fire, which inflicted ten casualties.[15]

LIEUTENANT LIFFITON, 3D PLATOON, COMPANY E: About 0100 the heavy-machine-gun section attached to Company F opened fire, and, periodically, riflemen fired and threw grenades. There was no definite attack on the positions, but I think it was an enemy probing patrol. Friendly flares were sent up continuously through the night. About 0600 hours on 6 April approximately fifteen 60mm enemy mortar rounds landed in Company E's perimeter, inflicting two casualties in my platoon. The first few rounds wounded several, and litter bearers were also wounded attempting to remove them. Later that day, as we moved down a ridgeline leading to the objective, I noticed four enemy dead with grenades clutched in their hands in front of the heavy-machine-gun positions.[16]

The 2d Battalion began the next day with a renewed attack on Hill 578. Major Jensen briefly describes that action.

On 6 April, Companies E and F sent out patrols and found the enemy to be on the hills to the east. Company G was moved up to the high ground with Companies E and F. On the way, the company suffered casualties from machine-gun fire and from snipers from Hill 578. A heavy artillery concentration was placed on the hill, and Company E took it without difficulty. It was not necessary to commit Companies F and G.[17]

Members of Company E add more details of the attack.

CAPTAIN TAIT, COMMANDING OFFICER, COMPANY E: At 0700 hours on 6 April, Company E was given the mission of securing Hill 578. While approaching the objective, we received sniper fire from a knoll about 400 yards to the northwest. The enemy resistance was eliminated by a concentration of mortar and artillery fire, and the knoll was taken by 1000. I had a concentration of 155mm howitzer fire placed on Hill 578, and, supported by a platoon as a base of fire, the 3d Platoon jumped off and secured Hill 578 against no enemy resistance. The 3d Platoon was ordered to stay on the hill while the rest of the company withdrew back to our night position.[18]

LIEUTENANT BRUMET, EXECUTIVE OFFICER, COMPANY E: Artillery and mortar fire was placed on a tabletop hill to the northwest of Hill 578, and the hill was secured by 1000. The 23d Regiment's S-3 requested that the 2d Battalion send one company to Hill 578. Company E attacked southeast after an artillery preparation and secured the objective with no enemy resistance by 1330 hours.[19]

LIEUTENANT LIFFITON, 3D PLATOON LEADER, COMPANY E: Company E moved over the previous day's objective, Hill 578, against no enemy opposition. The 3d Platoon moved on to a small nose to the south of Hill 578 and then received sniper fire from hills to the southeast. The platoon was forced to withdraw to the reverse slope before it could return fire. On the skyline several enemy soldiers were silhouetted. The exchange of fire lasted most of the morning, and by 1300 hours the enemy fire ceased. Heavy small-arms fire could be heard in the 3d Battalion, 23d Infantry Regiment's sector.[20]

Major Jensen describes the plan for the rest of the day and the next day.

In the afternoon the attack then swung north. Company G was sent out to make a strong reconnaissance in force, with the mission of contacting the enemy and then withdrawing. The battalion would then attack the enemy the following day. Company G made visual contact with the enemy, observing him on Hill 708 and in the Hach'on area. The company worked to the west and returned through the village of Muran-ni.[21]

Other members of the battalion provide additional details.

LIEUTENANT NANCE, COMMANDING OFFICER, COMPANY F: The battalion commander and his S-3 came up to the Company CP at 0900 hours on 6 April and gave us the plan of attack. Company E was to move about 800 yards to the east and secure an unnumbered hill. This was done after a brief firefight. Company G moved through Company F and through to another hill to the east. Shortly before dark, Company G pulled back to furnish defense for the battalion CP area. Company F remained in position all day and night without enemy contact. At 1500 hours, the battalion called for one platoon of infantry to accompany one platoon of tanks on a patrol up the road from the battalion CP to Muran-ni. The 1st Platoon was sent and, when it returned, reported no enemy contact.[22]

LIEUTENANT LIFFITON, 3D PLATOON LEADER, COMPANY E: At 1300 hours the company was given a series of objectives to the east, some in the 3d Battalion's sector. These were taken with no opposition after mortar and artillery fire was placed on them. The final objective was taken by the 3d Platoon at 1500 hours. About 1600 the company was ordered back into a perimeter with Company F, which did not move that day.[23]

LIEUTENANT BRUMET, EXECUTIVE OFFICER, COMPANY E: Companies E and F sent patrols northward to Such'ong-dong. The patrols were supported by artillery and 4.2-inch mortars and had no enemy contact. Company G sent a platoon-size patrol northward to Muran-ni but had no enemy contact. Company G later pulled back to their old positions. Company E moved over to Company F for the night. The battalion CP received some enemy artillery fire during the night.[24]

Major Jensen describes the 2d Battalion's plan and operations for 7 April.

The plan of attack on the enemy for 7 April called for Company G to move up the road through Muran-ni and attack Hill 708 from the west. Company E moved into a blocking position to the east astride the trail leading to Muran-ni. Company F remained in position to observe the enemy and to call for artillery. A heavy concentration of a battalion of artillery was placed on Hill 708, and Company G easily took the hill. Enemy dead were found on the ridge.

That afternoon Company G was left on the hill, and Company F was pulled to the village of Muran-ni to block to the southeast and to furnish patrols. Company E patrolled to the north and east. A tank-infantry patrol cleared the road of mines north of Togol and reported that the road ended at the 38th parallel. I sent my intelligence officer to verify this and received a report that enemy troops were occupying old South Korean defense positions. Later that afternoon, Company E moved to Muran-ni and tied into the battalion perimeter for the night.[25]

Other members of the battalion provide additional details of the day's activities.

LIEUTENANT NANCE, COMMANDING OFFICER, COMPANY E: At 0700 hours on 7 April, Company E moved out north on the ridgeline to set up a screening force for Company G's attack on Hill 708. The 1st Platoon was sent out to reconnoiter the villages of Naech'on and Hach'on to determine the presence of the enemy and to observe conditions of the road nets. The platoon returned by 1500 hours and reported that no enemy was contacted and that the road net was poor. At 1600 hours, Company E was ordered to move down the trail to the southwest and form a battalion perimeter with the other companies in the vicinity of Muran-ni. The night was quiet.[26]

LIEUTENANT BRUMET, EXECUTIVE OFFICER, COMPANY E: On 7 April, Company E moved down the ridgeline and noticed 150 to 200 enemy dead on the forward slope. They were approximately two weeks dead. Among the dead were some women nurses. Companies F and G moved forward all day with no enemy contact. Company G took Hill 708 and sent patrols to Naech'on. Company E sent patrols to Hach'on, and Company F sent a patrol to Hill 882 in the French Battalion's sector. The patrols returned about 1600 hours, and the battalion went into a perimeter defense at Muran-ni. Company F was on the left of town, and Company E was on the right with tanks. Company G remained on Hill 708. Word was received that French forces were at the Hwach'on Reservoir.[27]

LIEUTENANT NANCE, COMMANDING OFFICER, COMPANY F: On 7 April the battalion commander ordered Company F to remain in position in battalion reserve. Company E was to pull off their positions and go to the northwest. Simultaneously, Company G was to move up the road through Muran-ni and secure Hill 708. Company E jumped off at 0800, and Company F was ordered to send one platoon to occupy the positions Company E had vacated. About

1200 hours, the battalion commander ordered me to bring all of the company except the 1st Platoon to Muran-ni by the most direct route. The 1st Platoon worked with the tanks all day on patrols. The company arrived at Muran-ni at 1400 hours, and the battalion S-3 showed me the battalion defense plans for the night. The company was placed in a battalion perimeter around Muran-ni with Company E on the east and Company F on the west.

The 1st Platoon and tanks went up the road north of Muran-ni until it ended. Then Lieutenant Napier took a small patrol up across the 38th parallel and returned with no enemy contact. About 1430 hours the 2d Platoon was sent out on a patrol from the battalion CP to Hill 882 to contact the French Battalion. Contact was made, and the patrol returned by 1800 hours. The night was very quiet.[28]

The Thrust North: 2d Battalion,
23d Infantry, 8 April

Late on 7 April the French Battalion was concentrated around Hill 882 while the 2d Battalion, 23d Infantry, was at Muran-ni, with Company G holding Hill 708 to the north. Extensive ground and air reconnaissance, and interrogations of prisoners and civilians indicated few enemy forces to the immediate north of the 2d and French Battalions. Capt. John H. King, the S-2 of the 23d Infantry, summarizes the intelligence picture.

On 6 April the French Battalion apprehended civilian refugees coming through their positions, and extensive questioning revealed that they had observed 300 to 500 Chinese pulling back near the southwest tip of the Hwach'on Reservoir near Yuch'on-ni. They also said that a pass on the 38th parallel just north of the 2d Battalion, 23d Infantry, was clear of enemy forces. On 7 April a dismounted patrol confirmed the report.[29]

The French Battalion and the 2d Battalion, 23d Infantry Regiment, were ordered to attack north on 8 April. Major Jensen describes the 2d Battalion's plan and the ensuing actions.

On 8 April the 2d Battalion attacked north. The regimental

objective was to cut the road running from Hwach'on in the northwest to Ch'uyang-ni in the southeast. Company G was to push north up the ridgelines and secure Hill 654. Companies E and F, together with the attached tanks, were to push north up the valley paralleling the advance of Company G on the high ground. Company F was ordered to take Hill 811, and one platoon from Company F, together with Company E, was to secure a pass to the west at the 38th parallel.[30]

As Company G advanced on Hill 654, it encountered strong enemy resistance. Pvt. Milton L. Cagle, a member of the 3d Platoon, played a key role in overcoming the opposition. Soldiers of his unit describe what happened in their recommendation for award of the Distinguished Service Cross to him.

M. SGT. RALPH E. PATTEN: On the morning of 8 April, Company G was advancing over very mountainous terrain against well-dug-in positions. Fire was received from a pillbox approximately 200 yards to the left front. For the company to continue its advance it would be necessary for the pillbox to be destroyed. A squad of the 3d Platoon was given the mission. The squad was able to advance under cover to within a hundred yards of the enemy's position. The squad leader decided that the only way they could reach their objective would be to assault by rushes. As the squad exposed themselves, they were pinned down by fire from the pillbox. Private Cagle, a member of this squad, saw the hopeless situation of his comrades. With complete disregard for his own personal safety, he jumped up and ran swiftly toward the pillbox.

SGT. DOYLE A. COX: Pvt. Milton L. Cagle, a member of this squad, sized up the situation and realized that something must be done immediately or he and his comrades would be annihilated. Private Cagle, on his own, moved forward to within twenty yards of the pillbox, at which time he was pinned down by enemy rifle fire. Although he was mortally wounded at this time, he was able to throw several hand grenades into the enemy pillbox, thus destroying it. Due to Private Cagle's heroic action the company was able to advance with a minimum of casualties and secure its objective.

M. Sgt. Patten: Although Private Cagle was killed by enemy fire, he was able to silence the pillbox, allowing the company to move forward and saving the lives of the remainder of his squad.[31]

Major Jensen continues his description of the 2d Battalion's actions.

About 1030 I observed from the battalion OP approximately fifty enemy soldiers moving on to Hill 654. By this time a platoon from Company G was on the hill, and I ordered the platoon to withdraw. When the platoon had cleared the hill, I had artillery, 4.2-inch mortar, and tank fire placed on the ridge. After the fire was lifted, I ordered Company G to clear the hill. The company advanced to the first few slopes and then suffered casualties by sniper fire from a hill to the northeast. About twenty-five enemy dead were found on Hill 654. As Company G approached the summit of Hill 654, it spotted approximately 200–250 enemy moving northwest on the Hwach'on–Ch'uyang-ni road. Artillery fire was placed on the area, but we could not get an air strike.

By this time, Company F had secured Hill 811. Company G was then ordered to leave a platoon on Hill 654 and also to secure Hill 811, relieving a platoon from Company F. Upon receiving the report of enemy movement, I ordered Company F down the ridge to cut the road north of Hill 811 and to occupy the high ground just to the northwest of the road. This was accomplished by 1430 hours. That night Company F was astride the road, and Companies G and E were to the south and west.[32]

Lieutenant Miller, executive officer of Company G, describes his company's role in the fighting.

On 8 April at 0800 hours, Company G moved out in attack and secured Hill 654 by 1045. It was the commanding ridgeline overlooking a valley on the left and right. The valley on the right contained the road leading toward the Hwach'on Reservoir. When I first reached the crest of the hill I didn't notice any enemy movement in the valleys. We went forward along the ridgelines, making sure the enemy bunkers were clear. I looked down to the right, and at about 1,500 to 2,000 yards distance noticed two or three men coming up to a bridge and turning northeast up a draw. After that group came through, larger groups of fifteen or twenty went up into the same draw. I observed them for about thirty-five minutes and estimated a hundred had passed through. They were wearing pile caps and brown Chinese uniforms, but at the range I couldn't tell if they were friendly or enemy because the 3d Battalion was coming up on the high ground to the right of the valley.

I reported to the battalion that suspected enemy troops were moving up the valley disregarding the high ground. A confirmation came back from the battalion S-3, Captain Saeger, that there were no friendly troops in that vicinity. I tried to get artillery on them, but it apparently was not too effective due to the long range. Word must have been sent back through the 3d Battalion because artillery started hitting among them. I estimate that the artillery had approximately 30 percent effect on them; some had already gotten out. No vehicles were observed with them.

The company then moved out toward Hill 1031 along the ridgeline, and advance elements of the 3d Platoon received automatic-weapons fire from the objective. The 3d Platoon pressed the attack and placed machine-gun and 57mm recoilless-rifle fire from the Weapons Platoon on the enemy. The enemy dispersed to the northeast. At that time a platoon from Company F had secured the high ground dominating the road, and Company G took over the platoon's positions. Company G left one platoon on the hill, and the rest of the company withdrew around the battalion CP for the night. It snowed that night.[33]

Members of Companies E and F relate the details of their advance north on the left of Company G.

CAPTAIN TAIT, COMMANDING OFFICER, COMPANY E: At 0700 hours on 8 April, Company E traveled on the trail north of Muranni behind Company F. After crossing the 38th parallel, Company F cleared the high ground on the right of the trail, and Company E moved up through Company F to the pass. Company E secured the pass while Company F swung around the high ground on the right and secured the final battalion objective, the road connecting Hwach'on and Ch'uyang-ni. While guarding the pass at 1400 hours, the 2d Platoon leader notified me of a large unidentified group, about 500 individuals, in the low ground about 3,000 yards northwest of the pass. I notified the battalion S-3 and was told that they were friendly troops. Approximately fifteen minutes later Company E was in communication with them, and discovered that it was part of the French Battalion. Later I heard a call that the road was mined, and a later report said that they had run a jeep up the middle and were now clearing the shoulders the same way. Company E remained at the pass for the night.[34]

LIEUTENANT BRUMET, EXECUTIVE OFFICER, COMPANY E: On 8 April, Company E was given the mission of securing a defile on a north–south secondary road, and Companies F and G were to go down the ridgelines to the northeast. At 1000 hours Company F reported enemy small-arms fire coming from Hill 654. Tank and mortar fire was placed on the hill, and Company F secured it at 1030. Company G moved and secured Hill 811.

At 1010 hours, the 2d Battalion received a message from Company L of the 3d Battalion that enemy traffic was observed traveling northwest on the Hwach'on road about 2,000 yards west of Ch'uyang-ni. Company E stayed on the hill, which overlooked the north–south road, and Companies F and G, secured the Hwach'on road where it cut through a pass. Company F found booby traps made out of 82mm mortar rounds in old foxholes. The night was quiet.[35]

LIEUTENANT NANCE, COMMANDING OFFICER, COMPANY F: On the morning of 8 April Company F moved up the road northward, supported by a platoon of tanks. The tanks went up to where the road ended. Company F continued to secure the mountain pass. The battalion objective was the high hill mass in the vicinity of the Hwach'on–Ch'uyang-ni road due north of the pass. The pass was secured by 1200 hours with no enemy contact. Company G was sweeping north of Hill 708 along the ridgeline to Hill 654, where it had some enemy contact at 0900 hours. Company G's objective was Hill 811, but they failed to reach it. I sent the 3d Platoon to Hill 811 at about 1000 hours and secured it without enemy contact. About two companies of enemy troops were observed to the northeast on the Hwach'on–Ch'uyang-ni road. No enemy vehicles could be seen.

Company E reached the pass at about 1200 hours and was given the mission of securing it. Company G cleaned up their resistance and moved toward Hill 811. Company F was then given the mission of cutting the Hwach'on–Ch'uyang-ni road. The company moved from the pass and secured the high ground astride the road for the night. Company E spent the night north of the pass, and Company G was on Hill 811. The battalion CP remained at Muran-ni, but the battalion commander maintained an OP at the pass with Company E. A brush fire destroyed phone communications with the battalion CP, but we did have radio contact. The night was very quiet.[36]

SERGEANT FIRST CLASS LASTER, 3D PLATOON LEADER, COMPANY F: At 0730 hours on 8 April, Lieutenant Nance told me to move the 3d Platoon out from Muran-ni. The platoon moved about one mile and took a small hill to the right of the road and set up a defense until the 1st Platoon arrived at 0815. The company commander was on the OP to the rear and ordered my platoon to take Hill 811, the high ground to the right front. My platoon moved out at 0900 in a leapfrog manner with one squad covering the other. It was a very steep hill, and after an hour and a half climb the summit of Hill 811 was reached. Lieutenant Nance ordered me to secure the hill until relieved by Company G. The platoon remained in position until 1300 hours. Company G was approximately 400 yards down the ridge to the right of the 3d Platoon and was held up by a dug-in enemy machine gun. I was afraid of hitting Company G's men and wouldn't allow my men to fire a 3.5-inch rocket at the enemy position. Company G withdrew approximately forty-five minutes later, then attacked again and retook the ground.

A liaison plane circled the hill two or three times. I displayed the platoon's panel, and the plane left. When Company G reached the 3d Platoon's position at 1500 hours, I told the contact squad that I was taking my platoon on out the ridgeline to the left front to observe any possible enemy activity on the road. The platoon went about 150–200 yards and set up defense positions until Lieutenant Nance arrived. The road could be seen to the right and left front. At 1630, using binoculars, I spotted one group of ten to twelve North Koreans moving up a draw near a blown bridge to the northeast of Hill 811. Cpl. Ernest Townsend spotted approximately 150 to 200 troops on the road to the northeast. No vehicles were seen. I had picked up a report on the radio that vehicles were observed on the road, but I couldn't see them. Because of smoke and haze it was impossible to determine the nationality of the troops. I reported this to Lieutenant Nance, and about two hours later heavy artillery was hitting in the vicinity of the troops. When Lieutenant Nance arrived, the platoon pushed to the north about 200 yards to a little knoll, where I tried to point out the group to the lieutenant. I was unable to do so because of the artillery concentrations.[37]

CORPORAL TOWNSEND, 3D PLATOON, COMPANY E: I was a BAR man in the 3d Platoon of Company E. About 1400 hours on the 8th of April we reached the top of a high hill. Sergeant Laster gave me a pair of field glasses and told me to try to spot any gooks to the front. About 2,000 yards to the right front I spotted a group of about ninety moving southeast along the road. I hollered over to Sergeant Laster, and told him I spotted some troops down on the road. I didn't say enemy because I thought they were French. Some of them had helmet liners on, and some of them had the regular white gook uniform. I couldn't tell whether they were carrying weapons or not. Sergeant Laster thought they were gooks, and he called someone else to look at them, as I went back to my squad. I don't know what happened to them after that.[38]

Operation Swing: 2d Battalion, 23d Infantry, 9–12 April 1951

The relatively unopposed advance of the French and the 2d Battalion to the Hwach'on–Ch'uyang-ni road, along with the strong opposition in front of the 3d Battalion to the east, indicated the enemy's location. Captain King, the S-2 of the 23d Infantry Regiment, describes the intelligence picture.

From a study of aerial photographs and maps, plus the fact that there was no enemy contact in the western sector in front of the French and 2d Battalion, it was easily determined that the main enemy defense lines were on high ridges extending from the northwest near Nae-dong on the Hwach'on Reservoir to the southeast to the "Rock of Gibraltar" area near Ch'uyang-ni. Two ridges were used by the enemy. The second was 2,500 meters behind the first. Each ridge had at least a half-dozen small knolls, with many trenches and emplacements. It eventually took 155mm artillery fire with delayed fuses and 105mm artillery fire with VT to dislodge the enemy from their entrenchments.

Later, from captured prisoners of war and documents taken from enemy dead, it was determined that the 1st and 3d Regiments, 1st North Korean Division, were opposing the 23d Infantry Regiment. One prisoner was taken from the Reconnaissance Company of the 15th North Korean Division, and the 2d Battalion captured one Chinese (CCF) deserter.

It was the first time in the regiment's history in Korea that aerial photos were received in time to study enemy positions, make mosaics, and to generally be of use.[39]

Captain Selander, the S-3 of the 23d Infantry Regiment, describes the plan based on the emerging intelligence.

It became apparent at this time that the enemy was defending an area around Hill 1187. This was the first time during the attack toward the Hwach'on Reservoir that enemy lines actually developed. With the 3d Battalion unable to advance, it was planned that the entire regiment swing to the right with the 3d Battalion as the pivot. The 2d Battalion was to go to the north of the 3d Battalion over the summit of Hill 1187, and the French were to screen to the left along the edge of the reservoir. This operation was called Operation Swing.[40]

It was expeditious to plan to make a swinging movement to the east when the enemy main line of resistance developed, in order to attack the enemy defense line frontally rather than in depth going northward. The original plan of movement originated with Colonel John Chiles, the commanding officer of the 23d Infantry Regiment, and was approved by both the 2d Infantry Division and X Corps commanding generals. When the swinging movement took place, Colonel Chiles requested the 2d Reconnaissance Company of the 2d Infantry Division be sent to blocking positions at the western finger of the Hwach'on Reservoir. Platoon OPs were established on high ground overlooking the reservoir, and 81mm mortar fire was placed on several fishing boats and suspected enemy OPs. Later the Netherlands Battalion was sent at Colonel Chile's request to the road junction near Ch'uyang-ni to reinforce the position against a possible enemy counterattack from the east.[41]

With orders to push north, Major Jensen describes the 2d Battalion's operations on 9 April.
On 9 April the battalion again attacked north with the mission of securing Hill 856. Company E passed through Company F into the attack. The French Battalion had reported enemy moving to the north behind the hill, and artillery was placed on it from both the French and 2d Battalion sectors. All this time, the French could be seen moving in their sector. After the fire was lifted, Company E attempted to secure the objective but met very heavy resistance. The company fought most of the day but could make little progress. Company G was moved up to the vicinity of the pass on the Hwach'on road in readiness if needed, but the terrain was such that only one company could be committed. Company F remained at the pass; it was imperative that it be held because the entire right flank of the 2d Battalion was exposed. Company E was later withdrawn to the pass area for the night.[42]

Members of Company E describe the fight for Hill 856 on 9 April.
CAPTAIN TAIT, COMMANDING OFFICER, COMPANY E: At 0800 hours on 9 April, Company E moved through Company F's positions to attack Hill 856. The attack commenced about 1100, and by 1500 contact was made with the enemy defending the upper portions of the hill. Artillery was placed on the enemy but failed to dislodge them. I was ordered to withdraw Company E to the vicinity of Company F's perimeter at the pass and to tie in with them for the night.[43]

LIEUTENANT BRUMET, EXECUTIVE OFFICER, COMPANY E: At 0845 on 9 April, Company E joined Company F on the right of the pass, and Company G took over Company E's blocking positions. Company E was given the mission of securing Hill 856, and Company F was to support the attack from its original position at the pass. Friendly 105mm and 155mm artillery and 81mm and 4.2-inch mortar fire was placed on the objective for thirty minutes prior to the jump-off. At 1000 hours Company E attacked, and Company G was ordered to help Company F support the attack. At 1130 hours Company E reached the foot of the hill and received small-arms fire from the right and left front. The artillery continued to pound the hill, and the 3d Platoon started up and was again pinned down by small-arms fire. The 1st Platoon moved over to the ridge on the left to secure the flank of the 3d Platoon, and the company's mortars were set up at the foot of the hill and placed fire on the enemy positions.

At 1330 hours the battalion commander ordered the attack to continue forward, but Company E could not advance. Company F moved down the road to the east and up on a ridge [Hill 511] to support Company E. An air strike was requested on the hill but was not received. At 1600 hours Company E was ordered to withdraw to the high ground north of the pass, and artillery was placed on the objective. Company F moved south of the pass for the night.[44]

LIEUTENANT LIFFITON, 3D PLATOON LEADER, COMPANY E: At 0630 hours on 9 April, Company E swung up on a hill to the right and followed the ridges over to Company F's position astride a pass on the Hwach'on–Ch'uyang-ni road, arriving at 0930. The 3d Platoon moved out to a small knoll [Hill 571] where Hill 856 could be observed to the north. About an hour later the remainder of the company moved up with a section of heavy machine guns from Company H. All the FOs (artillery, 81mm mortar, and 4.2-inch mortar) were with the company.

The 3d Platoon, supported by the heavy machine guns, was ordered to take the hill. The battalion S-3, Captain Saeger, arrived and said no enemy was on the hill, and that the battalion had been observing the hill for several days and could not spot enemy movement. From the knoll, I had spotted at least three enemy soldiers moving on Hill 856. For over two hours, 155mm howitzer and 4.2-inch mortar fire was placed on the hill.

The 3d Platoon moved out at 1300 hours, going down to the right and swinging northeast up a gentler slope, hitting the hill from the right flank. There were a series of about three ridgelines, and when the platoon reached the first, scouts spotted three enemy moving north off the next ridgeline. I sent a squad over to investigate under cover of the platoon's light machine gun and riflemen. The enemy movement was reported by me, and the remainder of the company moved up. I didn't know that the company was following behind my platoon. The squad reconnoitered the area where the enemy was seen, and Captain Tait ordered another squad to be sent over. When the 2d Squad arrived, they received sniper fire from the ridge up which the company was approaching.

The company commander sent a 57mm recoilless-rifle squad forward, and two rounds were fired at the enemy. The squads also returned the enemy fire. After the enemy fire ceased, the 3d Platoon, followed by the remainder of the company minus the 1st Platoon, which stayed on the ridge, moved over to the right with the two squads. The 3d Platoon then moved about two-thirds of the way up a steep and rugged slope to a little rise, where I deployed a machine gun and a rifle squad. The rest of the platoon started forward approximately twenty-five yards and received automatic weapons and small-arms fire from both flanks. Several enemy soldiers up the hill to the direct front were throwing hand grenades down into the midst of the lead squad. There were no casualties, and the squad leader, Sergeant Erdman, threw three grenades back at the enemy. The 2d Platoon had moved up to a knoll below the 3d Platoon and was placing fire on the enemy. In the meantime I ordered the platoon to dig in.

The 1st Platoon moved up the ridgeline on the left and placed fire on the enemy soldiers who were throwing the grenades. Every time the 3d Platoon attempted to move, we were pinned down by the automatic-weapons fire. The company commander called for artillery and received very accurate fire. Some of the artillery rounds were landing thirty feet above my platoon. After the artillery barrage, my platoon attempted to move and again was pinned down. About 1600 hours, Captain Tait ordered my platoon to withdraw. The 1st and 2d Platoons were given the order to withdraw first. Two men were hit during the withdrawal. The 3d Platoon withdrew to the 2d Platoon's positions and set up covering fire until the wounded and dead were evacuated. All during this time the enemy was firing automatic weapons and small-arms fire from the top of the hill and flanks. About 1700 hours the platoon disengaged with the enemy, and by 1730 my platoon rejoined the company on the road at the base of the hill. The company moved and tied in with Company F astride the road. No enemy contact was made that night.[45]

SERGEANT ERDMAN, SQUAD LEADER, COMPANY E: On 9 April I had the lead squad in an attack on Hill 856. The squad arrived at the top of the ridgeline leading into the hill to the front. The lead scout spotted three North Korean soldiers on another nose to the right. The enemy saw my squad approaching and withdrew over the ridgeline. Lieutenant Liffiton, the 3d Platoon leader, ordered my squad to go forward and cross over to the nose to try to locate the enemy. No contact was made. The squad was then ordered to another knob to the right front. In the meantime, the rest of the platoon was following behind. The squad advanced up the ridgeline approximately fifty yards and then was pinned down by small-arms fire, rifle grenades, and hand grenades from the right, left, and direct front. The remainder of the platoon placed fire on the enemy, but the ridge was too small and had no cover available for reinforcements. Finally, after approximately one and a half hours, artillery was placed on the enemy. The entire 3d Platoon then withdrew under cover of protecting fire laid down by the 2d Platoon to the rear.[46]

LIEUTENANT DENNIS, 2D PLATOON LEADER, COMPANY E: On 9 April Company E, with heavy-machine-gun attachments from Company H, was ordered to attack Hill 856. Artillery and mortar fire was laid on the hill for about an hour, and about 1030 the company moved out with the 3d Platoon leading and the 2d Platoon in support. By 1430 hours, the 3d Platoon had advanced two-thirds of the way up the hill before it started to receive sniper fire and automatic-weapons fire from a high ridge to the right front. The 2d Platoon was to the left and right rear of the 3d Platoon, protecting the flanks. The 2d Platoon deployed and returned fire. One machine gunner was killed by sniper fire. Artillery fire was placed on the enemy, but further attempts to advance were repulsed by sniper fire. The firefight lasted about three hours, and then the platoons were ordered to withdraw. The 2d Platoon covered the withdrawal of the

3d Platoon with the exception of Lieutenant Liffiton and three men who were fighting a small rearguard action. The heavy-machine-gun section from Company H covered the withdrawal of the 2d Platoon. The platoon received sniper fire until it reached the flats at the base of the hill. It was necessary to make stretchers to evacuate the dead and wounded. The company withdrew back to the vicinity of Company F at the pass.[47]

While Company E was attacking Hill 856, Company F moved to clear the road to the east.

LIEUTENANT NANCE, COMMANDING OFFICER, COMPANY F: At 1000 hours on 9 April the battalion ordered me to send a platoon-size patrol down the road to the east. The patrol was to include a mine detail from the P&A Platoon and was to clear the road down to the battalion boundary with the 3d Battalion. The 3d Platoon was dispatched and found the road heavily mined and completely blasted away in several places. The mines were rotten, and the road had been blown for some time. There was no evidence of recent vehicular usage.[48]

SERGEANT FIRST CLASS LASTER, 3D PLATOON LEADER, COMPANY F: On 9 April the company commander told me to keep observing to the front. About 1000 hours, my platoon was ordered to accompany the P&A Platoon while they swept the road down to the right where the enemy had been spotted before. Along the mountainside bordering the road, many old wooden box–type antipersonnel mines were found. My platoon went down the road about five miles and could see air strikes to the right front in the 3d Battalion's sector. At about 1400 hours the 3d Platoon was ordered to return to the company perimeter immediately. We got back by 1600 hours. The company commander told me that it was a good thing I returned because the enemy was headed in the direction where the platoon had been.

In the meantime Company E was stopped in their attack by heavy small-arms fire and was forced to withdraw. Company F straddled the road that night with the 2d Platoon and 4th Platoon north of the road and the 1st and 3d Platoons south of the road. There was no enemy contact that night.[49]

On 10 April the 2d Battalion again attacked Hill 856, but this time there was little opposition, as Major Jensen relates.

On 10 April, Companies G and F were committed to secure Hill 856. Company G went up a sheer slope to the north, and Company F deployed to the right and went up another ridgeline. A heavy artillery concentration preceded the attack. Company G reached the objective by 1300 hours, and Company F reached the top by 1330 hours. No enemy opposition was encountered. The companies then patrolled north and northeast to the reservoir. A contact patrol was sent to meet the French Battalion on the left flank. The patrols advanced to a point about 1,000 meters short of the reservoir and returned.[50]

Lieutenant Brumet adds additional information.

On 10 April, Companies F and G were given the mission of taking Hill 856. At 1205 Company F went up a ridge on the right; Company G went up another ridge on the left leading into Hill 856. By 1400 hours the objective was secured without enemy contact. Company E remained in the same positions that day. Company F patrolled 2,000 yards to the northwest, and Company G to the north without contacting the enemy. The 2d Battalion tried to get tanks from the 3d Battalion's area up to the vicinity of the pass, but the road was blown. Companies G and F organized a perimeter defense on Hill 856 for the night, and Company E occupied the ground north and south of the pass. One platoon from Company E guarded the battalion CP. Company E had one section of 81mm mortars and one section of heavy machine guns, attached from Company H, set up on the pass facing eastward.[51]

On the following day, 11 April, the 2d Battalion was ordered to swing east. Major Jensen describes the situation.

At 0920 hours the 2d Battalion was ordered by the 23d Infantry regimental commander to swing east. I had a warning order before this from Colonel Chiles that such a wheeling movement was contemplated. The 2d Battalion had the dominating terrain in its sector during the approach northward, and it had to be secured before the swinging movement could take place. By this time the Hwach'on—

Ch'uyang-ni road had been repaired and cleared of mines, and tactical vehicles were able to move up through the French sector and over to the pass area.

Company E, followed by Company F, attacked north down a steep trail toward the battalion intermediate objective, a hill about halfway between Hill 856 and the objective on Hill 1187. I wanted to secure a line of departure before cutting up to our objective, Hill 1187. Company E advanced halfway up the battalion intermediate objective and met heavy enemy resistance. Three attempts to gain the position failed. Company F was then moved to the left to assist in the attack. The hill was worked over by artillery, and an air strike was made on the enemy positions using napalm. The TAC officer was at the 2d Battalion OP and directed the strike. The position was reduced, and Company E secured it. The company then moved north and secured a pass about 400 yards to the northeast. Company G provided the battalion CP defense. This was necessary because the pass area on the Hwach'on–Ch'uyang-ni road and the dominating ground had been left. The battalion mortars and tactical vehicles were also in the area.[52]

Other members of the battalion describe the fighting this day.

CAPTAIN TAIT, COMPANY E: On 10 April, Captain Sawyer returned from Rest and Recreation Leave and took over the company; I had been his replacement. On 11 April at 0700 hours, Company E left the battalion perimeter and went over the pass northward to take the objective, a hill about 3,000 yards northeast of Hill 856. At 1130 hours, when the company was approximately 150 yards from the objective, a platoon of enemy dug in on the crest of the hill and opened up with automatic weapons and small-arms fire on the 2d Platoon in the lead. Artillery and mortars were placed on the enemy positions, but the 2d Platoon was repulsed in a second attack on the hill. At 1400 hours, four F-80s napalmed and strafed the objective, and the 2d Platoon secured the hill on the third attempt. About seven enemy dead were found on the hill. Until nightfall, the company was subjected to light enemy mortar fire. The hill was found to have well-organized defensive positions with dug-in aid stations, bunkers, and foxholes.[53]

LIEUTENANT BRUMET, EXECUTIVE OFFICER, COMPANY E: At 0815 hours Companies E and F jumped off to secure Hill 1187, and Company E immediately received small-arms fire from the intermediate objective. The 2d Platoon was leading Company E, and the first squad had approached to within fifty yards of the objective when they encountered an estimated two platoons of enemy. The squad withdrew seventy-five yards while the 2d Platoon formed a base of fire. Artillery and mortar fire destroyed one enemy position, and the 2d Platoon tried to advance again but was immediately pinned down. The remainder of the company had set up a heavy base of fire to get them back, as there was no chance to maneuver. The platoon had to follow the ridgeline, and the firefight lasted thirty minutes.

In the meantime Company F was trying to advance up a ridge to the right but was making slow progress over adverse terrain. Company E called for air support and received two air strikes by four Corsairs and four F-80 jets, which napalmed, bombed, and strafed the objective. The air strike was directed by an SCR300 radio from the ground to a Mosquito L-5 liaison plane, which guided the planes. The target was marked by 57mm and 75mm recoilless-rifle smoke shells.

At 1300 hours Company E swept to the north and northeast to intercept enemy leaving the hill. We secured the hill by 1330 hours. Eight enemy dead were counted, and there were traces of fresh blood all around. Abandoned medical equipment was also found. Company F in the meantime was held up by enemy small-arms fire for twenty minutes, but finally tied in with Company E for the night. At 1815 hours, Company F received twenty to twenty-five enemy 82mm mortar rounds from the direct front, but suffered no casualties.[54]

LIEUTENANT LIFFITON, 3D PLATOON LEADER, COMPANY E: The 2d Platoon was ordered to take a hill to the north, with the 3d Platoon in support. An artillery and mortar preparation was placed on the target prior to the attack. About 1400 hours the 2d Platoon got halfway up the hill and received enemy small-arms and automatic-weapons fire from the front and both flanks. The 3d Platoon also received fire from the flanks, but we managed to set up a light machine gun and return fire on the enemy. Artillery was placed on the hill, and then an air strike using napalm and .50-caliber machine guns made a direct hit on the target. Firing ceased, and the hill was taken with Company E suffering no casualties. Companies E and F organized the hill for the night.[55]

Lieutenant Dennis, 2d Platoon, Company E: On 11 April the company attacked north to take a high hill. The 2d Platoon was the assault platoon. I deployed one rifle squad and the weapons squad to the right, covering the platoon's advance up the ridgeline. At about 1130 the leading squad received automatic-weapons fire from a small nose to the direct front. Captain Tait ordered me to withdraw the squad while artillery and mortar fire was placed on the enemy. This failed to dislodge the enemy, which I estimate was one platoon strong. A second attempt to move forward failed.

The company commander then ordered the platoon to withdraw farther down the slope while an air strike was placed on the enemy position. Approximately half an hour later, planes napalmed and strafed the enemy positions. The 2d Platoon again attacked up the ridgeline, and this time we didn't receive any enemy fire. Two enemy dead, including one North Korean officer, were found, and traces of fresh blood were seen leading to the northeast. The remainder of the company moved up and occupied the hill for the night.[56]

Lieutenant Nance, commanding officer, Company F: At 0800 hours Company E passed through Company F to secure a hill. Company F was in close support of Company E. Company E received heavy enemy automatic-weapons fire, but it was neutralized by an air strike and heavy artillery fire. Company E secured the objective at 1430 hours. Company F attempted to move around the right flank of Company E to seize Hill 1187 and received heavy automatic-weapons fire from a hill to the north. Company F set up the attached heavy-machine-gun section and engaged the enemy with machine-gun and artillery fire. Mortar ammunition was conserved during the day for use at night. I was ordered to hold and form a perimeter with Company E on the hill that they had just secured. During the night, both companies received sporadic mortar fire from the enemy.[57]

Sergeant First Class Laster, 3d Platoon leader, Com-

PANY F: At 0745 the company pushed off with the mission of taking Hill 1187. Company E was leading, Company F followed, and Company G brought up the rear of the advance. Company E had gone about one and a half miles and started up a knoll to the left front. About halfway up the hill, Company E received enemy small-arms and automatic-weapons fire from enemy bunkers on top of the ridge. Company F halted, along with Company E, while artillery and an air strike was placed on the hill. Company E then secured the hill, and Company F joined them on the top at 1500 hours. Company F pulled on about 500 yards to a high knoll on the ridgeline leading up to Hill 1187. About 1730, Company F was ordered to withdraw and establish a perimeter defense with Company E for the night.[58]

On the following day, 12 April, the 2d Battalion advanced on Hill 1187. Major Jensen describes the action.

On 12 April the 2d Battalion resumed the attack on Hill 1187. Company E protected the flank during the swinging movement by taking Hill 601 [2,000 meters west of Hill 1187] after air strikes were placed on the hill and on adjacent hills in the French sector. Artillery and mortar concentrations supported the attack of Companies F and G on Hill 1187. I personally directed mortar fire on the hill. Hill 1187 was taken without enemy resistance, although dead and traces of wounded were found on the hill. I believe that air and artillery were responsible for breaking the enemy resistance.[59]

Members of the 2d Battalion provide additional details about the operations on 12 April.

CAPTAIN TAIT, COMPANY E: On 12 April, Company E remained on the hill taken the day before and sent the 3d Platoon to patrol Hill 601. Before the patrol left, Hill 601 was bombed, strafed, napalmed, and shelled. When the hill was taken the platoon found another well-organized position, which was not manned. I think that the hill taken previously broke the enemy's main line of resistance.[60]

LIEUTENANT NANCE, COMMANDING OFFICER, COMPANY F: At 0800 hours Company F jumped off in attack on Hill 1187 and secured it by 1300 hours. After securing the hill, Company F sent a one-squad patrol from the 1st Platoon to notify Company K of the 3d Battalion that the hill had been taken. At 1700 hours Company G joined the company and established a perimeter for the night. The hill did not appear to have been occupied recently by the enemy. Leaves were on the trails, there were no tracks in the snow, and foxholes were filled.[61]

SERGEANT FIRST CLASS LASTER, 3D PLATOON LEADER, COMPANY F: The next morning the 3d Platoon led the company to a knoll overlooking Hill 1187 and set up a base of fire. Artillery and 4.2-inch mortar barrages were placed on Hill 1187. Company G was in position on the right of the 3d Platoon and also established a base of fire to support Company F's attack. At 1000 hours the company jumped off behind a rolling artillery barrage and went about 500 yards. The barrage was then lifted because of adverse terrain features. Company F climbed up a sheer slope and did not follow any path. The top was reached shortly after noon, and no enemy could be found. The enemy bunkers were facing eastward on the opposite slope of the company's approach. About 1500 hours a patrol from the 2d Platoon was sent out to contact the 3d Battalion of the 23d Infantry. Contact was made with a patrol from Company K. That night Companies G and F organized on Hill 1187.[62]

Advance in the South: 3d Battalion, 23d Infantry, 9–12 April

While the 2d Battalion had moved north across the Hwach'on–Ch'uyang-ni road and then swung east into the enemy defenses on Hills 856 and 1187, the 3d Battalion had dealt with the strong enemy position in the "Rock of Gibraltar" area that they had reached on 8 April. The 3d Battalion commander, Lieutenant Colonel Richardson, describes the situation on 9 and 10 April and how his battalion initially bypassed the "Rock of Gibraltar."

North of the Hwach'on–Ch'uyang-ni road, the North Korean defense line was at least ten miles in depth from the 38th parallel to the Hwach'on Reservoir. The defense positions were elaborate, including winterized dugouts equipped with stoves and sleeping quarters. On 9 April Companies I and L were in constant contact with an enemy who fought a superb delaying action. He evacuated all his dead and wounded. By dark the battalion had secured the high ground north and west of the important road junction at Ch'uyang-ni.

On 10 April, I decided to catch the enemy by surprise by changing the time of attack to 0500 hours. The maneuver was unique in that Company K attacked to the southeast to clear the hill mass called the "Rock of Gibraltar," and the remainder of the battalion attacked up the ridgeline to the northwest. By 1200 hours Company K had cleared its objective, inflicting heavy enemy casualties and capturing four enemy heavy machine guns, six automatic weapons, and large quantities of small-arms ammunition and grenades.

The attack of Companies I and L was slowed by a heavy fog, which limited visibility to 100 yards. Company K joined the battalion by 1300, and the advance continued. At 1600 hours the leading elements of the battalion came under enemy small-arms fire from an estimated enemy squad. Due to poor visibility and weather conditions the advance was halted, and a perimeter was established for the night.[63]

After the initial failure to capture the "Rock of Gibraltar" on 8 April, members of Company K describe the fighting for the hill over the next two days.

Lieutenant Hall, 1st Platoon leader, Company K: During the early morning hours of 9 April we could hear small-arms fire to the right. About 0800 hours Company K moved to the north in support of Company L. Company I was to the right and was held up by enemy automatic-weapons fire. At 1300 hours Company K, with the 3d Platoon leading, moved through Company L and pushed down a ridgeline toward the same hill my platoon had attempted to seize the day before. The platoon advanced 300 yards before it received enemy automatic-weapons fire from their front and left. The 2d Platoon laid a base of fire, and by 1730 hours the 3d Platoon carried their attack another hundred yards to a small knoll. The company consolidated the positions and tied in with Company L for the night.

On 10 April the 2d Platoon pushed through the 3d Platoon and saw six or seven enemy on the second ridgeline from the main objective. The enemy did not open fire. The platoon leader sent two squads to attack the hill with the weapons squad forming the base of fire. The hill was secured with no friendly casualties. Five or six enemy soldiers were killed in their foxholes by the use of grenades. By 1130 the main objective was taken with no further resistance. About 1400 hours Company K was relieved by Company B of the 1st Battalion, and it moved back and tied in on the left of Company L. That night I was evacuated to the aid station with a malarial fever.[64]

Sgt. Brown, 1st Platoon; SFC Glassman, 2d Platoon; and SFC Burgi, 3d Platoon, all Company K: On 9 April the 1st Platoon moved back across the river on the tanks and in doing so received enemy mortar fire. Company K moved out in support of Company L, whose objective was the high ground behind the "Rock of Gibraltar." After Company L had taken their objective about 1700 hours, the 1st Platoon and the 2d Platoon of Company K moved through Company L, while the 3d Platoon remained on the captured objective for several hours. The 1st and 2d Platoons were to sweep the ridgeline back to the "Rock of Gibraltar," but because of darkness they came back and tied in with Company L for the night. After dark the 3d Platoon joined the perimeter. During the night the enemy fired flares approximately fifty yards in front of the friendly positions, but there was no attack.

At 0800 hours on 10 April the 2d Platoon moved out to sweep the ridgeline back to the "Rock of Gibraltar." Before getting to the hill, two or three of the enemy were spotted moving around, and 81mm mortar fire was placed on them. Some of the enemy fled to the left down a ridgeline to the road. Just before reaching a small knoll, the platoon found five enemy in a dugout and killed them with grenades. The platoon had no further enemy opposition over to the main pillbox on the hill.

At 1300 hours Company A of the 1st Battalion came up from the road and relieved the company. Company K moved back to the high ground behind Company I. Company L was on the left flank. The companies formed a perimeter for the night and had no enemy contact.[65]

Members of Company L describe their role in the fighting on 9 and 10 April.

LIEUTENANT BARENKAMP, EXECUTIVE OFFICER, AND LIEUTEN- ANT PALMER, 2D PLATOON LEADER, BOTH COMPANY L: At 0800 hours on 9 April the company started up the ridge. The 1st and 2d Platoons advanced, covered by the 3d and 4th Platoons, which re- mained in position. The 1st Platoon got to within 150 to 200 yards of the main ridge, their objective, when they were pinned down by enemy small-arms fire from the right, left, and direct front. Com- pany I had advanced up their ridgeline but was also halted by enemy small-arms fire. Artillery was placed on the ridge all day, and at about 1600 hours Captain Jackson ordered the 2d Platoon up through the 1st Platoon to secure the ridge for the night. The pla- toon moved on the reverse slope and approached to within thirty yards of the ridge before being pinned down by two North Koreans with a BAR. The men in the platoon threw hand grenades at the enemy, and one North Korean got out of a foxhole and ran. The 2d Platoon started to check other foxholes and bayoneted some of the opposition in their positions. The 2d Platoon had enemy on their right and left flanks on the main ridgeline. Company K then passed through the 2d Platoon's positions and started approximately 1,000 yards down the right side of the ridge before receiving enemy machine-gun and automatic-weapons fire. I [Lieutenant Palmer] could see about fifteen enemy soldiers run off Company K's objec- tive, and the company secured a knoll to the right flank of Company L. The 1st and 3d Platoons of Company L moved up, secured the left side of the ridge, and tied in for the night. By this time the 2d Platoon had thirty men left.

Captain Jackson told Lieutenant Palmer not to have his platoon dig in because they may have to take the pillbox on the highest crest of the long ridge on which the companies were located. The pillbox had been bombarded by artillery, and air strikes had been placed on it. However, machine-gun and sniper fire was still coming from it into Company L's positions. By dark the enemy fire had lifted, and the 2d Platoon was not given the mission. The only enemy action that night was when Company K received light enemy 60mm mor- tar fire.

At 0400 hours on 10 April Captain Jackson notified Lieutenant Palmer to take the 2d Platoon at 0500 and move out to take the enemy pillbox. The platoon was to be followed by the 3d Platoon on call, and the 1st Platoon was to support the 2d Platoon's assault on the enemy pillbox.

Lieutenant Palmer instructed his men to fix bayonets, and the platoon moved out quietly. The 1st Squad proceeded up the ridge leading to the pillbox, and the 2d Squad proceeded up the right along the reverse slope. The platoon had traveled approximately 200 yards when the lead scouts saw two enemy soldiers burying another. The men couldn't bayonet the enemy and had to shoot them. One of the soldiers managed to get away and returned fire on the lead elements. The platoon advanced another 250 yards behind friendly artillery and 4.2-inch mortar fire and then notified the 3d Platoon to move out. The 2d Platoon moved on about a hundred yards to another small knoll and started to receive enemy machine-gun and automatic-weapons fire from fifty yards to their direct and left fronts. The 2d Platoon set up their machine gun and had fired approximately fifteen rounds when the weapon jammed. The 3d Platoon's machine gun was brought up and covered the ridge. Lieutenant Palmer instructed the lead squad to build up their fire and advance. The squad attacked and bayoneted one enemy machine gunner who had been stunned by the friendly artillery fire. The platoon continued their attack in spite of fire from the enemy pillbox. Lieutenant Palmer called back for the attached heavy-machine-gun section with the 1st Platoon, and after receiving the machine guns, placed fire on the slits of the pillbox. The lieutenant also requested Company I, on a ridge to the left front of Company L, to place fire on the pillbox. Captain Jackson also had 57mm recoilless-rifle fire placed on a slit of the pillbox.

The 2d Platoon pressed their attack under cover of small-arms fire, and reached a point within fifty yards of the pillbox before receiving sniper fire from a ridge to the right front about 500 yards away. Machine-gun fire was placed on the enemy snipers, and the platoon reached the pillbox. The men went to the slits, threw in two grenades, and then secured the pillbox. None of the enemy soldiers were killed in the pillbox, as they had fled down the reverse slope during the assault. The 3d Platoon and the 2d Platoon organized the captured positions. While the remainder of the company was approaching the position, approximately fifty rounds of enemy 82mm mortar fire landed in the area, killing one and wounding three men. During the assault on the pillbox the enemy suffered the loss of two heavy machine guns, two light machine guns, and six dead.

Captain Jackson had controlled the entire attack situation of the battalion for three days, and his recommendations were followed to the letter.[66]

MASTER SERGEANT WILLIAM M. SANFORD, 1ST PLATOON LEADER, COMPANY L: At 0800 hours on 9 April, the 1st Platoon attacked down the ridgeline to the left and immediately received very effective low trajectory automatic-weapons fire from a large pillbox 150 yards to the front. Some small-arms fire was coming from a ridgeline leading down to the "Rock of Gibraltar." Two air strikes and excellent artillery and heavy-mortar fire was placed on the pillbox, and the 1st Platoon moved up and secured it. The remainder of the company moved up and organized along the ridgeline. Captain Jackson then instructed the company not to dig in because another move was anticipated. Company K then moved through and cleared the ridgeline to the right after a brief firefight. The two companies tied in for the night. During the night, Company K received some 82mm mortar fire.

At 0400 hours on 10 April the 2d Platoon, led by Lieutenant Palmer, moved out to secure another pillbox on still higher ground along the ridgeline. The 1st Platoon was in support. By 1400 the objective was taken, and the company moved up and dug in. Approximately a half hour later, concentrated 82mm mortar fire came into the area, inflicting five casualties. At 2000 hours, approximately six rounds of 120mm mortar fire hit the positions, but the rest of the night was uneventful. The battalion secured the ridge for the night with Company K on the right and Company L on the left.[67]

SERGEANT FIRST CLASS CROCKETT, SQUAD LEADER, 3D PLATOON, COMPANY L: I joined the company on 9 April after being absent sick. On 10 April the 2d Platoon of Company L jumped off in the attack down a ridgeline. About 300 yards from the top the platoon received small-arms fire from two enemy soldiers. The 1st Platoon and 3d Platoon deployed and laid a base of fire for the attacking 2d Platoon. A heavy-machine-gun section from Company M was attached to the 2d and 3d Platoons.

I couldn't see the enemy, but the attacking elements were receiving small-arms fire from the ridge to the front. The 4th Platoon set up their 57mm recoilless rifle and fired directly on the objective, hitting both the forward and reverse slopes of the hill. When the fire lifted, Lieutenant Palmer sent one squad in a skirmish line to take both enemy-held pillboxes. The squad took the objectives without further enemy opposition. The enemy had withdrawn 150 yards to the hill directly in front of the pillboxes and started to put small-arms fire on the 2d Platoon. Lieutenant Palmer was wounded at this time. The rest of the company joined the 2d Platoon at the pillboxes and set up a perimeter.

Company I came up the ridge to the left of Company L and went on to the next ridge. Company L received enemy 82mm mortar fire at the pillboxes, killing one man and wounding another. Company I advanced seventy-five yards in front of Company L and received small-arms fire from their left, front, and right. Company I then passed through Company L into a little saddle where they were pinned down by small-arms fire from their left front. The company suffered several casualties from this enemy fire. About 1730 hours, Company I was ordered to pull back and tie in on the left of Company L down the ridgeline.

During the night, enemy 75mm self-propelled howitzer fire fell to the right front of Company L. Also that night, Lieutenant Kim, the ROK interpreter, heard over the SCR300 radio the North Korean battalion commander telling his company commanders to pull back 5,000 yards to Hill 8__. Captain Jackson, the Company L commander, tried to locate it on the map but couldn't find it. The remainder of the night was very quiet.[68]

PRIVATE FIRST CLASS RUSSELL, MACHINE GUNNER, 1ST PLATOON, COMPANY L: At 0800 hours on 9 April the 2d Platoon assaulted and secured the ground between the two companies [I and L, who had dug in the night before with enemy between them]. At 1000 hours the 1st Platoon then led a company attack on a hill to the front, approximately twenty-five to thirty yards from the Hwach'on–Ch'uyang-ni road. The lead squad was one-fourth the way up the hill before it received enemy small-arms fire from the right flank. I placed machine-gun fire on the enemy and forced them to withdraw. The platoon continued its advance and approached halfway up the ridgeline before it received accurate automatic-weapons and small-arms fire from the flanks and direct front. For approximately an hour the platoon returned fire, and suddenly the enemy fire from the right flank ceased. Captain Jackson ordered the company to retire to the right slope of the hill for protection and to dig in for the night. Company I was approaching up a ridge to the left, which led to the same objective, and was also engaged by the enemy. At 1800 several enemy soldiers were spotted on the skyline, and 60mm mortar fire was placed on them. There was no further enemy contact during the night.

At 0800 hours on 10 April the 2d Platoon attempted to secure the hill, but was pinned down by automatic-weapons, heavy-machine-gun, and small-arms fire after proceeding three-fourths the way toward the objective. The remainder of the company moved up and dug in for the night. Several small enemy probing attacks were repulsed in the early morning.[69]

CORPORAL NISHIDA, 1ST PLATOON, AND PRIVATE FIRST CLASS VICKERS, 2D PLATOON, BOTH COMPANY L: On 9 April, Company L moved out to take a hill but received small-arms and machine-gun fire from the right flank and left front. Company I was coming up the ridge to the left, but both outfits halted while air strikes were made on the enemy's positions. The enemy's stubborn resistance lasted all day. At 1700 hours the firing on the right had ceased, and the 2d Platoon was ordered up through the 1st and 3d Platoons. The platoon moved up with no enemy contact. Company K had pushed through to the right of Company L and had been held up for an hour. Thirty North Koreans were flushed out of a pillbox, and the companies organized on the hill for the night. Enemy 120mm mortar fire fell on the 1st and 3d Platoons' positions during the night.

On 10 April the company was alerted at 0430 hours, and at 0500 the 2d Platoon, followed by the 3d Platoon, moved out into attack down the ridgeline. The 1st Platoon formed a base of fire for the attacking platoons. About 0600, while it was still dark, Vickers saw two North Koreans carrying some dead about ten yards in front. Not being close enough to use his bayonet, he killed one with his rifle, and the other ran on up the hill.

About 0700, the leading elements of the company came up behind a large rock formation directly in the line of approach approximately thirty yards from open foxholes. The enemy threw hand grenades from the top of the rock formation and opened up with a machine gun. Vickers took cover behind the rock and killed the enemy machine gunner. A friendly machine gun to the rear gave the platoon overhead fire support. The lead squad was pinned down for thirty minutes and then received orders from Lieutenant Palmer to move forward. When the squad reached the enemy machine-gun position, they found the gun was removed, but the wheels were left in position. Machine-gun ammunition and grenades were abandoned by the enemy, and one machine-gun ammunition box had a red star on it.

The friendly machine gun placed fire to the left front while the platoon reorganized on the objective. The 2d Squad was put in the lead as the platoon went up to the high ground to take the pillbox. The 3d Platoon established positions on the rock mass and covered the 2d Platoon. At 1030 the platoon reached the pillbox, and enemy machine guns opened fire from the right front. Captain Jackson ordered the platoon to dig in and keep alert. The other two platoons moved up on the right. At 1120 the company received enemy 60mm mortar fire but remained in position the rest of the day and night without further enemy contact.[70]

Members of Company I describe their role in the fighting on 9 and 10 April.

CAPTAIN BARNITZ, COMMANDING OFFICER, COMPANY I: The next morning [9 April] at dawn Company L attacked the pillbox behind rolling artillery fire and secured it by 0600 hours. At 0800, Company I moved out through Company L and moved southeast following Company K. Company K took a high rocky hill mass, the "Rock of Gibraltar," and Company I stopped about 500 yards northwest and cleared the ridges on both sides. We found some dead

North Koreans. During this time, Company K thought a South Korean human carrier train approaching Company I was the enemy and opened fire on them, forcing them to take cover. At 1200 hours, Company I returned to the pillbox.

The company was then given the mission of securing a ridge about 400 yards south of Hill 705. At 1300 hours the 1st Platoon moved out around the edge of the pillbox and started up the ridgeline toward the objective. After going a short distance the platoon received heavy enemy small-arms and automatic-weapons fire from the ridge fingers to the right and left of the objective. Artillery and mortar fire was placed on the enemy positions but failed to dislodge him. Because of the heavy enemy fire and approaching darkness the battalion commander ordered Company I to tie in with Company L for the night.

On 10 April, Company I was given the mission of taking the same ridge and continuing to another ridge about 400 yards north of Hill 705. Both were secured by 1100 hours against no enemy opposition. A heavy artillery and mortar barrage preceded Company I's attack, and evidence of fresh blood and bandages indicated that the enemy had withdrawn during the barrage. Many grenades, and fresh ammunition dated 1950–51, were found. At about 1115 a heavy fog and drizzle set in, limiting observation to thirty to forty feet. Companies K and L then passed through Company I to attack another ridge to the front. The company remained in this position the rest of the day and night with no enemy contact. Companies K and L tied in with Company I for the night.[71]

Lieutenant Perdomo, 2d Platoon leader, Company I: On 9 April the 1st Platoon, led by Lieutenant Craig, was given the mission of clearing another ridge to the front. At about 1500 hours the 1st Platoon ran into a firefight. The enemy started to flank the platoon from the right, so Captain Barnitz ordered me to protect the right flank of the 1st Platoon. As the 3d Platoon started up the ridge, approximately half of the platoon was pinned down by machine-gun fire from Company L's sector. When this fire lifted, the platoon was pinned down again by eight short rounds of 105mm artillery fire. Finally the platoon maneuvered to where machine gun and BAR fire could be placed on the enemy. During the firefight, Lieutenant Griffith, the Company I executive officer, and two other men were hit. Lieutenant Craig, the 1st Platoon leader, called back to me to have me relay a message for artillery support. All the radios failed, and the word was not sent. When the firefight ceased, the platoons withdrew back to their original positions within the battalion perimeter. On 10 April Company I took the same ridge, which was the 3d Battalion's objective, against no enemy opposition.[72]

Lieutenant Rodgers, 4th Platoon leader, Company I: At 0430 hours on 9 April, after a fifteen-minute artillery barrage, Company L seized the pillbox and suffered three casualties from enemy machine-gun fire. Company I had no prior knowledge of Company L's attack. At 0630, Company I moved past the pillbox and turned right to assist the attack of Company K on a large pillbox on the high ground called the "Rock of Gibraltar." Company I secured both flanks of Company K during the attack, and Company K took the ground with two casualties.

Company I rejoined the battalion at 1400 hours and was ordered to secure the high ground to the front of Company L [about 1,000 yards south of Hill 703]. There were three small peaks, each separated by a draw, and each succeeding one a little higher. The 1st Platoon was assigned the mission, moved out, and had passed to the crest of the second peak before it received small-arms and machine-gun fire from the peak to the front. One man, Private Strobel, was wounded, and Lieutenant Griffith and a squad sergeant were wounded trying to rescue him. A medical aid man finally went out and brought the three back. Artillery and mortar fire was placed on the enemy position, but the battalion commander ordered the platoon to disengage with the enemy and withdraw back to the battalion perimeter near Company L's position.

The next day, 10 April, at 0800 hours, Company I secured the objective with no enemy opposition, swung to the right, and secured two more peaks. The company was covered by fire from tanks on the Ch'unch'on–Naep'yong-ni road. At 1430 Companies K and L were ordered through Company I to continue the attack, but snow and fog set in, limiting visibility. The battalion commander ordered the companies to hold the ground until the next day.[73]

Over the next two days, 11 and 12 April, the 3d Battalion's advance to the north continued, as Lieutenant Colonel Richardson relates.

The 3d Battalion moved out [on 11 April] with the mission of seizing and securing Hill 1031. There were only two routes of approach to the hill, and both were defended by the enemy. Previous air and agent reports stated that approximately 400 enemy troops were on Hill 1031. At 1100 hours [on 12 April] Company K reported contact with an estimated enemy squad approximately 1,000 meters south and west of the objective. Although the enemy had no apparent supporting weapons, he employed his small arms and automatic weapons so effectively as to halt the advance of Company K. After determining that Company K could not advance, at 1300 hours I committed Company L to the right in an effort to flank the enemy positions and permit the further advance of Company K.

A platoon from Company L gained the top of Hill 1031 without being detected by the enemy. One squad from the platoon assaulted an enemy pillbox along Company K's line of approach but was forced to withdraw. The pillbox was neutralized by Company L with 57mm recoilless-rifle fire. Company K moved up and secured its portion of the objective after dark. At 2330 hours Company I joined the remainder of the battalion on Hill 1031. Sporadic enemy small-arms fire continued until approximately 2400 hours.[74]

Members of the 3d Battalion recall the action to secure Hill 1031.

SGT. BROWN, SFC GLASSMAN, AND SFC BURGI, ALL COMPANY K: 11 April was very foggy, but at 0800 hours Company K jumped off down the ridgeline to the north and east through Company L. After advancing one mile, the lead squad received automatic-weapons fire from their direct front. The enemy withdrew, and the company advanced approximately 300 yards farther to higher ground. We thought it was the 3d Battalion objective, but were mistaken because of the fog and darkness. The company formed a three-platoon perimeter and was later joined by Company L. It snowed that night, but there was no enemy contact.

About 0800 hours on 12 April, the 3d Platoon moved out 800 or 900 yards and encountered two big flat rocks with a pass running between them. As the platoon started through the pass, approximately eight or nine enemy threw grenades down, and the platoon was forced to withdraw back to the left of the ridge. The remainder of the company formed a defense line while mortar fire was placed on the ridgeline and the rock formation. Air strikes were placed on the hill behind. The 2d Platoon then moved out in the attack with the 1st Platoon in support. The platoons received enemy automatic-weapons fire from the highest peak but finally secured the hill and tied in with Company L for the night. All during the night the company received automatic-weapons fire from a position seventy-five yards in front of the 3d Platoon. By early morning, mortar fire had silenced the enemy fire.[75]

LIEUTENANT BARENKAMP, EXECUTIVE OFFICER, AND LIEUTENANT PALMER, 2D PLATOON LEADER, COMPANY L: At 0800 hours on 11 April, Company I pushed off about 1,000 yards, secured the ground leading to Hill 1031, and swept the ridges to the right. Company K then passed through Company I to take Hill 1031, and Company L followed. Company I received a few enemy mortar rounds, but there was no further enemy contact. About 1630 hours the troops experienced a heavy snowstorm lasting about thirty minutes. Because of this, the attacking forces organized on the approaches to Hill 1031 and had no enemy contact that night.

At 0800 hours on 12 April, Company K was to go to the summit of Hill 1031 followed by Company L. Company I was to bring up the rear. As Company K advanced up the hill, their approach route went through two big rocks. About 1400 the lead platoon of the company got between the rocks and received enemy automatic-weapons fire and grenades from the top. Friendly artillery bombarded the hill and the ridges to the front. The battalion commander then ordered Company L to go up and assist Company K. Captain Jackson sent the 3d and 1st Platoons into the valley and had them go to the right of Company K. They were to climb up and hit the enemy on his right flank. The 3d Platoon met no enemy opposition in their advance, and at 1700 hours got into position to assault the top of the hill. SFC Crockett, with the lead squad, shot a North Korean trying to surrender, and the other North Koreans opened fire, forcing the squad to withdraw. The 3d Platoon sergeant, Sergeant Bagley, asked for volunteers to grenade the enemy out of their positions. SFC Crockett took six men and accomplished the mission. Twelve North Koreans were killed, and the pressure was taken off Company K, enabling it to advance again.

At 2200 hours Master Sergeant Sanford, the 1st Platoon sergeant, took a platoon-size patrol to contact a platoon from Company K. The platoon found two enemy dugouts and threw in grenades, which forced the enemy to flee, leaving behind some automatic weapons and ammunition. The platoon continued on about 400 yards and contacted the Company K patrol. The 1st Platoon dug in with Company K until Company I came up to tie in with the perimeter.[76]

MASTER SERGEANT SANFORD, 1ST PLATOON LEADER, COMPANY L: At 0800 hours on 11 April the 3d Battalion moved out in a column of companies—I, K, L—to secure a hill to the northeast. Company I secured the hill by 1330 after a brief firefight with an enemy machine gun. Company K then moved through Company I to a hill 500 yards to the front. Company L followed Company K and tied in for the night.

On 12 April Company K moved out to take Hill 1031. At 1130 it received automatic-weapons fire from the front and left flank. Until 1300 hours, Company K tried unsuccessfully to take the objective, but in spite of artillery and mortar fire the enemy was able to repulse each attack. Company L was then ordered to assist Company K.

Captain Jackson ordered the 3d Platoon to flank Hill 1031 by using a draw for cover and then advancing straight up the hill. The 1st Platoon was in close support. The 3d Platoon advanced to within 150 yards of the objective without being detected. Lieutenant Laemon, 3d Platoon leader, ordered one squad out as point. Sergeant Crockett, the squad leader, killed one North Korean, but other enemy soldiers on the ridge threw grenades at the squad. Lieutenant Laemon ordered the squad to withdraw while artillery and mortar fire was placed on the enemy. Approximately 100 to 150 enemy soldiers, some looking through field glasses, could be observed 250 yards to the right on another ridge. Approximately 200 rounds of 155mm artillery fire were placed on this group with excellent results.

With darkness approaching, Captain Jackson ordered the 3d Platoon to take the hill. Sergeant Bagley, the 3d Platoon sergeant, called for volunteers and received nine. Sergeant Crockett led the men out in squad column, moving from cover to cover and secured the ridge by grenading the enemy out of his positions.

At 1900 hours, the company commander ordered me to take the 1st Platoon and secure the ground separating Company L from Company K. He said that a patrol from Company K would be sent to contact the 1st Platoon. I requested that Company K stand fast and hold fire to prevent a possible firefight between the men. At 1930 the Company L patrol moved out and encountered enemy in two pillboxes. The men threw grenades into the openings and the enemy fled, abandoning their weapons. At 2030, contact was made with Company K, and the ridge was cleared. The 1st Platoon tied in between Companies K and L until Company I closed into the position at 0230 hours.[77]

SERGEANT FIRST CLASS CROCKETT, SQUAD LEADER, 3D PLATOON, COMPANY L: On 11 April the entire battalion moved forward without any opposition. Company I led the advance, followed by Company K, with Company L in reserve. A little small-arms fire was received by Company K during the later afternoon, but there was no further enemy contact. During the night, Company K was on the left ridge in front of Company I, and Company L was tied in on Company I's right front. Company L's right flank was open. The entire battalion sector was quiet during the night.

On 12 April, Company K led off the attack to a hill peak on the ridgeline, and Company L followed Company K. There was a huge rock, fifty feet high, on the ridge. Because of the terrain, Company K had to go by it. Enemy fire from the top of the rock formation pinned Company K down. Company L was pulled back down the ridge and ordered to flank the enemy. The 3d Platoon advanced down the ridgeline into a draw on the right and then started climbing up to the objective, which was the high peak of Hill 1187. The remainder of the company stayed at the bottom of the hill for support. Company K was also receiving fire from a saddle to the right front, but the 3d Platoon, in the meantime, was coming up the right flank. The platoon advanced as far as the saddle without receiving enemy fire. I took my squad through the saddle and spotted an enemy pillbox and several enemy soldiers in foxholes on either side. I threw a hand grenade into a hole, killing one of the enemy soldiers, and shot another. One North Korean remained in the hole and started to come out with his hands up, but then attempted to go for a weapon, so I shot him. The enemy soldiers in the pillbox were watching Company K, and I could see enemy BARs, machine guns, and automatic weapons. Some of the enemy approached a knoll overlooking my position and placed machine-gun and automatic-weapons fire on the squad. The enemy could not deploy their fire low enough to hit the squad, but started to throw hand grenades at us. The squad pulled back for protection, but I stayed by the pillbox and spotted three enemy soldiers in front of Company K, holding up their advance. I then returned to the platoon and had machine-gun fire placed on the enemy's positions. The enemy soldiers were killed, and Company K started to advance up the ridge.

The 3d Platoon leader was wounded, so the platoon sergeant asked for volunteers to assault the enemy positions. I had previously volunteered to lead such a group. Nine men volunteered, but only six were selected to accompany me back up the peak. My group, armed with three BARs and hand grenades, advanced up the ridge cautiously, in a crouching position. We knocked out the two pillboxes with hand grenades and forced the enemy to withdraw. After the enemy withdrew, the platoon came up and joined my group. The platoon placed BAR fire into another enemy pillbox farther down the ridge. The next morning a burp gun was found in the pillbox and there was blood all over the place. The entire company stayed overnight on the ridge. The company tied in with Company K, and at 0200 hours Company I came up to the ridge. The rest of the night was quiet.[78]

The capture of Hill 1031 by the 3d Battalion, combined with

the 2d Battalion capture of Hill 1187 to the north, hastened the
North Korean withdrawal already in progress. The 23d Infantry
Regiment's After Action Report sums up the end of the operation.

It was apparent that the regiment was confronting the main battle positions of the enemy. These positions ran generally south to southeast from the Hwach'on Reservoir to the Soyang River along sharp ridgelines that were the backbone of the Whitehead Mountains. Until this time the attack had been generally north, but with the discovery of the main defense line, it became clear that, by considering the reservoir as a barrier to the enemy, a lateral attack across the regimental sector with all elements of the command could be made. This plan was put into effect by moving the 2d Reconnaissance Company, who had arrived in the area two days earlier, to the west end of the reservoir, relieving the company of the French Battalion screening the northwest portion of the zone. The Netherlands Detachment, who had arrived on 10 April, took positions at the road junction [at Ch'uyang-ni] to protect the open right flank of the regiment.

After two days of pounding by the artillery and continuous pressure by the infantry, the enemy was defeated. The action was fierce and progress slow, but the issue was decided with the fall of Hills 1031 and 1187. Approximately 300 enemy soldiers, secure in their reveted positions, resisted stubbornly. Continuous pounding by the artillery, who fired more than 2,000 rounds in support, and the persistent maneuvering of the foot troops even as darkness was falling, broke the enemy defense, and they withdrew. There was no enemy to be found in front of our troops on the morning of 13 April, and no enemy contact had been made at the close of operations on 14 April.

Much credit for the success of the operation must be given to the supporting arms attached to the 23d Infantry for this operation. The artillery was used to the maximum of its capabilities. Targets were subjected to one- and two-battalion volleys and, on occasion, to time on target by the 37th, 15th, and 503d Field Artillery Battalions combined. More than 29,000 rounds were fired by the three battalions of artillery during this period. Companies A and B of the 2d Engineer Battalion toiled ceaselessly to clear roads, gun positions, and CP areas of mines and booby traps; to fill in craters; and, where necessary, to build new roads to allow the maximum supply support possible by vehicle. Without the efforts of these companies, in which fifteen men were killed or wounded by mines, this operation could not have been as successfully or as rapidly concluded.

Two enemy regiments were identified by prisoners of war taken in the operation, and estimates place 5,000 enemy in the sector cleared by the RCT. An estimated 1,913 casualties were inflicted on the enemy, with a counted total of 384 killed in action. Thirty-four prisoners were captured. This operation carried the 23d Infantry across the 38th parallel for the second time.[79]

Chapter 11

HWACH'ON DAM—
ATTACKS IN THE WEST

1st Cavalry Division, 9–10 April 1951

In early April, as the 23d Infantry Regiment of the 2d Division (X Corps) engaged in Operation Swing to clear the enemy from the southeastern end of the Hwach'on Reservoir, the 1st Cavalry Division (IX Corps) closed on Line Kansas at the western edge of the reservoir. The 7th Cavalry Regiment was the division's attacking force.

> *The advance moved forward over difficult terrain against weak opposition, as Lt. Col. John W. Callaway, commanding officer of the 2d Battalion, 7th Cavalry Regiment, describes.*

The enemy, even though in strongly prepared and well-organized positions, withdrew frequently in rout when his positions were aggressively attacked and partially taken. Friendly artillery, mortar, and tank fire was then able to be placed on those who were fleeing. It was noted in almost every encounter that the enemy was poorly armed. Some troops had no weapons or grenades. There were few automatic weapons. Machine-gun fire was sporadic and harassing in nature. Many captured weapons contained no sights. The enemy could have defended many of his positions had he chosen to do so and had he had the weapons. Approaches to enemy positions were made up narrow ridges. Envelopment meant moving 200 to 300 meters down, then up, sometimes over sheer cliffs. Enemy troops encountered were usually a delaying force, which withdrew when attacked. Operations were logistically difficult. Ammunition was hand-carried to positions 600 to 700 meters above the valley floor.

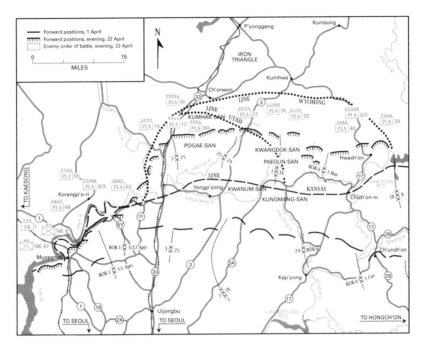

Operations Rugged and Dauntless, western front, 1–22 April 1951 (based on map in CMH manuscript, U.S. Army).

Evacuation was a serious problem, since three to seven hours were needed to evacuate a casualty from the hills.[1]

Reasons for the slow advance included rugged terrain, lack of roads, and resulting supply difficulties. Officers of the S-4 section of the 7th Cavalry Regiment describe the logistics situation.

CAPT. JAMES R. ELLINGSWORTH, S-4: The regimental advance toward Phase Line Kansas was made cautiously. The regimental mission was the destruction of the enemy. Taking ground was secondary.

The regimental sector had no roads, therefore no main supply route (MSR). Vehicles could not be utilized to transport supplies, even though Company B, 8th Engineer Combat Battalion, developed trails so that vehicles could be brought forward as far as possible. But the battalions eventually reached points where rations, ammunition, and water had to be hand-carried. Able-bodied Korean carriers were employed for this purpose. The Civilian Transportation Corps was organized to form companies of Korean bearers, and on 2 April, the 1st Cavalry Division drew one company, which was given to the 7th Cavalry Regiment. As the terrain became more difficult, the regiment requested another company. On the afternoon of 7 April our regiment received a second company. Two platoons of these companies worked with each battalion. The Greek Expeditionary Force was attached to the 7th Cavalry Regiment and was considered as the 4th Battalion.

The regiment reached Phase Line Kansas on 9 April. Orders for the relief of the regiment at 1600 hours on 10 April had been received.[2]

CAPT. CARLTON J. BARNES, ASSISTANT S-4: Two companies of Korean carriers were secured for the regiment, one on 2 April and one on 7 April. Each company had an authorized strength of 239, but the companies were understrength. It was necessary to hand carry supplies ten to fifteen air miles prior to arriving at the dam area. In order to transport supplies to the regimental positions in the vicinity of the Hwach'on Dam, a narrow, rocky road, little more than a trail, was utilized through the sector of the French Battalion [23d Infantry Regiment of the 2d Division] on the right. Only a jeep without a trailer was able to go over this route, which was named the French Pass.[3]

The right boundary of IX Corps, which on 4 April, at the beginning of Operation Rugged, had been shifted fifteen miles to the west, was shifted back three miles to the east on 6 April. This change gave the IX Corps and the 1st Cavalry Division the responsibility for capturing the Hwach'on Dam, which controlled the waters of the reservoir and the level of the Pukhan and Han Rivers. The release of water could have a significant effect on IX Corps operations. The IX Corps engineer study in early April highlights the problem.

The Hwach'on Reservoir is one of the largest in Korea. It covers thirteen square miles and has an estimated capacity of 19,140,000,000 cubic feet. The straight-line overflow-type dam is 275 feet high and has a spillway 826 feet long. The water level fluctuates between 512 and 594 feet above sea level and can attain a height of 32 feet above the spillway.

According to technical studies, it is believed that the enemy is incapable of breeching the dam by demolition. However, aerial observers have noted that the spillway gates are closed to their maximum extent, and that only a trickle of water is being released. It is entirely plausible that the enemy is trying to raise the level of the reservoir to its maximum elevation and subsequently release a flood of water by opening the penstocks and spillway gates. Interrogation of civilians in the Ch'unch'on area also indicates that the present water level of the river below the dam is well below normal for this time of year. This is another indication that the enemy may have such a plan in mind.

If the water in the reservoir were to reach its maximum height, and if all the gates and penstocks were opened simultaneously, an enormous flood of water would be released down the Pukhan River with the depth of water varying with the width of the channel at any particular point. In the portions of the river extending from the dam south to the Chich'on-ni area, the water may rise ten to twelve feet. In the Ch'unch'on flood plain area the river channels may be expected to rise approximately five feet, with inundation of the entire flood plain with about one foot of water, and a subsequent backing up of the river and streams in the entire area. The depth of the water in the narrow channel below Ch'unch'on may be expected to rise about five to eight feet.[4]

During the night of 8–9 April enemy forces resisting the advance of the 7th Cavalry Regiment abandoned their positions and withdrew. The next morning the waters of the Pukhan River began to rise. Staff officers of IX Corps describe the results.

MAJ. LINTON S. BOATWRIGHT, G-3 PLANS OFFICER: If the eighteen gates of the Hwach'on Dam were opened all at once, the water released would be capable of taking out most of the bridges across the Pukhan and Han Rivers. The river level would rise between ten and twelve feet. The sudden opening of all the gates by the enemy would inflict maximum damage to corps transportation.

The enemy opened only ten gates of the dam, and the maximum water rise has been only 4.9 feet. The enemy could open only ten gates; possibly not all are operable. There are penstocks and channels to run dynamos at the bottom of the dam, and if these were opened, the entire reservoir could be drained. This action could have split our forces from twelve hours to two days.[5]

MAJ. JAMES W. ROY, G-2 ANALYSIS OFFICER: By opening some of the gates of the Hwach'on Dam, the enemy partially and temporarily segregated corps troops on the east side of the Pukhan River from those on the west side. The rising water washed out one treadway bridge; the engineers took out one bridge on the lower Pukhan. To relieve pressure and lower the water level, the engineers opened the gates of the lower dam [Chongp'yong Reservoir Dam] on the Pukhan River. Opening the gates caused no damage and no loss of equipment.[6]

CAPT. GEORGE MINTZ, ENGINEER INTELLIGENCE OFFICER: The enemy opened only two-fifths of all the gates on the Hwach'on Dam. The water has actually risen a maximum of only seven feet. The gates on the dam can be operated manually and electrically. It takes approximately ten hours to lift one gate manually. The only reasonable explanation why the enemy did not open all the gates is that he started to and was unable to finish for an unknown reason.

The floating treadway bridge [east of Chich'on-ni], a key bridge across the Pukhan River, was disconnected on 10 April. This bridge was important because it is on the MSR, the only road from Ch'unch'on north to Hwach'on and eventually to Kumhwa, an important enemy center of communications and transportation. The bridge on the road from Ch'unch'on west to Kap'yong, also a treadway, was disconnected 10 April, then reopened to all traffic, less tanks. A bridge on the road southwest from Kap'yong was washed out. Of the five bridges across the Pukhan and Han Rivers, all were at one time disconnected and inoperable or washed out between 9 and 11 April. At this time (1700 hours on 11 April) two of the five are still out. One is of no tactical importance. But the other, southwest of Ch'unch'on, is of vital importance to corps operations.[7]

CAPT. ARNOLD FRANK, COMMANDING OFFICER OF THE IX

CORPS ENGINEER TECHNICAL INTELLIGENCE TEAM: The Hwach'on Dam had been closed, and water was permitted to build up in the reservoir. On the day before the dam was opened by the enemy [8 April], the water was up eighteen feet. From interrogation of prisoners of war, it was learned that at midnight, 8 April, an enemy company was ordered to open the gates. Two squads and five Korean employees of the dam power plant went up on the dam. The central power system was not working; therefore, in order to open the gates, which are ten meters wide and six meters high, auxiliary engines were used, or the gates were raised manually. Two gates were raised completely. Two gates were opened three-quarters of the way. The next six gates were opened slightly. I think that the enemy would have opened additional gates had he been able to do so.

Sufficient opening had been made, however, to release a large amount of water, and the water level on the river rose. It took four and a half hours for the water to flow from the Hwach'on Dam to Ch'unch'on. The IX Corps engineers took two bridges out so they would not be lost. In the meantime, friendly forces had opened the gates on the Chongp'yong Dam, lower on the river and on the same power system, to prevent a surge of water. Nevertheless, the engineers opened a bridge on the lower Pukhan.[8]

As the water level of the Pukhan River continued to rise on 9 April, the 7th Cavalry pushed forward to Line Kansas, about two miles south of the Hwach'on Dam, arriving there about noon. Earlier, the regiment had received word that it was to be relieved on Phase Line Kansas late on 10 April by the 1st Marine Division. Other elements of the 1st Cavalry Division were already moving out of the area. The regiment also had an "on order" mission from the 1st Cavalry Division to capture the Hwach'on Dam and had formed a special task force consisting of the 2d Battalion and the attached 4th Ranger Company. Staff officers of the division and the regiment describe the initial planning to capture the dam.

MAJ. JAMES H. WEBEL, S-3 OF THE 7TH CAVALRY REGIMENT: The mission of the 7th Cavalry Regiment was to advance to Phase Line Kansas, just short of the Hwach'on Reservoir area. This the regiment had accomplished when the G-3 of the 1st Cavalry Division instructed the regiment to continue the attack and, if possible, to seize the Hwach'on Dam. We inferred from this message that the area was not held in strength by the enemy, and that our regiment could easily overrun the dam.

The commanding officer of the 2d Battalion had already been briefed on the possibility of this mission while in a reserve area northeast of Ch'unch'on. For some time there had been talk of the possibility of task force action to seize the dam. On the day [7 April at 1600 hours] that the 4th Ranger Company became available to the 7th Cavalry Regiment, the regiment was alerted for the mission of destroying certain sluice gate mechanisms.

The 2d Battalion moved to an assembly area in the vicinity of Yuch'on-ni [on 8 April] to await orders for its commitment. The impression was that this mission would not be ordered for several days.[9]

LT. COL. JOHN CARLSON, G-3 OF THE 1ST CAVALRY DIVISION: On 7 or 8 April the original thought on the Hwach'on Dam operation was to send the Rangers up to destroy the floodgate machinery. The Rangers preferred to accomplish this mission as a night operation by proceeding across the reservoir on rubber boats. Division opposed this plan because of the distance the water voyage involved and because of the lack of available boats.

When the Chinese opened the floodgates it meant that a larger force would have to be sent to secure the dam while demolitions were placed. Division was instructed to be ready to take the dam or destroy it.[10]

CAPT. JOHN R. FLYNN, S-3 OF THE 2D BATTALION, 7TH CAVALRY: At the time the Rangers joined the 2d Battalion, the Hwach'on Dam mission was nebulous. Just what to do when friendly forces reached the dam remained doubtful to the very day of the attack. The commanding officer of the 4th Ranger Company had only a vague idea of what he was to do: what was he to destroy at the dam, or was he to destroy anything at all? His briefing had been cursory. I feel that an operation of this type requires planning in great detail; that planning should occupy at least four times the amount of time anticipated as necessary for the execution.[11]

The First Attempt, 9 April

The S-3 of the 7th Cavalry, Major Webel, describes the unit's operations on 9 April as they secured Phase Line Kansas and pushed forward toward the dam.

No enemy contact was made as the regiment took its objectives. The enemy had withdrawn across the Pukhan River during the night. Since the ridgeline along Phase Line Kansas was unoccupied, the division G-3 ordered the Hwach'on Dam to be seized, if possible, as a continuation of that day's operations.

The 2d Battalion pushed forward rapidly, meeting no resistance until it crossed the east–west road at the southern end of the neck of land [southwest of the dam]. At that point the enemy reacted. Enemy resistance came from a series of pillboxes, which were mutually supporting and extremely well constructed. These positions appeared to be part of original North Korean defenses in the dam area. The 2d Battalion commander then attempted to flank the enemy position by maneuvering to the west, toward terrain that offered a favorable approach. At this time intense enemy machine-gun and mortar fire was received from high ground west of the Pukhan River. It was evident that maneuvering in the vicinity of the river would be highly dangerous unless the enemy forces west of the Pukhan were eliminated by an attack against the high ground in that area.

The commanding officer of the attacking company was killed, and initial reports from that company indicated heavy casualties had been suffered. These reports proved to be false; there were only two casualties. Based on the reports, however, as well as on the fact that darkness was approaching, the attack was held up until the next morning. Permission to do so was granted. The 2d Battalion pulled into a defensive position for the night.[12]

Lieutenant Colonel Callaway, the commander of the 2d Battalion, provides more details of the action on 9 April.

On 8 April the battalion moved approximately seven miles, from regimental reserve to the Soomi area [about one mile east of Yuch'on-ni]. On this date the battalion was alerted to the mission of

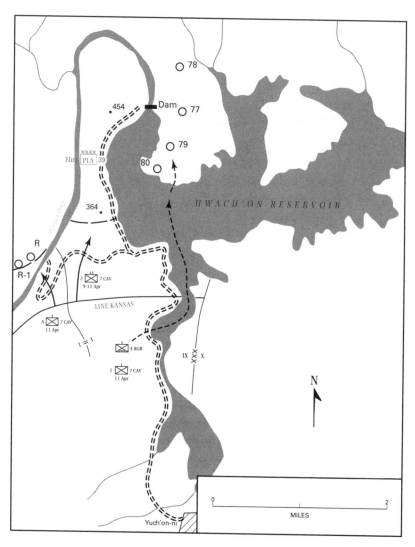

Hwach'on Dam, 9–11 April 1951 (based on map in CMH manuscript, U.S. Army).

seizing the dam. The battalion was informed that an engineer team from corps would be attached to the battalion to destroy the machinery or adjust the locks in the desired manner. Attached also were the Rangers, with the mission of actually seizing the dam for the engineer technical team.

On 9 April the battalion was ordered to seize the high ground along Phase Line Kansas. The plan was as follows: Company F would take the high ground on the right and continue the attack to the northeast; Company E would take the high ground on the left and await further instructions; Company G in reserve would clear the ridges adjoining the reservoir and open the road adjacent to the reservoir.

The battalion arrived on its objectives after a firefight in Yuch'on-ni, and after climbing 600 meters without encountering the enemy. Company F was on its objective at noon and was directed to go by the shortest route to the neck of land southwest of the dam and, if possible, take that ground west of the reservoir. I had received permission to continue the advance. Company E had more trouble with the terrain than Company F and was not yet on its objective.

Company F moved generally north. At 1500 the company reached the road on the southern edge of the neck of land without contacting the enemy. In the meantime I directed Company G to move down the road along the reservoir edge. I also directed the P&A Platoon to start repairing the craters to make the road passable for vehicles. This was done by the platoon and by Korean laborers. The only vehicles able to reach the 2d Battalion were jeeps without trailers. These vehicles were used to transport ammunition. By 1600 hours the road was opened north to where it bent back to the west at the edge of the reservoir. Company G stretched over the road, cleared the area, and the mortars and supporting weapons were able to get forward. The 2d Battalion at this time was beyond the range of 105mm howitzers and was operating at the extreme range of 155mm howitzers. This made battery dispersion greater than at normal range. The 8-inch howitzers were not yet in position to render support.

At approximately 1500, Company F moved across the east–west road at the southern end of the neck of land. There the company came under enemy fire from well-camouflaged positions believed to be west of the Pukhan River. Enemy mortar, machine-gun, and small-arms fire held up the company. The company, however, reported its position in error as being on the edge of the reservoir.

I had ordered Company E to clear the ridges northeast from its portion of Phase Line Kansas for approximately 2,000 yards, and it was moving up. From an observation post I noticed an enemy trench, which ran completely around the ridge forty feet above the water of the reservoir. I also observed pillboxes along the ridges, but I saw absolutely no enemy activity.

When Company F reported that it was pinned down and getting machine-gun fire from several directions, it also requested six litters. This indicated that the company had been ambushed or had suffered a considerable number of casualties. I called for an air strike and designated the target by having a white phosphorous round fired by a 75mm rifle. This target was selected because of Company F's reported position. In actuality, however, the company was below that point. Planes using rockets, machine guns, and napalm struck the target. It was then between 1700 and 1730, and I wanted Company F to continue across the area to the north while Company G moved over the road west and north. At this time I received word that the commanding officer of Company F was killed. Still badly needing six litters according to report, and pinned, the company could hope to withdraw only under cover of darkness. I decided to hold up the attack until the following morning.

I had the battalion move into an assembly area. I ordered Company G to move on the ridge in tight perimeter for the night. I instructed Company E to move to a position where it could assist Company F to withdraw. I also designated another officer to command Company F. I left my observation post about 1730 and traversed the extremely rough terrain, finally reaching the lead platoon of Company F at 1930 hours. I realized then that the company was considerably to the west of its reported position. The company was still receiving fire from west of the river. I called for counterbattery fire on these positions. Litters were brought forward, and after darkness the Company F platoon was withdrawn. There were only two casualties, one killed and one wounded. When the company withdrew I took back the wounded man who died en route. The litter was carried by native bearers over some cliffs that were almost vertical.[13]

Capt. Dorsey B. Anderson, the commander of the 4th Ranger Company, describes his unit's role in the operation and his own actions.

On 7 April, Lieutenant Colonel Carlson, G-3 of the 1st Cavalry Division, informed me that the 4th Ranger Company had been given the mission of making the Hwach'on Dam inoperative. On 8 April, accompanied by Major Wilson of the 8th Engineer Combat Battalion, I examined the dam at Chongp'yong so that I would be somewhat familiar with machinery presumed to be similar to that of the Hwach'on Dam. The dam machinery was not to be destroyed, but was to be rendered inoperative by blowing the cogs on the power wheel controlling the floodgates. I made detailed drawings and then secured the necessary demolitions from the 8th Engineer Battalion. On 9 April I made an aerial reconnaissance of the dam area. That afternoon I received word that the 4th Ranger Company was attacking, and I borrowed a helicopter from the 1st Cavalry Division and joined my company.

I arrived to find the 4th Ranger Company behind Company F, the attacking company in the battalion of the 7th Cavalry Regiment. When Company F secured the high ground on the neck of land west of the dam, the 4th Ranger Company was to move along the road on the eastern edge of the neck of land, place charges on the dam machinery, and secure the high ground east of the dam.

Company F did not accomplish its mission because no maneuver room existed. A front attack over two successive high points to the third and highest ground had to be made because of the water barrier on both sides of the neck. The 4th Ranger Company went into battalion reserve that night in a rice paddy where the road coming north from Yuch'on-ni bent back to the west.[14]

1st Lt. John S. Warren, executive officer, 4th Ranger Company, describes the activities of his company while Captain Anderson was absent.

The 4th Ranger Company departed the 5th Cavalry Regiment near Hongch'on at 1830 hours on 7 April and proceeded to the 7th Cavalry Regiment area. The company joined the regiment nine miles south of Yuch'on-ni at 2130. The company was sent to the 2d Battalion, 7th Cavalry, at that time in regimental reserve. I was briefed by the battalion S-3 and informed that the company would move to an area near Yuch'on-ni and prepare for the mission of closing the gates of the Hwach'on Dam. On 8 April the company departed the assembly area with the 2d Battalion and proceeded on foot to the vicinity of Yuch'on-ni.

At 0200 hours on 9 April the 1st and 3d Platoons moved from battalion reserve to fill a gap in the battalion perimeter of defense because small enemy activity had been noted in the vicinity. The platoons manned positions in the vicinity of the road. No enemy contact was made. At 0730 the battalion departed the assembly area to secure Phase Line Kansas. The departure was made with the Ranger company, Company F, Company E, headquarters company, Company H, and Company G, in that order. The initial mission of the 4th Ranger Company was to secure the low ground south of Line Kansas, which was to serve as an outpost for the battalion observation post. We secured our objective at 0815 without making enemy contact. Companies E and F secured Phase Line Kansas, with the 4th Ranger Company moving up to the right flank of Company F. This was accomplished by 1000 without making enemy contact.

Because no enemy had been encountered and because the objectives were secured at that early hour, the battalion commander decided to continue toward the objectives that had been scheduled for the following day's operations, so that the complete battalion mission would be terminated that same day. The original plan of action had been to set up a base of operations along Phase Line Kansas. The company commanders were briefed at 1030 hours. Company F was to move north along the ridgeline running up the middle of the neck of land west of the reservoir to Hill 454. Company E was to move north to the west of Company F, to the section of the ridge about 800 meters south of Hill 454. The 4th Ranger Company was then to move through Company E on the ridge and Company F on Hill 454 to the dam, secure the high ground east of the dam, with the further mission of closing the dam gates, two of which were partially open.

At 1500 hours Company F met heavy enemy fire and was halted, pinned down by enemy fire from high ground just north of the east–west road. The enemy fired at least three automatic weapons and 82mm mortars. Company E, attempting to continue from its position to its objective, was repelled by enemy fire from the same general location. The 4th Ranger Company was directly behind Company F and received three rounds of enemy mortar fire, which was not returned because Company F was in its line of fire. On order of the battalion commander, the 4th Ranger Company moved to an assembly area about two miles north of Yuch'on-ni to prepare for an amphibious assault mission to take the high ground on the peninsula west of the dam and also the dam. The company commander physically contacted the unit in its assembly area at approximately 2000 hours.[15]

The seizure of the dam, which at first appeared to be an easy task, now loomed as a formidable operation. Corps and division staff officers describe the problems, as they perceived them at their level.

LT. COL. JACOB SCHACTER, G-2, 1ST CAVALRY DIVISION: We had estimated an enemy regiment defending the Hwach'on Dam area, with one battalion occupying each of these three areas: the neck of land west of the reservoir, the high ground west of the river, and the peninsula east of the dam. This estimate was based on the number of mortars firing from these areas. Each area contained more than the normal number of mortars in support of a company, according to the enemy table of organization. Because enemy fires seemed well coordinated from all areas, it was thought that one enemy unit was established in defensive positions.

The 115th CCF Division was probably in this area. This unit had been in reserve, and was able to prepare excellent defensive positions. Reinforcements were moved in from the north.[16]

MAJOR BOATWRIGHT, G-3 PLANS OFFICER, IX CORPS: As judged by the amount of opposition to the 7th Cavalry Regiment, the enemy holding forces at the dam number at least a battalion. This enemy holding force has the advantage of terrain. To get to the west side of the dam, it is necessary to move up a narrow finger of land 1,000 yards wide—one long north–south hill, 4,000 to 5,000 yards in length, inclined upward toward the north. East of the dam, our forces have to cross the reservoir by boat and take other hills that overlook the reservoir.[17]

Guidance from commanders seems to have been unclear and misunderstood.

MAJ. GEN. WILLIAM M. HOGE, COMMANDER OF IX CORPS: Possession of the Hwach'on Dam gave the enemy the capability of releasing an amount of water that would be inconvenient for corps operations. The release of this water would not be disastrous in its effect, but it might slow down the corps advance. Therefore, the matter of seizing the dam and making it inoperative had been studied for about a week before the actual operation took place.

The 2d Infantry Division was at first considered for this mission, but when the 4th Ranger Company appeared on the scene, it seemed to be the perfect unit to accomplish this action. On the morning the 4th Ranger Company reported for duty, 8 April 1951, I directed the 1st Cavalry Division to make plans to utilize the Rangers and immobilize the dam. Although General Ridgway thought friendly forces would be able to remain in the dam area, I envisioned a raid-type operation, lasting from two to four hours, with the Rangers closing the floodgates, blasting the machinery in place, and withdrawing.

On the morning of 9 April I ordered the division to move up immediately. Instead of the battalion frontal attack that resulted, I thought the division could have accomplished the mission by sneaking the Rangers up the road on the western side of the reservoir. But the regiment failed to get started.[18]

COL. WILLIAM HARRIS, COMMANDING OFFICER OF THE 7TH CAVALRY REGIMENT: The mission against the Hwach'on Dam was not very clear at first, since the regiment was operating under the directive to kill the enemy rather than take ground. Later, the mission was clarified by General Palmer, the 1st Cavalry Division commander. The minimum mission was to get in and destroy the floodgates to prevent the enemy from tampering with them. The maximum mission was to take and hold the entire area until relieved, thus securing the dam.

A basic trouble was the lack of intelligence on enemy strength in three areas: the high ground west of the Pukhan River, the neck of land west of the reservoir, and the high ground east of the dam. It was not clear at first, but later it became apparent that the enemy forces on these three points could not be divided. Initially it was thought that if the two areas on the right were secured, the entire area could be held. This, however, was not so.

Seizing the dam was discussed about one week before the operation. In the regiment, some thought was given at that time to the operation. It was believed that a raid-type mission could be carried out while the regiment maintained Phase Line Kansas. On 9 April the Ranger company was informed of the possibility of their making an amphibious landing. Major Webel, the regiment's S-3, and Major Cochrane, the regimental executive officer, started to try to get assault boats on the afternoon of 9 April. Had the boats been available, I would probably have sent the Rangers across amphibiously on 10 April.

General Palmer, the 1st Cavalry Division commander, felt that if more daylight had been available on 9 April, the 2d Battalion might have reached the dam on that day, and additional forces could have been put up there to secure the area. I do not agree.

Throughout the operation a major concern of mine was supply, and particularly my supply of mortar ammunition. I was reluctant to commit a full attack on the dam due to my shortage of ammunition. The 105mm howitzers were not able to render support because of range. The 155mm howitzer batteries were operating at extreme range. Support by 8-inch howitzers came in later on 11 April. If 105mm precision fire had been available, it would have been able to quiet the area west of the Pukhan River. No air support was possible because of weather.[19]

The Second Attempt, 10 April

Major Webel, the S-3 of the 7th Cavalry, describes the preliminary activity on 9 April and the decision on 10 April to continue the attack along the narrow neck of land leading to the dam.

On 9 April, in preparation for a possible amphibious move, twenty boats and all available boat motors were requested from the

1st Cavalry Division engineers. The possibility of an amphibious move against the high ground east of the dam was discussed with the commanding officer of the 4th Ranger Company. It was agreed that in view of the distance over the open water in the face of dominating enemy positions, apparently strongly held, it would be best to have a night operation, with friendly forces on the initial objective as dawn broke. The Ranger commander concurred.

Despite the effort to bring boats forward, including hand-carry over the French Pass, which was wide enough only for jeep traffic, the 2d Battalion's commanding officer preferred to advance by land. Attacking with his own rifle companies on 10 April, he held the Ranger company ready to pass through and seize the dam after the high ground was secure.[20]

Captain Anderson of the 4th Ranger Company describes the planning and decisions from his perspective.

On 10 April my company assembled on the road east of and below the battalion observation post, while I consulted with the battalion commander. The battalion commander had one plan of attack, the one attempted to be executed the day before. This plan I labeled "Plan B."

I proposed two alternative plans. One, which I called "Plan A," was to cross the Ranger company by boat to some point on the peninsula east of the dam, secure the high ground during the hours of darkness, then move north on the peninsula to a point directly east of the dam in conjunction with the 2d Battalion attack northward on the narrow neck of land to the west of the dam. The Ranger company would, after securing the high ground, destroy the enemy on the southwest corner of the peninsula, later called Objective 80.

"Plan AA" would have the Ranger company land at night on the southern end of the peninsula, move north under cover of darkness, lay charges on the dam in darkness employing secrecy, stealth, and silence, move off the dam to the high ground east of the dam, explode the charges, and retire from the peninsula by daybreak.

I was of the opinion that this latter plan was the most logical and most feasible plan to destroy the dam mechanism. However, at the time of the operation, the mission was not clear. Clarification came over a period of time. This prevented clear-cut planning from the outset. At first the company was to destroy the dam machinery. Next, it was to secure the dam site. The third mission was to destroy the dam mechanism if the company was not able to secure and hold the high ground east of the dam.

The company was broken down into groups for training in specialized combat jobs. The demolition charges were made. The company was preparing for action under any plan.[21]

Lieutenant Colonel Callaway of the 2d Battalion provides his reasons for continuing the attack, and the results.

Returning to the battalion CP at 0100 hours on 10 April I drew up plans for the attack on the following day. Because Company F had suffered only two casualties, and because the enemy had withdrawn in the past from critical terrain, I ordered the attack to be continued. The advance would be made in a column of companies because of the narrow terrain, with Company G leading and Company E in support. When Company G seized the high ground on Hill 454, the Rangers would move along the road on the right side of the neck of land, cross the dam, and destroy the dam machinery. No engineer troops had arrived; none were on hand. But the Ranger company had demolitions and was prepared, upon seizure of the dam, to blast the mechanism on the gates. Company F was to send a platoon to protect the dam while the Rangers prepared the charges.

I prepared this plan to comply with a message relayed to me by regiment from the G-3 of the 1st Cavalry Division. This message, received the afternoon of 9 April, read as follows: "Be prepared to be relieved tomorrow [10 April]. Reference Task Force Callaway: Go up there if possible, stay there, do not get cut up, but do not withdraw unless necessary. If you can close locks, do so. If not sure how to operate, and likely to damage, leave them alone. Destroy machinery, if necessary to pull out."

My plan of defense after the dam was secured was to have a platoon of Company G hold the dam, while the Rangers held the high ground to the east, and Company F held the road west and south of the dam.

The attack jumped off at 0730 hours on 10 April, with Company G to move one platoon down a ridge to a position about halfway between Line Kansas and the east–west road. From there the platoon would support the rest of the company as it moved along the road up toward the enemy positions. I had managed to get a section of two 4.2-inch mortars, a section of 81mm mortars, and some 155mm artillery in support. Weather made air support impossible. The machine-gun section of the Heavy Weapons Company moved with the base platoon of Company G.

The platoon of Company G, attempting to advance to the point from which it could render support, came under murderous small-arms and mortar fire and was completely pinned down. The platoon could not move into the trenches in that area to render support. Again, enemy mortar and flat trajectory fire was received. The observation post group also received quite a bit of mortar fire, as did the area along the road. Enemy mortars could be heard firing, and artillery was directed against these positions. Friendly artillery and 4.2-inch mortar fire was also placed in front of the battalion. This had no effect on the enemy. Any forward movement of Company G brought accurate small-arms and machine-gun fire on the friendly troops.

I then ordered a platoon of Company E to move down the ridge about 300 meters east of Company G to support the Company G maneuvering element. These platoons of Company G moved along the forward slope of the ridge, utilizing the terrain for cover. This movement was held up when the commanding officer of Company G directed friendly fire to be placed across the road so that the support platoon wounded could be gotten to safety. After firing for thirty minutes this was accomplished. But the platoons were then low on ammunition, and a resupply was needed before the attack could continue. Ammunition was sent forward by native carriers. About one hour and thirty minutes was necessary to accomplish this resupply.

Under the protective fires from a platoon of Company E and another from Company G, one platoon succeeded in advancing to a series of trenches about two hundred yards south of the east–west road. But there the force came under intense small-arms fire from pillboxes and trenches on the ridge north of the east–west road and was unable to advance frontally. This platoon also received considerable enemy mortar and artillery fire from behind the ridge and across the Pukhan River to the northwest. Friendly 155mm artillery fire was being placed on the neck of land, on the dam area, and along the area where enemy mortars were located, with little apparent effect.

Despite continual efforts to move forward, the company was unable to advance. At darkness, the lead platoon withdrew to reserve positions, and Company E was moved to high ground south of the road on the right, while Company F tied in on the left. Company G received three rounds of enemy mortar fire while withdrawing and suffered twelve wounded in action. Total casualties suffered in the battalion numbered six KIA and twenty-seven WIA. The majority of these casualties were from enemy mortar fire.[22]

While the 2d Battalion continued to fight through the daylight hours of 10 April, the situation at higher headquarters remained confused, as commanders and staff officers relate.

MAJOR GENERAL HOGE, COMMANDER OF THE IX CORPS: At 1100 hours on 10 April, when the commanding general of the 1st Cavalry Division informed me [during a visit to the division] that they had not been able to capture the dam, I ordered a bona fide attempt. In the meantime, enemy resistance was building up in the dam area. Halfhearted efforts to secure the dam stirred up the enemy. The element of surprise had been lost. I ordered the division to take the dam before relief of the division was effected.[23]

LIEUTENANT COLONEL CARLSON, G-3 OF THE 1ST CAVALRY DIVISION: Corps wanted something done. Therefore, the 7th Cavalry Regiment was to go up on 10 April and secure the dam while the Rangers destroyed the machinery. Task Force Callaway was organized on 10 April, but this force failed to get across the road at the southern part of the neck of land west of the reservoir. The order was then received for the 1st Cavalry Division to be relieved by the Marine Division. These orders were interpreted as meaning relief also from the mission against the dam. At this time other elements of the division were being relieved. Late on the afternoon of 10 April General Palmer, commanding general of the 1st Cavalry Division, received a call from General Hoge, instructing the division to continue to the dam. This was transmitted to the 7th Cavalry Regiment.[24]

MAJOR WEBEL, S-3, 7TH CAVALRY REGIMENT: The 2d Battalion attacked throughout the day but was unable to advance. No air support was possible due to the lack of suitable weather. Information was then received that the regiment would be replaced by elements of the 1st Marine Division, and preparations were made for relief. Operations for the day terminated at 1700 hours. At the same time, orders were received that the dam would be taken before relief was effected.

The near-relief of the regiment had an unfortunate effect on the operation. Calling the mission off, then putting it on again had the result of confusing the troops. If the mission was important, it seems to me that it should have been assigned a unit that was going to remain in the area long enough to complete the mission. However, since the operation was called off, I think that the operation was apparently not too important. The battalion commanders, not entirely certain whether the dam was to be seized or relief of the regiment was to be effected, were looking over their shoulders.[25]

Mounting the Third Attempt

Colonel Harris describes the changed situation late on the afternoon of 10 April and considerations in his plan for attack.

On the afternoon of 10 April the mission was clarified. I could employ anything in the regiment to accomplish the mission. I pulled all the stops to attempt to get supplies. I thought that the peninsula across the reservoir was not strongly held. I believed that an amphibious landing would be successful. I wanted to contain and pin down the enemy in the neck of land west of the reservoir and make the amphibious operation the main effort. Then the neck of land could be attacked from the north, or the Rangers could move quickly to the dam, destroy the machinery, and withdraw.

The 1st Battalion was to make a diversionary feint [against the high ground west of the Pukhan River]. I wanted to put one company across the river. If there was no resistance, the company could remain on the high ground. But I never believed that the company would be able to get across. At the same time, the 2d Battalion holding attack could become the major effort any time the enemy crumbled.[26]

Major Webel provides additional details about the planning and about the requested support for the renewed attack.

Based on the stubborn and strong resistance of the enemy encountered on the two previous days, it was determined to launch a major effort to seize the dam. Because of the heavy casualties suffered in the attempt to overrun the enemy pillboxes, it was decided that an amphibious flanking maneuver was essential to success. Plans were laid, and the following items were requested from the 1st Cavalry Division: artillery priority; air priority to include one strike per hour; night B-26 bomber missions to strike east and west of the dam; Air Force smoke aircraft to be on standby for utilization on request to screen wherever necessary; and portable smoke generators as well as chemical smoke pots. Because of the difficulty of transporting amphibious craft in the mountain pass, it was requested that B-17 air-sea rescue craft drop two of their power launches on the reservoir inlet for use on the operation. Also requested were 150 life preservers, a repeat of a request made twenty-four hours earlier when the possibility of an amphibious operation was discussed. Because amphibious jeeps were not available, six DUKWs were requested. Since the French Pass was open only to jeep traffic, and since airlift was not possible, these DUKWs were to follow an armored task force that was given the mission of opening a road through the 23d Infantry Regiment sector (2d Infantry Division of X Corps) and thence northwest to the dam. Helicopters were requested to evacuate the wounded.

Of the above requests, air and artillery priority was granted. Smoke aircraft were denied. Smoke generators were not available. No B-17 aircraft were available. Life preservers were located some distance from the division, and trucks were dispatched to pick them up. Helicopters were promised. Twenty additional assault boats and more motors were promised. It was possible to bring nine engineer assault boats and six motors forward. In so doing, two jeeps were put out of commission. Only two of the motors worked. Based on a load of twelve men to a boat, however, it was still possible to lift the majority of the Ranger company over on these craft.[27]

Captain Ellingsworth, S-4 of the 7th Cavalry Regiment, describes the efforts to obtain support for the amphibious operation.

At 1800 hours on 10 April it was learned that relief would not be effected until after the Hwach'on Dam was secured. At that time the regiment began requesting assault boats, ammunition, and other equipment and supplies. A number of life belts were located with the 19th Engineer Combat Battalion near Hongch'on, and Captain Barnes drove down to secure them. When it was learned that the French Pass was congested, Lieutenant Cavanaugh, the regimental ammunition officer, was sent to establish a regimental ammunition and POL point on the southern side of the pass and to regulate the flow of these supplies.

Supplies were coming through the pass in great number during the night of 10–11 April. Boats were transported at 0100 and 0400 hours. They were hand carried and pushed on trailers up to the crest of the pass, then loaded on jeeps. The assault boats and motors were secured by the 8th Engineer Combat Battalion from a variety of sources in the vicinity of Ch'unch'on. About fifteen boats were sent through the road in the 23d Infantry Regiment, 2d Infantry Division, sector. The I&R Platoon of the 23d Infantry Regiment rendered security. One platoon from Company A, 2d Engineer Combat Battalion, filled craters in the road. On the night of 11 April, there were about thirty assault boats in the regimental area.

DUKWs were requested as reserve boats in case the engineer assault boats were sunk by the enemy while friendly forces were still across the reservoir. At that time DUKWs were being used by the 5th Marine Regiment. Two DUKWs were secured and sent from the pass to the reservoir at 0600; two more were sent at 0800, and two additional ones were sent later in the day.

Communications were so bad between forward and rear elements that the regimental support group was handicapped in anticipating needs and providing necessary logistical assistance. When the plan of amphibious assault was conceived, requests for the various items necessary for the operation came so rapidly that the support section found itself deluged. Had I been physically present during the planning of the operation, I could have coordinated the support much better. I had no idea how many troops were to cross the water, how long they would remain, the number of weapons and boats that were needed, how many boats leaked, how many motors worked, how much gas and oil would be necessary, and so on.[28]

Captain Barnes, the assistant S-4 of the 7th Cavalry Regiment, provides additional details.

On 9 April the regiment requested assault boats, outboard motors, and paddles. On the night of 10 April the regiment procured, through the division engineers, 20 boats, 10 motors, 180 paddles, and 20 air mattresses in lieu of life preservers. This equipment was sent through the pass on the first priority. From the southern side of the pass, the equipment had to be hand carried by Korean laborers across the mountain, then partially hand carried and partially jeep carried to the reservoir area.

At 0100 hours on 11 April, 160 life preservers were procured from the corps engineers. On 10 April about 400 smoke pots were requested through division. These were to arrive by air at 0900 hours on 11 April at Hoengsong, and a truck was dispatched to that location to secure them. The smoke pots did not arrive because bad weather canceled the flight. In the early morning hours of 11 April, an ASP [Ammunition Supply Point] and a POL supply point were established at the pass. DUKWs were requested from the division G-4, who began trying to secure them. Twenty additional boats and ten more motors were requested, but only fifteen boats and sixty-five paddles arrived from the division engineer. At noon on 11 April, word was received that six DUKWs had been made available by the 558th Amphibious Truck Company, which was working with the Marines. At 1330 hours on 11 April, fifteen assault boats and sixty-five paddles reached the southern side of the French Pass. All the battalion trains were instructed to send all their jeeps to the pass to transport this equipment to the companies. At 1700 hours the regiment received two DUKWs, and two more were on the way with ammunition loads. At 2030 hours on 11 April, word came that fifteen additional assault boats were available at an engineer battalion in the rear.

Ammunition resupply was a difficult problem. Supply personnel were continually trying to get 4.2-inch and 81mm mortar and 75mm rifle ammunition from the Army ASP to the troops. When the regimental S-3 requested demolitions, one demolition equipment set was received. Supply personnel continued to try and secure more TNT. At 1500 hours on 11 April, ammunition priority was received in this order: 4.2-inch mortar, 81mm mortar, .30-caliber machine gun, .30-caliber M-1 rifle, 60mm mortar, 75mm rifle, and 57mm rifle. The regimental S-3 requested an ammunition airdrop for the following day, and the division G-4 completed airdrop arrangements. At 1540 hours on 11 April an ASP opened at Ch'unch'on. Before this, ammunition had been secured from the IX Corps ASP at Hongch'on. Later we were permitted to secure ammunition from the Marines.

At 2000 hours on 11 April the road was opened through the 2d Infantry Division sector. Trucks could then transport supplies to the battalions. From the rear regimental CP, near the airstrip north of Ch'unch'on, to the reservoir area by way of this route was a distance of forty-two miles. At this time 4 DUKWs, two loaded with 4.2-inch ammunition and four outboard motors, and four 2½-ton trucks loaded with ammunition commenced the trip to the regimental area.[29]

Logistics officers at division and corps provide their perspectives on the supply effort in support of the 7th Cavalry.

MAJ. DAYTON F. CAPLE, ASSISTANT G-4, 1ST CAVALRY DIVISION: On 9 April the 1st Cavalry Division was preparing to move to army reserve. On 10 April the 5th Cavalry Regiment moved to the army reserve area, and trucks were committed to move personnel and equipment. On 10 and 11 April, the 8th Engineer Combat Battalion moved to the reserve area. Trucks utilized in these moves came from the three regiments, the field artillery battalion, the tank battalion, and the engineer battalion. Thus, most of the division trucks were tied up and were not readily available to support the Hwach'on Dam operation.

About 1300 hours on 10 April, arrangements were started to secure life preservers for use on a possible amphibious assault against the Hwach'on Dam. A representative was to fly to IX Corps with a requisition to get life preservers from the corps engineer dump near Yoju, about ninety air miles south of Ch'unch'on. This request, however, was canceled by the 7th Cavalry Regiment. Then at 1815 hours on 10 April the call came that life preservers would be needed. From the corps dump, 150 life preservers were hauled by truck to a point six miles north of Hongch'on by the corps engineers. The 7th Cavalry Regiment sent a truck to meet this shipment. After a run of several miles, the preservers had to be unloaded from the regimental truck to a jeep for further transport. By the time the life preservers arrived at the regimental area, it was too late for the Rangers to use them. They were, however, used by another company to reinforce the Rangers.

At 0035 hours on 11 April the first request for smoke came to the division. An amount of smoke was needed sufficient to cover 5,000 square meters for one hour. The estimated number needed was 625 small-type smoke pots, or 225 medium-size, or 187 large ones. There was no smoke available at any forward ASP. Twenty-five smoke pots were located at the ASP at Wonju. No smoke generators were in the immediate area. Captain Smith, the IX Corps assistant G-4, was contacted on this request. He investigated and found some smoke pots at Suwon, sixteen hours by road from the Hwach'on Dam area. At 0500 hours on 11 April arrangements were made for smoke to be air lifted to Hoengsong, to arrive at 0800 hours on 11 April. But all airfields in Japan and Korea were fogged in on 11 April, and no flights were possible. There were not enough artillery smoke shells to accomplish the mission.

A platoon of DUKWs had been acquired a week before to help the 1st Cavalry Division and the 1st Marine Division to cross the Soyang River north of Ch'unch'on. Six DUKWs were given to the 2d Infantry Division, and the 1st Cavalry Division retained control over six. On 10 April the 1st Cavalry Division gave its remaining six

DUKWs to the 1st Marine Division. On the morning of 11 April, through IX Corps, six DUKWs were gotten back. These were delivered to the 7th Cavalry Regiment on the evening of 11 April.

Rations had been hand carried by the 6th and 15th Civilian Transportation Companies (Korean) attached to the 7th Cavalry Regiment. About 400 Koreans transported ammunition, supplies, rations, and boats over the pass south of the dam area.

Ten outboard motors organic to engineer units were sent to the 7th Cavalry Regiment. Additional motors were gathered by the IX Corps engineers. By 2000 hours on 11 April, fifty-six boats had been furnished (thirty-five were at the site of the operation and twenty-one were at Ch'unch'on), and arrangements for fifty more had been made.

The 1st Marine Division ASP at Ch'unch'on furnished ammunition to the 7th Cavalry Regiment, and unused supplies were returned. In preparation for the possible continuation of the Hwach'on operation, preparations were made for an airdrop of ammunition on 12 April. At 1500 hours on 11 April, at the rate that 155mm howitzers were firing, only ten more hours of ammunition remained. Ammunition was then trucked up from Wonju.

About 1800 on 11 April, sufficient boats, rations, gas, oil, and ammunition were delivered over the road opened through the 23d Infantry Regiment's area that the operation could have continued for an additional day. Supply buildup continued during 11 April, so that when the operation was called off, supply was beginning to be adequate.[30]

MAJ. RUSSELL J. WILSON AND 1ST LT. C. K. GEORGEFF, 8TH ENGINEER COMBAT BATTALION, 1ST CAVALRY DIVISION: In anticipation of amphibious operations across the Pukhan and Soyang Rivers, the battalion had secured forty assault boats from the corps engineers. The battalion had also requisitioned and initially obtained at Ch'unch'on three infantry-support rafts (five double pontoons or ten boats), and one outboard motor per raft. This equipment was on hand for a week before the Hwach'on Dam operation. The equipment had been secured for use on the rivers because the battalion was not alerted to the Hwach'on Dam operation and had no idea of such action.

When the Hwach'on Dam operation assumed full-scale propor-
tions on the evening of 10 April, 50 percent of the assault boats and
three motors were already en route from Ch'unch'on to the army
reserve area. Equipment had been turned over to the Marines as relief was being effected. Battalion personnel were moving to the new
area. Fortunately, however, the battalion had radio communications
with the 7th Cavalry Regiment, and return of the assault boats could
be ordered. Ten boats could not be made available for the Hwach'on
operation because these craft were on the north side of the [Pukhan]
river, and the bridge was out. Ten boats and seven outboard motors
were sent from Ch'unch'on to the regiment on 10 April. On that day
a battalion convoy was intercepted, and three outboard motors were
taken off for shipment to the regiment. A radio message to the command post in the process of setting up in the new area ordered
twenty assault boats to be sent to the regiment.

On the morning of 11 April the 1st Marine Division was contacted. One motor and the promise of fifty boats were secured.
Corps engineers obtained commitment of fourteen additional boats.
Eleven outboard motors were delivered on 11 April, making a total
of twenty motors and thirty-five assault boats delivered to the
Hwach'on Reservoir. Mechanics trained to use engineer equipment
arrived in the operational area on the morning of 12 April, after the
operation had been canceled.

The trail over which supplies were carried was rocky, with large
boulders obstructing passage. Initially the regiment wanted the road
opened for jeeps. The first jeep traveled over the route on the evening
of 9 April. On 10 April the road was widened for artillery passage,
but the artillery did not reach this point. The road was eventually
opened for ¾-ton truck traffic. The amount of traffic on the road
and the weather made the road dangerous. The route was extremely
narrow, steep, and hazardous. It was little more than a trail. Yet this
was the only terrain where even a remote possibility existed for putting in a road. Lieutenant Georgeff was committed to the French
Pass to assist in every way possible the improvement of the route. He
had Company B of the 8th Engineer Battalion, two D-7s, and one
D-6 (dozers) to knock the road through. The road was so steep that
a vehicle could hardly get traction. Jeeps negotiated it with diffi-

culty. The majority of supplies for the 7th Cavalry Regiment came over this route. It was the only link between Ch'unch'on and the Hwach'on Reservoir area for the 1st Cavalry Division.[31]

Lt. Col. Thomas M. Magness Jr., IX Corps chemical officer: I learned for the first time at 1615 hours on 11 April that smoke pots were requested for the operation scheduled that morning. Incorrect channels were utilized by the 1st Cavalry Division and the IX Corps G-4 personnel to obtain chemical munitions. The G-4 of the 1st Cavalry contacted the G-4 of IX Corps, who contacted ordnance for the air delivery of smoke pots from Pusan. This was done in spite of the fact that there were advance chemical depot locations at Suwon and Chech'on, from which IX Corps units could draw chemical munitions not available at ASPs. Although sufficient smoke for the Hwach'on Dam operation was on hand at both Suwon and Chech'on, smoke pots were airlifted from Pusan to Hoengsong, only thirty-five miles forward from Chech'on. I surmise that this smoke was flown in C-54 planes, since these supplies were landed at Hoengsong, where a C-54 strip existed. Had the supplies been loaded in several C-47 planes, they could have been delivered at Hongch'on, nearer their ultimate destination. The smoke arrived two days late. However, even if advance planning had made smoke available at a forward area in time for use at the Hwach'on Reservoir, it would not have been possible to carry all the smoke pots to the reservoir area with the troops assigned the mission at the dam because of the logistical difficulties over that terrain.[32]

Despite the logistic shortfalls and other problems, the Rangers prepared to attack.

Chapter 12

HWACH'ON DAM—THE AMPHIBIOUS ASSAULT

1st Cavalry Division, 10–12 April 1951

While supply officers and engineers worked to obtain support, detailed planning and preparations for the amphibious operation proceeded. Captain Anderson explains the activity of the 4th Ranger Company.

That night [10–11 April] the Ranger company occupied a position on the battalion perimeter. I was called to the battalion and then summoned to a meeting of the regimental staff and the battalion commanders, which took place some time after 2200 hours on 10 April. I was told at that time that the 4th Ranger Company would cross the reservoir amphibiously, establish a beachhead, and move to the high ground on the peninsula, all under the cover of darkness. At daylight, a platoon would be sent to Objective 80 [in the southwest corner of the peninsula; see map on page 320] to destroy the enemy in that area. As the 2d Battalion moved north up the narrow neck of land, the Ranger company was to secure the high ground east of the dam, move to the dam, and prepare charges if we were unable to hold the site. A platoon from the 2d Battalion would actually secure the dam site itself, and the battalion would also send additional help if needed. This was the plan issued by the regimental S-3. I was told there would be ten boats with five motors. I later found nine boats and four motors.

The company had no knowledge of which plan would be issued, and the platoon leaders awaited my return for information. Upon my return to the company I informed the executive officer that "Plan AA" was in effect up to a certain point, and I instructed the executive officer to move the company from the perimeter to the embarking point. The company moved carefully off the steep hill it occupied.

The 3d Platoon was divided as follows: the 1st Squad, the initial landing element, was to be the "killer" squad, armed with knives, hand axes, grenades, pistols, and carbines. Its mission was to eliminate the enemy on the landing site as quickly and as quietly as possible. This group was led by Lieutenant Healy. The 1st Assault Team of another squad was to carry and place the demolitions. The other assault team of the same squad was to act as close support for the "killer" squad. The remaining squad of that platoon was to provide support for the "killer" squad and the demolition group. It was armed with BARs, sniper rifles, and machine guns. This group also had Ranger-type rifle grenades, which were 60mm shells wired to a grenade adapter and launched from a grenade launcher on the end of an M-1 rifle.

The 2d Platoon, to follow the 3d, was to be accompanied by the company headquarters and the attachments—the artillery forward observer party, the heavy mortar NCO and radio operator, the 81mm mortar NCO and radio operator from Company M of the 7th Cavalry, and the twenty-one-man machine-gun section from Company M.

Because of the shortage of assault boats, the 1st Platoon was to be carried over on the second lift. Lieutenant Warren, the executive officer, would come with the last portion in order to organize the embarking and landing sites, the resupply of ammunition, and the evacuation of the wounded. No attempt would be made to use the motors on the boats until the enemy discovered the presence of the landing force.

The following elements would be in support: a 75mm rifle section and a heavy-machine-gun section, attached to the Ranger company from Company M of the 7th Cavalry; one 81mm mortar platoon from the Greek Expeditionary Force Battalion; three 155mm howitzer batteries from the 1st Cavalry Division Artillery; and two 8-inch howitzer batteries from the 1st Marine Division.[1]

First Lieutenant Warren, executive officer of the 4th Ranger

Company, provides additional information about the previous planning for the operation and the final preparations.

At 0800 hours on 10 April, the 4th Ranger Company moved along the road toward the battalion observation post. The company commander went ahead to join the battalion commander. The company remained deployed along the road until 1200 hours, when the company commander contacted me and instructed me to move the company back to the battalion CP area to prepare for an amphibious operation that night. That afternoon the unit engaged in orientation and preparation for one of three feasible plans. These plans were lettered for convenience.

Plan "A" consisted of a night amphibious move to the peninsula east of the dam, to secure the beachhead under cover of darkness and to launch an attack at dawn or 0630 simultaneously with a coordinated attack by the 2d Battalion of the 7th Cavalry Regiment. The objective of the 4th Ranger Company was the high ground east of the dam, and the objective of the battalion was the high ground west of the dam.

Plan "AA" consisted of an amphibious move under cover of darkness to the peninsula to secure the high ground east of the dam without the coordinated assistance of the 2d Battalion. The 2d Battalion would attack at 0900 hours and would link up with the 4th Ranger Company on the high ground east of the dam.

Plan "B" would have Company E secure Hill 364 on the high ground west of the dam, Company F pass through Company E and secure Hill 459, and the 4th Ranger Company pass through both companies across the dam to secure the high ground to the east on the peninsula with the mission of closing the flood gates.

I was told that ten enemy soldiers had been noted on and around the dam. This was the only available information on enemy strength in that vicinity.

At 1630 hours on 10 April all three plans were canceled. At about 1700, the 4th Ranger Company moved from the battalion CP to the battalion OP [on the eastern end of the ridge along Phase Line Kansas, lying south of and overlooking the east–west road along the neck of land west of the reservoir] to tie in on the battalion perimeter defense, replacing Company G, which had shortly before received heavy enemy mortar fire. The 4th Ranger Company remained in defensive positions until 2400 hours. The company commander, at that time in conference with the battalion commander, then telephoned me to order the company to form and move to the battalion CP. Plan "AA" was to be put into operation.

The company closed into the battalion CP area by 0245 hours. Additional ammunition was issued at 0300 hours. The unit was then broken down among the assault boats. There were ten 10-man boats, one of which had a hole in the bottom and was therefore useless. Several outboard motors were attached. Manning crews, made up of line troops of the 7th Cavalry Regiment, rather than engineer troops, were inexperienced, and the departure was delayed.

The first element of the amphibious assault was to paddle across the reservoir for silence and surprise. The second element was to be motored over for speed. The motors were counted on. Yet the motors that worked were not powerful enough to transport the boats rapidly.[2]

The Amphibious Attack

1st Lt. Michael D. Healy led the initial assault element or "killer" squad across the reservoir onto the peninsula. He describes the action.

The company was in the battalion perimeter waiting for Captain Anderson to return with instructions on the expected operation against the Hwach'on Dam. Lieutenant Warren returned to the company and informed the officers that Plan "AA" was in effect. The company then stripped down to the bare essentials, left its equipment in bundles, and moved down the steep hill to the road. There Captain Anderson called the platoon leaders forward to the embarking point for a briefing.

I was informed that I would lead the "killer" squad and secure the landing on the other side of the reservoir. The number of enemy forces on the peninsula was unknown, but there would be no turning back once the company was on the water. Sergeant Garrett (the squad leader), a medical aid man, and ten men from the 1st Squad of the 3d Platoon departed with me at 0345 hours on 11 April. We paddled across using the compass for direction. At 0430 we landed on a rocky bank. I got out, pulled the boat up on shore, and the men debarked. I gave the medical aid man a flashlight with blackout cover to guide the following boats in. Then four men and I moved across the rice paddy adjacent to the landing site and searched out the landing area, while the remainder of the men fanned out. When I had gone about a hundred yards inland, Sergeant Sullivan reported that the remainder of the platoon was ashore. I ordered the squads to move up on the high ground on both flanks, and then put a machine gun on the right front flank on the high ground.

Assembling the "killer" squad, I moved inland. Shortly thereafter, Captain Anderson, who had moved over the ridge from the east side while I was proceeding up the west side, made contact with me.[3]

Captain Anderson describes the crossing and the initial contact with the enemy.

At 0345 hours on 11 April the initial elements of the company embarked. Lieutenant Healy arrived fifteen minutes before anyone else and secured the landing area with his "killer" squad. I arrived on the peninsula with the 2d Platoon and the attachments, and immediately started for the high ground. The 3d Platoon was joined about halfway toward Objective 79, a hill overlooking the reservoir about 500 yards north of the beach.

The first enemy troops were seen when the two platoons of the company were 125 yards from the crest of Objective 79. These enemy soldiers stood on the top of the hill, waving and shouting. The lead scouts, moving up, waved back and continued moving. An additional fifty yards were covered before the enemy group of six or eight soldiers gathered on the crest of the hill discovered the identity of the group. It was beginning to get light when the enemy opened fire from a range of about seventy-five yards.

No cover, trees, or ditches existed on the hill. The first burst of fire from an enemy light machine gun hit one man three times in the leg and killed the radio operator of the 81mm mortars. The platoons put fire on the enemy and continued moving by creeping and crawl-

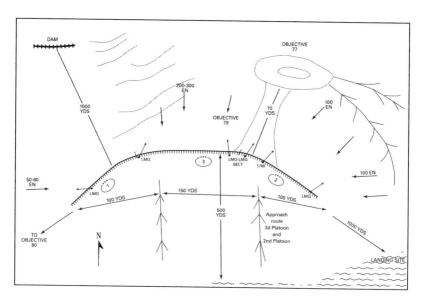

4th Ranger Company, 11 April 1951 (sketch based on Capt. Anderson interview in CMH manuscript, U.S. Army; not to scale).

ing in an attempt to reach grenade range. At that time an enemy machine gun opened up on the right front. The platoons continued to move up the left side of the ridge until an enemy machine gun from the left front and enemy snipers from the left flank pinned them down. The 3d Platoon's 57mm rifle knocked out the right machine gun after three or four rounds, and then shifted to the left, but it was not successful in searching out the gun position there.

In the meantime, Lieutenant Healy and the two lead scouts continued to the crest of the slope to the machine-gun position. Lieutenant Healy raised his head several times to draw fire to locate the gun position. Going to the right of the gun position, the group assaulted with grenades and small arms, knocking out the gun and killing the enemy. The remainder of the enemy group retreated, and the two platoons and the attachments moved up, secured the high ground, and consolidated on Objective 79 about 0615 hours.[4]

Other members of the 4th Ranger Company provide additional details of the crossing and the action to secure Objective 79.

Lieutenant Healy, 3d Platoon leader: When the enemy

troops discovered the identity of the group approaching Objective 79, they opened fire at a range of 200 yards from the top of the hill and from the right and left flanks. Corporal Krisco and I crawled up the hill under enemy fire. At an exposed place on the ridgeline we used our bodies as shields against enemy machine-gun fire so that those following could come through. Takach, Carbonel, Styles, and Macomber came through Krisco and me. Then all six of us worked our way up the hill to a position where a machine-gun nest could be grenaded. This nest was knocked out. Sergeants Robinson and Sullivan then led the machine-gun team to the hill and opened fire against the enemy machine guns. I continued to move to higher ground across the saddle, firing until the enemy forces on Objective 79 fled.[5]

1st Lt. Joseph W. Waterbury, 2d Platoon leader: As soon as the 3d Platoon was fifty yards out on the water, the 2d Platoon embarked in four boats, using one boat for each squad and the five-man 57mm rifle team. While on the water, the boats became separated, and the 2d Platoon landed at two separate sites after paddling across. I sent my 1st Squad to the high ground to secure the beach. The 3d Squad, 2d Squad, machine-gun team from the 1st Squad, and 57mm team, in that order, followed the 3d Platoon up the hill. The mortar crews of the 1st Squad remained on the beach.

When the 3d Platoon was halted by enemy fire, the 2d Platoon was unable to fire because the 3d Platoon was in its line of fire. I contacted the mortars and instructed them to shell the enemy hill. The 155mm artillery began firing at the same time. After the 3d Platoon reached the high ground and took the left portion of it, the 2d Platoon moved up and consolidated the right portion.[6]

M. Sgt. Eugene Lester, platoon sergeant of the 2d Platoon: The 2d Squad and I got into boats about 0400 hours and paddled across the reservoir. It was still dark, and the water was so foggy that my squad lost contact with the platoon. Although a 28-degree azimuth was plotted for the voyage across the reservoir, it was difficult to use the compass. I guided my boat by the hills on the ridgeline on the right flank. We observed silence going across the reservoir, and moved into a cove between two little finger ridges running down to the water. I noticed an enemy trench on the right finger and knew I was in the correct landing site according to the briefing I had received. Daylight began to arrive.

Eight men and I moved off the boat and searched out an adjacent hill, then spread out on the high ground. I physically contacted Captain Anderson and then physically contacted the remainder of the platoon and assembled the men. The 60mm mortar was set up near the landing site.

The 3d Platoon moved up the ridge with the 2d Platoon behind. I heard the enemy on top of the hill shout at the company, and the element of surprise continued until the men were about halfway up the hill. After the 3d Platoon had taken the hill, the 2d Platoon moved up and occupied its position about 0800 hours. The hill was set up for defense about 0830. The 57mm rifle joined and was placed into position on the right. At this time the 2d Platoon was receiving some enemy fire.[7]

SFC George E. Schroeder, communications sergeant, company headquarters: I boarded the sixth boat in the second wave. It contained the 155mm artillery forward observer, the 81mm and 4.2-inch mortar observers, the company medical aid man, the company runner, Captain Anderson, and myself. Everyone helped paddle the boat across the reservoir. When the boat reached the landing beach at daybreak, I led the forward observers 200 yards from the water and dispersed them.

The 2d Squad of the 2d Platoon landed in a boat just behind, and this group cleared the finger ridge to the left. Captain Anderson, the runner, and the heavy mortar observer cleared a house on the right finger ridge. Then the entire group proceeded toward Objective 79. About eighty yards from the top, I saw someone at the crest of the hill shouting at us. I at first thought it was someone from the 2d Platoon, but small-arms, then automatic-weapons fire was received from the hill.

The 3d Platoon's "killer" squad came forward, took the point, and started working up the hill until pinned down by enemy machine-gun fire. When the 57mm rifle knocked out the enemy machine-gun nest, the lead elements moved up and took the hill. Then the company headquarters group and the 1st Squad of the 3d Platoon moved to the top of the hill after the 3d Platoon radioed that it was secure. I set out a panel for aircraft, and the company took up defensive positions.[8]

SFC ROY J. MONTGOMERY, MACHINE-GUN SECTION LEADER, AND SGT. JOE L. BARNES, 81MM FORWARD OBSERVER, BOTH COMPANY M, 7TH CAVALRY: We were attached to the 4th Ranger Company, and crossed the reservoir and arrived on the beach with Captain Anderson, the Ranger company commander. It took the Rangers five minutes to get organized and move out. We accompanied Captain Anderson, joined another Ranger group, and came under enemy fire. One Ranger was wounded. Barnes's radio operator was killed. Montgomery laid down covering fire with his machine guns, firing at the enemy muzzle blasts. Before he could fire 750 rounds (three boxes), the Rangers were on top of the hill. It was just getting light.[9]

SGT. WILLIAM V. GOOLSBY, MEDICAL TECHNICIAN, COMPANY HEADQUARTERS, 4TH RANGER COMPANY: Medical preparations for the amphibious operation were very hasty. There were five medical aid kits in the company. One medical aid man operated with each platoon, and I worked with company headquarters. An extra aid man worked with the 3d Platoon and acted as an ammunition bearer for the machine gun. For the Musan-ni jump, ninety-six parachutists' medical aid kits had been issued to the 4th Ranger Company, and some of the men still had these kits. Each kit contained one morphine syrette, a tourniquet, and a Carlisle dressing.

I picked up a litter from the 2d Battalion aid station near the embarkation point. I embarked in Captain Anderson's boat, and on the other side of the reservoir I carried the litter off the boat and started up the finger ridge. I heard Sergeant Williams call to me as I was taking cover from enemy fire. Williams had four machine-gun bullets in his leg. I bandaged his leg, and then, since Williams had been given a shot of morphine by someone in the platoon, I accompanied him to the landing site where I dressed the wound again.

Lieutenant Johnson and part of the 1st Platoon arrived in boats, and I directed them into the landing cove. I then placed Williams in a boat to be evacuated by the coxswain. I informed Lieutenant Johnson where the company was. When I returned, I found the company had taken the high ground and was in position. I had left my litter on the hill when I dressed Williams's wound, but someone had moved it, and I could not locate it. I proceeded to the company headquarters where I found everyone digging in. Enemy mortar, mostly white phosphorus, was being received. Two men had been burned by white phosphorous and were waiting for medical attention.[10]

After the 3d and 2d Platoons crossed the reservoir, the boats returned for the second lift. The crossing of these elements is described by members of the unit.

LIEUTENANT WARREN, EXECUTIVE OFFICER OF THE 4TH RANGER COMPANY: The first element, led by Lieutenant Healy, departed the embarkation point at 0345. It consisted of the 2d and 3d Platoons and the company headquarters, except for me. The 1st Platoon, minus one squad, departed at 0700 under the command of Lieutenant Johnson. Due to motor failure, due again to inexperienced operators, the move was not made until daylight. The remainder of the second element departed at 0830 hours in two boats, with two motors working. This consisted of me with one squad of the 1st Platoon, a carrying party of ten Koreans, and a resupply of ammunition.

My boats were nearing the peninsula, 300 yards from shore, when we were fired upon by enemy automatic weapons from the peninsula. The boats moved eastward and attempted a second landing. Enemy machine guns and mortar fire from the peninsula caused the boats to move eastward again to seek a third landing site. Enemy fire was received a third time from the peninsula. The boats then returned to the embarkation point.[11]

1ST LT. JAMES L. JOHNSON, 1ST PLATOON LEADER, 4TH RANGER COMPANY: On the morning of 11 April my platoon's 57mm rifle section was attached to the 2d Platoon and moved out with the first wave. Approximately two hours after the 3d and 2d Platoons had departed across the reservoir, two boats returned to the embarkation point. I placed the 3d Squad, the 2d Assault Team of the 2d Squad (machine-gun crew), and the 1st Assault Team of the 1st Squad in these boats. I had received word from the company commander by radio that an ammunition resupply was necessary. So, I loaded the center of the boats with 57mm rifle, mortar, machine-gun, and M-1 rifle ammunition. I instructed the platoon sergeant and the remaining assault team on the beach to take the next boat that came back.

My group paddled across the reservoir during the early morning light between 0600 and 0700. My boat had a motor on it, but the motor did not work. As the boats were moving toward shore, they were guided into the landing site by Sergeant Goolsby, the medical aid man, who was waiting there to evacuate Sergeant Williams, who was wounded.[12]

M. SGT. DONALD G. LAVERTY, 1ST PLATOON SERGEANT, 4TH RANGER COMPANY: The officer in charge of the assault boats at the embarkation point, Lieutenant O'Reilly, informed me that the reason the outboard motors would not work was because they had not been test-run. Orders were in effect that upon daylight or upon enemy detection of the amphibious force, whichever came first, the motors in the boats would be operated for speed. Before then, silence was observed.

When the company departed, the men paddled across. On the return of the boats, after the enemy had discovered the Ranger landing force, it was attempted to get the motors started. Failing in this, the manning personnel paddled back. Then the 2d Squad of the 1st Platoon tried to get the motors started. They succeeded with two.

Lieutenant Johnson ordered me to remain with the 1st Assault Team of the 2d Squad. The remainder of the platoon departed in a double assault boat, which was two boats bolted together. I was to cross the reservoir later in a boat in the charge of Lieutenant Warren. With Lieutenant Warren, my assault team, and ammunition in the first boat, I started across the reservoir. A second boat contained six Korean carriers with Lieutenant Kim, the company interpreter, in charge, and with ammunition.

Halfway across the water, the boats met a returning boat carrying Sergeant Williams, who had been wounded on the first enemy burst of fire. Sergeant Williams and the coxswain were paddling back. Williams advised the boats to land in the cove near a house. As the boats headed for this cove, the morning mist disappeared, and the enemy fired on us from the left. We turned our boats to the right to attempt another landing site. Again enemy automatic-weapons fire was received from the front. The boats attempted a landing farther to the right, and again we received enemy automatic-weapons and mortar fire. At this point, the motor on the second boat stopped running. Since we were unable to find a place to land, the first boat picked up the second boat and towed it back to the point of departure.[13]

1ST LT. HUGH O'REILLY, EXECUTIVE OFFICER OF COMPANY B, 7TH CAVALRY: During the evening of 10 April, regiment asked the 1st Battalion to furnish five outboard motor operators. Five men of Company B, four men of Company D, and I volunteered. We were sent to the 2d Battalion CP where I received instructions to proceed to the beach. I was to organize the assault boats.

Arriving at the beach at 0100 hours on 11 April, I met the Ranger company commander and found ten boats delivered. One craft had a hole in the bottom and was unserviceable. Six motors were delivered, but I was informed that only four were serviceable. I had no opportunity to test-run the motors because of the secrecy of the operation. The Rangers were powered across the reservoir by paddles. No motors were to be used until the enemy discovered the Rangers and fired. There was one motor in the first wave, no motors in the second, three motors in the third. I placed a coxswain in each boat so that someone would remain with the craft. When the firing started, only one motor worked. This boat towed back several craft through small-arms and mortar fire. This occurred about daylight, 0530. I was notified that two boats had been hit, were sinking, and had been left on the other side of the reservoir. At this time I had a total of seven boats and one motor that worked.

About 0600 hours, ten more boats and three motors began to be delivered. I put the remainder of the Rangers in boats to be towed by the one motor, but this group was unable to land across the reservoir because of heavy enemy fire. This group returned.

The three motors delivered in the early morning were packed in crates. One motor had a smashed carburetor. No tools were delivered with the motors. I borrowed a wrench from the medical jeep so I could cannibalize inoperative motors. There were no extra spark plugs. Captain Osteen, the regimental assistant S-3, attempted to secure an outboard-motor mechanic about 0600, without success.

Three engineer enlisted men who accompanied these motors stated that they knew only how to start and stop them. They did their best, however, to get the motors working. I had amphibious training in a previous operation. My knowledge of outboard motors came from my fishing and boating on a recreational basis.[14]

Meanwhile, with only part of his company across and with enemy opposition stiffening, Captain Anderson describes the situation and his decision.

I decided to secure Objective 80 to the southwest, rather than move to Objective 77, the high ground to the immediate front of Objective 79 and opposite the dam to the west. I felt that if the company moved inland it might be cut off entirely from the beach by the enemy. The 1st Platoon had not yet landed, and boats attempting to come ashore were drawing intense machine-gun and mortar fire. I felt I was in a better position on Objective 79 to assist the landing of the remainder of my company than I would have been on Objective 77. I was convinced that if I had moved inland, the landing party would never have come ashore, and those on the peninsula would never have gotten off.

While waiting for the 1st Platoon to come ashore, I sent a patrol to overlook Objective 80. The landing of the 1st Platoon was assisted by friendly fire, and that platoon joined the company on Objective 79. I immediately sent the 1st Platoon to Objective 80. It encountered intense small-arms and mortar fire from a point just short of the objective. The platoon leader halted his platoon, made a reconnaissance, and sent a squad to the right to outflank the enemy position. But when enemy fire was received from the front, right, and rear, the platoon returned to the left of the group on Objective 79.[15]

Lieutenant Johnson, the 1st Platoon leader, provides more details about the attack on Objective 80.

I received instructions to move down the finger ridge to Objective 80, clearing the enemy. With two squads I had proceeded approximately 300 yards when we received enemy mortar and automatic-weapons fire. I set up a base of fire with one squad to fire on the enemy on Objective 80 and on a small ridge beyond Objective 80. This fire drove ten to fifteen enemy troops into their foxholes. I then called for artillery fire and directed it against the ridge beyond Objective 80.[16]

While the Rangers moved against Objective 80, the 7th Cavalry Regiment was in the process of beginning to move reinforcements across the reservoir. Major Webel, the S-3 of the 7th Cavalry Regiment, describes the situation from his perspective.

The Rangers were late in embarking due to the fact that they had to be pulled from their night defensive positions and marched to the embarkation site. The company commander also needed a certain amount of time to brief his men. The advance party of the Rangers was under way about 0320 hours on 11 April, and the main body departed shortly thereafter at 0340. Life preservers had not yet arrived, and thirty air mattresses were brought from the rear as a stopgap measure. The air mattresses were placed in each boat in case the boat was sunk. Two motors were working; the others did not function. It was not planned to use motors initially, because of the use of stealth. But it was desirable to have motors in case the landing force was discovered by the enemy.

At 0420 hours the advance guard of the Rangers landed without opposition, gaining complete surprise. Around 0600, sporadic machine-gun and small-arms fire was heard from the vicinity of the Ranger company's objective. The Ranger company reported being engaged by two enemy machine guns. These were quickly overrun, and the Rangers occupied and organized Objective 79, which provided excellent observation of the dam site and an excellent avenue of approach to the dam. At dawn the enemy found the Ranger company in his midst. The Rangers in turn found themselves surrounded. The assault craft bringing more Rangers and ammunition were taken under fire by enemy machine guns as they approached the beach. To avoid effective enemy machine-gun fire, a longer route to the landing beach was necessary. Four boats were nevertheless disabled by this fire. In the meantime, twenty additional boats and ten motors arrived about 0630–0700 hours. Unfortunately, none of the motors worked, and the one motor previously working ceased functioning. This left the amphibious force with one operable engine and twenty-nine assault boats. Life jackets arrived and were placed in the boats.

The Ranger company had originally been ordered to seize Objective 77, which dominated the ground on the ridgeline. However, the Rangers had reached Objective 79, just south of and below Objective 77. There the Rangers met strong resistance at daybreak. When the company commander asked whether to continue his attack or consolidate, he was ordered to consolidate what he had. About 0700 hours the 3d Battalion was ordered to move Company I without delay to reinforce the Rangers.

Company I had been purposely staged near the boats at 0600 hours to be in position to reinforce. The 3d Battalion immediately began the shuttling process of getting one company across the reservoir. This was a tedious operation over a long distance, made under enemy observation and without motors.

The enemy acted violently against the Rangers and immediately moved large numbers of troops from the west to reinforce the defense of the dam. Accurate artillery and mortar fire was placed on Objective 77 and Objective 78 [about 500 meters to the north of Objective 77] and also on enemy troops crossing the dam. A Ranger patrol of platoon strength was ordered to sweep southwest down the ridge [to Objective 80] to clean out a machine-gun nest. It was heavily engaged by enemy mortars and machine guns. After seizing an initial objective, the platoon was unable to proceed farther.

The regimental commander decided about 1000 hours to reinforce his amphibious landing. This decision was made in spite of the fact that movement of troops was limited by lack of motors. Furthermore, crossing a large number of troops who would be paddling under direct enemy machine-gun fire appeared to be an extremely risky thing. In the end, however, it was necessary to move troops this way to continue reinforcement.[17]

Before Company I could arrive, the enemy struck. Their assault began on the left against the Rangers' 1st Platoon, as Lieutenant Johnson relates.

Enemy mortar fire continued to be intense. I consolidated my two squads in position and was preparing to send one squad to the right of Objective 80 after the artillery fire lifted, when approximately fifty to sixty enemy troops attacked from my right. The enemy came within grenade distance of my position before he was beaten off. Sergeants Wilcoxson and Angland and corporals Chatta and Brexel did most of the effective firing against the attacking enemy.[18]

The enemy counterattacks soon spread from Lieutenant Johnson's platoon to the rest of the 4th Ranger Company. Captain Anderson describes the action.

The 1st Platoon then received an enemy counterattack of fifty to sixty men, which was repelled. I sent two squads from the 3d Platoon to assist the 1st Platoon, leaving the 3d Platoon machine-gun section and the company headquarters in the 3d Platoon positions.

The attack on the 1st Platoon was apparently a diversionary attack to draw the Ranger company out of position, and it was successful; immediately after the attack was repelled by the 1st Platoon and elements of the 3d Platoon, the 2d and 3d Platoon positions (the latter occupied only by company headquarters—one officer and four men) were attacked by 200 to 300 Chinese, who made no effort to use covering fire or utilize the terrain. The only enemy formation used was a mass formation of screaming, bugle-blowing Chinese. The enemy approached so closely and in such numbers that pistols were used effectively. This attack would have overwhelmed the company had it not been for accurate and intense fire delivered by the defenders. The defenders utilized machine guns, rifles, carbines, and, when ammunition ran low, pistols. I credit the artillery with placing fire with great effect; Lieutenant Forney, the 1st Cavalry Division Artillery forward observer, did great work. The 4.2-mortar observer with the 2d Platoon also did excellent work. The 81mm mortar observer, whose radio operator was the first man killed in this action, was too nervous to be effective. The intense attack lasted between thirty and forty-five minutes of actual hot and close fighting.

In the meantime the platoon leader of the 2d Platoon, whose radio had been knocked out early in the day, sent word to me that he was withdrawing slowly, under cover of his own fire. This was taking place until a grenade burst wounded the platoon leader, knocked him out of action, and rendered him temporarily in a state of shock. At that point the platoon broke, reappearing next on the beach. Four men of the platoon remained and joined the company headquarters. The platoon nevertheless took its dead and wounded with it, destroyed its 57mm rifle in position, and brought its machine gun and all its weapons out. The light-machine-gun section of Company M left its weapons and ammunition intact and moved off in disorder.

When the enemy attack was beaten back, a half box of machine gun ammunition was left. No BAR ammunition was left. An average of two clips of M-1 rifle ammo, 30 rounds per carbine, and seven to fourteen rounds of pistol ammunition remained. There were no grenades.

I pulled the 3d Squad of the 3d Platoon over to cover the 2d Platoon's former position, but the enemy was able to render my position untenable by enfiladed fire. I then asked regiment for permission to withdraw in view of my lack of ammunition, but I was informed that I would be joined by Company I, which was making an amphibious landing on the beach.[19]

Other soldiers of the 4th Ranger Company provide additional details of the Chinese assault.

LIEUTENANT JOHNSON, 1ST PLATOON LEADER: I sent Sergeant MacPherson's squad back to take the high ground to the rear of the platoon so it would not be outflanked. Under constant enemy mortar fire, I moved the other squad back to consolidate with MacPherson so the company could hold its perimeter on the high ground [Objective 79].[20]

LIEUTENANT HEALY, 3D PLATOON LEADER: I was informed by Captain Anderson that the 1st Platoon under Lieutenant Johnson was being attacked; he ordered me to move toward Objective 80 to aid Lieutenant Johnson. I shifted my platoon to the left, and met Johnson's men on their way back.

At this point Captain Anderson told me that he was being hit on his right flank because the 2d Platoon had been forced to withdraw. I moved my 3d Squad below the ridgeline and helped stop the intense enemy attack. In this action the aggressiveness of the lead elements was the vital factor in keeping the company moving. The company would have been pinned down for the rest of the day had it not been for the lead scouts and me.[21]

SERGEANT FIRST CLASS SCHROEDER, COMMUNICATIONS SERGEANT, COMPANY HEADQUARTERS: The 1st Platoon then sent an assault squad toward Objective 80 to clear it, but received machine-gun fire that pinned down the elements. The assault squad returned and reported an enemy mortar well dug in on Objective 80. The platoon leader instructed me to have the forward observer fire on this target. The FO moved to the 1st Platoon position for better observation. I then went back to company headquarters, which was still receiving small-arms and automatic-weapons fire from the high ground to the front. I was again sent to the 1st Platoon, this time with the 81mm mortar observer, to help knock out the enemy mortar that was constantly coming in.

I returned to the company headquarters about 1300. At 1330 the 1st Platoon called to inform Captain Anderson that the enemy was attacking. Captain Anderson directed part of the 3d Platoon to move toward the 1st Platoon to assist. Then the 2d Platoon reported heavy enemy fire. The company aid man went up on the ridgeline to observe and reported the enemy in attack. I moved up to the ridgeline and began firing at a range of eighty to ninety yards. The eight persons in the company headquarters position fired without stop for fifteen minutes. Then the 3d Platoon sent a squad over to assist the company headquarters group to repel the attack. At this time the 2d Platoon started moving back, bypassing the company headquarters group. A 2d Platoon BAR man came to notify the company headquarters that the 2d Platoon was falling back. About one squad of the 2d Platoon came over on the company headquarters position to help us. The company runner was sent to the beach to get the light-machine-gun section of Company M, which had been working with the 2d Platoon, to come back on the hill. One machine-gun crew came back with a tripod and ammunition, but no gun. At that point the enemy fell back.

The company was very low on ammunition, and Captain Anderson asked permission to withdraw. He was instructed to hold.

Captain Anderson then requested ammunition. He instructed his men to fix bayonets. We attached knives to our weapons.

In my opinion the company was saved by the 155mm artillery forward observer, who returned during the enemy attack from the 1st Platoon area and put fire on the attacking enemy. Shells dropped within seventy-five yards in front of the company. Then the artillery fire moved up in the hills toward the dam against enemy reinforcements who were observed moving toward the Ranger position. When the enemy fell back, the men on the ridge sniped at the retreating troops.[22]

SERGEANT BARNES, 81MM MORTAR FORWARD OBSERVER, COMPANY M, 7TH CAVALRY: When the Ranger 1st Platoon came up on the hill and swung to the left, I accompanied the platoon. My mortar fire, however, was a complete failure. The Greek Expeditionary Forces battalion was firing these mortars according to my direction. Sergeant Wilburn, on the M-10 plotting board at the fire direction center, computed for the GEF. But the mortars were way off target, and I could not get accurate fire.[23]

SFC MONTGOMERY, MACHINE-GUN SECTION LEADER, COMPANY M, 7TH CAVALRY: The 3d Platoon was in the center, the 2d Platoon on the right. I set up one gun in the center of the 2d Platoon sector, the other gun on the left flank of the 2d Platoon. The guns were picking off enemy snipers at a distance of 300 yards, when enemy soldiers jumped up ten yards in front of the company. An intense firefight took place, with the men firing .45 pistols, carbines, and any other available weapon. The 2d Platoon was forced to give way under the enemy attack. Artillery support was very close and marvelous.[24]

LIEUTENANT WATERBURY, 2D PLATOON LEADER: The 2d Platoon stayed in position until about 1430 under sporadic mortar, machine-gun, and sniper fire. The platoon killed fifteen enemy troops in a draw with BAR, small-arms, and mortar fire. The enemy seemed to be moving toward the beach, so the platoon fired at them at a range of 150 to 200 yards, and the 4.2-inch mortar forward observer called in very effective fire.

At about 1345 the platoon was running low on ammunition. Waiting for Company I to tie in on the right flank, I sent a five-man squad to the beach to secure it for Company I. When Company I arrived, it tied in on the right of the five-man squad, thinking this group was on the 2d Platoon position. About 1400 the enemy attacked in great strength. Someone in the 3d Squad on the high ground noticed that many enemy troops had infiltrated across the low ground to within twenty-five yards of the 2d Platoon position.

When the attack began, the 2d Platoon stood up on the ridgeline, in full view of the enemy, in order to fire effectively. The men were running out of ammunition. Approximately 200 enemy troops were rushing toward the platoon. At that time, three men and I were hit by a hand grenade. I was physically knocked down the hill. When I came to, I saw members of my platoon and of the Company M attachments running down the hill toward the beach.

My platoon sergeant tried to organize an orderly withdrawal. He could not communicate with Captain Anderson because early that morning my radio had gone out. The radio set received, but would not transmit. Part of my platoon moved over to Captain Anderson's position. The rest withdrew. The wounded and I withdrew to the assault team on the beach. Sergeant Lester organized that assault team and started back up the hill.[25]

MASTER SERGEANT LESTER, 2D PLATOON SERGEANT: With only four rounds of 57mm rifle ammunition left and the entire platoon low on ammunition, the platoon was conserving its ammunition. The enemy had withdrawn to Objective 77. When some enemy troops moved southeast from Objective 77, I put my machine gun on that movement and called for artillery on that point. I also directed the mortars to shell up and down the draw to the right front of the platoon.

About 1400 the enemy attacked the 2d Platoon, moving down in mass force from the right front. I noticed a tremendous number of enemy troops in front of the 3d Platoon sector. The enemy approached within grenade distance, and the 2d Platoon threw a great many grenades. At the time, two men were bringing up ammunition, and the right flank was consequently thin. In order to fire against the enemy it was necessary to stand on the skyline. Those who were wounded were dragged back into the draw for cover. The right flank had to be pulled back, and the 3d Squad was doing so, taking seven or eight wounded with them. Lieutenant Waterbury then led the wounded to the boats.

I met an ammunition-carrying party coming from the landing site. I organized this group and moved back up the hill with them. Before doing so, I contacted a platoon of Company I, which had just come over, and instructed them to pick up ammunition and come up the hill. I also directed two men from the assault team on the beach to aid the wounded. I then moved back up on the company position.[26]

SERGEANT GOOLSBY, MEDICAL TECHNICIAN, COMPANY HEADQUARTERS: When the 1st Platoon was attacked, no casualties were suffered. When the right flank (2d Platoon) began receiving an enemy attack, I was sent to the ridgeline to observe enemy activity. I reported that the enemy was preparing to attack the company headquarters position. The 2d Platoon started to pull back, and about four men came to the company headquarters to notify Captain Anderson that the enemy had overrun the 2d Platoon position. The artillery was then called in to aid in repelling the attack.

When Corporal Angarano was hit in the arm, he was pulled down into cover. I treated him for shock and tried to inject albumen, but Angarano's veins had collapsed, and he died from loss of blood. The 3d Platoon's medical aid man worked on Corporal Ligon, who was wounded in the lower stomach. They tried to give him albumen with little success, for the hill was very steep, and it was difficult to work. Ligon was treated for shock, and he seemed to be in fair condition. There was no way of evacuating him from the hill, for everyone had to be used to repel the enemy attack. PFC Young was in an exposed position with a BAR; he was hit in the head and died instantly.[27]

Company I Reinforces the Rangers

The movement of Company I across the reservoir was a slow process. The commander of the 3d Battalion, Lt. Col. Charles M. Hallden, describes the preparations and the crossing operation.

At 2100 hours on 10 April, I received the order at the regimental S-3 tent to move one reinforced company to the boat landing area.

This company was to be prepared to reinforce the Ranger company, which was to take Objective 77. I selected Company I, commanded by Captain Kennedy, by reason of rotation of companies for attack. Company I was ordered to move out at 0400 hours on 11 April to the boat landing area so that the company would be ready to embark at 0600. Captain Teague, the battalion S-2, was selected to pick up all boat operators and make certain the assault boats were in their proper places when reinforcement was necessary. The boat operators were men of the 7th Cavalry Regiment who stated they had had motorboat experience and volunteered for the job. The engineers did not supply boat operators. They furnished only the assault boats and ten motors for use on the boats. Approximately fifteen to twenty boats were in the area between 0400 and 0600 hours. When Company I arrived at the embarkation point, Captain Teague had fifteen boats and five motors in operational condition. The company waited for the order to embark and proceed to the Ranger area. As the men waited for the order to proceed, they were broken down into boat teams, ten men to a boat, and instructed on the proper method of getting in and out of the boat and in the use of the paddle and the life preservers.

At approximately 1000 hours I received the order to send Company I over. The remainder of the 3d Battalion was to be prepared to follow Company I, with me assuming control of the Rangers when I arrived on the peninsula across the reservoir. Only two motors operated at this time. Fifteen boats were on hand. Company I departed at 1045, after waiting for some time for more motors to get into operation. Two waves were formed of the 3d Platoon under Lieutenant Gappa. The executive officer of the 4th Ranger Company, Lieutenant Warren, accompanied Lieutenant Gappa. As the boats proceeded through the narrow inlet, enemy 81mm mortar rounds dropped into the water. The actual landing was made to the east of the point suggested by Lieutenant Warren.

The mission of Company I was to land amphibiously on the peninsula in order to make contact with the Rangers on Objective 79. The company then, in coordination with the Rangers, was to take Objective 77. A small group was to be left to defend the landing site. The Rangers had lost about four boats; I did not want to lose more.

The boats proceeded to the landing site, came under enemy small-arms fire, and landed. Upon debarkation, the initial group secured the beachhead and sent the boats back to pick up the remainder of Company I. The 3d Platoon then proceeded to enlarge the beachhead. It had taken the platoon one hour to get across the reservoir. While the boats were returning, Lieutenant Gappa maintained contact by radio with me, with Captain Kennedy, and with Captain Anderson, the Ranger company commander. When the 3d Platoon came under enemy machine-gun fire, Lieutenant Gappa requested that mortar fire be placed on the enemy. This was done. Captain Anderson reported on the radio that he saw Company I on the peninsula. Three or four hours were necessary to get the troops of Company I across the reservoir. The troops paddled since no motors were working.[28]

Members of the 7th Cavalry Regiment and the 4th Ranger Company provide additional details of the crossing operation.

CAPT. MORRIS M. TEAGUE JR., S-2 OF THE 3D BATTALION: My original mission as outlined was to pick up boats and crews at 0530 hours on 11 April at the 2d Battalion CP and move them to the beach. I was to organize Company I into boat teams and assault waves and act as beach master, test the motors, and arrange for ammunition resupply. Lieutenant Colonel Hallden gave me this mission about 2330 hours on 10 April because I had had amphibious and Ranger experience and training.

At 0515 hours, when I arrived at the point from which the Rangers had departed, I found all the boats being used by the Rangers and the Rangers in the process of crossing the reservoir. Boats unable to be utilized by the Rangers were jammed up on land. Jeeps were congested in the area. Enemy artillery and mortar fire added to the confusion. The regimental S-4 and I organized the area and cleared the congestion of vehicles, personnel, and equipment. I located another embarking site, which would be out of enemy observation. I halted Company I in that area and organized them into boat teams.

To preserve tactical integrity of the unit, I had the company divided into platoon-size waves, with ten men to a boat. I had the boats moved to the new site, and I began to stockpile ammunition. I used the P&A and S-2 sections of the 3d Battalion for assistance.

When I received the order for the company to embark between 1000 and 1100, only two motors were working. Six or seven paddle-boats were available. I had planned to have the motorboats reconnoiter and clear the beach for those that were paddled. I organized Lieutenant Gappa's platoon into two assault teams, and placed a BAR team in the bow of the two boats that had motors. I spoke with Lieutenant Warren of the 4th Ranger Company, who informed me that the beach was under enemy fire. I placed Lieutenant Warren in one of the boats. It took Lieutenant Gappa's platoon one hour and thirty minutes to paddle across the reservoir and take the beach under enemy small-arms and mortar fire.

The rest of the day I supervised the crossing operations. About 1600 hours the entire company was across the reservoir. Evacuation and resupply continued throughout the day. The landing beach was continuously swept by enemy small-arms and mortar fire.[29]

CAPT. THOMAS J. KENNEDY, COMMANDING OFFICER, COMPANY I: The battalion finished one phase of the general offensive movement and reached Phase Line Kansas. All equipment was loaded on vehicles, and the battalion awaited orders to move with the regiment into army reserve. At 1800 hours on 10 April the battalion actually started vehicles back to the rear area. Before the vehicles could clear the battalion area, the order was received to hold up. At 1900 hours, Company I was informed that another mission had been received. Vehicles were to be sent to the rear area for ammunition and rations. No one in the company knew what the mission was.

At 2300 hours I was ordered to report to battalion headquarters. There I received my mission for the following day. This was as follows: I was to be prepared to (1) move out amphibiously and assist the 4th Ranger Company on its mission; or (2) move over to the 2d Battalion area to (a) pass through the 2d Battalion and press the attack to the hill mass north of Hill 454 on the neck of land west of the dam; or (b) pass through the 2d Battalion after darkness and make a night attack on the same hill mass; or (c) move in and take over the same hill mass after the 2d Battalion had secured it.

At 0030 hours on 11 April, Company I was alerted to move at 0400 hours from the vicinity of Yuch'on-ni to a forward assembly area. At 0400 hours the company moved to this area, arriving at 0550. There the company awaited the order to perform whichever mission it would be called upon to do. Lieutenant Terry was sent to the regimental observation post to bring the order back. Heavy enemy mortar fire was coming into Company I's area, so the company moved for safety at 0830 to a sheltered cove. The company still did not know whether it would perform amphibiously or move into the 2d Battalion's area. At 0900 the company learned by radio that its mission was to make an amphibious landing on the peninsula across the reservoir, link up with the 4th Ranger Company, and attack Objective 77.

At approximately 1000 hours the company started to load its first wave. Although motors were to be used on the boats to cross the reservoir, only two motors worked. Six boats were paddled. The 3d Platoon, under Lieutenant Gappa and Sergeant Deaton, comprised the lead element.

Because the landing area was under enemy small-arms fire, the two powerboats were armed with a BAR in each bow. These were to be scout boats. One boat, however, turned out to be slower than the other. The first elements left shore at 1150 hours. Enemy mortar fire was received about halfway over. As the boats approached shore, additional enemy machine-gun and mortar fire was received. Automatic-weapons fire was received from the high ground on the peninsula. One boat received seven or eight bullet holes, and one man was wounded. The lead element went ashore to protect the landing of the paddleboats. Enemy troops were observed on a hill to the right. Lieutenant Gappa called for artillery fire, which silenced the enemy.

As the boats hit the beach the men moved out to secure it. The men in the first boat of the 3d Platoon, who had made the trip in fifty minutes, maneuvered to the high ground. The 1st Squad in front secured the high ground about thirty minutes before the slower motorboat reached shore. This boat made the voyage in one hour and thirty minutes.[30]

LIEUTENANT WARREN, EXECUTIVE OFFICER OF THE 4TH RANGER COMPANY: At 1030 the 3d Battalion commander contacted me and asked me to advise him on a landing site for Company I, which was going amphibiously in support of the 4th Ranger Company. I told him about a landing site and volunteered to go with the lead boat of Company I. The battalion commander proposed to use ten motors and twenty boats, each motor powering two boats. But only one outboard motor propelled one boat.

Company I departed with the 2d and 3d Platoons in the first wave; the 1st Platoon, company headquarters, and the 4th Ranger Company squad constituted the second wave. The boat carrying me landed under enemy machine-gun and sniper fire. The beachhead was immediately mortared by three rounds of 60mm shells. After the beachhead was secured, the 2d and 3d Platoons moved forward along the ridgeline to secure the beach for the following elements that arrived approximately at 1500 hours.[31]

After landing, Company I moved inland to attack Objective 77 and join the Rangers. Members of the unit describe what happened.

The 2d Platoon, after joining the 3d Platoon on the peninsula, waited for the remainder of the company to join. The 3d Platoon moved toward the company objective. The mission was to secure Objective 77 first, then link up with the Rangers. As the company headquarters, the company mortars, the balance of the 2d Platoon, and the forward observers in five boats approached shore, enemy mortar and machine-gun fire was received. The mortars were placed in position on the beach. Lieutenant Terry and Sergeant Bingham went forward to pick out targets. About 1400, the 1st Platoon brought the last Company I element across the reservoir.

The 3d Platoon started up the ridge toward the objective. The original idea had been to have Company I and the Rangers converge on Objective 77. Therefore, Company I started moving up the ridge to the right of the Rangers. But when the Rangers were counterattacked, Company I was ordered to connect with the Rangers first. This message was received at 1430. The ridge the company was pro-

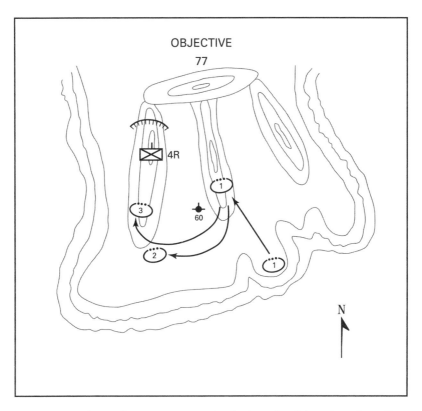

Company I, 7th Cavalry Regiment, 11 April 1951 (sketch based on Capt. Kennedy interview in CMH manuscript, U.S. Army; not to scale).

ceeding up would not permit connection with the Rangers unless the company proceeded through enemy territory. Therefore, the company pulled back and moved over to the left. The 2d Platoon moved into the 3d Platoon position to protect the right flank of the company. The 2d Platoon was ordered to hold until the balance of the company was on its way up the ridge. Then the platoon was to follow and join.

The 3d Platoon moved back around the hill and made contact with two platoons of the Ranger company. These platoons picked up ammunition on the beach for the Rangers, then guided the 3d Platoon of Company I to the Ranger company. No enemy contact was made moving up to the Rangers. On the hill, Company I took over the Ranger positions. Although the Rangers were to attack, ammunition supplies were low.[32]

The 7th Cavalry Regiment Attack

As the 4th Ranger Company, later joined by Company I, gained a foothold on the peninsula east of the dam and then struggled to beat off enemy counterattacks, the rest of the 7th Cavalry failed to achieve the hoped-for success in their attacks west of the dam. Major Webel, the S-3 of the 7th Cavalry, describes the situation.

The 2d Battalion jumped off at 0400 hours, moving north toward the enemy positions. At 0530 they came under intense machine-gun fire. Enemy mortar fire was received shortly thereafter. It was readily apparent that enemy machine guns were laid on the road that the 2d Battalion was moving on. Enemy outposts had alerted the defense to the 2d Battalion approach. The 2d Battalion, engaged by enemy pillboxes, was unable to advance. Even though heavy-machine-gun and mortar fire was directed against the enemy defenses, Company E was unable to move forward. The 2d Battalion artillery liaison officer adjusted 8-inch howitzer precision fire on enemy pillboxes to no avail. Many pillboxes were then visible because camouflage had been destroyed as a result of the artillery barrage. But the personnel in the boxes were not affected by friendly artillery fire. Because of poor visibility, air was unable to strike. Because of the road conditions no tanks could be brought forward. The 57mm and 75mm rifles were used to maximum extent, firing at the apertures of enemy pillboxes. Several pillboxes were hit by 8-inch fire, but no appreciable diminishing fire from the enemy resulted. It became readily apparent that the land west of the reservoir could not be taken without prohibitive losses.

During the early part of the engagement, one 76mm shell struck near the regimental observation post and killed the commanding officer of the heavy weapons company and three members of a 75mm rifle crew. Other personnel in this vicinity were wounded during the day.

Lieutenant Colonel Callaway, commander of the 2d Battalion, provides additional details.

I was then instructed to report to regiment to receive plans on an amphibious assault against the peninsula east of the dam. The plan as formulated committed the 2d Battalion to attack again in zone. The attack would be made prior to dawn so that a foothold would be secured before daylight. The Rangers would cross the water, attack and seize the high ground, and take the dam from the east. The 3d Battalion would reinforce the Rangers when necessary.

Jeeps bringing ammunition had to be pulled by bulldozer over the mountains. Large rocks on the route, slippery terrain, and heavy loads damaged several jeeps. Friendly units on the right of the regiment were also using this road, and supply problems were difficult. Evacuation of seriously wounded casualties was performed by helicopter from Yuch'on-ni. There was still no 105mm artillery support, and the 155mm batteries were firing at extreme range.

Company E, assigned the mission of attack, jumped off to the road at 0430 on 11 April and ran into an enemy outpost. The enemy forces opened fire from their well-defended positions. Despite darkness, the enemy fired effectively. Company E was unable to move forward even under cover of darkness. The Rangers had moved out undetected by the enemy and reached the high ground east of the dam before daylight. The Rangers then engaged the enemy in a small firefight, seized the objective, held it, and prepared to push on to the dam.

The 2d Battalion was unable to advance because of the limited maneuver space. Lieutenant Foster, platoon leader in Company G, who had been at Iwo Jima, reported receiving more mortar fire than against the Marines at Iwo Jima. Sergeant Sullivan, the acting platoon leader in Company E, stated that he never saw a position so well defended, except the Siegfried Line. Company E suffered twenty-five wounded. The Heavy Weapons company commander and two others were killed by artillery fire from west of the Pukhan River.

I considered moving a platoon of Company F amphibiously in an enveloping movement along the reservoir shore to the base of Hill 364. From there the platoon, moving under cover of smoke, would take the enemy position from the east, then descend on the enemy from his rear. I did not order this because all the available boats were being used to reinforce the Rangers.

Many enemy reinforcements were seen moving east across the dam into the peninsula against the Rangers. A prisoner stated that one enemy company was prepared to resist to the death. Other enemy elements were behind this company in depth. The prisoner stated that three 60mm mortars, eight light machine guns, and one heavy machine gun were in support.[33]

Captain Flynn, S-3 of the 2d Battalion, explains the problems involved in the attack plan.

About 1900 hours on 10 April, Major Webel, the regimental S-3, called and stated that the operation would take place on 11 April, with the 2d Battalion attacking over the same ground while the Ranger company moved across the reservoir. Major Webel stated that the objective would be taken at all costs. I believe that the operation was ill conceived due to the short planning time and because of the large enemy forces in the area. Colonel Callaway, the commander of the 2d Battalion, estimated that an enemy battalion opposed the 2d Battalion's advance.

A regimental conference took place between 2100 and 2300 hours on 10 April. At 0030 on 11 April the Ranger company prepared to move. This gave the Rangers two hours preparation, an inadequate amount of time. Company E of the 2d Battalion was ordered to depart its position at 0400 so that it could move to make enemy contact under cover of darkness. Company E was late, and enemy outposts picked up the company near the road at the southern end of the neck west of the reservoir. Company E was unable to make headway. Five or six men were lost on the initial assault. It was then planned to send a small group by boat to flank the enemy position between 1300 and 1400. But there was a shortage of boats and a lack of motors, and Company I was at that time in the process of reinforcing the Rangers. Although a platoon of Company E was on the beach and ready to go, such a move was impractical because of the need to get supplies across the reservoir to the Rangers and Company I.[34]

The 7th Cavalry's attack plan called for the 1st Battalion to make a diversionary attack across the Pukhan River while the 2d Battalion attacked the neck of land west of the dam. Capt. Carl W. Kueffer, S-3 of the 1st Battalion, describes the action of his battalion.

At 2000 hours on 10 April Major Malloy, the battalion executive officer and acting battalion commander, and I were instructed to report to regimental headquarters at 2100 hours. There the following mission was received: one reinforced rifle company was to cross the Pukhan River to seize Objective R and Objective R-1. Because the 2d Battalion had run into a large volume of enemy small-arms, automatic-weapons, and mortar fire from that area during 10 April, the regiment felt an advance northward to the dam was impossible unless this 1st Battalion diversionary attack was made. The 1st Battalion was also to support the 2d Battalion by fire.

At the battalion CP the following plan was worked out. Company A would cross the river. Elements of Company C would shift and occupy positions vacated by Company A. Company B was alerted to be prepared to move forward to support the 2d Battalion. Company D was to put its mortars and 75mm rifles in position to support Company A.

Company A moved out at 0745 hours on 11 April. A battalion observation post overlooking the area was established at 0800. Excellent observation of the objectives, the river, and the road would have been possible had the weather been good. But rain, snow, sleet, and fog hampered observation.

Company A advanced down steep slopes to the river and drew enemy fire at 0900. A squad sent to reconnoiter for crossing sites received a heavier volume of small-arms and machine-gun fire from the opposite bank each time it approached the river. The squad also found the river at a high level and the current swift. Because of the intense enemy small-arms fire, the squad was not able to get close to the river. Because of poor visibility, it was almost impossible to pick up enemy emplacements so that artillery and mortar fire could be directed against them.

The company never did get across the river. But artillery, 4.2-inch and 81mm mortar, 75mm rifle, and small-arms fire was placed on the opposite side of the river. Small-arms range was approximately 600 yards. The mortars fired at approximately 2,300 yards. The 75mm rifles fired at a range of between 600 and 1,000 yards.

At 1500 hours I informed the regimental S-3 that it was impossible to cross the river. I stated that I felt that by exposing Company A on this side of the river as a threat, the battalion was keeping the enemy occupied on that flank. Permission was granted to remain on this side of the river and to continue harassing fire. Because of failing visibility, I called the regimental S-3 and received permission to withdraw Company A at 1630 hours. A heavy snowstorm, fog, and sleet made it difficult for the companies to regain their original positions on the hills.

Although a map study was made, and although thought was given to crossing the river on boats, it was found impractical to carry boats over the mountains to the Pukhan. The building of rafts and the possibility of using air mattresses were also discussed, but it was felt that the current was too swift for such a crossing. The difficulties of the terrain were such that operations were very slow. Movement was most difficult.[35]

End of the Operation

With the 7th Cavalry's attacks stalled both east and west of the dam, the regiment began to reassess their options. Major Webel, the regimental S-3, describes the situation.

The Ranger company requested permission to withdraw because its ammunition was virtually exhausted. Permission was denied. Company I had already landed two platoons, and that company was instructed to move with speed to Objective 79 to assist the Rangers. In addition, intense heavy-mortar and artillery barrages were placed in front of the Ranger positions. One heavy-mortar barrage consisting of ten volleys of the heavy-mortar platoon fell in the center of an enemy attacking group and caused a great number of casualties. This fire support broke the enemy attack, although small groups continued to attempt to infiltrate the Ranger positions.

Company I, which had met a small Ranger element securing the beachhead, reported that it had linked up with the Rangers. The Ranger company commander reported no linkup. A check revealed that linkup had been made only with an outlying force. Necessary directions were given to Company I, which then continued to Objective 79.

When the two companies were tied in, there was no particular anxiety felt for the safety of the units despite enemy reinforcement east of the dam. There was, however, considerable doubt that these units could hold their positions without reinforcements and without a reliable and steady means of ammunition resupply and medical evacuation. It was almost a certainty that the enemy would attack in strength the night of 11–12 April. Because of the long water haul and the lack of motors, it was evident that the 3d Battalion would not be able to close north of the reservoir before darkness.

As the movement of troops and supplies progressed, a message from the 1st Cavalry Division informed the regiment that Korean Marines [attached to the 1st Marine Division] had arrived to relieve the 7th Cavalry Regiment on Line Kansas, but not on the neck of land west of the reservoir or on the high ground east of the dam. Colonel Harris was authorized at this time by the division to withdraw if he deemed such action advisable. At 1500 hours, with two motors in condition to operate most of the time, but ceasing to function from time to time, resulting in strings of five boats behind one motor and under continuous enemy fire, the regimental commander decided to pull back the forces that had crossed the reservoir and complete the regimental relief. Necessary orders were issued for Company I to protect the Ranger withdrawal, then to withdraw in turn to the mainland.[36]

Colonel Harris provides more details of his decision.
At 1200 hours on 11 April General Palmer called me and asked if I would recommend calling off the operation. I said no. Although I had given up the idea of securing the land, I still thought in terms of reinforcement so that the Rangers could perform the mission against the dam and withdraw under cover of darkness. At 1300 hours General Palmer called and gave permission to call off the operation. Between 1530 and 1600 the stubbornness of the enemy made me feel that the losses were more than the operation was worth. I ordered the troops across the reservoir to arrive at the beach on the peninsula at dark so that they could be evacuated under cover of darkness. The Rangers and Company I withdrew masterfully.[37]

Members of the 3d Battalion, 7th Cavalry, and the 4th Ranger Company describe the withdrawal.

LIEUTENANT COLONEL HALLDEN, 3D BATTALION COMMAND-ER: As elements of Company L were in boats and ready to move across the reservoir, the regimental commander phoned me at 1655 hours and ordered Company I and the Rangers pulled back. I ordered Company I to cover the Ranger withdrawal and to be the last to leave the beach. From then until 0130 on 12 April, when the last elements reached the initial embarkation point, the troops returned from the peninsula. Signal lights and radio communications guided the boats to shore. The last elements waited until fourteen boats were assembled for the final trip so that they would be able to defend in case of enemy attack. The weather that night was bitterly cold. A sleeting rain fell. The men operating the boats suffered from exposure.[38]

CAPTAIN TEAGUE, S-2 OF THE 3D BATTALION: Company L was brought to the embarkation site and was preparing to leave at 1730 to reinforce the Rangers and Company I, when it was decided that the friendly forces would withdraw from the peninsula. I moved back to the original embarkation point so that the returnees would not have to fight the current. I organized rescue teams, using Company L personnel as paddlers. Lashing five or six boats to a motorboat, I sent them to recover Company I and the Rangers. I marked the debarkation point with flashlights, and flashlights were used to signal between both shores. The night of 11 April was very dark. Evacuation of the companies was slow and without incident. At 0130 hours on 12 April all the men were back. Several enemy 120mm mortar shells came into the area, but caused no damage.[39]

CAPTAIN ANDERSON, COMMANDER OF THE 4TH RANGER COM-PANY: About 1630, as I was preparing to attack Objective 80, I received orders from the battalion S-3 to return to the landing site covered by Company I and return to the point of departure. The 4th Ranger Company moved off the mountain, carrying its dead and wounded. I was on the last boat and landed at the original embarkation point at 2030 hours.[40]

CAPTAIN KENNEDY, COMMANDER OF COMPANY I: As the 2d Platoon of Company I was moving up the hill, the order was received for Company I to cover the Ranger withdrawal, and then withdraw itself. Originally it was planned to have the 2d Platoon of Company

I cover the landing of Company L, which was to follow Company I. As the 3d Platoon took over the Ranger positions to cover the Ranger withdrawal, an enemy counterattack of an estimated sixty to seventy men was received. Company I fired all the ammunition it had and most of another basic load. An estimated forty-five enemy were killed. An ammunition detail from the 1st Platoon was sent to bring ammunition from the beach.

For the withdrawal the 3d Platoon held positions on Objective 79. The 2d Platoon came back and formed a strong line with the 1st Platoon across the ridge to the beach. The Rangers withdrew, one element at a time, while Company I covered. The Rangers carried out one wounded and two dead. Men were sent ahead to cut a trail for the litters. A boat was brought from the landing site to a point nearer the Ranger company so that the wounded could be loaded more easily.

After the wounded were loaded, the 3d Platoon joined the company on the beach. The Rangers cleared, and Company I remained on the beach without boats. They kept artillery directed on the enemy forces and put fire on the enemy attempting to fire on the company. When the boats, two of which were powerboats, returned, the 3d Platoon, the attached forward observers, and part of the 4th Platoon were loaded and sent back. The 1st and 2d Platoons remained on line on the beach to repel any enemy attack. At this time enemy sniper, machine-gun, and mortar fire was received. This fire was not too accurate, but two men were wounded. Friendly mortars threw out shells to discourage any enemy attack. It was then dark. It was raining, and the men were soaked. The wind was blowing hard. The beach was muddy. The company waited for enough boats so that everyone could be loaded on. By 2400 hours sufficient boats had returned. They were all paddleboats, each boat manned by two Company L men. Ammunition was stacked, and equipment was checked so that nothing would be left for the enemy. Everything was brought out.

The entire company was at the original point of embarkation at 0126 hours on 12 April. It was difficult to find the landing site due to darkness, and the boats steered according to flashlight signals. Private Studzman, who ran a powerboat continuously for twenty-four hours, did an excellent job. After a check was made to make certain that everyone was back, the company moved back to an assembly area under enemy mortar fire.[41]

A combat historian, 1st Lt. Martin Blumenson, who interviewed participants during and immediately following the operation, summed up the overall situation at the end.
Equipment and supplies had been building up to such an extent that on the evening of 11 April it appeared that sufficient materials were on hand to sustain the operation. By this time, however, the water level of the river was falling, and the immediate flood danger appeared to be past. The enemy positions were so well prepared and the enemy troops occupying these positions were of such number that it would have been necessary to commit a larger force to accomplish the mission. This was not desirable in view of the larger corps situation.

The following factors further rendered this operation difficult. Artillery support could be delivered only by 155mm and 8-inch howitzers firing at maximum range. Batteries of 105mm howitzers were outranged and could not be brought forward because of the terrain and the absence of roads suitable for vehicular traffic. The weather prevented air support and air supply, and obscured observation of enemy positions. The mission itself was not clear in some commanders' minds.[42]

With the completion of the withdrawal, as the Rangers and the 7th Cavalry moved to the rear into reserve, they had time to reflect on what had happened. Members of the units assess the operation.
COLONEL HARRIS, COMMANDING OFFICER OF THE 7TH CAVALRY REGIMENT: At the time of the withdrawal I did not realize how much the Chinese had been hurt. The entire mission was based on the assumption by Eighth Army and IX Corps that the enemy did not have the intention or capability of completely destroying the dam. The physical severity of the operations leading up to the dam was hard on the troops. The regiment had fought over extremely rugged terrain. The troops were therefore not fresh when they reached the reservoir area. The weather also conspired against the

operation. Snow and rain made for very poor visibility. One air strike in three days had been delivered. The main factor, however, was that this was an operation in which the tactical side was directed by the logistical difficulties.[43]

MAJOR WEBEL, S-3 OF THE 7TH CAVALRY: In my opinion, staff officers were prone to throw up their hands and say no when they received requests for devices or equipment of an unusual nature. The mission of the staff is to perform such duties.

The entire operation appeared to have little tactical benefit compared to the losses suffered. The sluice gates had been open for some time, and water in the reservoir was as low as it could go unless the penstocks were opened.

Scheduling the relief of a unit and assigning it a mission should not be done simultaneously, unless the relieving unit is to take over the ground taken. The Korean Marine Regiment would not relieve on the high ground at the dam because the ground was not defensible. The area to the west had to be secured before the dam site could be held.[44]

LIEUTENANT COLONEL CALLAWAY, COMMANDER OF THE 2D BATTALION: The battalion mistakes are as follows:

(1) A proper estimate of what the enemy planned to do and was prepared to do was lacking. I feel that a great deal more planning and coordination should have been accomplished before the operation commenced. One day should have been spent in reconnaissance. More time should have been given to the procurement of ammunition supply and an adequate number of boats. In short, the operation lacked adequate preparation.

(2) Company F gave the wrong coordinates of its position and prevented a much more effective air strike. In terrain such as this it was impossible for me to physically check my units. Too much time would be lost if such was done.

(3) The commander bases his estimate of the severity of an action on the number of casualties. When six litters were requested by Company F a short time after its attack commenced, I formed the opinion that the action was serious. Incorrect reports can affect the effectiveness of the battalion commander's decisions.

(4) In one case, a company commander moved with his base of

fire. He was pinned down with his base of fire so far from the maneuvering element that he was unable to bring the firepower of his entire company over the narrow company front. Such fire was necessary in attacking these strong enemy positions.

(5) All the company commanders of the battalion were pinned down at one time or another during this attack. One was killed attempting to rescue a wounded man. One was pinned down with his base of fire. One was pinned down behind his lead scout, and it took him several hours to get back to a position from which he could direct the operation. The company commanders must influence the action.

(6) Forward observers must be trained to remain close to the company commander so that they can be directed by the commander.

(7) The individual riflemen fired much too quickly for accurate aim. Many men fired indiscriminately. A resupply of ammunition was sometimes necessary after twenty minutes of combat. Resupply of ammunition slowed the impetus of attack and sometimes stopped the attack at a critical moment.

(8) Had tanks been available they would have had great effect on the enemy pillboxes. It seems to me that the regiment should have waited one more day before undertaking the operation. Although the 75mm rifles were used in very close support, they fired into pillbox apertures without effect. Baffle walls in the pillboxes or enemy reinforcements might account for this. The 75mm rifles employed at a distance of 1,000 yards might have been moved to within 400 yards of the enemy and possibly have been more effective. The 75mm rifle drew much enemy mortar and howitzer fire, thus indicating that the 75mm recoilless rifle is a very effective piece or that the enemy fired against the flash. Crews of the 57mm and 75mm rifles had to move continuously to avoid enemy fire.[45]

CAPTAIN ANDERSON, COMMANDER OF THE 4TH RANGER COMPANY: This mission could have been accomplished had plans been made in detail, equipment assembled a minimum of one day in advance, and rehearsal of the participants effected. The mission of the Ranger company was changed several times, indicating indecision of action. A definite mission must be established and made known to the combat leaders of the units to insure success of the operation.

The dam could have been made inoperative by the Ranger company if definite plans for the amphibious operation had been made. If the Ranger company had crossed the reservoir under cover of darkness on a raid basis, to get in and out quickly, fewer casualties would have resulted, and the mission would have been accomplished. The enemy was unaware of the presence of Ranger troops or of boats in his vicinity. Plans for the operation were released at 2300 hours; the operation commenced at 0300 the following morning. Plans for this type of operation must be very detailed. The troops should be rested and rehearsed beforehand.[46]

Lieutenant Colonel Hallden, 3d Battalion commander: This was a difficult operation, particularly since the men had never been trained for amphibious operations. Yet they performed capably. The most important element in this operation was control. I feel that Captain Anderson's coolness saved two platoons. Lieutenant Gappa's aggressiveness and Captain Kennedy's control of the men under him were very important to the success of the operation. The orderly withdrawal under constant enemy fire was handled very well.[47]

Chapter 13

THE HANT'AN RIVER CROSSING

24th Infantry Regiment, 10–12 April 1951

In the west, Operation Rugged saw the I Corps drive forward to the Hant'an River while the IX and X Corps pushed north to the Hwach'on Reservoir area in the east. After reaching Phase Line Kansas, the I Corps' 25th Infantry Division prepared to continue the advance when Operation Dauntless was launched. The 25th Division would open the new offensive with an assault crossing of the Hant'an River followed by a thrust toward the Iron Triangle area. Army combat historian Capt. Edward C. Williamson conducted a study of the ensuing operations of one of the division's regiments, the 24th Infantry. He summarizes the situation facing the unit and the attack plan.

Twelve miles south of Ch'orwon and twenty-five miles northeast of Uijongbu, the Hant'an River, a small tributary to the Imjin, flows in a generally east to west direction in the sector in which the 24th Infantry Regiment was to make its crossing. Here Hill 642, an almost vertical rocky mountain on the north bank of the Hant'an, dominated the terrain. An ungraded dirt trail ran north from across the Hant'an, where the Chinese had constructed a mud-branch cart bridge, and skirted the east side of Hill 642.

On 7 April 1951, the 24th Infantry Regiment of the 25th Infantry Division held positions south of the Hant'an River where the regiment had relieved the 35th Infantry Regiment. The Division Operation Order No. 30, issued at 1530 hours on 7 April, called for Operation Dauntless, in which the 24th Infantry Regiment would

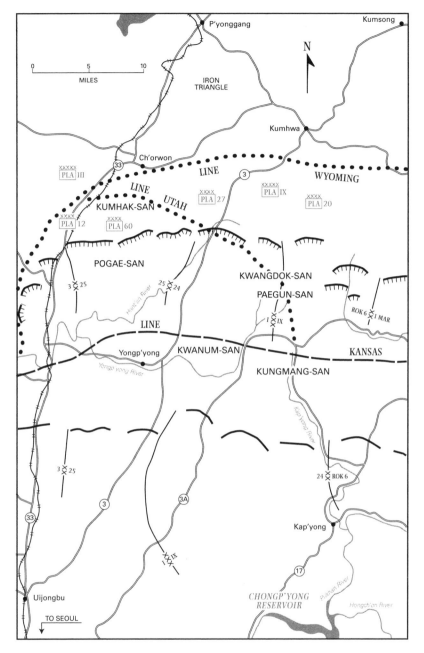

Operation Dauntless (based on map in CMH manuscript, U.S. Army).

attack on D-day at H-hour from positions along Line Kansas, cross the Hant'an River, and seize the hills north of the river. At 2300 hours on 9 April, I Corps informed all units that D-day and H-hour for Operation Dauntless would be 0700 hours on 11 April.

It was at first contemplated to send the 3d Battalion in behind the 1st Battalion but, because of the sheer wall of the bank of the Hant'an River, this was not practical. Therefore, it was decided to make the river the LD, and have the 3d Battalion cross the river, make an exit, and attack with three companies abreast up the three ridgelines leading to Hill 463. On the left flank of the 3d Battalion was the Turkish Brigade and on the right flank the 1st Battalion. The 2d Battalion was in reserve. Artillery supporting the 24th Infantry Regiment was the 159th Field Artillery Battalion (105mm) reinforced by the 176th Armored Field Artillery Battalion (105mm SP) and the 64th Field Artillery Battalion (105mm).[1]

From reconnaissance work, the attack plan was refined. Officers of the regiment describe the effort.

LT. COL. HUGH D. COLEMAN, EXECUTIVE OFFICER OF THE 24TH INFANTRY REGIMENT: Leaving the regimental CP at 1520 hours on 8 April I made a visual reconnaissance of the Hant'an River from the 3d Battalion's OP. By studying the terrain and the river, I discovered Chinese Communist Forces on the banks of the river. At that time a daylight attack had been planned, but I went back and told Colonel Britt, the 24th Infantry regimental commander, that we should make a night crossing, and I advised pounding Hills 642 and 463 and the village of Chikt'an [located about 200 yards east of the old bridge] on 9 and 10 April. There were two ways of crossing the river. The first was to cross at Chikt'an near the old bridge, and the second to move up an erosion ditch and walk to the river about 700 yards downstream [southwest] of Chikt'an. After studying very carefully, and making allowances for noise on the rocks, the exit on the banks, and the fifty enemy emplacements on the north side of the banks, I knew that walking up the river would mean heavy casualties.[2]

MAJ. JOSEPH BARANOWSKI, COMMANDER OF THE 1ST BATTALION, 24TH INFANTRY REGIMENT: The original attack order left D-day unannounced and H-hour to be chosen. To prepare, on 8 April

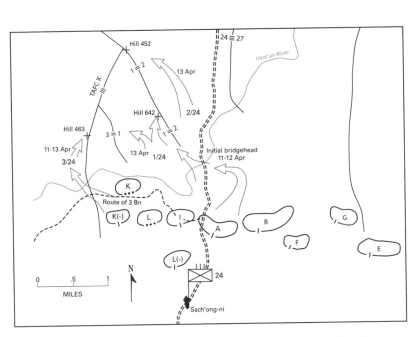

Operation Dauntless (based on map in CMH manuscript, U.S. Army).

I made a reconnaissance accompanied by the S-3, the artillery liaison officer, and an engineer group. I decided on a crossing site near Chikt'an, and engineers from the 65th Engineer Battalion were shown the bridge site. The reconnaissance was brief. On 9 April, two company commanders made their reconnaissance, and I issued the 1st Battalion attack order on the ground and outlined the plan. The mission was to take an initial bridgehead and attack Hill 383. I decided to cross at night because the limited area and observation made a daylight crossing impossible. Also a night crossing would have the element of surprise. A route was reconnoitered from Company A to the river and marked with engineer tape. The communications officer extended the OP line to the Battalion OP. Sherman tanks and AAA tracks in direct support laid wire to the 1st Battalion. I requested the tanks and AAA tracks to move up only upon request. Although I decided on no artillery preparation, plans were made for fires on call.[3]

MAJ. STANLEY P. SWARTZ, S-3 OF THE 3D BATTALION, 24TH INFANTRY REGIMENT: The biggest problem on the Hant'an River crossing was resupply. The 3d Battalion, 24th Infantry Regiment, crossed Hill 555, relieving the 2d Battalion, 35th Infantry Regiment, in position south of the Hant'an River on 7 April on Phase Line Kansas. The Turks were on the left, and the 1st Battalion, 24th Infantry Regiment, was on the right. We patrolled to the Hant'an for crossing sites and went on air reconnaissance to observe Hill 642. The company commanders and I went on the air reconnaissance. There were two possible crossings in our area, the rest of the riverbank being sheer rock cliff 50 to 150 yards high.[4]

The final plan for the 24th Infantry called for a surprise predawn attack with no immediate artillery preparation before the assault. The 1st Battalion was to cross on the right near the old bridge site at Chikt'an and seize the base of Hill 642, and the 3d Battalion was to cross about 3,500 yards to the left, capture Hill 463, and then assault Hill 642. The 2d Battalion was in reserve.

Major Baranowski, the 1st Battalion commander, briefly describes the river crossing of his unit on 11 April.

The assault company moved into the stream, breasting a strong current. The attack proceeded according to plan, with the beachhead seized by 0830 with a small semicircle to keep small-arms fire off the crossing. The two leading companies bypassed some enemy, and Company C, coming up in reserve, destroyed two light machine guns in the immediate area on the north side of the bridge crossing at 0830 hours.[5]

Company A was to lead the attack across the river and seize an initial objective, a hill about 800 yards in front of the crossing site. The company commander, 1st Lt. Gordon J. Lippman; the company executive officer, 1st Lt. David A. Freas; and the platoon sergeant of the 1st Platoon, SFC Willie M. Robinson, describe the action.[6]

1ST LT. LIPPMAN: At 2400 hours on 10 April, Company A began its movement to the LD. We assembled in a flat field, having walked and climbed for four hours. I sent a reconnaissance patrol led by SFC Robinson, 1st Platoon sergeant, and Sergeant Mitchell, 3d Platoon sergeant, with three men each down to the river to find

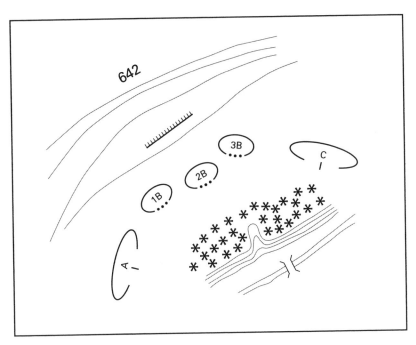

Assault on Hill 642 by Company B, 11–12 April 1951 (sketch based on Capt. Mayo interview in CMH manuscript, U.S. Army; not to scale).

a route to move the men. The patrol was to proceed to the V, and when it arrived at that point the six men were to cross the river and get up on the lip of the bank. A rainy, windy night made it easy to conceal movement.

SFC ROBINSON: I left Lieutenant Lippman, found a route across the river, and picked a crossing site that wasn't deep. I tried to throw some logs across a thirty-foot gap in a bombed-out bridge but was not able to throw the logs across as the time was running short. I detailed three men to wade across the river and ordered them to the lip. When they got across they lay with their feet in the water and didn't go to the lip. Sergeant Mitchell and I then came back and reported to Lieutenant Lippman. At 0425 hours Company A dropped packs.

LIEUTENANT LIPPMAN: Then the sergeants picked up their platoons. The 1st Platoon led off down the trail. Company headquarters was behind the 1st Platoon. At 0435 hours, the head of the column reached the river. The A&P Platoon, which had the job of bridging the gap in the bridge, arrived at 0425 hours with timbers and found the estimate missed by fifteen feet.

MAJOR BARANOWSKI: On 10 April a patrol had been sent to measure the missing span in the bridge with tape. They measured it at twenty feet. Assault elements accompanied by the Pioneer and Ammunition Platoon, carrying two sixteen-feet timbers, found the missing span to be thirty feet wide.

LIEUTENANT FREAS: I picked up the A&P Platoon and took them to the river. Korean laborers carried out the first plank, but it was not long enough. I then asked SFC Robinson to hold up. In about two minutes Lieutenant Lippman came up.

LIEUTENANT LIPPMAN: I knew they didn't have the time for the bridge to be repaired so I jumped in the river with SFC Robinson to the left of the old Chinese cart bridge of mud covered with logs. The river was waist deep, 125 feet wide, and swift running. The 1st Platoon followed closely. Several of the men fell into the water, and equipment that fell into the water included one machine gun, two cans of ammunition, and several weapons. I stood on the bank and prodded the 1st Platoon and a good share of the 3d Platoon into the cut at 0450 hours.

SFC ROBINSON: As we were going up the V, someone challenged us in Chinese. All guys stopped, and no one said a word at that time. About fifty hand grenades and machine-gun fire then came in. One man, Private Logan, was killed. At that time I heard Lieutenant Lippman order us to move to the left. We wanted to take that hill before daylight, and we maneuvered to the left the best way we could.

LIEUTENANT LIPPMAN: I was speaking to the people behind. The SCR536 was wet, and there was no inter-platoon communications except voice. An enemy machine gun was firing from the right front.

LIEUTENANT FREAS: Machine-gun bullets were landing between Company A and the bridge.

LIEUTENANT LIPPMAN: Although machine-gun fire was denying Company A the use of the cut, there were no casualties. I knew we would have to move to the shelter of the lip, and I feared the machine gun would hinder the rest of Company A from crossing the river. I estimated the enemy fired a belt in bursts. We moved into a pine grove, which we had spotted the day before on reconnaissance. The men were each carrying a basic load: the riflemen had three bandoliers, a rifle belt with ten clips (80 rounds), and six mixed hand grenades. In addition, the men carried one round for a crew-served weapon or a box of .30-caliber machine-gun ammunition. This was standard through the battalion due to the time element of getting the bridge in and ammunition resupply up.

We reached the pine grove at 0510, being disorganized because of the dark. I gave the men ten minutes to reorganize while I cased the situation. At the end of the time, Lieutenant Freas had brought up a portion of the 2d and 4th Platoons. At 0520 came the first gray of dawn. With an open field to cross, I ordered Sergeant Paul with the 2d Platoon to take the first finger [leading to Hill 642]. Lieutenant Freas came up and left with the 2d Platoon in line of skirmishers. I watched Sergeant Paul lead. SFC Robinson arrived with nine men and was sent back for the rest at 0525. He reported back at 0530, on the run and bringing several more, with the rest still in the cut. I gave SFC Robinson the mortar section, fifteen to twenty men, and the company headquarters, ten to twelve men, and told him to proceed to the original objective [about 800 yards in front of the crossing site]. I kept only a runner and the SCR300 radio operator. I set up the three 60mm mortars on the edge of the pine grove to support either of the two units sent out. The enemy machine gun first mentioned began firing on the 2d Platoon. I then desired to move the rest of the people out of the pine grove. I could see the 2d Platoon on top of the first knoll; I moved to the left with the 4.2-inch mortar observer, the SCR300 radio operator, the 81mm observer, and a runner. By SCR536, I asked SFC Robinson his location and assumed he was on top of the ridge, which he wasn't.

SFC ROBINSON: I left Lieutenant Lippman, moved out across the open field, got on the left side of the finger, called Lieutenant Lippman, and asked did he want me to keep moving. I reported not receiving machine-gun fire from the top of the hill.

LIEUTENANT LIPPMAN: I climbed the knoll and found that SFC Robinson was to the left. I reached the military crest, started receiving hand grenades, and was fired at by three automatic rifles, two burp guns, a collection of four to five rifles, and hand grenades eight feet from the top of the knoll at 0550 hours. The hand grenades were stick and concussion types. With the 3d Platoon on a finger to the right rear, Company A had two-thirds coverage of the knoll. The 3d Platoon could only get fifteen yards from the military crest. I tried to send three men to the left; they got one halfway around the knoll, ran into small arms, automatic weapons, and hand grenades, and returned. The Korean interpreter was brought up. Fire was held up, and the interpreter called for the Chinese to surrender. In answer, the Chinese fired all their weapons from their holes and threw hand grenades. Fifteen men advanced on the holes; however, the machine gunner couldn't get close enough to fire.

SFC ROBINSON: Lieutenant Lippman said, "Get down a base of fire," and he tossed a WP grenade into a hole. When his hand grenades ran out he threw his pistol and requested a bandolier of ammunition from me. Returning to a hole on the top, he was hit by a fragmentation grenade as he approached the hole. I told him he was hit, and he said, "We have got to get our objective." I saw he was losing too much blood and asked him to go down, but he kept on fighting; he finally left to get the 3.5-inch bazooka and flamethrower, which arrived at 0615.

LIEUTENANT LIPPMAN: I went back down the hill and found Lieutenant Freas with the rest of the platoon.

LIEUTENANT FREAS: We crossed the open ground and started up the nose opposite the pine grove, running into a few holes. A machine gun opened up, and Sergeant Paul was hit by a hand grenade from a hole on the forward part of the hill. A machine gun from the rear was firing. We continued up the ridge until it became perpendicular, then we swung to the left toward the initial objective, moved across a ridge clearing four or five CCF out of holes, and had started up the hill when Lieutenant Lippman arrived. He told us to hold up, and we formed a line to hold the ground to the right.

LIEUTENANT LIPPMAN: We got the 3.5-inch rocket launcher to the top of the hill. I then turned Company A over to Lieutenant Freas and went to the 1st Battalion aid station.

SFC ROBINSON: By the time the 3.5-inch rocket launcher and flamethrower came up, we had secured the knoll.

LIEUTENANT LIPPMAN: The hill was secured at 0715. Tanks firing on top of Hill 642 neutralized the main defenses. The tanks from Company B, 89th Tank Battalion, gave overhead support and were reinforced by Battery D, 21st AAA Battalion. Faulty ammunition fell short. On the way to the aid station I met Company B in the pine grove. A bulldozer was working at the crossing site, and the 65th Engineer Combat Battalion was about to start the bridge. I arrived at the aid station at 0830 and found nineteen wounded from Company A there. Two from Company A were killed.

LIEUTENANT FREAS: I took charge of Company A and reported to the 1st Battalion that we were on the initial objective. I then took a rough count and found we had seventy-eight men. Twenty more men arrived shortly thereafter. I checked the ammunition, contacted the S-3, and checked on the machine gun to our rear. I then ordered SFC Robinson to go down a finger to the river and check the area of the wide bend in the river. I moved the 2d Platoon up the finger to connect with Company B. The S-3 called and told Company A to hold fast because Company B was not yet up. At 1500 the 2d Platoon sent word that Company B was up. I moved to the high point in the ridge and met Captain Mayo, who was moving Company B's 1st Platoon up.[6]

Company C followed Company A to the river. The company commander, 1st Lt. Edward H. Russ, describes Company C's crossing.

It was still dark at 0415 hours on 11 April when Company C got to the Hant'an River. There had been very little firing up until then. We started to cross the river in single file. The preceding company, Company A, had placed timbers in the gap of the Chinese mud cart bridge. As we approached the bridge we began receiving automatic-weapons fire from the opposite shore, and I proceeded on across the bridge with the 1st Platoon. A few of the 1st Platoon jumped off the bridge and waded across. Upon reaching the opposite shore, the 1st Platoon fanned out to the right, and we worked our way up the steep rocky cliff and proceeded to lay down a base of fire on the automatic weapons that had been firing on the bridge site.

The 1st Platoons of Companies A and B were pinned down by the bridge. That discouraged the balance of Company C from crossing. By this time it was becoming a little light. The enemy was covering the bridge well. I went back to get the remainder of the company. By exercising strong command discipline, despite the automatic-weapons fire, the company was moved across the bridge.

Our primary mission was to cover the right flank of the bridgehead. The 1st Platoon was still under heavy automatic-weapons and sniper fire. I sent two platoons under Lieutenant Sheffey around the right flank, bypassing the 1st Platoon, which was engaging the enemy. At 0730 we got a call from Company B that some of the 1st Platoon fire was striking in the Company B zone. Captain Mayo, the Company B commander, offered to send back a platoon to help Company C's 1st Platoon. I decided, however, that the 1st Platoon could handle the situation if Company B would move on and tie in on the right flank of the two platoons under Lieutenant Sheffey. By this time the 1st Platoon was running low on ammunition and hand grenades. We redivided the ammunition and sent a squad to the right flank, crawling and running in behind the enemy. In the meantime, a pack train led by Warrant Officer Lewis arrived with ammunition at 0830 hours.

Having received a resupply of ammunition, I placed a machine gun and a BAR in position to fire on two enemy bunkers, taking the remainder of the 1st Platoon around the right flank to join the 1st Squad. At this time the enemy, estimated as a platoon, was throwing ten to twelve satchel charges and hand grenades. About 200 hand grenades were thrown by the enemy in the morning. I received a call from Lieutenant Sheffey at 1000 hours. He had taken his objective and tied in with Company B. I decided on a flanking assault of the enemy strongpoint. The men, the 1st Platoon with sixteen men remaining, were deployed in a skirmish line. By crawling forward, using maximum fire, and throwing hand grenades, after being driven back several times by enemy hand-grenade barrages, we were able to reduce the bunkers and knock out the strongpoint at

1030–1100 hours. Engineer charges, placed on a bunker during the attack, failed to detonate. We captured several new British Bren guns and counted twenty-three enemy killed in action. We lost one killed and twelve wounded in action.

A portable flamethrower would have saved time and lives. Our flamethrower man straggled 500 yards from the start of the attack. Ammunition discipline should be stressed during training. The discipline of moving through a hand-grenade barrage should be practiced and taught in training. It is an art. You must get up, move, and close with the enemy. Within ten feet of the enemy you are through his effective hand grenade range.

After securing the right flank, we dispatched patrols to seek a route up Hill 642.[7]

Two soldiers from Company C, Sgt. Frank W. Howard, 4th Platoon sergeant, and M. Sgt. Marcellus S. Gray, 2d Platoon leader, provide more details of the crossing.

MASTER SERGEANT GRAY: We jumped off at midnight on 10 April and walked 2,000 yards to the south bank of the Hant'an River, arriving there at 0500 hours. The enemy had the bridge and the draw there covered by automatic-weapons fire, causing the men to halt by the old Chinese footbridge.

SERGEANT HOWARD: There were a few scattered mortars, not much small arms. A lot of automatic-weapons fire was coming from the center of Hill 642.

MASTER SERGEANT GRAY: Directly north of the crossing, about 700 yards away, automatic weapons were firing. At daybreak the Chinese could see Company C crossing the bridge. Some men were wounded on the bridge and were holding up the advance. One soldier fell in the river wounded, and because of the swift current would have drowned, but another one jumped in and hauled him out. After crossing the bridge we advanced toward a steep cliff with fire coming in. We managed to get on top of the cliff with three 57mm recoilless rifles and two light .30-caliber machine guns. White phosphorous rifle grenades were then shot into bunkers fifty to seventy-five yards to our front. The automatic-weapons fire continued to come in from five or six different directions. At about 1000 hours the 2d Platoon swung to the right. The 2d and 3d Platoons proceeded to take the ground on the right, 1,000 yards from the crossing, engaging in a firefight. There was little resistance until we hit two small hills and started to set up a defensive position. At 1200 I went from the 2d Platoon to the 3d Platoon and on the way back looked fifteen feet away and spied a Chinese soldier. I ran back to the 2d Platoon and, with the 3d Platoon, attacked the enemy, estimated as a platoon, killing fifteen and causing the rest to withdraw. The enemy troops were well dug in, and hand grenades were used on the holes.[8]

Company B followed Companies A and C. Their part in the action is described by Capt. Steven B. Mayo, company commander; SFC Willard B. Smith, 3d Platoon leader; Cpl. Carey Lewis, 4th Squad leader of the 3d Platoon; and SFC Walter C. Fitzgerald, 2d Platoon sergeant.

CAPTAIN MAYO: I made a reconnaissance on 10 April with my platoon leaders and sergeants. At 0900 hours we could see the bridgehead and the mountain. I pointed out the fingers to the left front of the bridgehead that we would occupy. Company B came over the hill behind Company A at night at 0430 hours; it was still dark. Planks were down on the old bridge, and Company B crossed the bridge with one Korean interpreter being wounded. I placed a heavy .30-caliber machine gun in a V in the bank. Company B crossed the river to the low ridge, regrouped at 0700 hours, and did not fire a round. I pointed out the objective. Open ground lay 700 yards to the front. The 1st Platoon on the left walked slowly to a finger without being fired on. The 2d Platoon also advanced without being fired on, but the 3d Platoon caught hostile fire, losing one friendly KIA in a small firefight with an estimated company. I established an OP and secured the initial objective by 1300 hours. At this time Company C on the right had a platoon in a firefight.

SFC FITZGERALD: The 2d Platoon led Company B across the Hant'an River at 0500, part of the men wading and part walking the bridge; the first two squads walked the bridge. As day broke, three enemy machine guns fired on the bridge. At 0520 Captain Mayo moved the company up to a pine grove where he assigned the objective.

SFC SMITH: We moved out the night of 10 April south of the Hant'an River. We lost communication when the artillery forward observer lost contact with the leading elements of Company B. We wandered around, discovered the trail, and at daybreak found Major Baranowski, who told me where the objective was. The 3d Platoon reached the low ground where Company C and Company A on the bank were receiving small-arms fire. The 3d Platoon crossed the bridge at 0630 hours. We received the order for the attack in a pine grove. We used a flamethrower in the attack on Chinese pillboxes.

CORPORAL LEWIS: I got lost following communication wire; white engineer tape initially marked the route. After crossing the Hant'an, I proceeded up the hill, spotted a Chinese in a bunker, and killed him with my M-1 rifle.[9]

Meanwhile to the west, the 3d Battalion of the 24th Infantry Regiment, with the mission of seizing Hills 463 and 642 [see map on page 383], was having a more difficult time. Major Swartz, the S-3 of the 3d Battalion, summarizes their crossing.

The 3d Battalion started moving up at 1700 hours on 10 April and crossed the LD, which was the Hant'an River, at midnight. It took three hours to walk to the crossing. The water was swifter than hell and chest deep. It was rough crossing the river, and we lost an estimated two men drowned. One platoon of Company K was partly disorganized. The order of crossing was Company K, then Company L, with Company I in reserve. One platoon of Company L secured the bridgehead. Company K moved on Hill 463. The remaining elements also advanced. Company K and Company L had a platoon each on top of Hill 463, and some units were on the ridgeline of Hill 642. Dawn came at 0600 hours. The plan was for Company K to go up the saddle between Hills 642 and 463 and put in a block to the west on the ridgeline while Company L passed through to Hill 642. Company I was to remain behind to hold the river crossing. At daylight the CCF counterattacked. At 0730 hours

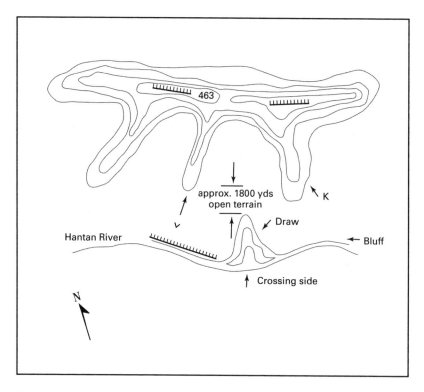

Hant'an River crossing by the 3d Battalion, 11 April 1951 (sketch based on Maj. Swartz interview in CMH manuscript, U.S. Army; not to scale).

Company K was pinned down and driven back across the river by machine-gun, automatic-weapons, and mortar fire. It took three hours to carry a litter back to the aid station, and it took a three-hour haul to get the supplies up. The companies came back across the river by infiltration.[10]

1st Lt. John L. Herren, Company K commander, provides more details.

We approached the left flank. There were three fingers going up a ridge in the saddle connecting Hill 463 with Hill 642. We had progressed with slight opposition up to within assaulting range of the crest. Between 0630 and 0700 we had been receiving automatic-weapons fire from the top of Hill 463, from the right flank, and from Hill 642. Fire increased extensively from five machine guns on top of the ridge, ten BARs and Bren guns, plus three automatic machine guns. From daylight to 1000 hours, 250 to 300 enemy mortar rounds came in. Company K had the 1st Platoon on the right, the 2d Platoon on the left, and the 3d Platoon with the light machine guns as a base of fire. The Chinese, in platoon size, made a fanatical banzai attack with burp guns and grenades, yelling and running. One was shot by three men and continued twenty yards before he dropped dead. The 2d Platoon was forced to withdraw. A .30-caliber light machine gunner was killed at his gun, and his replacement was wounded. The 2d Platoon leader had his carbine blown out of his hand. Under these circumstances the 2d Platoon had to withdraw. Four were killed in action against an estimated fifty Chinese killed. The 1st Platoon held and continued to hold until I was informed the left flank was exposed and enemy were moving to that flank. After checking with the 3d Battalion commander, Lt. Col. William P. Mouchet, and receiving an order to hold off, if it was at all possible that the 1st Platoon could remain in position, it became necessary between 0930 and 1000, due to the enemy flanking movement, to order their withdrawal back to the foot of the hill. From there they infiltrated back to the river. The river crossing was under fire. It was necessary to move in short dashes. One man was killed in crossing. We assembled all men and were told to await further orders.[11]

An artillery liaison officer at the 3d Battalion's observation post south of the Hant'an River, 1st Lt. Scott K. Cleage, provides the perspective from his location.

The first crossing on 11 April was made without incident. All three companies of the 3d Battalion went into position for the attack. There had been a radio blackout ordered by the 3d Battalion commander. At approximately 0700 hours we got our first report from the companies, which were meeting resistance. That was the first time we knew they were in trouble. At approximately 0900 we found out the companies had run into real trouble and had started pulling back to the crossing site. The terrain obscured the OP from the crossing site. The companies went down the river and came across in the Turkish Brigade area. At that time, Lieutenant Colonel Mouchet, the 3d Battalion commander, went down and took personal command. The companies were pretty well scattered out, and it took quite some time to reorganize them—in fact, the rest of the day.[12]

The 24th Infantry Regiment's executive officer, Lieutenant Colonel Coleman, summarizes the 3d Battalion's effort.

When the crossing was made, floodgates had been opened by the enemy, deepening the river two to three feet during the night. A cable was stretched across, and the 3d Battalion crossed at 0400 hours on 11 April, reaching its objective at 0645. Here the CCF woke up and drove Company L from Hill 463 and forced Companies I and K back with heavy losses, 240 men from the 3d Battalion being reported missing. The 3d Battalion recrossed to the south bank of the river and reorganized.[13]

The problems in the 3d Battalion's sector affected the 1st Battalion, as Major Baranowski, the 1st Battalion commanding officer, relates.

The 3d Battalion was in trouble and was unable to climb the ridge. At 1200 hours I crossed the river. No further orders came to the 1st Battalion until 1600, when the regimental commander directed that previous orders be disregarded and that Hill 642 be seized from the present initial bridgehead by frontal assault. A reconnaissance patrol, which was initiated for possible routes up the cliff, found the only suitable route on the west side on a ridgeline running north–south. I discussed the route with the regimental commander, pointing out that the right flank would be exposed, with the danger of no tenable defensive position at darkness. It was decided to move Company E to the right of the bridgehead in order to concentrate the entire 1st Battalion on the ridge. Company C was given the mission of blocking to the west to aid the 3d Battalion.[14]

Members of the 1st Battalion provide additional details of the events in their sector for the remainder of 11 April.

LIEUTENANT FREAS, COMPANY A: I was told to hold fast for the night. The company CP was on top of the initial objective. The S-3 ordered me at dark to send out a patrol to find the best route to the top. I called SFC Robinson and had him take ten men and go two fingers down along the river.

SFC ROBINSON, COMPANY A: I climbed about 300 yards, found a possible route, returned, and reported that a trail led up the hill.

LIEUTENANT FREAS, COMPANY A: I called the S-3 and told him of the trail and finger, which offered the best approach. I again requested ammunition, which arrived well after dark with the bedrolls. The men dug in and did not occupy the Chinese dugouts, which were full of dead and were flea infested. We remained there for the night. It rained during the night; the temperature was 40 degrees.[15]

CAPTAIN MAYO, COMPANY B: At 1400 hours the battalion commander ordered me to secure the hill. Company B moved up the ridge until it reached the rocks. I then tried the finger to the right and called the battalion commander, who ordered me to withdraw the company and reorganize. On 11 April, Company B had one killed and one wounded in action.[16]

MASTER SERGEANT GRAY, COMPANY C: The 1st Platoon joined the 2d and 3d Platoons in position for the night. The 2d Platoon lost five WIA and three to four others suffered from concussion grenades. There were ten to fifteen WIA in the company. After 1900–2000 hours Company C set up for the night, receiving an order to shift to the left flank of the 1st Battalion to replace Company B, which was moving forward. The 2d Platoon of Company C went to occupy a high hill with the company on one side. A sniper continued to toss grenades on the hill for half an hour. When an attempt to silence him with the 57mm recoilless rifle failed, a volunteer crew of six men reached his hole under covering fire and dropped some WP and HE grenades in the hole. After that Company C buttoned up for the night.[17]

During the day's fighting, Company B of the 89th Tank Battalion provided close support for the 1st Battalion. 1st Lt. Orval Belcher, the company commander, provides details of their part in the action.

At 0500 hours on 11 April the 1st Battalion, 24th Infantry Regiment, supported by Company B, 89th Tank Battalion, moved across the Hant'an River under cover of darkness so as to ensure the element of surprise. At the crack of dawn the fingers to the top of Hill 642 had been secured. Company B, 89th Tank Battalion, had the 1st Platoon on the right, the 3d Platoon in the center, and the 2d Platoon on the left. Tank firing started at 0500 when the infantry received the first shot. At 0600 the tanks started to fire at the top of Hill 642 on orders of the 1st Battalion commander. By 0800, the seventeen Sherman M4A3E8 tanks had fired their basic loads of 72 rounds per tank. I pulled the 1st Platoon back for resupply, and the 2d and 3d Platoons continued to fire. As soon as the 1st Platoon reloaded, it moved up on the left flank to support the 3d Battalion, which had started to attack at midnight. After having all platoons resupplied, the tanks continued to fire at the Chinese soldiers on the skyline. As the rounds hit the individual Chinese you could see them disintegrate. When Company B, 24th Infantry Regiment, got almost on top it started receiving grenades. Company B got in touch with the 2d Platoon of tanks for close support, which came within forty yards. At 1330 Company B ran into a reinforced pillbox in solid rock. The tanks used three rounds of AP to knock out the pillbox. As the Chinese troops left the pillbox they were destroyed with HE rounds from the tanks. Major Baranowski ordered Company B, 24th Infantry, to withdraw to the fingers. During the night the tanks were called on to fire on different targets. Moonbeam (searchlights) lighted the targets.[18]

During the night the 1st Battalion prepared to resume the attack the next day. The plan was for Company A to lead the assault, followed by Company B, with Company C remaining on the low ground.

Lieutenant Freas, the acting commander of Company A and the only officer left in the company, describes the attack on 12 April.

On 12 April we were up at 0600, ate chow at 0615, and moved out at 0700. I placed the 1st Platoon in the lead, followed by the 3d Platoon, company headquarters, then the 4th Platoon with the 2d Platoon bringing up the rear. At 0700 we were at the bottom of the knoll. The machine-gun section from Company D left for Company

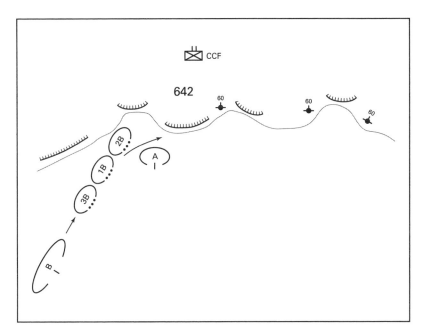

Assault on Hill 642 by Company B, 24th Infantry Regiment, 12 April 1951 (sketch based on Capt. Mayo interview in CMH manuscript, U.S. Army; not to scale).

B. The point for Company A, consisting of two men, went to the ridge and started up. I ordered the 2d Platoon to climb the next ridge to the left, which they did. SFC Robinson got one-third of the way up the hill when the going became slow. From there to halfway up, the trail was steep; from halfway to the top it was rocky. The men climbed hand-over-hand. A squad of the 3d Platoon was sent to the valley between the company and the 2d Platoon and began climbing a ridge that rose out of the valley forming a finger. At 0940–1000 hours, while we were approximately two-thirds or three-fourths of the way up, we received what was either machine-gun or automatic-weapons fire. Visual contact was lost with the 2d Platoon. The SCR 536 radio communication was poor. The 2d Platoon was receiving machine-gun fire from the right and left flanks. The BAR man returned the fire. An enemy machine gun was firing from the short valley finger. We brought a machine gun to the 1st Platoon to fire on the right flank, and the enemy firing stopped.

The 1st Platoon continued to move. I sent a runner to the 3d Platoon. The runner went twenty-five yards when a sniper fired at him. We failed to locate the sniper, and we left the trail and went to the right around the rocks. I ordered the 2d Platoon to get on top of the ridge. Company A continued up the finger, bearing to the right a hundred yards from the top. About ten hand grenades were then tossed at the lead men from concealed enemy positions from the right front. I got the rest of the 1st Platoon up and organized a group of five men to start toward the higher rocks. Automatic-rifle fire came from the direct front. The ground was gently sloping for fifty yards, and then became sheer. Part of the 3d Platoon started up the cut, and hand grenades rolled down on them. An enemy BAR pinned down the 1st Platoon, part of which withdrew in an attempt to climb around the rocks. The 1st Platoon machine gun set up to cover the next finger to the right from which we still received hand grenades, although we failed to see any CCF except a Chinese with a BAR. At 1500 hours another group of the 1st Platoon attempted to go around the rocks, and fifteen to twenty hand grenades fell on them. Better than half of the men withdrew to lower ground.

Company A continued to receive hand grenades despite friendly machine-gun fire. The SCR300 radio was lost. I ordered the tank fire from the rear stopped. The enemy machine gun on the right flank opened up again between 1515 and 1530. I picked up a violet smoke grenade to mark it and looked for the 536 radio operator, who was shot. He handed me the radio. I notified Captain Mayo, who relayed the message to the tanks to fire at the violet smoke. The tank fire did not silence the enemy. Corporal Cooper, an 81mm mortar observer, came up with an SCR300 radio, and I reestablished contact with the 1st Battalion. The 1st Battalion directed me to get the ground before dark. The 1st Platoon started up and was forced to withdraw by hand grenades. Corporal Cooper and I remained by the rocks. We saw a Chinese head in the rocks. The Chinese threw four hand grenades, three of which hit me, one in the face. I withdrew and ordered Master Sergeant Marshall, the 4th Platoon sergeant, to take over the company at 1630. The 2d Platoon was still off to the left, and if possible the rest of the company was to join them. Company B was seventy-five to one hundred yards below Company A. I returned down the hill, meeting Lieutenant Williams from Company B, who was climbing the hill to take over Company A. I then continued through Company B to the rear.[19]

Major Baranowski summarizes the situation and his decision. Company A led up the ridgeline followed by Company B. At nightfall Company A was barely on top, being held up by small-arms fire and hand grenades coming from the left of the 1st Battalion. That night the units of the 1st Battalion were pretty well beat up. Since the two officers with Company A were wounded, I sent an officer from Company B to command Company A and decided to pass Company B through Company A.[20]

Members of Company B describe their entry into the fight late on 12 April.

CAPTAIN MAYO: At 0700 hours on 12 April the 1st Battalion started up the mountain. Company A in front ran into small-arms and mortar fire 200 yards from the top, losing three killed and twenty-two wounded in action. The company commander, Lieutenant Freas, was wounded between 1600 and 1700 in the afternoon and evacuated. Company B lost a .50-caliber MG section, and Lieutenant Ford, the artillery forward observer, was hit at 1800 and evacuated. Since Company A was without an officer, Major Baranowski ordered me to send Lieutenant Williams to take over Company A at 2000 hours, the company being 200 yards from the top. "Joe" had holes on the top and was rolling down hand grenades. From two holes came automatic-weapons fire. The last peak had a mortar firing. I prepared defenses, pulling Company A around to make a 5th Platoon. Company A no longer had a radio. Major Baranowski said that Company C would move up from the bottom of the ridge and hook in with Company B's left flank. Small-arms and hand grenade firing continued until 0300 on 13 April.

SFC SMITH: We moved out across a dip and up the range, running one man at a time. Enemy small arms and automatic weapons slowed the advance and made control difficult. In the rear, one man was shot in the foot and one man in the breast. We took cover constantly. A 3.5 gunner fell fifteen feet down the mountain, when he was hit by a mortar blast. My goodness, we could hardly breathe around there. We placed a panel on the left side of the ridge where it could be seen by Company C. I ordered my platoon, "If you're not hit, move." I observed ten to fifteen Chinese moving to the west and south.

CAPTAIN MAYO: I had trouble seeing the enemy snipers.

SFC FITZGERALD: After bedding down, I was told by Captain Mayo to get a squad to the top. We started at 1800, meeting small arms and hand grenades. One hundred yards from the top the Chinese rolled hand grenades down, forcing the platoon to take cover under a rock. The hand grenades continued to come until 0300 to 0400, when all at once they stopped. Two enemy heavy .30-caliber machine guns were knocked out by tank fire at 1830 hours.

SERGEANT CAMPBELL: The squad was not able to reach the top of the hill that evening but went up the next morning.

CORPORAL LEWIS: The 3d Platoon, in rear of the 2d Platoon, set up for the night and received mortar fire.[21]

Meanwhile the rest of the 24th Infantry had been struggling to overcome the enemy opposition, but to no avail. Other members of the regiment describe their role in the fighting on 12 April.

LIEUTENANT COLONEL COLEMAN, EXECUTIVE OFFICER OF THE 24TH INFANTRY REGIMENT: At 0700 on 12 April the 3d Battalion jumped off for the second time. Prisoners said that an enemy regiment was in the area with a battalion extending from Hill 463 to Hill 642. The 3d Battalion was able to cross the river and form a line but could not knock the enemy off the hill. The CCF used mainly hand grenades in defending the hill, which had to be taken by frontal assault. About 2,300 rounds of artillery and 4.2-mortar fire had little effect except to pin down the enemy. The attitude of the Chinese was disdainful, as they walked the three- to five-feet-wide peak of Hill 463 for 300 meters all during the day. Artillery failed to knock them off. Finally at 1700 in the afternoon I placed tanks on them. The first CCF hit by a ricochet was knocked fifty feet in the air with a CCF radio on his back, and the rest scampered off the peak. However, they continued to feed reinforcements over the hill. The tanks also fired into bunkers on Hill 463. During the day the air OP spotted 400 to 500 Chinese on the north side of Hill 463. Three of the air strikes attacked this enemy concentration, dispersing it to the north. The air OP directed artillery VT-shell fire on the enemy concentration.[22]

MAJOR SWARTZ, S-3 OF THE 3D BATTALION, 24TH INFANTRY REGIMENT: The 3d Battalion jumped off at 0700 hours in the order Company I, Company L, and Company K. They reached within thirty-five to forty yards of the top, running into periodic machine-gun and mortar fire. Enemy fire periodically interdicted the crossing. We advanced to Hill 463. Small-arms and automatic-weapons fire pinned down the 3d Battalion despite continued effort by air strikes and artillery support. A patrol from Company L led by Lieutenant Ames reached a position fifteen yards from the top only to be repulsed by CCF standing on the top throwing hand grenades. Because of casualties and failure to take the hill, the 3d Battalion was ordered to withdraw on 12 April.[23]

LIEUTENANT CLEAGE, ARTILLERY LIAISON OFFICER WITH THE 3D BATTALION: On D+1 [12 April] the attack jumped off at 0600 hours at the same crossing site. The attack was launched behind a fifteen-minute artillery preparation. The crossing was made under light enemy fire. Companies I and K made the crossing. The approach to the high ground was made, and they had started to ascend when they got their first enemy fire from automatic weapons and small arms. The advance was very slow. The peak of Hill 463 was kept under constant artillery fire, mostly VT. From my OP we could observe enemy activity in an estimated two-company strength. By approximately 1200 hours the enemy resistance had stiffened to the extent that all companies were pinned down. Between 1400 and 1500 I called for a second preparation of fifteen minutes with two battalions, 600 rounds, intense fire. The infantry advanced beautifully in close coordination with the artillery. By 1600 they had advanced to within seventy-five yards of the highest peak. At that time I was told to cease fire because of the proximity of troops. I observed the Chinese on the top throwing hand grenades. That intense grenade dropping by fifty Chinese continued until dusk at 1700. The Chinese were constantly under heavy fire from our 75mm and 57mm recoilless rifles and our heavy machine guns, but they still continued to fight. At 1645 the 3d Battalion commander was ordered to pull back and button up across the river for the evening. At that time I was requested to give covering fire for the orderly withdrawal, which I did. The troops went into their original positions.[24]

Lieutenant Belcher, the commander of Company B, 89th Tank Battalion, describes his unit's role in fighting on 12 April and the plan for the following day.

At dawn the next morning [12 April] I was told to lay down a twenty-minute preparation, and the 1st Battalion jumped off, fighting all day. The 2d and 3d Tank Platoons crossed the river during the day. The 1st Battalion jumped off to go to the top. The CCF reinforced the top from the north along the ridgeline. Company A got to the top and called for close tank support. All men in Company A crouched when a round was fired. The 1st Battalion on the second day held a small outpost on top of the hill and split the hill.

The second night [12–13 April], I received orders to send the 1st Platoon through the Turk area to support the 3d Battalion. The next morning I called the 1st Platoon back to support the 1st Battalion. All three tank platoons were now across the Hant'an. The order was for the tanks to jump down the valley the next morning [13 April]. The 2d Battalion was to go up the right ridge, the 1st Battalion was to go up in the center, and the 3d Battalion was to move up on the left.[25]

The 24th Infantry's main attack on 13 April was with the 1st Battalion in the center, led by Company B. Members of the unit describe their role in the fighting.

CAPTAIN MAYO: I ordered Company A to come down and Company B to continue, with the 3d Platoon leading. I sent Company A to neutralize fire on the left and to contact the 3d Battalion. SFC Fitzgerald went up ahead, climbing rocks and moving a hundred yards up the ridge. Here the 2d Platoon halted, and the 3d Platoon went through to the next peak fifty yards distant, where small-arms fire was coming from an enemy emplacement. The 1st Platoon bazooka and the 57mm recoilless rifle fired on the emplacement. Two squads went into a plateau.

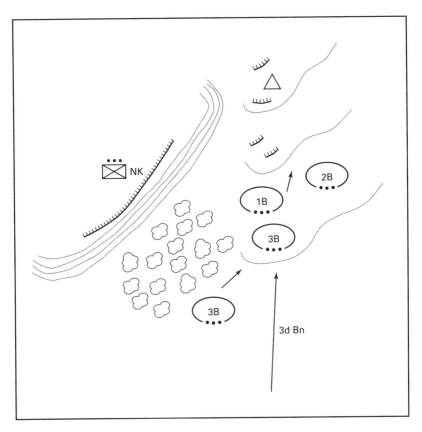

Assault on Hill 642 by Company B, 24th Infantry Regiment, 13 April 1951 (sketch based on Capt. Mayo interview in CMH manuscript, U.S. Army; not to scale).

SFC SMITH: I took a squad at 1000 hours and went along the left of the ridge, crawling, and captured the emplacements. The Chinese held fire until the squad got close. PFC Swanson killed two Chinese, and other members of the 3d Platoon killed three, one being killed while setting off a bangalore torpedo.

CAPTAIN MAYO: The 3d Battalion moved up at 1500, taking over the old Company B positions. When Company B was pinned down by fire from a ridge to the northwest, a machine gun from Company K opened up on the enemy. Lieutenant Newhouse set up an OP.

LIEUTENANT NEWHOUSE: I established an OP near the top of

Hill 643 at 1200 hours. Company B was receiving heavy automatic-weapons and mortar fire from a ridge about 300 yards to the northwest. I picked up two machine-gun emplacements and four 60mm mortar positions and brought artillery fire using delay fuze and WP. This silenced the automatic-weapons and mortar fire. When the battery would fire, the platoon covering me would fire all weapons so I could rise up and observe the fire.

SERGEANT CAMPBELL: I came up a hundred yards with a squad.

SFC SMITH: Moving up the ridge in a dispersed formation, the squad bypassed Chinese. They returned to kill three, and then moved forward up the ridge.

CAPTAIN MAYO: At 1600 we were held up, getting nowhere. The 3d Platoon reached the last rock before the top of the hill. The 2d Platoon deployed to the rear. The 1st Platoon moved to the right flank. In the final action, the 57mm recoilless rifle and the 3.5-inch rocket launcher were brought up. SFC Fitzgerald on the left was pinned down. The 2d Platoon was on the right.

LIEUTENANT NEWHOUSE: We couldn't use artillery on the top. It was too close. PFC Swanson closed with the enemy with hand grenades.

CAPTAIN MAYO: I yelled, "Squad who takes the top will get a five-gallon tin of water." Men ran up the trail; nine in the 1st Squad of the 3d Platoon ran to the top at 1755. SFC Fitzgerald's platoon gave covering fire. PFC Swanson closed with the enemy with hand grenades. Overhead fire by Corporal Carey Lewis ended the day's action. Company B set up defenses but could not make contact with the 2d Battalion because of one ridge. The next morning, Company B moved downhill and contacted the 2d Battalion.

PFC WOODWARD: After SFC Smith got hit, I was told to bring up a BAR and a 3.5-inch rocket launcher. I laid down a base of fire. A machine gun came up between 1630–1730 hours. We had been promised some water for going across the knoll. We got the water.

CAPTAIN MAYO: Company B suffered three killed and forty-four wounded in action and evacuated.

LIEUTENANT NEWHOUSE: Company B was full of initiative, down to the privates.[26]

Major Baranowski summarizes the 1st Battalion's fight on 13 April.

The pack train of fifty native packers moved up at 0400, carrying ammunition in sufficient time for the attack. Company B passed through Company A at 0630, making a junction with the 2d Battalion at 1000. Meanwhile, Company A moved up behind Company B, blocking to the west along the ridge, with Company C on fingers by the river moving to the west and contacting the 3d Battalion. The end of organized resistance on Hill 642 by the enemy occurred at 1100 hours.

During the movement on the ridge, the 1st Battalion used 4.2-inch mortars, 81mm mortars, and 3.5-inch rocket launchers firing in front of the lead elements. There was good communication by radio and wire. The .50-caliber AAA tracks fired under the tank commander. Friendly losses were eight killed and ninety-two wounded in action, mostly by fragmentation grenades. Enemy losses were six captured, fifty KIA (counted), and one hundred KIA (estimated).[27]

On the left, the 3d Battalion crossed the river for the third time and advanced up Hill 463 against light opposition. The hill was secured about 1000 hours, and the 3d Battalion pushed eastward to Hill 642 and joined the 1st Battalion. On the right, the 2d Battalion also moved up Hill 642 to link up with the other two battalions. With the Chinese defenses along the Hant'an finally broken, the 24th Infantry Regiment continued its advance slowly to the north in step with other units of the 25th Infantry Division toward the objectives for Operation Dauntless.

CONCLUSION

UN forces continued to push north as Operation Dauntless unfolded. In the 25th Infantry Division sector, the 24th Infantry Regiment, flanked by the Turkish Brigade on the left and the 27th Infantry Regiment on the right, gained the Pogae-san high ground south of Ch'orwan after crossing the Hant'an River. To their east, the 24th Infantry Division of I Corps and the 6th ROK and 1st Marine Divisions of IX Corps kept pace. The enemy offered sporadic resistance and fell back before the UN advance.

The beginning of Operation Dauntless on 11 April also saw important changes in the UN command structure in the Far East. Gen. MacArthur had not quietly accepted President Truman's restrictions on the conduct of the Korean War. MacArthur voiced his concerns to the press, timing his comments to ensure the maximum disruption of a peace initiative by Washington directed at the Chinese Communists. Additionally, MacArthur wrote a letter outlining his criticisms of administration policy to Congressman Joseph Martin, the House Minority Leader. When Martin read the letter on the floor of the House of Representatives on 5 April, Truman decided that MacArthur must go. Secretary of Defense George C. Marshall and Chairman of the Joint Chiefs of Staff, Gen. Omar Bradley, recommended that MacArthur be replaced by Ridgway and that Lt. Gen. James A. Van Fleet become the Eighth Army commander. Communication interruptions botched the carefully arranged timing of the announcement of the relief, and MacArthur was informed that he had been fired through a news broadcast the afternoon of 11

April. Ridgway, touring the front lines, received the news late on 11 April and, the next day, flew to Japan for a quick meeting with MacArthur. Ridgway then returned to Korea to oversee Operation Dauntless until Van Fleet's arrival on 14 April.

Gen. Van Fleet was an experienced combat veteran. He commanded a machine-gun battalion in World War I in the Meuse-Argonne offensive, and in World War II he led an infantry regiment ashore on Utah Beach on D-day. Within nine months of the Normandy landings, he rose to corps command, an astoundingly rapid rise in rank. After the war, as commander of the U.S. Joint Military Advisory and Planning Group in Greece, he oversaw the defeat of a Communist insurgency and the creation of a modern Greek army. The situation that he faced upon his arrival in Korea was unsettled, but he was confident of dealing with it.

Ridgway's limited offensives, launched in January 1951, had not only regained most of South Korea and crossed the 38th parallel back into North Korea, but the successful operations had also done much to restore the confidence and fighting spirit of the UN forces. The gains, however, could be deceptive, for the enemy had conducted a skillful delaying action while continuing his buildup for a renewed offensive. Repeated UN attempts to trap significant portions of enemy forces failed. The Chinese and North Koreans' tactics emphasized defending the rugged terrain in order to force the UN into costly assaults, while stalling pursuit and disrupting supply operations with liberal use of mines. The harsh weather, rugged terrain, and lack of roads combined to assist the enemy. The future fighting ability of the ROK army units, which had been the prime target for previous Communist attacks, remained a great unknown.

Ridgway turned over command to Van Fleet late on 14 April 1951. The only restriction Ridgway placed on Van Fleet was that he must gain permission before advancing north of the combined Wyoming and Kansas Lines, the designated objective lines for Operation Dauntless. Otherwise Van Fleet would operate under the same guidelines in Korea as Ridgway had: namely, that the objective of combat operations was to inflict high losses on the enemy while keeping UN losses to a minimum, and that substantial reinforcements should not be expected. The war would remain limited, both in scope and in United States resources committed to the effort.

Van Fleet immediately undertook an inspection tour of the units of his new command. Reflecting his recognition of the need to improve the effectiveness of the ROK army, but also stemming from his recent experience in Greece in a similar effort, he first visited the ROK sector in the eastern part of Korea. Although he found that there was little enemy activity in the area, he learned firsthand the supply problems in Korea when he saw that one entire ROK division was being supplied by air and carrying parties because of a lack of roads. To the west, the U.S. X Corps was consolidating along Line Kansas after the opposition in their front had disappeared in mid-April. Patrols north of Line Kansas found no significant enemy forces. West of the Hwach'on Reservoir, IX Corps was advancing north of Line Kansas to connect with Line Utah along the I Corps boundary, but here too there was a noticeable absence of enemy forces in strength. In I Corps, the 25th Infantry Division was nearing Line Utah about five miles south of Ch'orwon, but in this area immediately south of the Iron Triangle, resistance was stiffer. West of the 25th Division, the rest of I Corps manned defensive positions stretching along the Imjin River to its junction with the Han River northwest of Seoul.

Intelligence reports indicated that enemy offensive preparations were nearing completion, and although an attack could be expected at any time, there was no sign of major enemy forces moving forward into attack positions. Van Fleet suspected that the enemy might be trying to lure the UN forces into a trap, but he directed that Operation Dauntless continue on 21 April in the I Corps and IX Corps sector to Line Wyoming on the southern edge of the Iron Triangle.

The UN advance on 21 April again failed to encounter large enemy forces. On 22 April, ROK Marines captured the Hwach'on Dam that had earlier frustrated the efforts of the 1st Cavalry Division. But on the same day, across the front, captured enemy soldiers from newly arrived units indicated that the Chinese and North Koreans were moving forward for their expected attack. Aerial reconnaissance quickly identified the forward shift of the enemy, but air attacks failed to stop the troop movements. Warnings were sent to UN forces, and soon after sunset, under a full moon, the enemy launched their long-awaited assault. The question of how the UN forces would withstand the heavy attacks of their well-prepared foe was soon to be answered.

NOTES

1. Korea and the Cold War World

1. For more detail on events covered in this chapter, the following may be consulted: William T. Bowers, *The Line: Combat in Korea, January–February 1951* (Lexington: University Press of Kentucky, 2008); Bevin Alexander, *Korea: The First War We Lost* (New York: Hippocrene, 2000); Roy E. Appleman, *Ridgway Duels for Korea* (College Station: Texas A&M University Press, 1990); Clay Blair, *The Forgotten War* (New York: Doubleday, 1987); William T. Bowers, William M. Hammond, George L. MacGarrigle, *Black Soldier, White Army: The 24th Infantry Regiment in Korea* (Washington, D.C.: U.S. Army Center of Military History, 1996); Albert E. Cowdrey, *The Medics' War* (Washington, D.C.: U.S. Army Center of Military History, 1987); T. R. Fehrenbach, *This Kind of War: A Study in Unpreparedness* (New York: Macmillan, 1962); Steven Hugh Lee, *The Korean War,* Seminar Studies in History (Harlow, England: Pearson Education Limited, 2001); David Halberstam, *The Coldest Winter: America and the Korean War* (New York: Hyperion, 2007); Kenneth E. Hamburger, *Leadership in the Crucible: The Korean War Battles of Twin Tunnels and Chipyong-ni* (College Station: Texas A&M University Press, 2003); Spencer C. Tucker, ed., *Encyclopedia of the Korean War* (New York: Checkmark Books/Facts on File, 2002); and Stanley Sandler, *The Korean War: An Encyclopedia* (New York: Garland, 1995). The most comprehensive account of U.S. Army military operations during these months is Billy C. Mossman, *Ebb and Flow, November 1950–July 1951* (Washington, D.C.: U.S. Army Center of Military History, 1990), while the overall UN and U.S. strategy in Korea is covered in James F. Schnabel, *Policy and Direction: The First Year* (Washington, D.C.: U.S. Center of Military History, 1972).

For the personal perspective of the new commanding general, Eighth U.S. Army, on the challenges and plans after he assumed command late in December 1950, see Gen. Matthew B. Ridgway's *The Korean War* (Garden City, N.Y.: Doubleday, 1967). Gen. J. Lawton Collins provides his views as the Army Chief of Staff and member of the Joint Chiefs of Staff during these trying days in his *War in Peacetime: The History and Lessons of Korea* (Boston: Houghton Mifflin, 1969). Gen. Omar Bradley, then the chairman of the Joint Chiefs of Staff, was intimately involved in the high-level decisions, which are laid out in Omar N. Bradley and Clay Blair, *A General's Life* (New York: Simon and Schuster, 1983), especially pp. 569–663. D. Clayton James covers the actions of Gen. Douglas MacArthur in the third volume of his biography, *The Years of MacArthur*, vol. 3: *Triumph and Disaster, 1945–1964* (Boston: Houghton Mifflin Company, 1985), pp. 518–604. *Memoirs by Harry S. Truman*, vol. 2: *Years of Trial and Hope* (Garden City, N.Y.: Doubleday, 1956), provides the president's views on all aspects of the Korean War.

The South Korean experiences in the war can be found in the three volumes compiled by the Institute of Military History of the Republic of Korea's Ministry of National Defense, *The Korean War* (Lincoln: University of Nebraska Press, 2000–2001). A very personal view of these years is found in the memoirs of South Korean Gen. Paik Sun Yup, *From Pusan to Panmunjom: Wartime Memoirs of the Republic of Korea's First Four-Star General* (Washington: Brassey's, 1992).

For Soviet, Chinese Communist, and North Korean perspectives, see Sergei N. Goncharov, John W. Lewis, and Xue Litai, *Uncertain Partners: Stalin, Mao, and the Korean War* (Stanford, Calif.: Stanford University Press, 1993); Xiaoming Zhang, *Red Wings over the Yalu: China, the Soviet Union, and the Air War in Korea* (College Station: Texas A&M University Press, 2002); Xiaobing Li, *A History of the Modern Chinese Army* (Lexington: University Press of Kentucky, 2007); Xiaobing Li, Allan R. Millett, and Bin Yu, trans. and eds., *Mao's Generals Remember Korea* (Lawrence: University Press of Kansas, 2001); Shu Guang Zhang, *Mao's Military Romanticism: China and the Korean War, 1950–1953* (Lawrence: University Press of Kansas, 1995); and Russell Spurr, *Enter the Dragon: China's Undeclared War against the U.S. in Korea, 1950–51* (New York: Newmarket Press, 1988).

2. For the best study of the Fiscal Year 1950 defense budget debate, see the classic account by Warner R. Schilling, "The Politics of National Defense: Fiscal 1950," in Warner R. Schilling, Paul Y. Ham-

mond, and Glenn H. Snyder, eds., *Strategy, Politics, and Defense Budgets* (New York: Columbia University Press, 1962), pp. 5–266.

3. In addition to the United States, the following provided combat troops: United Kingdom, Canada, Turkey, Australia, New Zealand, France, Belgium, Colombia, Ethiopia, Greece, Netherlands, Philippines, Thailand, and Luxembourg; medical support was provided by India, Denmark, Italy, Norway, and Sweden. See Tucker, *Encyclopedia of the Korean War*, p. 681.

4. The connection between NSC 68 and the military buildup following the beginning of the Korean conflict has been covered in a number of sources. One of the most recent is David T. Fautua, "The 'Long Pull' Army: NSC 68, the Korean War, and the Creation of the Cold War U.S. Army," *The Journal of Military History* 61 (January 1997), pp. 1, 93–120. See also Ernest R. May, *American Cold War Strategy: Interpreting NSC 68* (New York: Bedford Books, 1993). Older but still useful works are Paul Y. Hammond, "NSC-68: Prologue to Rearmament," in Schilling, Hammond, and Snyder, eds., *Strategy, Politics, and Defense Budgets*, pp. 267–378; Samuel P. Huntington, "NSC 68 and Rearmament, 1950–1952," in *The Common Defense: Strategic Programs in National Politics* (New York: Columbia University Press, 1961), pp. 47–64; and Stephen E. Ambrose, *Rise to Globalism* (New York: Penguin, 1976).

5. For more details on Ridgway's sudden assignment to Korea and meeting with MacArthur in Tokyo, see Ridgway's *The Korean War*, pp. 79–83.

6. Schnabel, *Policy and Direction: The First Year*, pp. 294–295, 298–300, 310–314; Mossman, *Ebb and Flow*, pp. 230–237; Bradley, *A General's Life*, p. 612; Truman, *Years of Trial and Hope*, pp. 386, 419, 432–433, 436.

7. Rad, C 53167, MacArthur for JCS, 10 January 1951, as quoted in Schnabel, *Policy and Direction*, p. 322.

8. Schnabel, *Policy and Direction*, pp. 325–330; Mossman, *Ebb and Flow*, pp. 230–237.

9. Cowdrey, *The Medics' War*, p. 156; see also Alexander, *Korea: The First War We Lost*, p. 396.

10. Mossman, *Ebb and Flow*, pp. 234–235; Ridgway, *The Korean War*, pp. 90–91; Collins, *War in Peacetime*, p. 257.

11. Cowdrey, *The Medics' War*, pp. 325–326. In May 1951, following the greatest disruptions from the North Korean invasion in the summer of 1950 and the Chinese intervention in late 1950, the estimate was 4.5 million displaced persons in South Korea.

2. Grenade Hill

1. Narrative, Capt. Pierce W. Briscoe, Ms. 8–5.1A BA 15, Grenade Hill, CMH.

2. Interview, Capt. Freemont B. Hodson Jr., with Capt. Pierce W. Briscoe, 22 July 1951, Ms. 8–5.1A BA 15, CMH. Capt. Pierce W. Briscoe also conducted all of the remaining interviews in this chapter, which are found in Ms. 15, CMH.

3. Interview, 1st Lt. Jack D. Thomas, 22 July 1951.

4. Interview, 1st Lt. James F. Greer, 22 July 1951.

5. Interview, Thomas, 22 July 1951.

6. Interviews, Sgt. Thomas G. Cline, Cpl. Lawrence D. Swift, and SFC Clyde J. Ging, 22 July 1951.

7. Quad 50 and twin 40 were antiaircraft weapons used for infantry support. The quad 50 was an M-16 half-track (armored vehicle with wheels in the front and tracks in the rear) mounting four .50-caliber machine guns that could be fired simultaneously. The twin 40 was the M-19 tracked vehicle (light tank chassis) mounting two Bofors 40mm automatic cannon.

8. Interview, Hodson, 22 July 1951.

9. The SCR300, an FM radio with a range of 1–3 miles and weight of 40 pounds, was used to communicate between company and battalion.

10. Interview, Thomas, 22 July 1951.

11. Interview, Greer, 22 July 1951.

12. Interviews, Cline, Swift, and Ging, 22 July 1951.

13. Interview, Thomas, 22 July 1951.

14. Interviews, SFC Santos L. Alecea, Sgt. Jimmy R. Hintz, and Cpl. Archie W. Fowler, 22 July 1951.

15. Interviews, SFC Don R. LeSieur, Cpl. Richard H. Neihardt, and Cpl. Joe W. Powell, 22 July 1951.

16. The SCR536 radio, a short-range (1 mile) AM radio weighing about 10 pounds, was used to communicate between platoons and company headquarters.

17. Interview, Greer, 22 July 1951.

18. Interviews, LeSieur, Neihardt, and Powell, 22 July 1951.

19. Interviews, Alecea, Hintz, and Fowler, 22 July 1951.

20. Interviews, Cline, Swift, and Ging, 22 July 1951.

21. Interview, Greer, 22 July 1951.

22. Interview, Hodson, 22 July 1951.

23. Interview, Greer, 22 July 1951.

24. Interviews, Alecea, Hintz, and Fowler, 22 July 1951.

25. Interviews, Cline, Swift, and Ging, 22 July 1951.

26. Interview, Thomas, 22 July 1951.

27. Interview, Hodson, 22 July 1951.

28. Interviews, LeSieur, Neihardt, and Powell, 22 July 1951.

29. Interview, Hodson, 22 July 1951.

30. Interviews, LeSieur, Neihardt, and Powell, 22 July 1951; casualties for Company L are from interview, Greer, 22 July 1951.

3. Breaking the Hongch'on Defense Line

1. Interview, Maj. Charles J. Parziale with 1st Lt. Martin Blumenson, 7 April 1951, Ms. 8–5.1A BA 30, Breaking the Hongch'on Defense Line, CMH. Lt. Blumenson also conducted the remaining interviews in this chapter, which are found in Ms. 30 at CMH.

2. Interview, Capt. Robert J. Cook, 5 April 1951.

3. Interview, Parziale, 7 April 1951.

4. Interview, Capt. James V. Marsh, 5 April 1951.

5. Interview, Capt. Edward R. Stevens, 7 April 1951.

6. Interview, Parziale, 7 April 1951.

7. Ibid.

8. Interview, Marsh, 5 April 1951.

9. Ibid.

10. 1st Lt. Alma G. Longstroth, S-2, 3d Battalion, 5th Cavalry Regiment, Evaluation of Enemy Positions on Song-chi Mountain and Its Southern Slopes, 4 April 1951, in Ms. 8–5.1A BA 30, CMH.

11. Interview, Parziale, 7 April 1951.

12. Interview, Marsh, 5 April 1951.

13. Interview, Capt. R. M. Lohela, 6 April 1951.

14. Interview, Cook, 5 April 1951.

15. Interview, Parziale, 7 April 1951.

16. Interview, Lohela, 6 April 1951.

17. Interview, Parziale, 7 April 1951.

18. Interview, Cook, 5 April 1951.

19. Interview, 1st Lt. James W. Kent, 5 April 1951.

20. Interview, Cook, 5 April 1951.

21. Interview, 1st Sgt. George M. Baker, 6 April 1951.

22. Interview, Cook, 5 April 1951.

23. Interviews, Marsh (5 April 1951), Lohela (6 April 1951), and Cook (5 April 1951).

24. Interviews, Lohela (6 April 1951), Cook (5 April 1951), Marsh (5 April 1951), and Parziale (7 April 1951).

25. Interview, Lohela, 6 April 1951.

26. Interviews, Parziale and Stevens, both 7 April 1951.

27. Extract, S2-S3 Journal, 3d Battalion, 5th Cavalry Regiment, Entry for 2120 hours, 18 March 1951 in Ms. 8–5.1A BA 30, CMH.

28. Interview, Cook, 5 April 1951.

29. Interview, Stevens, 7 April 1951.

30. Interviews, Stevens (7 April 1951), Lohela (6 April 1951), Longstroth (7 April 1951), and Parziale (7 April 1951).

31. Interview, Maj. Charles E. Harris, 9 April 1951.

32. Interview, Lt. Col. Robert J. Natzel, 10 April 1951.

4. Supporting the Attack

1. Interview, Maj. Charles E. Harris with 1st Lt. Martin Blumenson, 9 April 1951, Ms. 8–5.1A BA 30, CMH. Lt. Blumenson also conducted the remaining interviews in this chapter, which are contained in Ms. 30 at CMH.

2. Interview, Maj. James M. Gibson, 8 April 1951.

3. Interview, 1st Lt. Henry S. Watcke, 7 April 1951.

4. Interview, WOJG Jimmie D. Spencer, 7 April 1951.

5. Interview, 1st Sgt. Arnold E. Mitchell, 7 April 1951.

6. Interview, WOJG Thomas J. Sherman, 6 April 1951.

7. Interview, 1st Lt. James W. Kent, 6 April 1951.

8. Interview, CWO Clarence J. Umberger, 6 April 1951.

9. Interview, SFC Carl P. Michael, 6 April 1951.

10. Interviews, LtJG Robert M. Adams and 1st Lt. Bill T. Wilson, both 5 April 1951.

11. Interviews, PFCs J. C. Weston and Vern Tidwell, both 5 April 1951.

5. Operation Tomahawk

1. Interview, Col. George H. Gerhart with Capt. William T. Crawford Jr., 8 April 1951, Ms. 8–5.1A BA 1, Operation Tomahawk, CMH. The remaining interviews in this chapter are also from Ms. 1 at CMH.

2. Interview, Maj. Raymond H. Ross with Capt. William T. Crawford Jr., 12 April 1951.

3. Interview, Lt. Col. Thomas H. Lane with Capt. William T. Crawford Jr., 10 April 1951.

4. Narrative Report, Capt. Edward C. Williamson, Book II, Operation Tomahawk, 22–29 March 1951, in Ms. 8–5.1A BA 1, Operation Tomahawk, CMH.

5. Interview, Gerhart with Crawford, 8 April 1951.

6. Interview, Ross with Crawford, 12 April 1951.

7. Appendix A (Intelligence Estimate) to Annex 1 to OPLAN 7, 674th Airborne FA Battalion, 21 March 1951 in Ms. 8–5.1A BA 1, Operation Tomahawk, CMH.

8. Appendix B (Tactical Study of Terrain and Weather) to Annex 1 to OPLAN 7, 674th Airborne FA Battalion, 21 March 1951 in Ms. 8–5.1A BA 1, Operation Tomahawk, CMH.

9. Interview, Lt. Col. Harry F. Lambert with Capt. Edward C. Williamson, 8 April 1951.

10. Interview, Maj. Joseph E. Jenkins with Capt. William T. Crawford Jr., 11 April 1951.

11. Interview, Lane with Crawford, 10 April 1951.

12. Interview, Capt. Alvin Ash with Capt. William T. Crawford Jr., 12 April 1951.

13. Interview, Maj. Thomas P. Mulvey with Capt. William T. Crawford Jr., 8 April 1951.

14. Interview, Capt. Charles E. Weddle with Capt. William T. Crawford Jr., 8 April 1951.

15. Interview, Gerhart with Crawford, 8 April 1951.

16. Interview, Lt. Col. J. P. Connor with Capt. Edward C. Williamson, 12 April 1951.

17. Interview, M. Sgt. Yen Chin Chow with Capt. Edward C. Williamson, 11 April 1951.

18. Interview, Capt. Dorsey B. Anderson with 1st Lt. Martin Blumenson, 14 April 1951.

19. Interview, Mulvey with Crawford, 8 April 1951.

20. Interview, SFC Adasius Karwasa with Capt. Edward C. Williamson, 16 April 1951.

21. Interview, Maj. Vernon W. Froelich with Capt. William T. Crawford Jr., 9 April 1951.

22. Interview, Maj. Charles M. Holland with Capt. Edward C. Williamson, 13 April 1951.

23. Interview, Gerhart with Crawford, 8 April 1951.

24. Interview, 1st Lt. Leo R. Gulick with Capt. Edward C. Williamson, 14 April 1951.

25. Interview, Maj. Ronald C. Speirs with Capt. Edward C. Williamson, 12 April 1951.

26. Interview, Sgt. Charles P. McDonald with Capt. Edward C. Williamson, 10 April 1951.

27. Interview, 2d Lt. Melvin C. Strawser with Capt. Edward C. Williamson, 11 April 1951.

28. Interview, 2d Lt. Everett Mackley with Capt. Edward C. Williamson, 11 April 1951.

29. Interview, M. Sgt. Neal A. Perkins with Capt. Edward C. Williamson, 11 April 1951.

30. Interview, Capt. John E. Strever Jr., with Capt. Edward C. Williamson, 11 April 1951.

31. Interview, 1st Lt. Edward F. Gernette with Capt. Edward C. Williamson, 11 April 1951.

32. Interview, Capt. Thomas J. Watkins with Capt. Edward C. Williamson, 12 April 1951.

33. Interview, Capt. Robert A. Chabot with Capt. Edward C. Williamson, 13 April 1951.

34. Interview, PFC William Coker with Capt. Edward C. Williamson, 13 April 1951.

35. Interview, 1st Lt. James E. Hanlin with Capt. Edward C. Williamson, 14 April 1951.

36. Interviews, Sgts. Walter E. Chaney, Robert J. Wotherspoon, and Percy L. McDaniel with Capt. Edward C. Williamson, 13 April 1951.

37. Interview, Capt. Daniel L. Melvin with Capt. Edward C. Williamson, 10 April 1951.

38. Interview, Cpl. Norman I. Fullerton with Capt. Edward C. Williamson, 10 April 1951.

39. Interview, Capt. Rolland A. Dessert with Capt. Edward C. Williamson, 10 April 1951.

40. Interview, Gerhart with Crawford, 8 April 1951.

41. The SCR619 radio is an artillery version of the SCR300.

42. Interview, Weddle with Crawford, 8 April 1951.

43. Interview, Holland with Williamson, 13 April 1951.

44. Interview, 1st Lt. Jesmond D. Balmer with Capt. Edward C. Williamson, 9 April 1951.

45. Interview, 1st Lt. James E. Hanlin with Capt. Edward C. Williamson, 14 April 1951.

46. Interviews, Chaney, Wotherspoon, and McDaniel with Williamson, 13 April 1951.

47. Interview, Holland with Williamson, 13 April 1951.

48. Interview, Connor with Williamson, 14 April 1951.

49. Interview, 2d Lt. Edward J. Whelan with Capt. Edward C. Williamson, 14 April 1951.

50. Interview, SFC George G. Lane with Capt. Edward C. Williamson, 14 April 1951.

51. Interview, 1st Lt. Rudy V. Paraiso with Capt. Edward C. Williamson, 15 April 1951.

52. Interviews, 1st Lt. Donald L. Roberts, SFC Ross C. Duncan, and SFC Raymond Morris with Capt. Edward C. Williamson, 15 April 1951.

53. Interview, 1st Lt. Jack W. Von Steiegel with Capt. Edward C. Williamson, 16 April 1951.

54. Interview, 1st Lt. J. L. Beasley with Capt. Edward C. Williamson, 15 April 1951.

55. Interview, Jenkins with Crawford, 11 April 1951.

56. Letter, Maj. Burnside E. Hoffman to Commanding Officer, 674th Airborne FA Battalion, 8 April 1951, Subj. Parachute Operation Munsan-ni, 23 March 1951 in Ms. 8–5.1A BA 1, Operation Tomahawk, CMH.

57. Interview, Lane with Crawford, 10 April 1951.

58. Interview, Mulvey with Crawford, 8 April 1951.

59. Interview, Lambert with Williamson, 8 April 1951.

60. Interview, Capt. Bertram K. Gorwitz with Capt. Edward C. Williamson, 15 April 1951.

61. Interview, Karwasa with Williamson, 16 April 1951.

62. Interview, Ross with Crawford, 12 April 1951.

63. Interview, Anderson with Blumenson, 14 April 1951.

64. Interview, 1st Lt. George H. Lehmer with Capt. Edward C. Williamson, 12 April 1951.

6. Task Force Growdon

1. Narrative Report, Capt. Edward C. Williamson, Task Force Growdon, 21–27 March 1951, Ms. 8–5.1A BA 63, Task Force Growdon, CMH.

2. Interview, SFC Daniel Crough with Capt. Edward C. Williamson, 3 April 1951, Ms. 8–5.1A BA 63, Task Force Growdon, CMH. Unless otherwise noted, Capt. Williamson also conducted the other interviews in this chapter, which are contained in Ms. 63 at CMH.

3. Interview, Capt. Joseph F. Landers, 3 April 1951.

4. Interview, CWO Michael Pineda, 3 April 1951.

5. Interview, 1st Lt. Arthur Keeley, 3 April 1951.

6. Narrative Report, Capt. Williamson, Ms. 63, CMH.

7. Interview, Capt. Jack G. Moss, 3 April 1951.

8. Interview, M. Sgt. Billy M. Skiles, 20 April 1951.

9. Interview, SFC Laverne Cordry, 20 April 1951.

10. Interview, Moss, 3 April 1951.

11. Interview, Skiles, 20 April 1951.

12. Summary of Operations, Task Force Growdon, 211340 March to 271200 March, 271200 March 1951, in Ms. 8–5.1A BA 63, CMH.

13. Interview, Maj. Thomas Cleary, 30 March 1951.

14. Interview, Moss, 3 April 1951.

15. Interview, 1st Lt. Robert H. Turner, 31 March 1951.

16. Interview, Moss, 3 April 1951.

17. Interview, Keeley, 3 April 1951.

18. Narrative Report, Capt. Williamson, Ms. 63, CMH.

19. Summary of Operations, Task Force Growdon, 271200 March 1951, in Ms. 63, CMH.

20. Interview, 1st Lt. James McNiff, 31 March 1951.

21. Summary of Operations, Task Force Growdon, 271200 March 1951, in Ms. 63, CMH.

22. Interview, Keeley, 3 April 1951.

23. Interview, Maj. Joseph E. Jenkins with Capt. William T. Crawford Jr., 11 April 1951, Ms. 8–5.1A BA 1, Operation Tomahawk, CMH.

24. Interview, Lt. Col. Thomas H. Lane with Capt. William T. Crawford Jr., 10 April 1951, Ms. 8–5.1A BA 1, Operation Tomahawk, CMH.

7. The Advance East

1. Interview, Capt. Charles E. Weddle with Capt. William T. Crawford Jr., 8 April 1951, Ms. 8–5.1A BA 1, Operation Tomahawk, CMH. Unless otherwise noted, all other interviews in this chapter are from Ms. 1 at CMH.

2. Summary of Operations, Task Force Growdon, 271200 March 1951, in Ms. 63, CMH.

3. Interview, Capt. John Wahl with Capt. Edward C. Williamson, 8 April 1951.

4. Summary of Operations, Task Force Growdon, 271200 March 1951, in Ms. 63, CMH.

5. Interview, Lt. Col. Harry F. Lambert with Capt. Edward C. Williamson, 8 April 1951.

6. Interview, Capt. Dorsey B. Anderson with 1st Lt. Martin Blumenson, 14 April 1951.

7. Interview, 1st Lt. Ward C. Goessling Jr. with Capt. Edward C. Williamson, 16 April 1951.

8. Interview, Capt. John E. Strever with Capt. Edward C. Williamson, 11 April 1951.

9. Interview, Capt. Thomas J. Watkins with Capt. Edward C. Williamson, 12 April 1951.

10. Interview, 1st Lt. J. L. Beasley with Capt. Edward C. Williamson, 15 April 1951.

11. Interview, 1st Lt. Donald L. Roberts with Capt. Edward C. Williamson, 15 April 1951.

12. Interview, 1st Lt. Donald L. Roberts and SFC Ross C. Duncan with Capt. Edward C. Williamson, 15 April 1951.

13. Interview, 1st Lt. Daniel L. Baldwin with Capt. Edward C. Williamson, 14 April 1951.

14. Interview, Lt. Col. J. P. Connor with Capt. Edward C. Williamson, 12 April 1951.

15. Interview, 2d Lt. Edward J. Whelan with Capt. Edward C. Williamson, 14 April 1951.

16. Interview, SFC George G. Lane with Capt. Edward C. Williamson, 14 April 1951.

17. Interview, 1st Lt. Rudy V. Paraiso with Capt. Edward C. Williamson, 15 April 1951.

18. Interview, M. Sgt. Othon Valent with Capt. Edward C. Williamson, 14 April 1951.

19. Interview, 1st Lt. Leo F. Siefert with Capt. Edward C. Williamson, 14 April 1951.

20. Interview, Lane with Williamson, 14 April 1951.

21. Interview, Whelan with Williamson, 14 April 1951.

22. Interview, Paraiso with Williamson, 15 April 1951.

23. Interview, Roberts with Williamson, 15 April 1951.

24. Interview, Beasley with Williamson, 15 April 1951.

25. Interview, Roberts with Williamson, 15 April 1951.

26. Interview, Connor with Williamson, 12 April 1951.

27. Award Case Files, Eugene Estep and Ervin L. Muldoon, Distinguished Service Cross (Posthumous), RG 500, Eighth Army, Boxes 1246 (Estep) and 1269 (Muldoon), NA. In the first quote from Sgt. Hinebaugh, the first paragraph is from his statement in Muldoon's award recommendation and the second paragraph is from his statement in Estep's award recommendation. Hinebaugh was the only eyewitness who provided statements for both award recommendations.

28. Interview, Sgt. Charles P. McDonald with Capt. Edward C. Williamson, 10 April 1951.

29. Interview, 2d Lt. Melvin C. Strawser with Capt. Edward C. Williamson, 11 April 1951.

30. Interview, M. Sgt. Neal A. Perkins with Capt. Edward C. Williamson, 11 April 1951.

31. Interview, 2d Lt. Everett Mackley with Capt. Edward C. Williamson, 11 April 1951.

32. Interview, 1st Lt. James J. Coghlan with Capt. Edward C. Williamson, 16 April 1951.

33. Interview, Capt. Nick Garcia with Capt. Edward C. Williamson, 11 April 1951.

34. Interview, Goessling with Williamson, 16 April 1951.

35. Interview, Strever with Williamson, 11 April 1951.

36. Interview, SFC James E. Hoeh with Capt. Edward C. Williamson, 12 April 1951.

37. Interview, Watkins with Williamson, 12 April 1951.

38. Interview, Maj. Charles M. Holland with Capt. Edward C. Williamson, 13 April 1951.

39. Interview, Capt. Robert A. Chabot with Capt. Edward C. Williamson, 13 April 1951.

40. Narrative Report, Operation Tomahawk, 22–29 March 1951, Capt. Edward C. Williamson, Ms. 8–5.1A BA 1, Operation Tomahawk, CMH.

41. Interview, Capt. Billy F. Pendergrass with Capt. Edward C. Williamson, 10 April 1951.

42. Extract, Daily Journal, 23–28 March 1951, Engineer Company, 187th Airborne RCT, in Ms. 8–5.1A BA 1, Operation Tomahawk, CMH.

43. Interview, Weddle with Crawford Jr., 8 April 1951.

44. Interview, Col. George H. Gerhart with Capt. William T. Crawford Jr., 8 April 1951.

45. Interview, Lane with Crawford, 10 April 1951.

46. Interview, Anderson with Blumenson, 14 April 1951.

8. Cutting the Uijongbu Road

1. Interview, Maj. Charles M. Holland with Captain Edward C. Williamson, 13 April 1951, Ms. 8–5.1A BA 1, Operation Tomahawk, CMH. All interviews in this chapter are from Ms. 1 at CMH.

2. Interview, Capt. Daniel L. Melvin with Capt. Edward C. Williamson, 10 April 1951.

3. Interview, Holland with Williamson, 13 April 1951.

4. Interview, Capt. Rolland A. Dessert with Capt. Edward C. Williamson, 10 April 1951.

5. Interview, PFC Milton Eisenhauer with Capt. Edward C. Williamson, 10 April 1951.

6. Interview, Holland with Williamson, 13 April 1951.

7. Interview, Dessert with Williamson, 10 April 1951.

8. Interview, 1st Lt. Samuel P. Muse with Capt. Edward C. Williamson, 15 April 1951.

9. Interview, Roberts with Williamson, 15 April 1951.

10. Interview, SFC Manuel M. Garza with Capt. Edward C. Williamson, 15 April 1951.

11. Interview, M. Sgt. Elbert V. Ritch with Capt. Edward C. Williamson, 15 April 1951.

12. Interview, SFC Troy U. Gilley with Capt. Edward C. Williamson, 15 April 1951.

13. Interview, SFC Raymond Morris with Capt. Edward C. Williamson, 15 April 1951.

14. Interview, Paraiso with Williamson, 15 April 1951.

15. Interview, Roberts with Williamson, 15 April 1951.

16. Interview, Goessling with Williamson, 16 April 1951.

17. Interview, McDonald with Williamson, 10 April 1951.

18. Interview, Chabot with Williamson, 13 April 1951.

19. Interview, Dessert with Williamson, 10 April 1951.

20. Interview, 1st Lt. Jesmond D. Balmer with Capt. Edward C. Williamson, 9 April 1951.

21. Report, Action on Hill 228, 1st Lt. Edward C. Radcliff, 6 April 1951 in Ms. 8–5.1A BA 1, Operation Tomahawk, CMH.

22. Interview, Garcia with Williamson, 11 April 1951.

23. Interview, Strawser with Williamson, 11 April 1951.

24. Interview, Perkins with Williamson, 11 April 1951.

25. Interview, Coghlan with Williamson, 16 April 1951.

26. Interview, Hoeh with Williamson, 12 April 1951.

27. Award Case File, M. Sgt. Clarence A. Peterson, Distinguished Service Cross (Posthumous), RG 500, Eighth Army, Box 1273, NA.

28. Interview, McDonald with Williamson, 10 April 1951.

29. Interview, Strever with Williamson, 11 April 1951.

30. Report, Action on Hill 228, 1st Lt. Edward C. Radcliff, 6 April 1951 in Ms. 1, CMH.

31. Interview, Lambert with Williamson, 8 April 1951.

32. Interview, Roberts with Williamson, 15 April 1951.

33. Interview, Ritch with Williamson, 15 April 1951.

34. Interview, Paraiso with Williamson, 15 April 1951.

35. Interview, Strever with Williamson, 11 April 1951.

36. Interview, McDonald with Williamson, 10 April 1951.

37. Interview, 1st Lt. William L. Clark with Capt. Edward C. Williamson, 16 April 1951.

38. Interview, Holland with Williamson, 13 April 1951.

39. Interview, Wotherspoon with Williamson, 13 April 1951.

40. Interview, Chaney with Williamson, 13 April 1951.

41. Interview, Sgt. Frederick Conrad with Capt. Edward C. Williamson, 7 April 1951.

42. Interview, Chabot with Williamson, 13 April 1951.

43. Interview, Balmer with Williamson, 9 April 1951.

44. Interview, Dessert with Williamson, 10 April 1951.

45. Interview, Watkins with Williamson, 12 April 1951.

46. Interview, Holland with Williamson, 13 April 1951.

47. Interview, Sgt. Howard Houston with Capt. Edward C. Williamson, 14 April 1951.

48. Interview, Balmer with Williamson, 9 April 1951.

49. Interview, 1st Lt. James E. Hanlin with Capt. Edward C. Williamson, 14 April 1951.

50. Interview, SFC William L. Dumas with Capt. Edward C. Williamson, 14 April 1951.

51. Interview, McDaniel with Williamson, 13 April 1951.

52. Interview, Chaney with Williamson, 13 April 1951.

53. Interview, Wotherspoon with Williamson, 13 April 1951.

54. Interview, Sgt. Clark J. Tanner with Capt. Edward C. Williamson, 8 April 1951.

55. Interview, Holland with Williamson, 13 April 1951.

56. Interview, Melvin with Williamson, 10 April 1951.

57. Interview, Pvt. Roland J. Lemay with Capt. Edward C. Williamson, 10 April 1951.

58. Interview, Dessert with Williamson, 10 April 1951.

59. Interview, Holland with Williamson, 13 April 1951.

60. Interview, Anderson with Blumenson, 14 April 1951.

61. Interview, McDonald with Williamson, 10 April 1951.

62. Interview, Strever with Williamson, 11 April 1951.

63. Interview, Hoeh with Williamson, 12 April 1951.

64. Interview, M. Sgt. Yen Chin Chow with Capt. Edward C. Williamson, 11 April 1951.

65. Interview, 1st Lt. Edward F. Gernette with Capt. Edward C. Williamson, 11 April 1951.

66. Interview, Cpl. James T. Pitts with Capt. Edward C. Williamson, 11 April 1951.

67. Interview, Watkins with Williamson, 12 April 1951.

68. Interview, McDonald with Williamson, 10 April 1951.

69. Interview, Connor with Williamson, 12 April 1951.

70. Interview, Muse with Williamson, 15 April 1951.

71. Interview, Lane with Williamson, 14 April 1951.

72. Interview, Muse with Williamson, 15 April 1951.

73. Interview, Lane with Williamson, 14 April 1951.

74. Interview, Roberts with Williamson, 15 April 1951.

75. Interview, Siefert with Williamson, 14 April 1951.

76. Award Case File, Cpl. Lawrence Norman Gardner, Distinguished Service Cross (Posthumous), RG 500, Box 1249, NA.

77. Ibid.

78. Interview, Valent with Williamson, 14 April 1951.

79. Interview, Von Steigel with Williamson, 16 April 1951.

80. Interview, Connor with Williamson, 12 April 1951.

81. Interview, Maj. Raymond H. Ross with Capt. William T. Crawford Jr., 12 April 1951.

9. Operation Swing—The Push to the East

1. After Action Report of the 23d RCT Operation, 4–12 April 1951, 23d Infantry, n.d., in Ms. 8–5.1A BA 85, Operation Swing, CMH.

2. Forward, 1st Lt. John Mewha, Ms. 8–5.1A BA 85, Operation Swing, CMH.

3. Narrative, 1st Lt. John Mewha, pp. 1–3, Ms. 8–5.1A BA 26, Recon Dailey, CMH.

4. Interview, Capt. John H. King with 1st Lt. John Mewha, 4 May 1951, Ms. 8–5.1A BA 85, Operation Swing, CMH. Unless otherwise noted, Lt. Mewha conducted all of the interviews in this and the next chapter, which are contained in Ms. 85 at CMH.

5. Interview, Capt. Stanley W. Selander, 5 May 1951.

6. Interview, Lt. Col. Beverly T. Richardson, 7 May 1951.

7. Interview, 2d Lt. Walter E. Rodgers, 5 May 1951. Other participants state that Company I was in the rear as the battalion advanced.

8. Interview, 1st Lt. Vivious M. Hall, 8 May 1951.

9. Interviews, Sgt. Jack P. Brown, SFC George H. Glassman, and SFC Robert G. Burgi, 8 May 1951.

10. Interviews, 1st Lt. William P. Barenkamp and 1st Lt. Richard A. Palmer, 6 May 1951.

11. Interview, Richardson, 7 May 1951.

12. Interview, Rodgers, 5 May 1951.

13. Interview, Hall, 8 May 1951.

14. Interview, M. Sgt. George D. Chamberlain, 8 May 1951.

15. Interviews, Brown, Glassman, and Burgi, 8 May 1951.

16. Interviews, Barenkamp and Palmer, 6 May 1951.

17. Interview, PFC David E. Russell, 6 May 1951.

18. Interviews, Cpl. Harry N. Nishida and PFC Edward L. Vickers, 9 May 1951.

19. Extracts from rough draft of 3d Battalion After Action Report, for Period 3 April 1951 to 28 April 1951, n.d., Ms. 8–5.1A BA 85, Operation Swing, CMH.

20. Interview, Richardson, 7 May 1951.

21. Interviews, Barenkamp and Palmer, 6 May 1951.

22. Interviews, Nishida and Vickers, 9 May 1951.

23. Interview, Richardson, 7 May 1951.

24. Interview, Capt. Gerald W. Barnitz, 5 May 1951.

25. Interview, Rodgers, 5 May 1951.

26. Interview, 1st Lt. Jose L. Perdomo, 6 May 1951. Capt. Barnitz and Lts. Rodgers and Perdomo all indicate that the attack on Hill 663 was on 6 April. All other interviews and the official reports of the unit, including the daily journal of the 2d Division, clearly show that the attack was on 7 April.

27. Interviews, Barenkamp and Palmer, 6 May 1951.

28. Interviews, Nishida and Vickers, 9 May 1951.

29. Interview, Russell, 6 May 1951. PFC Russell states that the attack on Hill 663 took place on 8 April; other records and eyewitness accounts clearly show the attack was on 7 April.

30. Interview, Chamberlain, 8 May 1951.

31. Interviews, Brown, Glassman, and Burgi, 8 May 1951.

32. Interview, Richardson, 7 May 1951.

33. Interview, Hall, 8 May 1951.

34. Interview, Chamberlain, 8 May 1951.

35. Interviews, Brown, Glassman, and Burgi, 8 May 1951.

36. Interviews, M. Sgt. Warren F. Dailey, Sgt. Earl J. Cayemberg, and Cpl. Elmer L. Bartley with 1st Lt. John Mewha, 5 September 1951, Ms. 8–5.1A BA 26, Recon Dailey, CMH.

37. Interview, Capt. John N. Botkin with 1st Lt. John Mewha, 7 September 1951, Ms. 8–5.1A BA 26, Recon Dailey, CMH.

38. Interview, Capt. Kermit H. Selvig, 12 May 1951.

39. Interview, 1st Lt. James B. Schryver, 13 May 1951.

40. Interview, M. Sgt. Fillman B. Leaphart, 12 May 1951.

10. Operation Swing—The Thrust North and the "Swing"

1. Interview, Maj. Lloyd K. Jensen with 1st Lt. John Mewha, 10 May 1951, Ms. 8–5.1A BA 85, Operation Swing, CMH. Lt. Mewha conducted the remaining interviews in this chapter, which are contained in Ms. 85 at CMH.

2. Interview, 1st Lt. Chester C. Brumet, 9 May 1951.

3. Interview, 1st Lt. Marvin L. Nance, 9 May 1951.

4. Interview, 1st Lt. Donald O. Miller, 11 May 1951.

5. Interview, Jensen, 10 May 1951.

6. Interview, Nance, 9 May 1951.

7. Interview, 1st Lt. Robert W. Engberg, 9 May 1951.

8. Interview, SFC James T. Laster, 10 May 1951.

9. Interview, Capt. Lawrence Tait, 11 May 1951.

10. Interview, 2d Lt. Ralston K. Dennis, 12 May 1951.

11. Interview, 1st Lt. William T. Liffiton, 11 May 1951.

12. Interview, Engberg, 9 May 1951.

13. Interview, Laster, 10 May 1951.

14. Interview, Nance, 9 May 1951.

15. Interview, Brumet, 9 May 1951.

16. Interview, Liffiton, 11 May 1951.

17. Interview, Jensen, 10 May 1951.

18. Interview, Tait, 11 May 1951.

19. Interview, Brumet, 9 May 1951.

20. Interview, Liffiton, 11 May 1951.

21. Interview, Jensen, 10 May 1951.

22. Interview, Nance, 9 May 1951.

23. Interview, Liffiton, 11 May 1951.

24. Interview, Brumet, 9 May 1951.

25. Interview, Jensen, 10 May 1951.

26. Interview, Nance, 9 May 1951.

27. Interview, Brumet, 9 May 1951.

28. Interview, Nance, 9 May 1951.

29. Interview, King, 4 May 1951.

30. Interview, Jensen, 10 May 1951.

31. Award Case File, Pvt. Milton L. Cagle, RG 500, Eighth Army, Box 1237, NA.

32. Interview, Jensen, 10 May 1951.

33. Interview, Miller, 11 May 1951.

34. Interview, Tait, 11 May 1951.

35. Interview, Brumet, 9 May 1951.

36. Interview, Nance, 9 May 1951.

37. Interview, Laster, 10 May 1951.

38. Interview, Cpl. Ernest A. Townsend, 10 May 1951.

39. Interview, King, 4 May 1951.

40. Interview, Selander, 5 May 1951.

41. Interview, Selander, 13 May 1951.

42. Interview, Jensen, 10 May 1951.

43. Interview, Tait, 11 May 1951. Tait states that Company E attacked Hill 811, an obvious error since the map coordinates given are for Hill 856. On some maps Hill 856 is identified as Hill 859.

44. Interview, Brumet, 9 May 1951.

45. Interview, Liffiton, 11 May 1951. Liffiton also refers to Hill 811 but gives the map coordinates for Hill 856.

46. Interview, Sgt. Lawrence W. Erdman, 11 May 1951.

47. Interview, Dennis, 12 May 1951.

48. Interview, Nance, 9 May 1951.

49. Interview, Laster, 10 May 1951.

50. Interview, Jensen, 10 May 1951.

51. Interview, Brumet, 9 May 1951.

52. Interview, Jensen, 10 May 1951.

53. Interview, Tait, 11 May 1951. A number of the interviews for members of Companies E and F contain many discrepancies in the dates for events of 10–13 April. Changes have been made in the interviews as inserted in this chapter to bring the dates in line with unit journals and daily operation reports with accompanying overlays.

54. Interview, Brumet, 9 May 1951.

55. Interview, Liffiton, 11 May 1951.

56. Interview, Dennis, 12 May 1951.

57. Interview, Nance, 9 May 1951.

58. Interview, Laster, 10 May 1951.

59. Interview, Jensen, 10 May 1951.

60. Interview, Tait, 11 May 1951.

61. Interview, Nance, 9 May 1951.

62. Interview, Laster, 10 May 1951.

63. Interview, Richardson, 7 May 1951.

64. Interview, Hall, 8 May 1951.

65. Interviews, Brown, Glassman, and Burgi, 8 May 1951.

66. Interviews, Barenkamp and Palmer, 6 May 1951.

67. Interview, M. Sgt. William M. Sanford, 6 May 1951.

68. Interview, SFC Van Crockett, 7 May 1951.

69. Interview, Russell, 6 May 1951.

70. Interviews, Nishida and Vickers, 9 May 1951.

71. Interview, Barnitz, 5 May 1951.

72. Interview, Perdomo, 6 May 1951.

73. Interview, Rodgers, 5 May 1951.

74. Interview, Richardson, 7 May 1951. Richardson mistakenly compresses the action to take Hill 1031 into one day, 11 April, instead of 11–12 April.

75. Interviews, Brown, Glassman, and Burgi, 8 May 1951.

76. Interviews, Barenkamp and Palmer, 6 May 1951.

77. Interview, Sanford, 6 May 1951.

78. Interview, Crockett, 7 May 1951.

79. After Action Report of the 23d RCT Operation, 4–12 April 1951, 23d Infantry, n.d., in Ms. 8–5.1A BA 85, Operation Swing, CMH.

11. Hwach'on Dam—Attacks in the West

1. Interview, Lt. Col. John W. Callaway with 1st Lt. Martin Blumenson, 17 April 1951, Ms. 8–5.1A BA 34, Hwach'on Dam, CMH. Unless otherwise indicated, all interviews in this chapter and the next chapter were conducted by Lieutenant Blumenson and are contained in Ms. 34 at CMH.

2. Interview, Capt. James R. Ellingsworth, 17 April 1951.

3. Interview, Capt. Carlton J. Barnes, 17 April 1951.

4. Engineer section, IX Corps, Engineer Study of Hwach'on Reservoir and Dam, 4 April 1951, Annex 1 to Periodic Intelligence Report (PIR) 190, IX Corps, Ms. 8–5.1A BA 34, Hwach'on Dam, Tab 40, CMH. See also C. Van B. Sawin, assistant corps engineer, HQ IX Corps, Subj.: Hwach'on Dam, 7 April 1951, which is a discussion paper of methods of preventing the raising or destroying of Hwach'on Dam gates, in Ms. 8–5.1A BA 34, Hwach'on Dam, Tab 42, CMH.

5. Interview, Maj. Linton S. Boatwright, 11 April 1951.

6. Interview, Maj. James W. Roy, 11 April 1951.

7. Interview, Capt. George Mintz, 11 April 1951.

8. Interview, Capt. Arnold Frank, 15 April 1951.

9. Interview, Maj. James H. Webel, 11 April 1951.

10. Interview, Lt. Col. John Carlson, 11 April 1951.

11. Interview, Capt. John R. Flynn, 11 April 1951.

12. Interview, Webel, 11 April 1951.

13. Interview, Callaway, 17 April 1951.

14. Interview, Capt. Dorsey B. Anderson, 13 April 1951.

15. Interview, 1st Lt. John S. Warren, 13 April 1951.

16. Interview, Lt. Col. Jacob Shacter, 18 April 1951.

17. Interview, Boatwright, 11 April 1951.

18. Interview, Maj. Gen. William H. [M.] Hoge, 15 April 1951.

19. Interview, Col. William Harris, 18 April 1951.

20. Interview, Webel, 11 April 1951.

21. Interview, Anderson, 13 April 1951.

22. Interview, Callaway, 17 April 1951.

23. Interview, Hoge, 15 April 1951.

24. Interview, Carlson, 11 April 1951.

25. Interview, Webel, 11 April 1951.

26. Interview, Harris, 18 April 1951.

27. Interview, Webel, 11 April 1951.

28. Interview, Ellingsworth, 17 April 1951.

29. Interview, Barnes, 17 April 1951.

30. Interview, Maj. Dayton F. Caple, 18 April 1951.

31. Interviews, Maj. Russell J. Wilson and 1st Lt. C. K. Georgeff, 18 April 1951.

32. Interview, Lt. Col. Thomas M. Magness Jr., 11 April 1951.

12. Hwach'on Dam—The Amphibious Assault

1. Interview, Anderson, 13 April 1951.

2. Interview, Warren, 13 April 1951.

3. Interview, 1st Lt. Michael D. Healy and M. Sgt. G. D. Sullivan, 13 April 1951.

4. Interview, Anderson, 13 April 1951.

5. Interview, 1st Lt. Healy and M. Sgt. Sullivan, 13 April 1951.

6. Interview, 1st Lt. Joseph W. Waterbury, 14 April 1951.

7. Interview, M. Sgt. Eugene Lester, 14 April 1951.

8. Interview, SFC George E. Schroeder, 14 April 1951.

9. Interviews, SFC Roy J. Montgomery and Sgt. Joe L. Barnes, 16 April 1951.

10. Interview, Sgt. William V. Goolsby, 14 April 1951.

11. Interview, Warren, 13 April 1951.

12. Interview, 1st Lt. James L. Johnson, 13 April 1951.

13. Interview, M. Sgt. Donald G. Laverty, 14 April 1951.

14. Interview, 1st Lt. Hugh O'Reilly, 17 April 1951.

15. Interview, Anderson, 13 April 1951.

16. Interview, Johnson, 13 April 1951.

17. Interview, Webel, 16 April 1951.

18. Interview, Johnson, 13 April 1951.

19. Interview, Anderson, 13 April 1951.

20. Interview, Johnson, 13 April 1951.

21. Interviews, Healy and Sullivan, 13 April 1951.

22. Interview, Schroeder, 14 April 1951.

23. Interviews, Montgomery and Barnes, 16 April 1951.

24. Ibid.

25. Interview, Waterbury, 14 April 1951.

26. Interview, Lester, 14 April 1951.

27. Interview, Goolsby, 14 April 1951.

28. Interview, Lt. Col. Charles H. Hallden, 16 April 1951.

29. Interview, Capt. Morris M. Teague Jr., 16 April 1951.

30. Interviews, Capt. Thomas J. Kennedy, 1st Lt. Robert B. Easter, 1st Lt. Harry B. Seward Jr., 1st Lt. William E. Terry, M. Sgt. Douglas Deaton, and 1st Sgt. James D. Williams, 16 April 1951.

31. Interview, Warren, 13 April 1951.

32. Interviews, Kennedy, Easter, Seward, Terry, Deaton, and Williams, 16 April 1951.

33. Interview, Callaway, 17 April 1951.

34. Interview, Flynn, 17 April 1951.

35. Interview, Capt. Carl W. Kueffer, 17 April 1951.

36. Interview, Webel, 16 April 1951.

37. Interview, Harris, 18 April 1951.

38. Interview, Hallden, 16 April 1951.

39. Interview, Teague, 16 April 1951.

40. Interview, Anderson, 13 April 1951.

41. Interviews, Kennedy, Easter, Seward, Terry, Deaton, and Williams, 16 April 1951.

42. Hwach'on Dam Resume, 1st Lt. Martin Blumenson, no date, in Ms. 8–5.1A BA 34, Hwach'on Dam, CMH.

43. Interview, Harris, 18 April 1951.

44. Interview, Webel, 16 April 1951.

45. Interview, Callaway, 17 April 1951.

46. Interview, Anderson, 13 April 1951.

47. Interview, Hallden, 16 April 1951.

13. The Hant'an River Crossing

1. Narrative Report, Hant'an River Crossing, 10–13 April 1951, Capt. Edward C. Williamson, no date, Ms. 8–5.1A BA 65, Hant'an River Crossing, CMH.

2. Interview, Lt. Col. Hugh D. Coleman with Capt. Edward C. Williamson, 13 June 1951, Ms. 8–5.1A BA 65, Hant'an River Crossing, CMH. Unless otherwise noted, Capt. Williamson conducted the interviews in this chapter, which are contained in Ms. 65, CMH.

3. Interview, Maj. Joseph Baranowski, 12 June 1951.

4. Interview, Maj. Stanley P. Swartz, 13 June 1951.

5. Interview, Baranowski, 12 June 1951.

6. Interviews, 1st Lt. Gordon J. Lippman, 1st Lt. David A. Freas, SFC Willie M. Robinson, 11 June 1951.

7. Interview, 1st Lt. Edward H. Russ, 21 June 1951.

8. Interviews, Sgt. Frank W. Howard and M. Sgt. Marcellus S. Gray, 15 June 1951.

9. Interviews, Capt. Steven B. Mayo, 2d Lt. Jesse P. Newhouse, SFC Willard B. Smith, Cpl. Carey Lewis, SFC Walter C. Fitzgerald, Sgt. William Campbell, PFC Winston Woodard Jr., 12 June 1951.

10. Interview, Swartz, 13 June 1951.

11. Interview, 1st Lt. John L. Herren, 13 June 1951.

12. Interview, 1st Lt. Scott K. Cleage, 20 June 1951.

13. Interview, Coleman, 13 June 1951.

14. Interview, Baranowski, 12 June 1951.

15. Interviews, Freas and Robinson, 11 June 1951.

16. Interview, Mayo, 12 June 1951.

17. Interview, Gray, 15 June 1951.

18. Interview, 1st Lt. Orval Belcher, 16 June 1951.

19. Interview, Freas, 11 June 1951.

20. Interview, Baranowski, 12 June 1951.

21. Interviews, Mayo, Newhouse, Smith, Lewis, Fitzgerald, Campbell, and Woodard, 12 June 1951.

22. Interview, Coleman, 13 June 1951.

23. Interview, Swartz, 13 June 1951.

24. Interview, Cleage, 20 June 1951.

25. Interview, Belcher, 16 June 1951.

26. Interviews, Mayo, Newhouse, Smith, Lewis, Fitzgerald, Campbell, and Woodard, 12 June 1951.

27. Interview, Baranowski, 12 June 1951.

BIBLIOGRAPHICAL ESSAY

This work is based primarily on the interviews, documents, and detailed operational resumes that U.S. Army military historians assigned to the historical detachments of the Military History Section, Headquarters, Eighth U.S. Army Korea (EUSAK), U.S. Army Forces, Far East (USAFFE), collected during the Korean War. The various historical detachments completed their interviews and studies within weeks or months of the operations covered and submitted them as Section IV, After Action Interviews, of EUSAK's Command Reports. These reports were then collected at Headquarters, U.S. Army Forces, Far East, and also sent to the Office of the Chief of Military History, Department of the Army, in Washington, D.C., for use in preparing the official history of the U.S. Army in the Korean War. Today, the Historical Resources Branch, Field Programs and Historical Services Division, U.S. Army Center of Military History (CMH), at Fort McNair in Washington, D.C., holds copies of these interviews and studies. This volume is based on the operational interviews and studies listed below.

Other primary sources were used to supplement the interviews in the Center of Military History's Korean War holdings. These sources include unit historical files and reports from Record Group 407 and award case files from Record Group 500, all held by the National Archives at College Park, Maryland. Other primary sources are given in the chapter notes.

There is a substantial and growing body of secondary material on the Korean War. Only a few of the major titles are noted here, as a starting point for those readers who desire to explore additional material about this conflict. For an introduction to the historiography of the war and bibliography, see Allan R. Millett, "The Korean War: A 50-

Year Critical Historiography," *Journal of Strategic Studies* 24 (March 2001): 188–224, and Allan R. Millett, *The Korean War: The Essential Bibliography* (Washington, D.C.: Potomac Books, 2007). Millett should also be consulted on the background of the war; see Allan R. Millett, *The War for Korea, 1945–1950: A House Burning* (Lawrence: University Press of Kansas, 2005). For information on the U.S. Army in the years between the conclusion of World War II and the beginning of the Korean War, see William W. Epley, *America's First Cold War Army, 1945–1950* (Arlington, Va.: Association of the U.S. Army, Land Warfare Paper No. 15, 1993); and Thomas D. Boettcher, *First Call: The Making of the Modern U.S. Military, 1945–1953* (Boston: Little, Brown, 1992).

The U.S. Army published a number of excellent official histories covering military operations. These include the series United States Army in the Korean War, consisting of the following volumes: Roy E. Appleman, *South to the Naktong, North to the Yalu* (Washington, D.C.: U.S. Army Center of Military History, 1961); James F. Schnabel, *Policy and Direction: The First Year* (Washington, D.C.: U.S. Army Center of Military History, 1972); Billy C. Mossman, *Ebb and Flow, November 1950–July 1951* (Washington, D.C.: U.S. Army Center of Military History, 1990); and Walter G. Hermes, *Truce Tent and Fighting Front* (Washington, D.C.: U.S. Army Center of Military History, 1992).

The U.S. Army also published a number of monographs on the Korean War. Of special interest for small unit combat actions is Russell A. Gugeler, *Combat Actions in Korea* (Washington, D.C.: U.S. Army Center of Military History, 1987). A work covering the background on the U.S. Army in Japan before the war and the experiences of the 24th Infantry, the last segregated infantry regiment in the U.S. Army, is William T. Bowers, William M. Hammond, and George L. MacGarrigle, eds., *Black Soldier, White Army: The 24th Infantry Regiment in Korea* (Washington, D.C.: U.S. Army Center of Military History, 1996). For an outline of U.S. efforts to develop the Republic of Korea Army (ROKA) before and during the conflict, see Robert K. Sawyer, *Military Advisors in Korea: KMAG in Peace and War* (Washington, D.C.: U.S. Army Center of Military History, 1988).

The U.S. Marine Corps official history is covered in Lynn Montross et al., *History of U.S. Marine Operations in Korea, 1950–1953*, 5 vols. (Washington, D.C.: Marine Corps Historical Branch, 1954–1972). The other services published one-volume histories of their service during the Korean War; see James A. Field Jr., *History of United States*

Naval Operations in Korea (Washington, D.C.: Director of Naval History, 1962); and Robert F. Futrell, *The United States Air Force in Korea, 1950–1953*, rev. ed. (Washington, D.C.: Office of the Chief of Air Force History, 1983).

At the higher echelons of command, Gen. Matthew B. Ridgway's *The Korean War* (Garden City, N.Y.: Doubleday, 1967) provides his perspective as commanding general of the Eighth U.S. Army during the operations covered in this volume. Gen. J. Lawton Collin in his *War in Peacetime: The History and Lessons of Korea* (Boston: Houghton Mifflin, 1969) gives the view from Washington, where he served as Chief of Staff of the U.S. Army and a member of the Joint Chiefs of Staff. Omar N. Bradley and Clay Blair, *A General's Life* (New York: Simon and Schuster, 1983) provides the views and experiences of the chairman of the Joint Chiefs of Staff during this period. D. Clayton James provides coverage of Gen. Douglas MacArthur's actions in Korea and the Far East in the third volume of his biography, *The Years of MacArthur*, vol. 3: *Triumph and Disaster, 1945–1964* (Boston: Houghton Mifflin, 1985). *Memoirs by Harry S. Truman*, vol. 2: *Years of Trial and Hope* (Garden City, N.Y.: Doubleday, 1956) recounts the president's actions and thoughts throughout the Korean War.

Among the plentiful secondary works covering the military aspects of the war that are not part of the official histories, of note are Roy E. Appleman, *Ridgway Duels for Korea* (College Station: Texas A&M University Press, 1990), which provides considerable detail on the period covered by the combat interviews in this work, and Clay Blair, *The Forgotten War: America in Korea* (Times Books, 1987), which is based on numerous interviews with commanders at regimental level and above and provides a unique view of the war from those levels. Other works drawn largely from personal accounts of the war include Rod Paschall, *Witness to War: Korea* (New York: Berkley Publishing Group, 1995); Allan R. Millett, *Their War for Korea: American, Asian, and European Combatants and Civilians, 1945–53* (Washington, D.C.: Brassey's, 2002); John Toland, *In Mortal Combat: Korea, 1950–1953* (New York: William Morrow, 1991); Richard A. Perry and Xiaobing Li, *Voices from the Korean War: Personal Stories of American, Korean, and Chinese Soldiers* (Lexington: University Press of Kentucky, 2004); and David Halberstam, *The Coldest Winter: America and the Korean War* (New York: Hyperion, 2007). Retired U.S. Army historian Col. Kenneth E. Hamburger has provided the best detailed operational study of the pivotal fights at the Twin Tunnels and Chip'yong-ni in his *Leader-*

ship in the Crucible: The Korean War Battles of Twin Tunnels and Chipyong-ni (College Station: Texas A&M University Press, 2003).

Spencer C. Tucker, ed., *Encyclopedia of the Korean War* (New York: Checkmark Books/Facts on File, 2002), and Stanley Sandler, *The Korean War: An Encyclopedia* (New York: Garland, 1995), provide a wealth of information on the war in Korea.

Works covering the South Korean perspective of the war include the three volumes published by the Institute of Military History of the Republic of Korea's Ministry of National Defense, *The Korean War* (Lincoln: University of Nebraska Press, 2000–2001), and the memoirs of South Korean Gen. Paik Sun Yup, *From Pusan to Panmunjom: Wartime Memoirs of the Republic of Korea's First Four-Star General* (Washington, D.C.: Brassey's, 1992).

The story of the war from the view of North Korea and her allies is gradually becoming more complete, but there is still much that remains unclear. Much of the material is from the Chinese perspective; see, for example, Sergei N. Goncharov, John W. Lewis, and Xue Litai, eds., *Uncertain Partners: Stalin, Mao and the Korean War* (Stanford, Calif.: Stanford University Press, 1993); Xiaoming Zhang, *Red Wings over the Yalu: China, the Soviet Union, and the Air War in Korea* (College Station: Texas A&M University Press, 2002); Xiaobing Li, *A History of the Modern Chinese Army* (Lexington: University Press of Kentucky, 2007); Xiaobing Li, Allan R. Millett, and Bin Yu, trans. and eds., *Mao's Generals Remember Korea* (Lawrence: University Press of Kansas, 2001); Shu Guang Zhang, *Mao's Military Romanticism: China and the Korean War, 1950–1953* (Lawrence: University Press of Kansas, 1995); and Russell Spurr, *Enter the Dragon: China's Undeclared War against the U.S. in Korea, 1950–51* (New York: Newmarket Press, 1988).

Operational interviews and studies on which this volume is based include the following: No. 8–5.1A BA 1, Operation Tomahawk, Capt. William T. Crawford Jr., 7th Historical Detachment, May 1951, also cited as Ms. 1; No. 8–5.1A BA 15, Grenade Hill, Capt. Pierce W. Briscoe, 2d Historical Detachment, June 1951, also cited as Ms. 15; No. 8–5.1A BA 26, "Recon Dailey," 2–8 April 1951, 2d Engineer Combat Battalion, 2d U.S. Infantry Division, 1st Lt. John Mewha, 8th Historical Detachment, [April 1951], also cited as Ms. 26; No. 8–5.1A BA 30, Breaking the Hongch'on Defense Line, 1st Lt. Martin Blumenson, 3d Historical Detachment, March 1951, also cited as Ms. 30; No. 8–5.1A BA 34, Hwach'on Dam, 1st Lt. Martin Blumenson, 3d Historical Detachment, April 1951, also cited as Ms. 34; No. 8–5.1A BA 63, Task Force Growdon, Capt. Edward C. Williamson, 4th Historical Detachment, March 1951, also cited as Ms. 63; No. 8–5.1A BA 65, Hant'an River Crossing, Capt. Edward C. Williamson, 4th Historical Detachment, May 1951, also cited as Ms. 65; and No. 8–5.1A BA 85, Operation Swing, 1st Lt. John Mewha, 8th Historical Detachment, May 1951, also cited as Ms. 85.

INDEX